Anglo Saxon

Paganism

History
and
Beliefs

Jamie Lang

Publication: ©2021 James Alastair Lang

Front and Back Cover Art: ©2021 Lynne Harling
Illustrations (pages 134, 216, 248, 280, 281): ©2021 Lynne Harling

ISBN: 9798736420438
First published 2021

A Note on Art Works

The original art in this volume, including that used for the front and back covers, and the five internal illustrations as listed by page number above, are by Lynne Harling.

The front cover picture shows the goddess Freya (with references to her falcon form). The back cover picture shows Loki holding one of his children: the eight-legged foal Sleipnir.

Larger digital versions of this book's original art works (free of the book's text overlays) may be viewed at:

anglosaxonpagans.co.uk

The website also contains information on how to obtain prints of these art works.

Synopsis

When Anglo-Saxon tribes first settled in Britain in the mid fifth century CE, their beliefs, though varied and developing over time, were essentially pagan and polytheistic. The history of the ways in which the early English understood their world is told here in terms of both the character of specific deities they followed, and the broader nature of their pre-Christian culture.

Key themes include the ways in which Anglo-Saxon paganism differed from Scandinavian (Viking) spirituality, and how early English deities compared to those of other early polytheistic cultures, such as the Greek and Sumerian. In order to better comprehend the pagan Anglo-Saxon mind-set, basic Germanic materialist philosophy is contrasted with aspects of ancient Greek idealist philosophy, in particular neoplatonism, and related changing perceptions of the goddess Hecate. Loki's role as an agent of cultural dissent and gender diversity is analysed, and differing views of life after death reviewed.

Particular attention is paid to what the Old English Beowulf poem might tell us about English tribal foundation myths, and chapters on the uses of runes and the place of trees in pagan culture are also included. The author seeks to make a case that the early English revered the divine feminine to a degree not found in either Scandinavian paganism or Roman Christianity. As part of this analysis eight north European myths are adapted, retold in short story formats, and evaluated in terms of what they can tell us about key features of early English pagan belief.

Early Anglo-Saxon ways of looking at and understanding the world were complex, sophisticated, diverse and pluralistic, and very different from 21st century belief systems. This book seeks to help us comprehend the thought processes of the early English living in Britain one and a half thousand years ago.

This book is dedicated to all those who encouraged and inspired its writing. My especially heartfelt thanks go to Lynne, who produced so much truly magnificent, high quality artwork for me. Anwen is both my chosen (front cover) face of the goddess Freya, and our "Airy Fairy" Queen of Sheffield – thank you. Ann is a listening, advising, encouraging, empathetic, motivating, priestess of Sheffield's Goddess Temple – my thanks for everything. Graham's proofreading skills and dedication proved invaluable (any remaining textual oddities are down to me alone). Christina broadened my interests by introducing me to both the goddess Inanna and Greek philosophy, thereby having a major influence on the writing of this book. Mark first introduced me to the Sheffield Pagan Pathways group, facilitated by Rachel and John, which over two decades has been continually and positively stimulating. Many thanks to you all, and to my wife Isilda, sons Jamie and Stephen, daughters in law Julia and Kirstin, and all my friends who have, sometimes perhaps without even knowing it, through your friendship, support, and goodwill – also helped produce this book.

Jamie Lang
Sheffield 2021

Contents Page

Preface

A Note on Letters and Spellings

It will be noticed that the spelling of Old English and Norse names is not consistent throughout this volume. This reflects common practice, in that different authors use more or less modernised versions of such place and personal names, as well as other terms. Scyld Scefing for example (the subject of chapter 2) is sometimes written in modern English as Shield Sheafing, which is more recognisable to 21st century eyes, but retains the likely original Old English pronunciation. Wherever possible (access to appropriate computer fonts allowing) letter types and spellings in quotations have been maintained in their original form. It is hoped that in most cases variations in names and terms will not obscure meaning, as such variations are quite limited, usually restricted to the use (or not) of accents, and the use (or not) of Old English letters no longer current in modern English. The latter are few in number, the most commonly used being shown in the table below. In Old as in modern English pronunciation varied according to both place and time, but a rough guide is given below.

Old English	Case	Modern English
Þ	upper	th (as in *think*)
þ	lower	
Ð	upper	th (as in *the*)
ð	lower	
Æ	upper	e (as in *egg*)
æ	lower	

Anglo-Saxon Paganism - *Introduction*

Why on earth would anybody want to read a book about Anglo-Saxon paganism? Or indeed, write one? The answer, I think, is that what this is really about is how we look at and understand the world we live in, how that was once very different, and whether there might be aspects of that older worldview which might still be useful to us in the 21st century.

Looking backwards in order to better understand the world might at first be thought likely to prove rather retrograde, negative, and ultimately not that useful. However even a glance at the possible thought processes of people living up to two millennia ago quickly reveals their concerns with some remarkably modern-looking concepts, such as pluralism, diversity, the balancing of individual and collective freedoms, and issues of sexual and gender related power.

It also quickly becomes clear that the pre-Christian Anglo-Saxon worldview cannot be fully understood in isolation, but is more effectively considered in the context of relationships with the polytheistic experiences of other peoples more distant in terms of both place and time. The great north European goddess Freya for example turns out to have much in common with ancient Sumerian comprehension of the goddess Inanna up to 5,000 years ago.

We also need to recognise that there was never just one single, unitary form of Anglo-Saxon paganism. One of the first things revealed in any study of the development of early English thought processes is that they were both diverse and ever-changing. This is not surprising given that one of the fundamental aspects of virtually all forms of paganism is its pluralism, expressed through polytheism, and often also through an understanding that recognised not just one world, but many. For pagans the universe could be more accurately described as a multiverse.

A key concern of this book is to review variations in north European pre-Christian beliefs, in particular aspects of pagan understanding which may have been less or more emphasised in Anglo-Saxon societies than in the generally better-known Scandinavian stories of the gods, and to consider why this might be. Much can be learned from looking at differences in the comprehension of Æsir and Vanir gods, and by considering stories such as Beowulf and the less well-known tale of Scyld Scefing, which stem from well before the writing down of Nordic myths in the 13th century.

In order to get closer to the essential spirit of paganism, and through that better to understand the specifics of the Anglo-Saxon version, it is useful to compare and contrast, in hopefully relatively simple terms, fundamental philosophical issues. It is argued in this book that pagan worldviews are closely tied to philosophical materialism, and that this fundamentally reflects ancient peoples' deep roots in worlds perceived and directly experienced as physically and spiritually real. The development of an alternative speculative and idealist philosophy by Greek philosophers such as Plato, it is argued, amounted to the abandonment of paganism, and acted as the precursor for the adoption of Christianity in the Roman-Greek empire, and its subsequent outlawing of polytheistic practices.

Greek idealist philosophy later came to be imposed, through the Christian church, in northern Europe, including what was by then becoming England. The Greek idealist worldview is fundamentally at odds with the pagan materialist understanding of fundamental issues such as the true nature of reality and the significance of death, and therefore also how to more fully comprehend life and the worlds we live in. This brings us back to the question: why read a book about Anglo-Saxon paganism? Because it is worth considering whether or not Anglo-Saxon pagans might have understood the complex nature of reality better than we do.

Chapter 1 – *The Anglo-Saxon Outlook*

The world that early (pre-8th century CE) Anglo-Saxons inhabited was very different from that of the 21st century. They experienced the world differently, and consequently their outlook, or way of looking at and understanding the world, necessarily differed from our own. We all adapt to our own experiences of living in order to be able to survive better, to cope more effectively with the varied challenges which life throws up for us. For rational, thinking beings our ability to adapt successfully to those challenges requires us to be able to put them into some kind of comprehensible context. In order to feel that we can act effectively, we need to believe that we can understand, at least in general terms, how the world works. Day to day decision making and practical acts, we sense, will function at a qualitatively better level, if we can place them correctly 'in the scheme of things'. If we can make some attempt at understanding how the world works at fundamental and higher levels, then the quality of our own individual, family and collective 'tribal' lives will be enhanced. Whether or not we consciously rationalise it, we need a cosmology – a *Weltanschauung*[*], or way of looking at the world.

Given that it is desirable - indeed possibly ultimately essential in order to survive - for us to adopt a cosmology, how do we do this, and how did the early Anglo-Saxons do it? We and they do or did it by looking around us, by taking into account what our senses reveal to us, and then mentally processing that information in order to identify key facts and patterns, in the hope or belief that doing so will enable us to make the 'right' decisions and to act effectively.

As part of this learning process we discover that our ability to comprehend reality, the material and physical world, is imperfect. As a result, despite all our best efforts, we make mistakes. We try to learn from those mistakes, and sometimes we do, but nevertheless experience teaches us that we will never be able to avoid making mistakes altogether, that our senses and mental faculties can never become perfect. Our cosmologies will forever remain flawed. And precisely because our ways of looking at the world always remain imperfect, so we tend to remain open to adapting, changing and

---

[*] Weltanschauung: *"A comprehensive conception or image of the universe and of humanity's relation to it"* - www.dictionary.com

(hopefully) improving them.

This must certainly have been the case with the early Anglo-Saxons, just as it is in the 21st century. The first step in understanding our Anglo-Saxon ancestors' belief systems must be to recognise that they were never static, or everywhere identical, either over time or in geographical terms. We can certainly identify specific key factors – for example polytheism – but interest in specific god/desses and their nature will have waxed and waned over time and in differing tribal contexts. If your tribe migrates from a landlocked, mountainous homeland to a flat, coastal area, the perceived importance of sea god/desses is apt to increase. If generations of peaceful agricultural abundance are jeopardised by the sudden appearance of violent raiders stealing your food stocks, guardian spirits are likely to be asked to get their swords out of storage.

This first chapter therefore starts by looking at the arrival, settlement and expansion of Anglo-Saxon tribes in Britain from the mid-5th century CE, considering (initially in broad terms only) where they came from and why, where their pre-existing pagan polytheistic belief systems originated, and the likely impacts of their history and migration on that pagan cosmology.

Anglo-Saxon Timeline

The table in the appendix to this chapter summarises the arrival and expansion of the Anglo-Saxons in Britain, from their initial importation in the role of mercenaries paid by the Romans in the third and fourth centuries CE to guard the south-eastern coasts against raiders, to the death in battle of King Harold in 1066. Although the first Anglo-Saxons to set foot in Britain may have arrived in the third century, they were initially settled here under Roman and subsequent British rule. The Romans pulled out of Britain in the year 407 CE.

When the Romans left they created a power vacuum in Britain. Imperial law and order vanished along with the legions, and the British tribes were soon fighting amongst themselves. From the year 428 one of the British tribal leaders, Vortigern, attempted to bolster his own military position by inviting Saxons to come to Britain to fight for him in greater numbers. These Saxon mercenaries however discovered that their British employers were much less reliable paymasters than the Romans had been and, unpaid, rose in revolt.

By the mid-6th century power in the south and east of Britain was increasingly passing from Britons to Saxons, a process which continued to attract further Saxon migration from mainland Europe. Despite being vastly outnumbered by the indigenous British population, widespread Saxon settlement and expansion was successful. In 552 the first English Kingdom of Wessex was proclaimed at Salisbury, followed by a second (Kent) in 555.

It seems certain that this sixth century migration eventually involved not just male warriors but their families as well, for (Old) English remained the spoken language of the newcomers, even though as late as the year 600 it is estimated that the British population still outnumbered the Anglo-Saxon by ten to one (750,000 against 75,000). Anglo-Saxon children in what was to become England grew up learning to speak only English from their mothers. Where intermarriage between invading male warriors and native women did take place more widely, for example when Vikings later settled in the Isle of Man, children tended to retain (not necessarily exclusively) their mother's tongue.

News of the successful Saxon acquisition of land in southern Britain obviously reached the Germanic tribes back home in mainland Europe, for Saxon expansion in the south was soon being matched by Anglo settlement in the east of Britain. It was said that the migration of the Angles to eastern Britain was so extensive - again clearly involving women and children as well as men - that it led to the complete depopulation of their previous home in Jutland (modern day southern Denmark and northern Germany).

As Angles and Saxons arrived in greater numbers the tribes expanded westwards across most of what is now England, though indigenous British tribes remained independent (and Welsh speaking) in the far west – what is now Wales and Cornwall. The maps below show the approximate extent of the Anglo-Saxon conquest and settlement between 500 and 800 CE, with predominantly Anglo-Saxon areas shaded in grey.

At the same time as the Anglo-Saxons were conquering much of Britain, so too were the Anglo-Saxons being gradually conquered – by what was to them the new incoming religion of Christianity. The first English Anglo-Saxon kingdom to convert to Christianity was Kent in the year 597. The last was Sussex in 680. These dates mark the official conversion of ruling kings, from when their subjects too would be expected to follow suit and allow themselves to be baptised. However there is substantial evidence that pagan beliefs and outlook continued

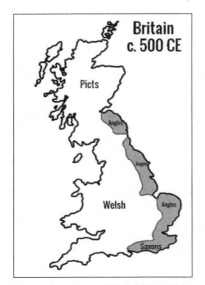

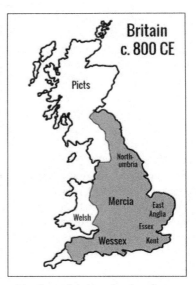

to survive alongside official Christian ideology for hundreds of years, and this will be considered in subsequent chapters.

In order to better understand the conversion of the Anglo-Saxons to Christianity, and how that impacted on the Anglo-Saxon *Weltanschauung* or way of looking at the world, it makes sense to first consider the composition of that earlier pagan Anglo-Saxon world outlook. Pagan Anglo-Saxon England was a pre-literate society. Their world outlook will certainly have been reflected in their storytelling, but those stories unfortunately remain largely inaccessible to us, as they were not written down, but instead passed down orally. What we do have in written form are some of the stories told by the north European cousins of the English Anglo-Saxons – the Scandinavian 'Vikings'. Their paganism survived until a later date, with Iceland not being converted to Christianity until 1000 CE.

It seems certain that versions of these same 'Viking' pagan stories were known to the early English, for the English recognised the same god/desses as the Vikings, or at least very similar versions of some of them, for example Thor (Thunor to the English) with his magical hammer acting as the common people's lightening god of war against the giants. Similarly Odin, the devious, patriarchal god of battle to the Vikings, to the English was Woden, the magically wise wanderer. Subsequent chapters will review the relationship between Viking and Anglo-Saxon interpretations of the god/desses (particularly chapter 4 on the Vanir, and chapter 9 on Freya), but for now a start may be made by looking at just two of the pagan Viking stories that have come down to us in written form. Both involve goddesses: the story of a magical golden necklace in which Freya appears, and the tale of Sif's hair.

First Storytelling - *The Breeze Necklace* [†]

The flaming dominion of magic can be fanned into life by the flowing energies stored in gold. Catherine knew that; she felt it in her bones. The sun goddess herself breathed rays of heat and light into gold. The breath of the goddess was the transforming breeze of magic, the gentle zephyr of empowerment. The runes could teach her. The rune Ansuz [ᚨ], the letter 'a', the runic out-breath of a god/dess, could give her empowered speech – spell casting.

Catherine was still young, but eager to learn. Her body had become that of a woman, but in her village she still lived with her family. Her people had a small farm, but since she had been a little girl, Catherine had wanted more. In her dreams at night she sensed an emotional and spiritual breeze blowing. It came from the world of the Light Elves, from Freya and Frey, goddess and god of fertility and growth. This night breeze, the breath and secret whispered wisdom of the gods, told her to study and to learn, to become whole and sovereign through discovery, healing, empathy, compassion, and ability to protect. *"Look for the Breeze Necklace"*, something in her dreams told her, *"and learn the magical out-breaths inherent in the spoken powers of the runes"*. Were these the words of the god Frey, she wondered? Could they be trusted? Or was this the trickster god Loki impersonating wisdom in her mind?

One dark winter night, leaving the family cats sleeping soundly on her bed, Catherine ventured out, away from her village, wandering away through snow covered fields, walking into the mountains. After some time, before the dawn, she took shelter in a cave entrance, finding herself in a large, dank cavern. Feeling her way, she descended

[†] The stories of *The Breeze Necklace* and *Sif Golden Hair* as presented here have been adapted by the author. Versions closer to those first written down in the thirteenth century can be found in various publications, e.g. *Norse Myths*, by Kevin Crossley-Holland, Penguin 1982.

down a steep and stony path, drawn onwards by a faint red light and a hint of warmth.

Catherine paused and stood listening. She heard water dripping into rock pools. And then a distant tapping noise. Her heartbeats aligned themselves to the rhythm of the tapping, measuring her longing. Somehow she felt that here she could find her magical Breeze Necklace of gold. She continued onwards, down into the strengthening underground light, now flickering and turning fiery.

Eventually she stepped into a large cavern which, it quickly became obvious, was a smithy of the Dark Elves, those also known as dwarves, small in stature and saturnine in temperament, but famed for their skill in working gold. An intense heat emanated from a glowing furnace in the centre of the cavern, around which stood four dwarves.

When she realized what the dwarves were working on, Catherine gasped in delight. She saw an almost completed, wondrous necklace of gold, incised with magical patterning – runes potentially both warding and active. She stared at the workings of the dwarves, wondering from where their knowledge of the runes had come. Hearing Catherine's astonished exhalation, the four dwarves turned and stared. Just as Catherine was mesmerised by the magical splendour of the gold, so they became enraptured by Catherine's feminine beauty. *"Dvalin, at your service!"* announced the first Dark Elf. The others too gave their names: Alfrigg, Berling and Grerr.

At first she did not understand that to the Dark Elves the runes were patterns and letters, but little more. They had sought to imbue the necklace with their own dark, male magic, but they didn't see the vast and complex potential of the gold so worked. Catherine knew instinctively that she could take that basic male magic, and transform it into something else. From base metal that is gold, she could create things much more valuable than material wealth. In her hands the golden runes might bring light of knowledge, spells of physical, emotional, and spiritual healing, and ultimately new life itself.

Dimly she perceived that the dwarves would never do these things, never bring the rune-incised gold to its full potential, because they remained blinded by its material value as a worked object, a great creation of dwarven art, beautiful and valuable in both visual and monetary terms but, once forged, static and apparently dead. She ached to bring the runes to life, to interact with them, to be able to use them not only as adornment, but as living magical gifts to those in need: women and men who could be made more fertile, healed of physical, emotional and psychic pain, or be given opportunities to learn and create in many varied ways.

In desperation Catherine offered to buy the necklace... but the dwarves pointed out that they had spent their lives acquiring wealth – they had no need of yet more coins. But, they told her, there was a way the necklace could be hers. *"Stay, and have a drink with us,"* they said, *"and we'll discuss it. Don't worry, we'll look after you."* Later in the evening, when she was already drunk and confused, they named their price. Or at least, the first instalment. Dvalin led her to his bed, coveting her charm. He took possession of her body, placating his physical desires.

The next day Catherine was ill and hung over, but now it was Alfrigg's turn. With a knowing wink from Dvalin, he insisted that she stagger to her feet, and eat and drink with him, *"to make her feel better"*. By evening she hardly knew where she was any more. This time it was Alfrigg who took the beautiful young woman to his bed, and had his way with her. And the next day and night it was Berling's turn, and then finally, amidst much laughter from his three companions, the fourth day and night belonged to Grerr. By which time, Catherine no longer knew where she was, with whom, or what was happening to her.

On the fifth day, used and abused, she was evicted from the forge by the dwarves. Laughing loudly amongst themselves they dragged her, almost senseless, to the surface, and dropped her on the path outside the cave entrance to their underground labyrinth. They called her *"whore"*, but - loudly proclaiming that they were honourable men of their word - also threw their golden necklace on to her prostrate body. *"Don't say we didn't pay you... whore!"* Dvalin shouted, cursing her for her expensive, seductive, attractiveness. *"And don't come back, we've had our fill of you!"* Alfrigg moaned as the dwarves departed, leaving Catherine wounded and alone.

Someone was watching. As the barely conscious young woman tried in vain to struggle to her feet, she sensed a presence. At first it was all round her: in the sky above, and the ground below; in the trees, in the wind. In the Breeze. And then She came, walking gently down the path towards Catherine: an embodiment of warmth, a mature woman. There was an intensity about this approaching figure, a healing, healthy protectiveness. Catherine attempted to stand, but was too weak. Instead the woman bent down, embraced her, and gently lifted her to a sitting position, where she could at least breathe more easily.

After some time had passed, Catherine began to feel well again. At first she was bemused by the taut power of the arm muscles holding her. Then she noted a sword hanging in a sheath from a leather belt around the woman's skirt. At last, with sudden vision, she knew her protector: Freya, love, sun, and warrior Goddess. Catherine's spirit re-awoke. Her soul danced and basked in the forbidden fruit of knowing that she, yes she, and all women, live in the image of goddesses... with all her imperfection, her pain and abuse, she was loved.

Escorting Catherine back to her village Freya explained: "*I was travelling the nine worlds and I saw you. I saw that you know true beauty, the energy that is in golden sunlight, in the warmth of the sun's rays. You know that solar energy, through the magic of the runes, can give knowledge, wisdom, understanding; that it can heal the body, the emotions, and the spirit. And I can tell you: that's not all those golden etchings in your Breeze Necklace can do. Learn to use those runes aright, and they can, at your spoken words, transmute active evil into impotent immobility.*"

Later, as time passed, Catherine learned much about the runes and their solar energies. Until one day - one pre-dawn - she returned to the mountain cave entrance to the dwarves' underground labyrinth. Wearing her golden Breeze Necklace, and speaking runic enchantments on every out-breath, she drew Dvalin, Alfrigg, Berling and Grerr to the surface - attracting them with spells of lust for both gold and sexual pleasure.

On to the path they came, greedy for yet more wealth and beauty to be despoiled. But as they emerged, so too did the sun from beyond the horizon. Freya's light rays, her solar energies, quickly turned the stunned dwarves to petrified stone, absorbing their body heat, and changing their fiery hot blood to frozen ice. The runic etchings on Catherine's golden Breeze Necklace glowed for a few moments, then faded to become once again just etched metal... awaiting any future need for spells to be spoken.

Second Storytelling - *Sif Golden Hair*

Somehow Loki the shape-changer got into the goddess Sif's locked bedroom at night. As was often the case Thor, her husband, was away in the East, fighting off the attacks of the frost giants. Silently Loki smiled to himself as he pulled out a razor-sharp, curved blade, and moved to Sif's bedside. Thor's wife was breathing deeply and easily, quite dead to worldly sorrows. Loki raised his knife. With quick, deft strokes he lopped off Sif's head of hair - her famous hair which as she moved rippled and gleamed, changing from shade of gold to shade of gold like swaying corn. Sif murmured in her sleep, but failed to awaken. The hair left on her cropped head stood up like short, ugly corn stubble.

The next morning Thor returned from battle to find his wife's head shorn, and her blue eyes brimming with tears. Loki the well-known trickster quickly found himself suspected, and was soon dangling a foot off the ground, his neck held in Thor's powerful grasp. *"Only a joke,"* whined Loki. *"It was only a joke."*

"Well, what are you going to do about it?" demanded Thor.

"I... I, I'll replace the hair," yelped Loki. *"I promise. I'll make it good. I'll go to the dwarves. They'll know what to do".*

"You'll make it good... or else," thundered Thor as he threw Loki violently to the ground, *"or else... I'll break every bone in your body!"*

Loki straightened his clothes, and smoothed down his long hair. Then quick as a flash he winked at Thor and ran from Asgard, away over Bifrost the rainbow bridge, and headed downwards into the lands of the dark elves. He picked his way around a chain of chilly potholes, skirting wide, darkly shining pools of water, until he reached a great cave. This was home to the two sons of Ivaldi the dark elf.

Loki the sly explained to the dwarves the reason for his journey, though somehow managing to avoid explaining precisely how Sif had come to lose her hair. *"You dwarves are such skilled metal workers,"* he said, *"and only the sons of Ivaldi the smith could spin real gold as fine as Sif's hair, and imbue it with magic strong enough to let it grow on her head".*

"Oh yes, and what do we get out of this?" was all the dark elf sons of Ivaldi could be bothered to ask Loki.

"You will have the thanks of Sif and Thor, and the friendship of many gods," responded Loki. *"That counts for a great deal you know. And, more than that, I give you my oath that I'll repay you in full measure when you have need of my services."*

The dwarves understood that Loki was really offering them nothing more than promises, but they considered that they were still likely to make a profit on the bargain, since the most they could lose would be a little labour and a few ounces of gold. So, still grumbling, they piled wood on to the furnace in the corner of their cave. Then one dwarf worked the bellows, while the other began to hammer and spin the gold. Loki watched and marvelled, his eyes flickering red and green in the firelight.

The sons of Ivaldi the smith made a long wave of fine golden strands and, as they worked, they muttered magical spells over them. Soon the golden hair hung over Loki's outstretched arm like a single shining sheet, and yet a breath of air was enough to ruffle it.

When the trickster returned to Asgard, the gods gathered to see what he'd been up to. *"This gift,"* said the schemer simply, *"I owe to you Sif,"* and he showed the goddess the skein of flowing golden hair which he had brought back with him from the lands of the dark elves. *"As soon as you lift this to your head,"* he explained to Sif, *"it will take root there and turn to pure growing gold. You will be no less beautiful than you were before."*

Thor's wife took the hair from Loki, whilst her husband looked on. She fingered the fineness, and turned it over and over, finally slowly raising it to her head. The magic worked just as Loki promised, and Sif smiled as a shout of joy erupted from the watching gods.

North European Cosmology – *Brief Outline*

Storytelling can be rich in meaning, both clear and implied. As soon as we immerse ourselves in the tales of Sif's hair and the Breeze necklace, we find ourselves in a world (or worlds) very different from our own everyday domain. Firstly this is a world where mankind is not the only intelligent, speaking, thinking, rational animal. The gods are real, as are other beings such as dark elves, light elves, and frost giants. This is not a single, relatively simple and comprehensible universe, but a complex multiverse of various worlds (traditionally nine of them).

Secondly, the laws of nature are different here. Magic too is real, and effective when properly studied. Sounds, letters, symbols, words: all can be directly employed as powerful tools. Both spoken and written words and symbols can be immediately potent in breath-taking ways above and beyond earthly rhetoric. Runes are not mere letters, but tell their own stories.

Having said this, it must also be acknowledged that the worlds of gods, elves, and giants, though different from our own, are far from being totally foreign to us. These beings, even the gods themselves, are a long way from acting as representatives of the kind of immaculate divinity attributed by monotheists to a perfect God. Neither Asgard (home to the Æsir tribe of gods such as Odin), nor Vanaheim (land of the Vanir deities such as Freya), constitute any kind of eternal heavenly paradise. In fact the worlds of the north European gods are much more like our earth than the Christian heaven. The gods are complex, changeable, evolving individuals, all different from each other not just in physical terms, but also in moral and spiritual matters. They too all have their own outlook. And perhaps crucially, they are not without or beyond gender. Female and male interests sometimes conflict for the goddesses and gods just as much as they do for women and men. Sex remains of vital interest to the gods, for they exist in worlds not purely spiritual, but just as material as our own. Their worlds too are subject to factors as diverse as ever-changing weather, the seasons, fascination with beauty, desire for material wealth, love, and war.

The early, pre-Christian north European *Weltanschauung* then was above all pluralistic and diverse. Their culture, when still pagan, was largely pre-literate, but it is no coincidence that when that culture's ethos did eventually come to be recorded in writing a few hundred years after Christianisation[‡], no trace of any Bible-like single 'indisputable' holy text was found to be set in print. Instead it was ancient Storytelling that was remembered, with all that form's complexities, uncertainties, and moral variability.

The surviving stories may appear multifaceted and initially more entertaining than didactic, but they do also provide underlying detailed, fundamental structural forms to the early pagan world view. Worlds may be plural, but they are not infinite in number – there are nine of them, and each world has its specific role. They are:

- Nifelheim   - land of the frost giants
- Jötenheim   - home to the rock giants
- Muspelheim   - residence of the fire giants
- Helheim   - abode of goddess Hel (and the dead)
- Midgard   - (middle) Earth
- Svartalfheim - dwelling place of the dark elves
- Alfheim   - domicile of the light elves

---

‡ See the Poetic Edda (anonymous sources), Snorri Sturluson's prose Edda, Icelandic Sagas, Beowulf and other Old English literature.

- Vanaheim   - seat of the Vanir god/desses
- Asgard   - fortress world of the Æsir god/desses

All the nine worlds are also connected to each other, and it is possible to travel between the worlds (though it helps to be a god). The worlds are held in the branches of the 'World Tree' Yggdrasil, which itself has its own cosmology and ecology: its roots are continually threatened and gnawed at by the dragon Nídhögg, but also nourished and refreshed by water from the spring or pool of Hvergelmir at its base. The waters of Hvergelmir are in turn renewed by dew falling form the branches of the World Tree, shaken as they are by the squirrel Ratatosk who runs up and down Yggdrasil carrying messages and insults between Nídhögg at its base and an eagle who inhabits the top of the tree. Four stags also wander about between the tree's branches, nibbling at its foliage, and innumerable snakes swim and slither around Hvergelmir.

The hall of the three Norns themselves [the north European destiny-weaving 'Fates' of the past (Urd), present (Verdandi), and what yet might come about or need to be done (Skuld)] is situated close by Hvergelmir as well, as they play out time on their looms, creating and manipulating the *Wyrd*, the magical concept that everything is connected (directly or indirectly) to everything else, creating potentially infinite knock-on effects for every action.

Such is the geography of pagan northern Europe's cosmology, but it also has an epochal narrative. In the beginning, before the nine worlds even existed, there was only fire and ice, and between them nothing, just a yawning gap (the *Ginnungagap*). But then the fire touched the ice, and they reacted against each other, sparking off new energies, creating the first fertile female living being: Audhumla the primeval cow. Audhumla licked a still frozen salty ice block, thereby – like a cow licking her new born – freeing and giving life to the giant Buri, who became the forefather of the Æsir gods. She also fed a frost giant, Ymir, with her milk. Ymir though, as an unlicked, unshaped frost giant, was an enemy of the gods. Buri's children (the Æsir Odin, Vili and Vé) grew up to slay Ymir, and from his flesh they made the earth, from his bones our rocks and mountains, from his blood the seas and lakes, and from his hollowed skull they created the sky.

That was how things began, but after many exploits through the ages, many adventures of gods, goddesses, human beings, elves, giants, and so many other living beings... things must also end. There is no immortality, neither for gods nor for mankind. Through the ages the frost, rock and fire giants struggle to destroy everything, all life, intending to leave once again only the primeval energies of fire and ice triumphant. And they will succeed. In the final battle between giants and gods, at Ragnarok, the giants will win, and both the gods and mankind will be destroyed. Those heroic human warriors who lived again in Odin's hall of Valhalla will be summoned to that final battle… to die, alongside the gods. However, then a new cosmological cycle must begin: a new unspoiled world will arise from beneath the sea, and a few individuals, such as Thor's sons Magni and Móði, will be found to have survived after all.

That in summary constitutes the material and temporal cosmology of pre-Christian north European storytelling of the kind that the early English were no doubt familiar with, for the English tribes (Angles, Saxons, Jutes and others) migrated from those parts of southern Scandinavia and northern Germany where these cosmological stories originated. The stories gave form and structure to the pagan world outlook. They express in mental shorthand the need to be able to describe the most fundamental experiences of living and existing. In order to achieve this, the attempt to make the cosmos comprehensible necessarily involves much simplification and perhaps the first stirrings of universalisation – that demand of the human mind that material reality be conceived as conforming to the limited human imagination, rather than the mind admitting its limited ability to comprehend complex and plural material realities.

In reality, there are not just nine worlds, but a potentially infinite number. However the recognition that worlds are plural was at least some kind of an acknowledgement of the limits of human cognition. Subsequent post-pagan philosophical trends have largely tended not to expand this admittedly restricted world outlook, but on the contrary to further limit cosmological learning by reducing even nine worlds in number: often down either to three (a celestial heaven, earth herself, and an underworld of some kind), or even to one – a single universe in which all things may at last come to be perceived as being at least potentially scientifically fully understandable.

It is surely possible that the greater diversity of the early pagan world view is actually more in line with the material realities of a plural multiverse, than any modern day scientific or monotheistic universalism. After all, much of the complexity and depth of 'reality' will surely forever remain beyond accurate analysis by both gods and mankind, given the limited nature of the sensory perception, imagination, and learning ability of all living beings. This will be looked at again in chapter 11 in a discussion of Hecate used to emphasise key aspects of north European pagan materialist philosophy by comparing and contrasting it with Greek Neo-Platonist idealism.

Chapter 1 Appendix - *Anglo-Saxon Timeline*

Year/Time	Pre-Anglo-Saxon Era (<428 CE)
3rd and 4th Centuries	'Saxon Shore' coastal forts established on south eastern coasts of Britain by Angle, Saxon and Jutish mercenaries paid by Romans to fight raiders.
313	'Edict of Toleration' proclaimed at Milan - Christianity legalised in the Roman Empire.
337	Roman Emperor Constantine baptised a Christian on his death bed.
407	Emperor Constantine III withdraws last Roman troops from Britain.
410	Emperor Honorius rejects British pleas to Rome for aid to end British lawlessness.

Year/Time	Early Anglo-Saxon Era (428 - 650) – Pagan English Kingdoms Established
428	British leader Vortigern invites Anglo-Saxon pagan mercenaries led by Hengist and Horsa to fight for him in Britain.
428-600	Further English settlement from European mainland.
441	Vortigern fails to pay Anglo-Saxons, who rise in rebellion.
442(?)	Hengist slaughters 300 top British tribal leaders at "peace conference".
442-515/37	Anglo-Saxon pagan kingdoms expand from south east; Britons retreat westwards.
460-515/37	British anti-English resistance led by Ambrosious Aurelianus (and then Arthur?).
515-537(?)	Arthur reputedly killed at battle of Camlann (site uncertain).
552	English Kingdom of Wessex proclaimed at Salisbury.
555	English Kingdom of Kent established.
597(?)	King Aethelbehrt of Kent marries Christian Frankish princess Bertha.
597	Augustine sent by Rome to preach Christianity in Kent; baptises King Aethelbehrt.
600	*Estim. English population (pagan): 75,000. Estim. Britons (many Christian): 750,000.*
632-655	Penda pagan King of Mercia (descendent of Woden) - tolerates all gods, inc. Christ.

Year/Time	Middle Anglo-Saxon Era (600-800) – Gradual Christianisation of England
<650	Pagan burials continue in Kent, despite ruling class adoption of Christianity.
604	King Raedwald of East Anglia persuaded by King Aethelbehrt of Kent to accept Christianity, but Raedwald maintains toleration of paganism.
617	Kingdom of Essex renounces Christianity and returns to paganism.
625	Pagan/Christian King Raedwald of East Anglia given high pagan burial with grave treasure at Sutton Hoo barrow.
627	King Edwin of Northumbria converts to Christianity - declares war on pagan Mercia.
633	Pagan Mercia victorious. King Edwin slain in battle.
653	Sigeburt 'Sanctus', King of Essex, converts to Christianity
655	Pagan King Penda of Mercia dies in battle. Succeeded by Christian son Paeda.
680	Last English pagan kingdom - Sussex - forced to convert.
680-1066	Aristocracy Christianised. Church outlaws paganism, e.g. the naming of gods in spells and poems, veneration of trees, woods, rivers, mountains, and "black magic".

Year/Time	Late Anglo-Saxon Era (800-1066) – Pagan Gods Return with Vikings
793	"Fiery Dragons" reported flying in Northumbria, prior to first Viking raid at Lindisfarne.
865-880	Danish rule of Northumbria, East Mercia, and East Anglia ("Danelaw"). Recognised by English in 878. In return - Danish ruler Guthrum accepts Christian baptism.
899	Death of King Alfred of Wessex.
920	Edward of Wessex becomes king of all England south of the Humber.
925-927	New King Athelstan of Wessex conquers Northumbria - England is united.
930 (approx.)	Erection of Gosforth Cross, Cumbria - inc. pagan and Christian motifs.
1000	Icelandic Council agrees conversion to Christianity (private paganism tolerated).
1016-1035	Dane Cnut (Christian) King of all England.
1066	Harold, last Anglo-Saxon English king, killed at Hastings.

Chapter 2 –
The Legend of Scyld Scefing

Despite the fact that his story is referenced in the prologue to the famous Old English poem Beowulf (see the appendix to this chapter), one of the primary but least well known Anglo-Saxon stories is the legend of Scyld Scefing (pronounced 'Shield Sheafing'). Scyld is a figure from the very earliest known period of Anglo-Saxon mythology, going back thousands of years to well before the migration to Britain. He is both divine and mortal – not semi-divine (half man and half god), but fully both a man and a god. He is a Van, i.e. a member of Freya and Frey's Vanir tribe of gods (not Odin's Æsir) and, as is typical of the Vanir, is associated (primarily) with fertility – of the land, animals, and mankind - and (secondarily) with leadership qualities, including fighting and warfare abilities.

His name means 'Shield son of Sheaf'. Shef is an early form of the Old English word 'sceáf' or 'sheaf' (as in a sheaf of grain), and the 'ing' suffix indicates 'of'. He is the son, in mythological terms, of Shef, who was said to be the first ever patriarch or founder of the English Yngling, Angle and Heathobard tribes, who later in his life also came to be acknowledged by north German Saxons. As he lived in the very early pre-tribal-migration period (precisely when is considered later in this chapter), the story of his life is set not in modern day England, but in what is now southern Sweden, Denmark, and northern Germany (Schleswig-Holstein and north-west Saxony).

Third Storytelling - *The Legend of Scyld Scefing*

This is a story which is estimated to be anything up to about 4,000 years old! It was certainly a very long time ago, before ever the English came to England, when one day a ship was seen sailing near the coast of Skåne in southern Sweden. It was spotted approaching the land without being propelled by either oars or sail. The incoming tide brought the ship to the beach, and a young boy was found lying in it, asleep, with his head on a sheaf of grain. He was surrounded by treasures of various kinds, farmers' tools, spears, and coats of mail. The boat itself was royally appointed and beautifully decorated. Who he was and where he came from nobody had any idea, yet although

---

the people of Skåne were poverty stricken, and struggled even to feed themselves, the young child was received as if he were a kinsman, and was given the most constant and tender care. As he came with a sheaf of grain to their country the people of Skåne called him Shef, their word for sheaf.

At this time there were several tribes living in Skåne and surrounding areas, including the Skjöldungs (later called Danes after their first king, Dan), the Heathobards, the Angles, and the Ynglings (with the last three being seen as ancestors of the English). These tribes generally lived amicably together, so much so that inter-marriage became common between them, particularly between the Angles and the Ynglings. Shef grew up among these people, and soon became their benefactor, teaching them many new skills they had previously had no knowledge of. Under Shef's guidance their tending of the land improved immeasurably, resulting in better crops and better fed, healthier animals on their farms. Shef taught people to acknowledge and value the spirits of land and forest, the land-wights. The spirits responded well to being shown new respect, and soon Skåne developed into a place of plenty, with abundant food for all.

Recognising Shef's knowledge and skills, as soon as he was old enough the tribes of Skåne elected Shef to be their joint king. He ruled most honourably for many years.* Just as the sheaf of grain and farmers' tools found in Shef's boat had proved to be omens of improved agricultural fertility, so the spears and coats of mail in the boat turned out to be indicators of better military abilities. The new abundance of the land in Skåne soon attracted the attention of neighbouring warlike tribes, but Shef taught his peoples advanced weapon training and warfare techniques, and they successfully defended their newfound wealth. In fact northern Saxon tribes too came to acknowledge Shef as their liege lord.

Just as important as Shef's military abilities, and his sharing of new knowledge about how to live in peace and abundance with the spirits of the land, were his cultural and educational skills. He encouraged storytelling, and soon the spoken poetry of Skåne's skalds became renowned even far beyond that land's boundaries. Tales of heroic derring-do, and great love stories, not only kept people royally

---

* The Beowulf poem calls this character Scyld, son of Sceaf, and makes Beowulf the son of Scyld, with the grandson of the boy who came with the sheaf being Halfdan, king of the Danes.

entertained around the evening and winter fires in the mead halls, but also recounted the histories of gods, goddesses, giants, and the many tribes of Midgard.

On top of all this, Shef's sharing of his knowledge (which came from who knows where, or possibly the gods themselves?) extended also to healing and other magical abilities. He encouraged the women of the tribes in particular to study magical practices, and develop their own spells and skills using shamanic spirit travelling and guidance techniques, divinatory powers associated with energy symbols called runes, and rhythmicly chanted and sung incantations known as 'galdr'.

When Shef eventually died he was far advanced in age. In accordance with his own directions, after death his body was borne down to the coast where he had landed as a child. There in a little harbour was found again the same boat in which he had arrived. Glittering with hoar-frost and ice, and rising and falling with the swell of the waves, apparently eager to return to the sea, the boat was waiting to receive the dead king. Out of love for the goddesses and gods who had surely sent Shef to them, around his body the grateful and sorrowing Skjöldungs, Angles, Heathobards, Ynglings and Saxons laid no fewer treasures than those with which Shef had arrived so many years before; gifts for gifts. When all was ready the boat went out to sea, again unguided by oar or sail, never to be seen again.

Analysis of the Legend - *Who was Shield Sheafing?*

Unsurprisingly for such an ancient legend more than one version of the story has survived. This has led in particular to some confusion about the identity of the child in the mysterious boat. Is he

- Shef, or
- Is he Shield son of Shef, i.e. Shield Sheafing?

It seems probable that the confusion arises because there were originally not one but two legends, one being a fertility myth concerning *Shef* (or Sheaf), and another being an heroic myth concerning a warrior figure: *Shield*. Gale Owen points out that:

> *"Scyld Scefing, the legendary king whose career and ship funeral form the unforgettable prologue to Beowulf, himself evolved from a fertility myth. He was evidently a composite figure, embodying in his name the two qualities essential for the successful survival of a people*

— military might (shield) and agricultural prosperity (sheaf).

"The story of a child who came over the ocean evidently belonged to the character named Sheaf or Scef, a fertility figure who was believed to have appeared from the unknown and brought prosperity. This tradition is preserved in the Chronicle of Æðelweard (c.1000) and in a twelfth century account by William of Malmesbury... To Sceaf there was attributed a son named Beow, a word which means Barley, supporting the possibility that a fertility myth lies behind the legend of Sceaf." [1]

In Beowulf, Denmark's first royal family was descended from Shef through his son Scyld — called Skjöld in Danish. And Shef (or Skjöld) is not only the progenitor of the Skjöldungs (the Danes), but also of the Ynglings (the English). The word Skjöld meant "the protecting one," "the shielding one". It is the Beowulf version of Shef's identity, i.e. *Shield son of Shef* or *Shield Sheafing* that is best known today as the small child who miraculously arrived in the boat on the beach, but commentators such as Viktor Rydberg,[2] Kathleen Herbert[3] and Gale Owen[4] believe that originally the child in the story was the fertility figure *Shef*, not his son *Shield*. They believe that Shef's son, Shield, and in some versions Shield's son Beow or 'Barley', were much later inventions of Alfred the Great's scribes, who that Christian king required should prove his descent from both Woden (to Alfred an ancestor who had once been considered a god) and ultimately from the biblical Adam. Achieving this for the king necessitated increasing the number of royal generations of ancestors; hence Shield was declared to be the son of Shef. As Kathleen Herbert explains:

"The royal house of Wessex... was at that time the champion of Christendom against the heathen Vikings. Yet the first ancestor of the dynasty was Woden. This did not bother them in the least... What worried them was that they could not count so many generations... [as to] reach back to Adam. Their scholars... set that right by adding in the requisite number of legendary heroes from Old English poetry and tradition. The three highest names on the new list... are

- *Scef (Shef - Sheaf), "who was born in Noah's Ark"*
- *Scyld (Shield), his son, and*
- *Beow (Barley), his [Scyld's] son. This is*

> *the being, later known as John*
> *Barleycorn, whose passion, death and*
> *resurrection are told in a folk song."* [5]

At least in Alfred the Great's Wessex Shef retained his position as a royal ancestor, even if his relations had to be reinvented so as to be linked back to Adam. Elsewhere the required Christianisation of pagan myths resulted, in the early Middle Ages, in:

> *"Shef being displaced from his status as original*
> *patriarch of the royal families of Sweden, Denmark,*
> *Angeln, Saxony, and England* [except Wessex]*, by the*
> *"scholastic fiction"* [6] *of 'Trojans' supposedly migrating*
> *to these lands from Asia* [Turkey] *- under the leadership*
> *of non-other than Odin!*

> *"This view seems first to have been established in*
> *England after this country had been converted to*
> *Christianity. The Æsir god Woden (Odin) was there*
> *placed at the head of the royal genealogies of the*
> *chronicles, except in Wessex, where Shef was allowed*
> *to retain his old position, and where Odin had to*
> *content himself with a secondary place in the*
> *genealogy.*

> *"From England this same distortion of the myth was also*
> *eventually recorded in later Nordic sources, following*
> *the spread of Christian culture to Scandinavia. Skjöld*
> *(Shield), Shef's son, was changed into a son of Odin.*
> *Yngvi, who as the progenitor of the Ynglings is identical*
> *with Shef - and whose very name, perhaps, was*
> *conceived as an epithet indicating Shef's tender age*
> *when he came to the coast of Skåne - is confounded*
> *with Frey and styled Yngvi-Frey. And he, too, is called a*
> *son of Odin, although Frey is actually a son of Njörd*
> *and belongs to another race of gods altogether, the*
> *Vanir, and not Odin's Æsir."* [7]

Like the god Heimdal, who was originally perceived by the English Angle, Heathobard and Yngling tribes to be a member of the Vanir, Shef too had his reported identity later changed by Christian and Nordic sources.

- Heimdal was originally perceived as a Van god, a key male fertility figure and divine fore-father of mankind, as well as the bringer of enhanced material abundance through the introduction of skilled tool-making, agriculture, and the division of labour by social class, but was later relegated by Christian Nordic skalds to become a member of Odin's Æsir, whose limited role it became to guard the rainbow bridge to Asgard (*Bifrost*) from attack by giants.

- Similarly Shef was originally acknowledged as both a Vanir god and a mortal king of the Heathobard , Yngling and Angle English tribes, seen – like Heimdal – as a divine fore-father of mankind, and as the bringer of enhanced material abundance through the introduction of skilled tool-making, agriculture and, in Shef's case, military victory. Like Heimdal too, Shef was later relegated by Christian (in this case Anglo-Saxon) storytellers to a very much more limited role as one of Odin's many sons and warriors.

The similarities between Shef and Heimdal – and the reasons for them – will be looked at again later in this chapter.

Shef - *God of Fertility and Culture*

To the early English pagan tribes the corn sheaf was a symbol of the Vanir Earth Mother goddess, Nerthus, in her form as goddess of the harvest. Mother Earth produced the food so essential to survival, and so nurtured us all. In return mankind, her children, loved and celebrated her through the fertility rituals associated with harvest festivals – which were no doubt a bit wilder, freer and generally more fun than sanitised modern-day versions!

The English tribes (Heathobard, Yngling and Angle) saw themselves as the mortal children of the Vanir gods. Shef was both a god (a Van) and the original mortal progenitor or patriarch of Ynglings, Heathobards, Angles and Sköldungs (Danes). The story of Shef, Heimdal and Rig – which will be looked at later in this chapter – makes this understanding of the tribes as the mortal children of the Vanir very clear indeed.

Although seeing themselves as the mortal children of the Vanir gods, there is no doubt that the early English also acknowledged the existence of the Æsir; after all the early history of the Vanir practically begins with their war against Asgard and the Æsir. The cause of the war indicates key differences between the perceived Vanir (and English tribal) world outlook on the one hand, and that of the Æsir and their human followers on the other. The Vanir included knowledgeable and powerful female practitioners of magic, said to be skilled in the ancient supernatural art of *seidr*, a form of sorcery generally only available to goddesses (and women). The uses of seidr were said to include foretelling the fates of men and women, cursing someone with bad luck, illness, or even death, and depriving people of both wisdom and power, or the granting of wisdom and power to others.

It seems though that the Æsir despised seidr and its practitioners, and particularly resented the fact that it was wielded by females. The Æsir were ruled by a single male, their "All-father" patriarch: Odin. Odin taught the Æsir that the use of seidr was dishonourable, and especially so for male gods and men (in Viking society its use by men may have been associated with frowned-upon effeminate homosexuality). However, apart from his disdain of goddesses and women, Odin's real reason for his loudly expressed rejection of seidr was that in reality he lusted after gaining its power for himself. Furious that as a male god he could not acquire such feminine skills, his anger drove him to whip up hatred of those female Vanir who did use it. He launched a witch-hunt.

Ancient storytellers related how a leading Vanir witch named Gullveig was dragged by the Æsir to Odin's hall, where he judged her and condemned Gullveig to be burned alive, having found her guilty of *"practising seidr in a trance, always to the delight of wicked women"*.[8] To Odin's and the Æsir's despair however, despite doubling and tripling their murderous efforts, despite both burning her alive and running her through with their spears, Gullveig's female magic proved too powerful for the Æsir, and she survived:

> *"They stabbed at Gullveig with spears,*
> *And they burned her in Odin's hall,*
> *Thrice they burned the thrice-born girl,*
> *Many times, not once, but still she lived."* [12]

Although Gullveig lived to tell the tale, when Freya and the other leading Vanir heard it, they were outraged, and declared war on the Aesir, besieging Asgard, and wearing down its fortress walls. In the end Odin was forced to sue for peace, but he saw this as his big chance to finally gain what he had really been after all along: the magical powers of seidr. As part of the peace terms hostages were exchanged by both sides, and Freya left Vanaheim to stay at Asgard for a while, in fact long enough – Odin insisted – for Freya to teach him some seidr skills! Freya agreed to this, and suddenly the use of seidr was no longer 'dishonourable', or at least not by the "All-father" – it is said that he unsurprisingly thereafter still let it be known that, amongst males, its powers were to continue to be restricted to his personal use alone.

It should be noted though that the early English understanding of the character of Woden, said to be their incarnation of the Norse god Odin, seems to go back to an earlier, less misogynistic, pre-Viking age:

> *"The Old English 'waelcyrge' were vastly different from the Norse Valkyrie. Woden was not concerned with organising vast battalions of dead warriors, but more with walking the rolling downs, and watching over his (living) people."* [9]

The early English in fact, although clearly aware of Odin and the Æsir, and whilst hardly disdaining issues of war, sorcery, and military survival, remained much more focused on the crucial importance of fertility, and in particular Vanir fertility goddesses and gods, and their vital roles in blessing agriculture and harvests. So important was this to the English, that survivals of these beliefs could still be found even a thousand years after the first arrival of Christianity amongst the English in Britain:

> *"In England we can find examples of the veneration of the sheaf, and the goddess who gave birth to the sheaf, continuing until the mechanisation and industrialisation of farming destroyed most of the old rituals. On September 14th 1598 a party of German visitors was going towards Eton:*
>
> > '...by lucky chance we fell in with the country folk celebrating the harvest-home. The last sheaf had been crowned with flowers and they had attached it to a magnificently robed image, which perhaps they meant to represent Ceres [Roman goddess of the corn harvest]. They carried her hither and thither with much noise... shouting through the streets until they came to the barn.' [10]
>
> *"To classically educated scholars from one end of Europe to the other, all the old gods appeared in their Roman forms. At least they recognised that the Harvest Queen was a goddess, not a corn dolly. Whatever she is called: Ceres, Harvest Queen, Earth Mother... or Nerthus, she is the special goddess of the English".* [11]

Nerthus, as Mother Earth the "special goddess of the English", is the mother of the Vanir fertility gods *par excellence* Freya and Frey (their father being Njörd, a god of the seas, the wind, fishing, and material wealth and prosperity). Shef was sent to the pre-migration

Heathobard, Yngling and Angle tribes in southern Sweden and neighbouring areas primarily as a Vanir blessing of their fertility:

"Yngvi-Shef, the son of a deity transformed into a man, was both a Vanir god and mythical progenitor of the Yngling tribe. Accordingly every member of the Yngling tribe and every descendant of Shef may be styled a daughter/son of Frey. The gifts which Shef brings with him to the ancient peoples of Skåne, Angeln, Saxony and elsewhere - the treasures, tools and weapons which reference the Vanir god Njörd's riches, and the sheaf of grain which is Frey's symbol - are all gifts from the Vanir, and Shef's rule was accordingly peaceful, and rich in blessings." [12]

The author Gale Owen argues that 'Yngvi-Shef' (as Ing and/or Sceaf) were remembered as heroic mythological figure/s in Anglo-Saxon England, and that whilst direct evidence of Anglo-Saxon reverence of pagan female fertility figures is harder to come across, nevertheless they must also have revered an Earth Mother goddess:

"In Germanic mythology we find fertility cults associated with either gods or goddesses, sometimes with both, as in the case of the twins Freyr and Freyja, children of Njörd and his sister [Nerthus]. In England we have ample evidence for the cult of Freyr, and it is clear that the names of Ing and Sceaf were long remembered in association with heroes. We do not have the names of any fertility goddesses from Anglo-Saxon England, but it is clear that... like most pagan peoples, the Anglo-Saxons acknowledged an Earth Mother whose favour was essential if they were to survive. Before the coming of Christianity she may have been worshipped with elaborate rituals such as Tacitus associates with Nerthus." [13]

However Gale Owen's assertion that *"We do not have the names of any fertility goddesses from Anglo-Saxon England"* appears to ignore Eostre, the goddess after whom Easter is named:

"Bede describes Eostre as a goddess of the light of the rising sun, a young female dressed in a short tunic, wearing a hood with hare's ears, and carrying round a silver disk on which could be seen an image of the moon. According to Bede the name Easter is derived from the Germanic 'Eostur-monath' – dawn month, the

beginning of the new cycle of life, springtime when the plants recover from their dormant state of winter sleep." [14]

Understanding Easter as the month of the English goddess Eostre, the month of the new cycle of life, surely makes it very clear that Eostre was indeed a goddess of fruitfulness, and another good example of the English tribes' focus on the blessings of divine female fertility. There is no recorded evidence that Eostre was a member of the Vanir, but given that she fits the general English and Vanir concern with the fertility of the land, animals and mankind, it does seem quite likely.

The Religious Role of Kings

When discussing kings of the very early English it should be noted that the kingly role was not static but evolved over the centuries. The general trend seems to have been for the kingly leadership role to become less collective and more autocratic as tribes grew in population size, amalgamated with neighbouring peoples through marriage or conquest, and the geographical area ruled by each king gradually expanded, whilst the number of competing kingdoms slowly declined. For a very long time English kingship was not automatically hereditary. Kings had to be elected or at least approved by a council of nobles or 'wise men' – the Witenaġemot or *Witan*. This remained the case amongst post-migration Anglo-Saxon realms in Britain, though the Witan tended to become less truly autonomous and more formalised over time, as the remuneration and coercive capacities of royal families increased with the growing size and resources of their domains.

Nevertheless in the pre-Christian period the authority of pagan kings to rule their peoples depended not just on coercive and remunerative capacity, but also on their being perceived as legitimate by their followers, which in turn depended in large part on those rulers being seen to be favoured (or not) by the gods. The favour of the gods could be requested through religious rituals and sacrifice, with the chances of success depending in part on the degree of expertise exercised in such matters by tribal priestesses and priests.

As noted above, for the Vanir-respecting early English, divine fertility blessings were of the utmost importance for the tribes' very survival, the key to the avoidance of starvation. A king presiding over failed harvests was likely to be deposed for having lost the trust of the gods. For a king to maximise his chances of personal survival, and those of his tribe, he needed divine favour, and the power to appeal effectively for that favour was believed to lie mainly with women skilled in shamanic trance, divination, and the magical seidr arts. Kings were dependent not just upon the male Witan, but also upon the priestesses of their tribe, a mutual female-male granting and exchange of power which would eventually be ended with the dominance of patriarchal Christianity.

> "Leadership of the king in religious matters must go back to heathen times. Kings and tribal chiefs no doubt figured in sacrificial and other pagan ceremonies. They habitually surrounded themselves with councillors who fulfilled... both the ritual function of priests and the advisory capacity of cabinet ministers. A king of ancient times had two main responsibilities – to keep his people fed and to ensure military victory (cf. the dual symbolism of king Scyld Scefing). The first of these needs, which concerned the cyclic planting and harvesting of crops and the breeding and killing of beasts, was presumably satisfied by the seasonal sacrifices and feasts. Warfare, less regular in its occurrence, was prefaced by divination." [15]

For a pagan English king to be successful in his dual role as the perceived provider of both sufficient food and security he needed to

- Firstly, keep on good terms with the Vanir goddesses, such as Nerthus (Mother Earth), in order to keep his people fed, and
- Secondly, liaise closely with tribal priestesses, who were not only intermediaries with the goddesses and gods, but whom he also needed to guide him through their female shamanic and runic divinatory skills, especially when it came to political and military matters.

The general early Germanic veneration of the special holiness of women, especially strong amongst the Vanir-respecting English Yngling and Angle tribes, was noted by the Romans:

> "Tacitus[16] stresses that the Germans believed that there was something especially holy about women as a sex... that they had special prophetic powers, that men consulted them, and followed their advice on matters of politics and war. The English seem to have conformed to the general Germanic pattern... except

for one thing... The noteworthy characteristic of the English, to foreign eyes, was that they were goddess worshippers; they looked on the earth as their mother. They did not leave this relationship behind when they crossed over to another part of the earth. [17]

'They worship in common Nerthus, that is Terra Mater (the Earth Mother), and believe she intervenes in human affairs and goes on progress through the tribes'." [18]

Scyld Scefing's Dual Role as King

Given all the emphasis on the importance of Shef (or Scyld Scefing) as a bringer of fertility to lands and peoples, where does the 'shield' element of his name fit in? We know that Shef became king, and that the king's role was both religious and military. However another possibility, considered by Kathleen Herbert, is that the circular form of the shield, in addition to its obvious defensive military function, might also have referenced the sun, that other Vanir fertility goddess (whether Freya or Sol) so essential to the Earth Mother's ability to feed her children through the successful generation of food crops. In Germanic culture and mythology the sun is female and the moon male.

> *"Looking at the sequence: Sheaf, Shield, Barley in the Wessex genealogy, it is easy to see why the barleycorn sown at the New Year ploughing should be seen as the offspring of last year's harvested sheaf – but why did a shield come between? ...In Bronze Age*[†] *pictures, sun-discs are used as shields by stick-like male figures. They are also placed with ritual boats. The sun is needed to bring the crops. The story of the wonder child from overseas contains some lost myth or ritual. If this was originally a celebration of the coming of agriculture to the north, with the miraculous enrichment that this must have brought to human life, then it could go back*

[†] Bronze Age: *"The European Bronze Age is characterized by bronze artefacts and the use of bronze implements... It starts with the Aegean Bronze Age in 3200 BC, and spans the entire 2nd millennium BC in Northern Europe, lasting until c. 600 BCE."* [Wikipedia]

*as far as 2,500 BCE, which is about the time when this
knowledge and skill developed in Old Anglia..."* [19]

The idea that the 'shield' element in Scyld Scefing's name could
originally (about 4,500 years ago) have referred to the sun, prior to
becoming associated with physical protection, is certainly an attractive
one. It makes sense to suppose that Scyld Scefing's perceived function
as divine patriarch and fertility totem of the very early English tribes
would originate with storytelling remembrances of the hugely
beneficial impact that the arrival of agriculture must have had for the
quality of life of those tribes so very long ago.

The Vanir - *the Sea, and Ship Funerals*

It is significant that Shef arrives mysteriously from across the sea.
That the boat which brings him is richly decorated, and yet has neither
sails nor oars, but still somehow travels untroubled across the waves,
suggests that it has come from some other world altogether,
apparently magically and inexplicably guided to the shores of Skåne.
The early English believed that Vanaheim, the homeland of the Vanir
goddesses and gods, was to be found across the seas in the very far
west. They might well have speculated that the young child found in
the magical boat had indeed been sent to them from divine Vanaheim,
and that therefore they would be wise to keep him well looked after.
Viktor Rydberg goes into some detail to show that the decision to love
and protect the child in the boat was indeed a sensible one, explaining
in detail how the young Van offspring had been prepared for his
journey to, and for life in, the mortal world:

> *"As a young boy... [Shef] was sent by the Vanir to the
> southern shores of Scandinavia with the gifts of
> knowledge, learning and culture. 'Hyndla's Lay' tells
> how nine sisters amongst these friendly divinities
> prepared the child for its important mission, after he
> had been born in the outermost regions of the earth.[20]
> For his mission the child had to be equipped with
> strength, endurance, and wisdom. The nine sisters
> therefore gave him a triple heathen-mythic drink –
> firstly a potion of forgetfulness able to allay sorrow.
> What the child tasted next was the mead of inspiration
> and wisdom - the very highest of spiritual gifts. Finally
> he drank water sourced from pools around whose rush-*

bordered edge the reeds of poetry grow.[21] All these
liquids came from the subterranean fountains which
water the world tree Yggdrasil itself, sustaining the
spiritual and physical life of the universe.

"When the child had been strengthened in this manner
for his great mission, he was laid sleeping in the
decorated ship, given the grain-sheaf for his pillow, and
numerous treasures were placed around him. It is
certain that there were not only weapons and
ornaments, but also workmen's tools. Amongst other
things Scef brought the fire-auger[22] to primeval man
who until that time had lived without the blessings
produced by the sacred fire.[23]" [24]

It was said that the Van god Njörd's coastal home was bordered by
a beach on which resided a flock of sacred swans which sang to him,
and that divine swans of the same species also swam in the waters
which nourished the roots of the World Tree Yggdrasil, which
supported all the nine worlds and all life. There is a north German
version of the Shef legend which presents the child's boat as arriving
drawn over the waves by one of these swans.

"Shef comes from across the sea. Vanaheim (homeland
of the Vanir gods such as Freya and Frey) was thought
to be situated on the other side of it, in the same
direction as the sea god Ægir's palace in the great
western ocean. Njörd's home Nóatún is also situated in
the West, on a strand beyond which sacred swans sing.

"In a faded memory of Shef, preserved in the folktales of
the Lower Rhine and the Netherlands, there comes to a
poverty-stricken people a boat in which there lies a
sleeping youth. This boat is, like Shef's, without sails or
oars, but is drawn over the surging waves by a swan.
Sacred swans of this sort are said to be descended from
that pair which swim in the waters of the Norn Urd's
fountain, which nourishes the World Tree Yggdrasil.
Thus the descendants of these swans that sing outside
the Vanir palace of Nóatún, and their arrival on the
shores of our world of Midgard at Skåne, are connected
to Shef, and the cultural riches given to the Danes,
Angles, Saxons, Swedes and English (Ynglings) by the
Vanir gods." [25]

That Shef's original homeland had indeed been otherworldly

Vanaheim would have appeared to storytelling audiences to have been confirmed by the reappearance of his boat upon the king's death, and its bearing him away back across the sea. This would have been something of a departure from the more usual form of royal ship funeral involving either interment of the ship on land or, less frequently, its being set fire to at sea, but close enough to the coast for the living to witness the inferno.

That Shef's boat should be perceived as being capable of having borne him from another world would not have surprised Anglo-Saxon storytelling audiences, for ships were generally recognised as vehicles which sailed off in to the far unknown, and sometimes returned from what to most people remained mysterious foreign lands. It seemed natural enough that those unknowable alien destinations might also include otherworldly ports, so much so, as the archaeological evidence at Sutton Hoo, Oseberg and elsewhere shows us, some very important Anglo-Saxon and Nordic burials – those of kings or high priestesses – took the form of ship inhumations. The dead king or priestess was prepared for their journey to another world beyond the grave by being interred inside a ship, along with many treasures and tools which it was thought might be useful to them in their new life. Hence it is no great surprise to find that when Alfred the Great later demanded of his scribes that they provide his people with evidence of his having been appointed to rule by the Christian God himself, they did so by inventing a royal ancestry going all the way back – *via Shef* – to that other very special ship: Noah's Ark:

> "The genealogists of the West Saxon kings... transformed Scyld, Sceaf, Beow and other legendary characters into ancestors... the semi-fictional pedigree of most Anglo-Saxon kings went back to Woden... the list concludes with Bedwig [Beow, Barley], son of Sceaf, who...
>
> 'is the son of Noah; he was born in Noah's Ark'.
>
> "Thus Sceaf, a fertility figure, was, like Freyr and his father [Njörd], associated with a ship. Possibly Nerthus, the fertility goddess whose rites Tacitus describes, was also linked with a ship, for the author mentions... that some of the Suebi worshipped a goddess whom he identifies with the Egyptian Isis... Nerthus, or Mother Earth." [26]

Most commentators seem agreed that Scyld Scefing's ship funeral as described in the Old English *Beowulf* poem corresponds quite accurately in most, but not quite all, respects, with actual historically evidenced ship funerals:

"The ship funeral is a rite which certainly took place in the Germanic world, as archaeological evidence proves. It was a ritual associated with the death of kings and chiefs and involved the provision of grave goods just as elaborate as the poem [Beowulf] suggests. The funeral of Scyld Scefing seems to be fictional only in the detail that the ship laden with treasure is set adrift at sea... it is unlikely that the mourners might face the anti-climax of finding the funeral ship coming back in on the next tide, or worse, the humiliation of losing their nation's treasure to an enemy if the funeral ship drifted to foreign shores...

"From other literature and from archaeology we can see that in practice the role of the ship was more symbolic than in Scyld Scefing's special case. Since the soul departed... the body was prepared for a journey. It was laid in a ship with the elaborate equipment the dead man[27] would need for life in the next world appropriate to his rank; but the whole was not set aimlessly adrift. If it was towed out to sea it was set on fire. Alternatively it could remain on land, where it was burned on a pyre or buried in the earth." [28]

North European pagan ship burials were *not* only about preparing a king or high priestess for the journey to a new life. The attendant religious ritual was also associated with recognising and strengthening relationships between pagan peoples and their gods:

"From an archaeological point of view, the royal rite of ship funeral in East Anglia is seen as signalling dynastic allegiance with Scandinavia... Yngling traditions seem to provide an analogy, for according to Snorri Sturluson, the establishment of the rite of mound inhumation was attributed to the dynasty's founder, the divine figure Yngvi-Freyr:

"After Freyr had been buried in a mound at Uppsala, many chiefs made mounds no less than standing stones to the memory of their kinsmen". [29]

"The enactment of this particular burial rite was understood by those who believed themselves to be his descendants to be a re-enactment of Freyr's mythic

precedent, so affirming their allegiance to him." [30]

"The rite of mound burial in the Northlands would seem to have entailed, in the words of Mircea Eliade:

> "Repetition of an archetypal action performed *'in illo tempore'* ['at that time', or 'in times gone by'] by ancestors or gods... By its repetition, the act coincides with its archetype, and time is abolished." [31]

"The implication is that the legend of Scyld Scefing in Beowulf represents a version of a story told to explain the mythic origin and purpose of the Old English royal rite of the ship funeral." [32]

Note the phrase *"and time is abolished"*. Ironically - time was only abolished temporarily(!), i.e. while the magic of ritual took place. But whilst the ritual was taking place the space between worlds could overlap, and the presence of the gods was felt. This was particularly so at the funeral of a king, as Anglo-Saxon kings believed themselves to be descended from the gods (whether Shef or later Woden). With the magical temporary abolition of time, those ancestors, including the divine ones, could again actually be present to witness the passing of another generation from Midgard to another world:

> *"We have evidence... that the West Saxon kings of the late 9th and 10th centuries regarded themselves as descendants of the same Danish royal family which we meet in Beowulf... The legend itself was... not native to Wessex. Its nautical character suggests that it is more likely to have been fostered by a seafaring people. Wessex appears to have been a landlocked realm... until its expansion southwards in the latter half of the 7th century... The origin legend of the hero from over the sea moreover appears to have incorporated aspects of ancient English fertility myth."* [33]

Pagan funeral ritual was not just about recognising and strengthening the relationship between tribal leader figures (such as high priestesses and kings) and the gods. Every member of such a priestess's or king's tribe would have felt themselves associated with the worlds of the gods, and especially strongly so when witnessing or participating in religious ritual. Although the boundaries between the worlds could be thinned or even temporarily abolished by such practices, the world of the Vanir ultimately remained not merely mysterious, but never fully comprehensible to mortal mankind, whether kings or peasants. Beyond a certain point, in this world even magic must have its limits, as the gods and their worlds are actually beyond full human cognition:

> "[There is] *a direct relationship between Scyld's legendary advent and his ship funeral... the form of his departure mirrors the form of his arrival; the one explains the other... the symbolic roles of the ship and its voyages from and to the unknown are primary; having originally functioned as Scyld's cradle, bearing him from the unknown over the sea to the Danes, it becomes at the end his funerary vessel, returning him to the unknown. The implication is that the references to the sea... are more symbolic than literal... Scyld's last voyage clearly realises a return to his mysterious place of origin.*
>
> > "Men under heavens' shifting skies,
> > Though skilled in counsel,
> > Cannot surely say who unshipped that cargo."
> > [Beowulf - lines 43-45]
>
> *"These lines state explicitly that the ultimate destination of Scyld's funeral ship is beyond the knowledge of the wisest and the strongest of men. The limits of mere human knowledge are similarly defined a little later in the poem when we hear of the supernatural movements of ... the monster Grendel:* "no man can know whither such wending demons glide". *The ultimate destination of Scyld's funeral vessel is... unknowable precisely because it is beyond mortal cognition."* [34]

Sam Newton explains that whilst the burial of a ship, and its covering by a mound of earth, might appear to imply that its use as a means of transport was ending, in fact to the early English pagan mind ships were chosen to encompass the bodies of the dead for precisely the opposite reason. Their transportation function was not ending, but being transformed to operate on a higher plane, so as to facilitate travel from this world to an otherworld:

> *"Scyld's last voyage should be understood as a realisation of a poetic ideal... This notion of the ship as a means of crossing the boundary between worlds... certainly seems to apply in the majestic ceremony implied by the contents of Mound One at Sutton Hoo, even though here the vessel was interred... Interment...*

need not have contradicted the suggested symbolic function of the vessel at all, [and] although the suggested symbolism of Scyld's last voyage is not incompatible with Christian thought, the context here... is primarily pagan." [35]

Shef - *and Heimdal*

Viktor Rydberg argues that Heimdal, seen in later Nordic myth as the Æsir's guard of Asgard's rainbow bridge, and Shef, are in fact one and the same. Heimdal, he maintains, was originally one of the Vanir tribe of gods, along with Freyja, Freyr, Njörd, Nerthus and others. Heimdal/Shef's primary and key role, he says, was not the later defence of Asgard against the giants, but rather the much earlier fathering of children with mortal couples, a process which brought to mankind both

- A certain unity and identity of interests between the Vanir gods and mortals, or at least the tribes of Skåne, whose later generations could legitimately claim divine ancestry, *and*
- The rich cultural fertility associated with Shef's arrival in Skåne, including such things already mentioned as the development of agriculture, military skills, poetic learning, and now also the further development of productive and social wealth of all kinds (material and intellectual) through the development of the division of labour and the creation of social classes.

   "The Vanir most prominent in the myths are Njörd, Frey, and Heimdal. Though an Æsir god by adoption, Heimdal is like Njörd and Frey a Vanir god by birth and birthplace, and is accordingly called both áss and van.
   Meanwhile these three divinities, definitely named Vanir, are only a few out of many. The Vanir constituted a numerous clan, strong enough to wage a victorious war against the Æsir. Who among them was Shef-Yngvi?
   "Of Heimdal, and of him alone among the gods, it is related that he lived for a time among men as a mortal man, and that he performed that which is attributed to Shef - that is,

organised and elevated human society and
became the progenitor of royal families in
Midgard. The god Heimdal, having assumed
the name Rig, fathered with a mortal woman
a son who was given the title of Jarl [lord or
earl], *who in turn became the father to Dan,*
given the title of Konr [king]. *Rig is*
grandfather to Dan, who is a Skjöldung.
Heimdal-Rig is thus the father of the
progenitor of the Skjöldungs, and it is the
story of the divine origin of the Skjöldungs
'Rigsthula' gives us when it tells of Heimdal as
Jarl's father and the first king's grandfather.
But the progenitor of the Skjöldungs is,
according to both Anglo-Saxon and the
northern sources, Shef. Thus Heimdal and Shef
are identical." [36]

Shef - *Civilisation and the Class System*

Rydberg brings together the stories of Shef and Heimdal-Rig, by asserting that Heimdal-Rig surely did not suddenly descend from Asgard as a god, appearing uninvited from nowhere to sleep with mortal women and father children with them. Rather, Rydberg suggests, he got to know mankind first by growing up amongst them as the child Shef... no doubt developing his flirting and seduction skills in his teenage years, before being allowed into mortal women's beds!

"The boy [Shef] *grew up among the inhabitants of the*
Skåne coast and, when he reached manhood, human
civilisation developed rapidly under his influence.
Different social classes, each with their distinct
functions, appeared. In 'Rigsthula', we find him
journeying along
"green paths, from house to house, in that land which
his presence has blessed."
"Here he is called Rig - it is true of him as of nearly all
mythological persons, that he has several names - but
the introduction to the poem [Rigsthula] *informs us*
that the person so called is the god Heimdal.
"Civilisation was now fully established. The people were

settled, they span and wove, and their skilled hands produced many things. They worked as smiths, ploughed the fields, baked bread, and Heimdal instructed them in runes. Different homes showed different customs and various degrees of wealth, but happiness prevailed everywhere.

"Heimdal visited Ai's and Edda's unpretentious home, was hospitably received, and remained there three days. Nine months later a son called Thrall was born to this family. Heimdal then visited Afi's and Amma's well-kept house, and nine months after that visit a son called Karl (churl) was born in that household. Finally Rig took himself to Fadir's and Moder's elegant home. There, nine months later, a son called Jarl (lord) was born. Thus the three Teutonic classes - thralls, freemen, and nobility - received divine sanction from Heimdal-Rig." [37]

Churls, it should be noted, are not 'churlish' but 'freemen', usually tenant farmers rather than landowners, at least in Nordic Scandinavian society. The *Rigsthula* poem is Norse, not Anglo-Saxon. Social class divisions continued to develop and become more complex over time, especially in Anglo-Saxon England. *Rigsthula's* original three classes - aristocracy, freemen and thralls (slaves) – became four or five in Nordic areas later, and up to ten or more in more highly developed Anglo-Saxon England,[38] and that is without counting 'the religious' (priests, monks, nuns etc.) as a separate social class.

Rydberg continues by further explaining that although 'Teutonic' men and women can legitimately describe themselves as children of the gods, they are nevertheless still nothing more than fully human; they are not themselves gods:

"In the account of Rig's visit to the three different homes lies the mythological concept of a common father, an idea which should not be overlooked when human heroes are described as sons of gods in the myths and heroic sagas. They are sons of the gods and, at the same time, mortal men. Their lineage, starting with Ask and Embla, was not interrupted by the intervention of the visiting god, nor did it generate any kind of half-divine, half-human being.

"The Teutonic patriarch Mannus was, according to Tacitus, the son of a god and the grandson of the

goddess Earth. Nevertheless he was, as his name indicates, in the full physical sense of the word, a man, and besides his divine father, also had a human father. Men and women of all classes are the descendants of Ask and Embla, as Völuspa's *skald describes them gathered around the seeress when she was to present to them a history of the world's development, and commanded silence with the formula:*

'Listen now, all you peoples of sacred origin, great and
small, children of Heimdal.' [39]

So, all members of these tribes 'of sacred origin' are the children of the god Shef/Heimdal, at least in the limited sense that he is their distant spiritual ancestor. However Rydberg (and Tacitus) are also clear that even Mannus, who was much more directly *"the son of a god and grandson of the goddess Earth"* (Nerthus), had *"besides his divine father also a human father"*.

How is it possible for someone to have two fathers? What this surely must mean is that *Rigsthula's* skald is speaking to us in figurative, poetic terms, not literal ones. In the poem the three individual, named human fathers and husbands of the named individual mortal women remain the true physical fathers of their children. What Shef/Heimdal is doing is giving those children gifts of knowledge and abilities required to successfully fulfil specific social functions, and hence promote human society in general, and its ability to further engender abundance and fertility in all its forms, whether agricultural, martial, intellectual, or spiritual.[40]

Scyld Scefing – *Essential Anglo-Saxon Paganism*

In conclusion it can be said that although the ancient legend of Scyld Scefing is not as well known as the stories of the north European gods and goddesses recorded by Snorri Sturluson in Iceland in the thirteenth century, it is key to understanding some of the basic differences and similarities between early (pre-migration) Anglo-Saxon and later Scandinavian pagan Weltanschauungen (ways of looking at the worlds). Key points include:

- The legend of Shield Sheafing is an extremely old story, going back well before the migration of the Anglo-Saxons and associated tribes to Britain about 1,500 years ago.
- A key aspect of the legend is its celebration of the abundance

brought about by the development of agriculture, estimated to have reached northern Europe about 2,500 BCE – so about 4,500 years ago.

- The migrating tribes – Heathobards, Ynglings, Angles, Jutes and Saxons, later to become the English - recognised primarily the Vanir as their gods, and in some senses saw themselves as descendants of the Vanir, especially Shef/Heimdal.
- The early English tribes, later called Anglo-Saxons, also knew of Odin's Æsir gods, but saw them differently from the way the Vikings later understood the Æsir; for the English Woden was a wandering mystic, not Odin the capricious military leader collecting the battle dead together ready to die again at the end of the world.
- Heimdal was seen as one of the Vanir, and for the Anglo-Saxons was the same as their divine ancestor Shef, not the warrior-guard of Asgard's rainbow bridge as he later came to be presented by Viking skalds.
- For the pagan early English, there was always less emphasis on military aspects of the divine, and instead a much greater interest in
    o Fertility issues, especially of the land
    o 'Cultural development' – relating to the improvement of knowledge and skills in areas such as crop cultivation, hand tool manufacture, military abilities, and poetry and storytelling
    o Goddesses as life-giving forces, especially Nerthus as a vital Mother Earth figure, and possibly also sun goddesses.
- The magical, healing, divinatory, and divine-intercessionary roles of women and priestesses were highly valued.

The above list of key points is not an exhaustive record of everything that differentiated early Anglo-Saxon paganism from its later Scandinavian counterpart, for although many important points can be found in the Scyld Scefing story, there are also other unique aspects of early English paganism which are not present there. Additional key aspects discussed in subsequent chapters include Anglo-Saxon perceptions of the goddesses, in particular the 'great goddess' Freya, and attitudes to issues such as gender fluidity, dissent, death, and materialist philosophy.

Chapter 2 Appendix –
Scyld Scefing in *Beowulf* *

Listen now!
Was it not Scyld Scefing who shook the halls,
Took mead benches, taught encroaching foes
To fear him,
He who, found in childhood, had lacked even clothing.
Yet he lived, and prospered,
Grew in strength and stature under the heavens,
Until even those tribes settled on neighbouring sea coasts,
Over the whale road,
All – obeyed him and gave tribute.
He was a good king!
At the hour shaped for him Scyld departed.
They carried him out to the edge of the sea,
His sworn comrades in arms, as he had himself directed them
While yet he wielded his words, Warden of the Scyldings,
Beloved folk-founder; long had he ruled.
A boat with a ringed neck rode in the haven,
Icy, eager to be away, the atheling's vessel,
And there they laid out their lord and master,
Dispenser of coiled gold,
In the waist of the ship, in majesty by the mast.
A mound of treasures
From far countries was fetched aboard her...
The hoard was no less great
Than those gifts he had received
From they who at the outset
Had adventured him over seas
Alone, a small child.
High overhead they hoisted and fixed
A banner of beaten gold.
With bitter hearts and mourning mood
They gave him to the flood,
Let the seas take him.
Men under heavens' shifting skies,
Though skilled in counsel,
Cannot surely say who unshipped that cargo.

---

* Excerpt slightly adapted from: *Beowulf*, Penguin Classics, London, 1973, orig.
  trans. Michael Alexander (lines 1-23; 30-45)

Chapter 3 –
Beowulf: the Pagan Legacy

In seeking to illuminate the pagan world view of the early English, Beowulf is an important source. It is one of the earliest surviving major literary works in Old English, and in throwing significant light on the origins and attitudes of the English tribes – before they came to what became England – is useful in illustrating key differences between early English and later Viking/Scandinavian pagan cultures. This is particularly true of the sub-plot involving Freawaru and Ingeld (see later in this chapter). Although written down by a Christian poet in the 9th or 10th century, its origins go back to pagan times, perhaps around the mid-7th century, with some events possibly relating to even earlier periods. As part of its wonderfully poetic and heroic storytelling Beowulf deals in elemental themes including *"death, divine power, horror, exultation, disgrace, personal devotion,* [and] *fame."* [41]

In discussing Beowulf it is first worth noting that (for most of us) it is a work in translation (from Old English) that is being reviewed. As with all translation this immediately opens up questions of tone and accuracy of meaning, potentially raising questions about the reliability of interpretations of the 'true' sense of the text. This is valid to a lesser extent for all criticism of any work of literature, even when not in translation, but nevertheless examples of how differences in translation may affect perceived meaning, and perceptions of the pre- and post-conversion Anglo-Saxon world outlook, will be included here. In particular the sometimes conflicting analyses in the classic translations of Beowulf by J. R. R. Tolkien (author of *Lord of the Rings* and Oxford University Professor of Anglo-Saxon) and Seamus Heaney (Irish poet and 1995 winner of the Nobel Prize for Literature) will be considered.

Tolkien himself said that *"Too many people are willing to form, and even to print, opinions of this greatest of the surviving works of ancient English poetic art after reading only... a translation"*,[42] but that didn't stop him offering his own translation!

Before considering later in this chapter what this might mean when it comes to interpreting the early English pagan world outlook, here is just one brief technical instance of the problems of translation. One of the problematic areas can be the Anglo-Saxon (and Norse) use of 'kennings' or poetic metaphor phrases. A well-known example is the referencing of the sea by calling it the "whale road". Heaney uses this "whale road" translation (e.g. line 10 of his *Beowulf*) for the Old English word "hronrad". Tolkien however says *"It is quite incorrect to translate it* [hronrad] *as 'whale road'"*[43], explaining that "hron" is not 'whale' at all, but a dolphin (a whale being "hwael" in Old English), and "rad" he says is not a noun meaning 'a road' either, but rather a verb meaning 'to ride'. This might seem to invalidate Heaney's "whale road" translation... but then Tolkien in his own translation comes up with *"over the sea where the whale rides"*.[44]

Part of the problem is that Heaney attempts a poetic, artistic translation, as true as possible in rhythm and sound to the original Old English, while Tolkien does not do that at all. Instead he concentrates always on accuracy of meaning, because as a university lecturer in Old English he was concerned to help his students' literal understanding of the language. As the result of these different approaches Tolkien ends up with 2,669 lines of prose in his translation, whilst from the same original text Heaney comes up with 3,182 lines of poetry.

Over and above technical issues of this sort, the sense of translations can also be significantly affected by the translator's own world outlook and ideological concerns. Tolkien was a Christian who seems to have found within himself some degree of poignant empathy for pre-Christian English paganism growing out of his Anglo-Saxon cultural and Old English language studies. He therefore experiences Beowulf as an elegy, sympathetic with times past now gone forever. In this he sees himself identifying with the post-migration but still pagan early English, seeing them remembering and perhaps even yearning for their old pre-migration homelands and experiences. For the early English in Britain, he says, the

> *"poem is like a play in a room through the windows of which a distant view can be seen over a large part of the English traditions about the world of their original home".* [45]

For Seamus Heaney on the other hand Beowulf remains a more straightforward fantasy adventure story and "heroic narrative". He claims that

> *"People living in England during... the poet's own day... knew no more than we do now of ghoulish flesh-eating demons, of flying, fire-breathing dragons... [they] may have known little more... about great pagan cremation funerals, or about acts of huge and selfless heroism."* [46]

It appears that Heaney, when he imagines an Anglo-Saxon Beowulf audience, casts his mind back only to the late Anglo-Saxon period when England was already (at least formally) Christian. The more apparently ardent Christian Tolkien on the other hand, when he imagines an Anglo-Saxon Beowulf audience, casts his mind back further, envisaging an earlier period when the post-migration English were still pagan. He does this because he is keen to try to understand the pre-Christian mind-set – a concern discussed in more detail later in this chapter.

In any case Heaney's contention that the Anglo-Saxons *"knew no more than we do now of... fire-breathing dragons"* perhaps underestimates early English visionary credence. Certainly it underestimates that of the pre-Christian English. They were definitely able to experience the very gods themselves in their landscape, never mind mere dragons.

> *"English topographical place-names... that mention supernatural creatures such as elves, monsters, demons or giants etc. are rare but informative, associating such creatures with fissures and hollows, openings in the ground, pools and wet places, ancient monuments and ruins... the whole landscape was...* 'sacred and numinous' *to greater and lesser extents... The existence of fields and groves dedicated to specific deities is attested to by a range of place names...* Feld (field) and Leah (grove) occur several times in combination with gods' names such as Woden, Thunor and Tiw... These sites presumably functioned as places of belief or cult locations where sacred activities might have been carried out."* [47]

The differences in the ways that Tolkien and Heaney envisage the Anglo-Saxon Beowulf audience are linked to the relationship between the historical setting of the story itself, and the imagined audiences. For Heaney the poem is illustrative of a

> *"Christian understanding of... a pagan Germanic society governed by an heroic code of honour, one where the attainment of a name for warrior-prowess among the living overwhelms any concern about the soul's destiny in the afterlife".* [48]

Tolkien would agree, but also try to dig a bit deeper into understanding that pagan apparent lack of concern about the soul's destiny – again a concern discussed in more detail later in this chapter, and more generally in chapters 13 and 14.

What Heaney and Tolkien definitely do fully agree on is that the story is partly historical, but partly also fiction, and that it is no longer possible to be always sure which is which. Beowulf was written in England - but set in Denmark, because English tribes, clans and dynasties (known as, Angles, Jutes, Heathobards, Ynglings and by other names over time) were living there before they migrated to Britain (possibly following military defeat by the Danes, creating a need to find a new homeland or live in subjugation). Nevertheless Beowulf is not a history of the English. To the extent that it is historical and not fiction, it is a history of Scandinavian tribes (Danish Scyldings and Swedish Geats), as remembered by the English, but not a history of the English themselves (Beowulf is not English, but a Geat). This allows creative space for English storytellers to extend the narrative beyond relatively simple heroic adventures in history into the magical, spiritually important, and simultaneously entertaining realms of the fairy story, encompassing additional themes which speak more directly to English pagan mystical concerns.

Early English World Views – *Pagan and Christian*

In order to review survivals of the early English pagan world view in Beowulf, it is worth first summarising the story line. The tale seems to relate events from the fifth and sixth centuries CE, but to have been composed much later (Tolkien's 'best guess' for the date of composition is 797 CE [49]), and not to have been set down in writing until the 9th or 10th century. Tolkien was also clear that Beowulf as a character was *"unhistorical, at any rate as an actual member of the Geatish royal house"* [50] but suggests that in terms of the story he must have been born around the year 495, and arrived at King Hrothgar's hall of Heorot about age 20 in 515, when Hrothgar would have already been about sixty years old. Beowulf's name means 'war-wolf'. The story of Beowulf's life as set out in the poem is summarised very briefly below.

The Story of Beowulf

Beowulf, a hero of the Geats, comes to the aid of Hrothgar, the king of the Danes, whose great hall, Heorot, is plagued by the monster Grendel. Beowulf kills Grendel with his bare hands, and later also Grendel's mother with a giant's sword that he finds in her lair. Later in his life, Beowulf himself becomes king of the Geats, and finds his realm terrorized by a dragon. Beowulf finally slays the dragon, but is mortally wounded in the struggle. He is cremated and a burial mound is erected in his honour by the sea.

By the late ninth or early tenth century when the Beowulf story was probably finally being recorded in writing, England had been formally Christian for over two centuries, although paganism was far from forgotten. Not only did aspects of it survive informally in sub-aristocratic Anglo-Saxon culture[*], but the more strident paganism of Scandinavian Viking raiders and settlers also continued to be well known. It was only towards the end of the ninth century that Guthrum, Viking king of the English 'Danelaw' (Northumbria, East Mercia, and East Anglia) accepted Christian baptism, and it seems likely that not only did many Danes remain only superficially Christian for some time afterwards, but that

> "The presence of Scandinavians in England in the late Viking age could have caused a resurgence of the Anglo-Saxon cult. If we acknowledge that this paganism included concepts of mentality and world view on a general level and not just belief in its narrowest sense, it is clear that the depositions of weapons, jewellery and tools [into rivers, lakes and pools] from mainly the ninth and tenth century could be expressions of a new blossoming of cultural paganism. This tradition of mobilising specific landscape features through ritual acts had its roots in pre-Scandinavian Anglo-Saxon England, revitalised in the fusion of Anglo-Saxon and Scandinavian traditions.

[*] See elsewhere in this volume, especially later in this chapter and chapter 8, *Trees in Anglo-Saxon England*.

> *The objects deposited in this period were of distinct Anglo-Saxon as well as Scandinavian types... several of these objects have Anglo-Saxon runic inscriptions. Thus, the acts of deposition were most likely shared ritual practices."* [51]

Given then that paganism was not forgotten at the time when Beowulf was written down, the Christian storyteller/s who recorded this poem dealing with pre-Christian times and events clearly needed to be conscious of how they might best present paganism to their audience, and would be aware of a requirement and responsibility to do so within a Christian context. They sought to achieve this by reminding readers and listeners that, in the view of the Church, it was Christianity which first brought realistic hope of personal salvation and an eternal afterlife in heaven to mankind. Prior to that there had been only the 'false hope' of paganism.

> *"Sometimes at pagan shrines they vowed*
> *Offerings to idols, swore oaths*
> *That the killer of souls might come to their aid*
> *And save the people. That was their way,*
> *Their heathen hope; deep in their hearts*
> *They remembered Hell."* [52]

Christian commentary repeatedly sees pagans as being without hope, by which they mean without hope of an eternal afterlife of the individual soul – because this is granted by the one (individual) God to (individual) Christians only. It is not guaranteed, but good Christians may hope for salvation. Hence 'false gods' or *"idols"*, seen as the work of the Devil, are the *"killer of souls"*. It is unclear how this reconciles with the eternal damnation of undead souls implied in the allegation that *"deep in their hearts"* even pagans somehow *"remembered Hell"*, unless perhaps damnation is here being presented as eternal death (without eventual resurrection) rather than eternal suffering in the flames of the Christian Hell.

Tolkien claims of the Christian Beowulf poet that *"he knew one thing clearly: those days were heathen – heathen, noble and hopeless".*[53] This appears to imply that Tolkien thought the poet saw pagans as being entirely without hope, but this is clearly not the case. Rather, the poet laments what he perceives as the <u>false</u> hope of the heathens, i.e. their trust in 'false' gods and idols, the "killer of souls".

For the English pagan however it would have been the Christian concept of salvation that was a false hope. Pagans did not dream of individual 'salvation' and eternal life. Observation of nature taught them that the price of life is death. Death is 'the debt which must be paid' at the end of life. Without that no life would be possible, for life is change, not eternal stasis. Pagans did of course have hope: of a good life and a good death, and that their reputation might live on after them.

> *"Cattle die,*
> *Kinsmen die,*
> *The self dies too;*
> *I know one thing*
> *That never dies:*
> *The repute of each of the dead."* [54]

Even in Scandinavian Æsir-orientated paganism, warriors killed in battle, although they might go to Valhalla, did so only to pay their debt of life by dying heroically in the final battle against chaotic entropy at the end of the worlds. And in English Vanir/fertility based paganism the seasonal cycle of the year, and the cycle of life, are based on collective and pluralistic (not merely individual) birth/life/death/birth progressions. It seems that the Christian Beowulf poet was aware of this when he wrote of pagans hoping that *"the killer of souls might come to their aid, and save the people"*, i.e. that the entire people or tribe's salvation was the collective issue for pagans, not themselves as individual souls.

Similarly the collective and pluralistic nature of north European paganism differentiated it not only from the Christian emphasis on the fate of the individual soul, but in rejecting that individualism also denied any form of universalism and associated intolerance of alternative world views. It was never a single religion of 'the book', interpreted as unchangeable and inviolable rules, but rather a fluid and ever-changing range of beliefs tied not to any one spiritual or worldly leader, but rather to whole peoples' multiple, varied, at times no doubt contradictory, and certainly ever developing and adapting understandings.

Stephen Pollington sees this as a key difference between Germanic paganism and those (most often monotheistic) religions which claim eternal and universal applicability:

> *"Germanic religion was of a type termed 'folk', 'ethnic',*
> *or 'natural', as distinct from the 'universal' and*
> *'revealed' or 'prophetic' religions such as Christianity,*
> *Islam, Buddhism and Zoroastrianism. Prophetic*
> *religions differ from each other in the matter of*
> *doctrine and belief, in the importance assigned to this*

or that prophet, and in the details of the creeds espoused. None of these factors are of relevance to folk religions, because the latter define themselves in terms of ethnocultural rather than doctrinal terms. In effect, the primary object of devotion in a folk religion is the community..." [55]

This issue is looked at further at the end of this chapter through analysis of the Beowulf poet's treatment of the Freawaru and Ingeld legend.

Ancestors and the Dead in Beowulf

Christian Anglo-Saxons were faced with a conceptual conundrum concerning their generally revered forebears: was it really conceivable that members of their own families, their own noble and respected ancestors, might be condemned to all the eternal tortures of Hell simply because they were pagans, even though they had never had any opportunity to hear 'the word of God'? Did being pagan mean that you were, by definition, not 'saved', and so denied entry to heaven? The answer is not entirely clear, but for the Beowulf poet at least it seems that they were indeed condemned to Hell if, in their ignorance of God, they put their trust in the devil and the domain of demons:

"Cursed is he
Who in times of trouble has to thrust his soul
In the fire's embrace, forfeiting help;
He has nowhere to turn." [56]

Tolkien summarises the Christian view of pagan ancestors as follows: *"The 'leading idea' is that noble pagans of the past who had not heard the Gospel, knew of the existence of Almighty God, recognised him as 'good'... but were (by the Fall) still cut off from Him, so that in time of woe they became filled with despair... that was the hour when they were specially open to the snares of the Devil: they prayed to idols and false gods for help"*.[57] He also points out that although *"In Beowulf there is Hell... there is practically no clear reference to Heaven as its opposite... the characters within the poem do not understand heaven, or have hope of it. They refer to* Hell, *an originally pagan word"*.[58]

In Beowulf the monster Grendel, says the poet, had a "heathen soul" which, upon physical death, goes to the Christian Hell.[59] Tolkien sees this as the poet simply updating the alleged pagan concept of

'Hel' as being a place of punishment to which all who fail to gain entry to Odin's Valhalla are condemned:

> "Punishment of the wicked is certainly contemplated in Old Norse... 'heathen mythology', and the poem Völuspá reserves a place of torment for them; though Hell, like Hades, was the 'hidden land' of all the dead – apart from the Odinic conception of Valhöll".[60]

In this though, Tolkien is simply wrong. As Hilda Ellis's book 'The Road to Hel' makes clear, north European pagans had several ideas about where the souls of the dead might go, but Hel as a place of torment played very little role:

> "There appear to be two main conceptions about the fate of the dead: either they enter the realm of the gods, or they continue to dwell within the earth itself... The idea of an underground realm does not stand out... as an alternative to the realm of the gods and the grave-mound; the references to an underworld are vague, and there are no descriptions of such a realm...[61] In none of these stories is any attempt made to present the Underworld as a place of retribution and punishment. Snorri, it is true, attempts to make Hel such a place, but his interpretation is likely to be chiefly due to Christian teaching... but he is not convincing".[62]

This appears to be an example of Christians (ancient and modern) either misunderstanding or deliberately misrepresenting Anglo-Saxon and Scandinavian paganism. The misunderstanding or misrepresentation originates with the Christian teaching that individual souls face an eternal afterlife, and that by default that endless afterlife will consist of continual torture and pain, unless the individual can obtain salvation by giving their soul to the one true God. Clearly if that is your belief then the fate of your ancestors who never had a chance to hear that teaching of salvation must be seen to be grim indeed. At best, everlasting salvation in heaven will not have been achieved and, unlike deceased Christians, the pagan dead will stay dead, their souls destroyed without hope of resurrection. And at worst, those pagan dead who put their trust in idols and false gods will not only fail to get into heaven, but will also face the perpetual flames of the Christian Hell.

That is how Christians saw the pagan world view, but it is not how pagans themselves conceived of such existential questions. For the pagan the question of a need for salvation did not arise, because the individual soul was not conceived of as potentially living forever. Although limited afterlives of one kind or another (with Odin in Valhalla, in Freya's hall of Sessrumnir, to some time-limited degree as a spirit under the earth in a grave mound, or in the goddess Hel's chthonic realm) were possible, their duration was restricted – ultimately by the end of the worlds in the final battle against the forces of chaos at Ragnarok. And, while they lasted, such afterlives were more likely to involve feasting, drinking, and general merrymaking than being painfully tortured by the one God or (for pagans) his alter ego the devil. Individuals would best survive death by being remembered by their descendants through heroic and poetic storytelling, which would illuminate their earthly lives not merely in individual terms, but more importantly in how they served the collective fate of their people or tribe. For pagans the Christian need to illuminate a supposed dark fate of their ancestors after death did not arise. Instead there was a more positive emphasis on remembering, celebrating, and praising the achievements of their lives.

For the Christian Beowulf poet however such issues had to be dealt with. In addition to the question of personal salvation, Tolkien sees him as attempting to provide a Christian solution to the perceived philosophical and existential problem of despair: the heathen belief that ultimately everything must perish, even the gods themselves, in the final battle against the forces of chaos: *"The northern gods... are on the right side, though it is not the side that wins. The winning side is chaos and unreason".*[63] Tolkien explains that in the pagan view:

> *"The monsters had been the foes of the gods [and] the captains of men, and within Time the monsters would win... [For Christians however] the monsters remained the enemy of mankind, the infantry of the old war, and became inevitably the enemies of the one God... [but] the tragedy of the great temporal defeat remains for a while potent, but ceases to be finally important... [as] there appears a possibility of eternal victory (or eternal defeat), and the real battle is between the soul and its adversaries".*[64]

For the Beowulf poet and Tolkien then the Christian message is: Christ has brought about an alternative to the despair of inevitable collective defeat and death in the temporal, material world. That alternative is the salvation of an eternal afterlife, beyond the temporal, material world, not for all, but for those individuals who will surrender their soul to the one God. But again, this is Christians delving for answers to a problem of their own making, not a problem for pagans. Christians saw the pagan conceptions of death, the end of individual life, and the end of the worlds at Ragnarok, as expressions of despair. Pagans saw things very differently.

For the pagan life was less about the individual and more about the collective, both in the sense of the tribe, and in the cycle of life (and death) experienced through the generations. The meaning of life was to be found not in the seeking of everlasting heavenly joy and perfection for individual souls, but rather in individuals' celebration of the significant progress through life of their children, their family and tribe, and in recognition of deceased ancestors. With so much to celebrate, despair was hardly the key issue Christians imagined it to be. Individuals would die, and any souls' afterlives would also eventually be ended, but this was what made change, progress, and new, different lives possible. Children and grandchildren would be born and supersede parents. Similarly even after Ragnarok, new worlds would replace old. For pagans when the end of the worlds comes about:

> "The sun turns black, land sinks into the sea;
> The bright stars scatter from the sky.
> Flame flickers up against the World-Tree;
> Fire flies high against heaven itself." [65]

But that is followed by:

> "She sees rising up a second time
> The earth from the ocean, ever-green;
> The cataracts tumble, an eagle flies above,
> Hunting fish along the fell." [66]

Early English World Views – *Fate and Wyrd*

Having looked at the pagan and Christian Anglo-Saxon understanding of the philosophical concepts of hope and despair, as mediated through doctrines of salvation and everlasting life (for Christians) and death and new birth cycles (for pagans), this analysis of early English world views can be usefully extended by reviewing the pagan concept of the *Wyrd*, and its relationship to the perception of fate.

Old English had a range of words covering different aspects of the idea of 'fate'. In terms of an inevitable future, the word *'orlæg'* might be used, or perhaps *'metodgesceaft'* or simply *'metod'* meaning an absolute fate decreed by God. The term 'Wyrd' is also often translated as 'fate', but any investigation of this Anglo-Saxon term soon reveals some significant complexity of meaning deriving from the way the pagan English envisaged the worlds. Far from implying a simple inevitability, the *Wyrd* was much more about the intricacy of the inter-relationship of everything, rather in the nature of the chaos theory 'butterfly effect' in which *"a small change in one state of a deterministic nonlinear system can result in large differences in a later state"* [67], or to put it another way *"A butterfly flaps its wings in the Amazonian jungle, and subsequently a storm ravages half of Europe".*[68]

Seamus Heaney translates Beowulf's definitive statement on the matter as *"Fate goes ever as fate must"* [69]. Tolkien's translation is similar but importantly acknowledges the Anglo-Saxon concept of fate as being feminine: *"Fate goeth ever as she must."* [70] The original Old English line in Beowulf is *"Gæð a Wyrd swa hio scel"* or *"Wyrd* always goes as *she* shall".[71]

Bernard Cornwell in his series of Anglo-Saxon novels *The 'Last Kingdom'* (also a Netflix TV series) allocates an apparently equally deterministic understanding of fate to his main character Uhtred, whose motto is the Old English *"Wyrd bið ful āræd"*, which he translates as *"Fate is inexorable"*. It might be better to allow a subtly different translation: "fate is relentless".[72] 'Inexorable' means 'unalterable' or 'unavoidable", terms which clearly derive from the Christian concept of fate as the irreversible Will of God. But in Anglo-Saxon that is *'metod'*, not *'wyrd'*. Cornwell has taken the phrase *Wyrd bið ful āræd* from Old English poem *The Wanderer*, contained in the tenth century *Exeter Book*. The same *Exeter Book* also contains another verse, *The Rhyming Poem*, which has a different line about fate: *"Me þæt wyrd gewæf"* or "Wyrd wove this for me".[73] One of the key aspects of *Wyrd* is that unlike *Metod* it is happening and changing all the time. Far from being inexorable or unalterable it (or more accurately *she*) is weaving still, forever connecting threads in complex new ways:

> *"The idea of Wyrd, or something close to this, can be found worldwide in various forms, but you will see it most clearly as the Fates, the Norns and the Wyrd Sisters – a name made famous by Terry Pratchett."* [74]

In Cornwell's 'Last Kingdom' *"Fate is inexorable"*. In Heaney's Beowulf *"Fate goes ever as fate must"*, which sounds equally inexorable. But Tolkien's recognition that *Wyrd* is a feminine noun[75] in Old English changes everything. *Metod* (fate as decreed by God) is masculine, as of course is the early Christian God. However the word being used in Beowulf is *Wyrd*, of which Tolkien says *"it is difficult to determine in any given passage containing 'wyrd'... what precisely it means".*[76] This *Wyrd* feminine complexity contrasts strongly with the fixed and absolute nature of the Christian male God's *metod*. For Tolkien Wyrd *"means 'a happening, event'... and can be spoken of as a 'power' or an ordinance in itself"* – i.e. Wyrd is a force independent of God's will, neither 'inexorable' as Bernard Cornwell would have it, nor inevitable. The Christian poet tries to square the circle of this traditional pagan understanding of *Wyrd*, says Tolkien, by acknowledging its independence - but then insisting on seeing it as subordinate to *'Metod'* as determined by God.[77]

Wyrd as an independent force is evidenced again when Beowulf remembers earlier fights he had had with monsters of the deep:

> *"Often, for undaunted courage*
> *Fate spares the man it has not already marked.*
> *However it had occurred, my sword had killed*
> *Nine sea monsters."* [78]

Tolkien comments that this seems, at first glance, to be *"as completely an 'illogical' reference to Fate as could be devised".*[79] How can Fate be Fate if it/she keeps changing her mind? The answer is of course that it is not Christian Fate, or the Will of God, that is being referred to, but *Wyrd*. He explains that

> *"This is... an assertion not only of the worth in itself of*
> *the human will (and courage), but also of its practical*
> *effect... that is, actually a denial of absolute Fate...*
> [stemming] *ultimately from popular rather than*
> *'heroic' or aristocratic language... Wyrd is not*
> *philosophic Fate, but fortune or chance".*[80]

Unfortunately this seems to be a case of going from one extreme to another. No doubt Tolkien is correct in divining that the concept of Wyrd derives originally from popular rather than aristocratic language and culture, but he surely goes too far in attempting to reduce *Wyrd* to mere fortune or chance. Wyrd is about the woven interconnection of all things, rather in the nature of an early English vision of pluralist reality as something rather like the 21st century World Wide Web. However Tolkien refutes this:

> *"The concept of the 'weaving of destiny' (by the Parcae,*
> *Norns, Valkyries) ...has become a mere figure of speech.*

> *Personally I doubt very much whether the use of*
> *'weave' in this connexion had ever been anything more.*
> *There has been a great deal of mystification,*
> *inaccuracy, and fanciful 'web-weaving' in all*
> *discussions of 'mythology'".*[81]

Tolkien backs up his view by stating that the Norns, as women, could only spin, and not weave, as weaving allegedly *"remained largely a masculine craft"*.[82] It seems clear though that in Beowulf *Wyrd* could allow the defeat of apparently inexorable fate and prolong a person's life, even when faced with nine sea monsters wishing to eclipse it. The 'web of destiny' in Beowulf is not shown as fixed, but as being constantly woven with newly spun threads, implying that the future is never fully determined; e.g. human courage can impact on the web and change 'fate'. In any case, whether or not weaving *"remained largely a masculine craft"*, is irrelevant to the usefulness of the woven web as a metaphor for understanding the concept of the Wyrd. In reality (e.g. in 18th and early 19th century England) weaving remained a complex process often requiring both female and male participation – with weavers' cottages being organised on a home industry, family basis.

Tolkien's denial of the concept of the web of the wyrd appears to explain why Heaney's *"But the Lord was weaving a victory on his war-loom for the Weather-Geats"*[83] becomes, in Tolkien's translation, *"God granted them a victorious fortune in battle, even to those Geatish warriors..."* [84] The original Old English text says *"Ac him dryhten forgeaf, wígspéda gewiofu Wedera léodum"* ("But to them the Lord granted the woven-destiny of war-luck - to the Wederas' men").[85] So in this case it is Heaney who sticks much more closely to the original text. Tolkien does recognise in his "Commentary" that *wígspéda gewiofu* is literally victory in battle as the *"product of weaving (together)"*, but his denial of the web of the Wyrd causes him to justify his failure to translate literally or accurately, on the alleged grounds that *"the pictorial 'figure' of weaving, in connection with 'fate', was obsolescent, and soon ceased to be current"*.[86]

At the end of the poem of course Beowulf, like all of us, must meet his doom, but now at last the Christian poet seems to acknowledge the hero's pagan 'fate'; there is no mention of any form of personal salvation, only an ending. When Beowulf goes to face the dragon, he says

> *"what occurs... between the two of us*
> *Will turn out as fate, [the] overseer of men, decides".*[87]

This time there is no mention of the will of God, perhaps because when the hero Beowulf dies, the Christian poet can allow that unhappy event to remain the result of pagan Wyrd, rather than God's will? The outcome is reported as:

> *"That final day was the first time*
> *When Beowulf fought and fate denied him*
> *Glory in battle...*
> *So every man must yield*
> *The leasehold of his days".*[88]

This passage seems more reminiscent of the Norns determining the length of life than it does of the will of God, particularly the idea than every man only has a 'leasehold on his days', i.e. that the gift of life from the Norns ultimately incurs a debt which must be paid: that of death.

In true pagan style however, there is one form of immortality granted by poet and people to Beowulf: his renown shall live on after him, his story told through the ages. The final lines of the poem extoll his virtues, which clearly do not include Christian humility, but do benefit his people collectively rather than himself alone:

> *"Of all the kings upon the earth,*
> *He was the man most gracious and fair-minded,*
> *Kindest to his people, and keenest to win fame".*[89]

The Anglo-Saxon View of the Gods

When Beowulf and the Geats sail from modern day southern Sweden and land their ships in Denmark to come to the aid of King Hrothgar, a Danish coastguard horseman *"shakes his spear overhead when addressing the strangers who have landed".* [90] This is a threat of potential armed resistance if required. Actually throwing the spear over the strangers' heads would be a traditional call to Odin, leader and 'All-father' of the Æsir gods, to witness a declaration of war. Who were these followers of Odin and the Æsir, these Geats?

Tolkien links the Geats with both the Goths and Odin:

> *"Many... points connect the Goths (Gotan) and the*
> *Géatas (Old Norse 'Gautar').*
>
>> *(a) The Géatas/Gautar occupied an area in the*
>> *south of what is now Sweden. The Goths*
>> *came from Sweden, and their name survives*
>> *in Gotland, the large island off its east coast*

(b) *The two names are beyond doubt connected in origin...*

(c) *The name Gautr is in Old Norse a frequent name for the god Odin (Woden), whose cult was especially connected with Goths.*

(d) *...Odin/Woden was evidently originally a wind or storm god... the Géatas are called Weder-Géatas or simply Wederas: Wind Géatas, or wind-folk.*[91]

So the Geats (or Géatas, or Gautar) were a Gothic tribe from modern day southern Sweden, and were closely associated with Odin. However although this tale is the life story of a great Æsir and Odin following Swedish Geat leader (Beowulf), most of the action in the first part of the poem is set in Hrothgar's Denmark , and the tale is being told for an Anglo-Saxon audience, by an Anglo-Saxon scop (skald or storyteller). The pre-migration Anglo-Saxons (Angles, Jutes, Heathobards etc.) had also been living in Denmark during the period when the Beowulf story is set, and are believed to have been Vanir-followers. Perhaps unsurprisingly then allusions to the gods in the Beowulf poem often reference the Vanir rather than the Æsir.

The arms worn by Beowulf's men serve as a good example of this, as they were important in identifying them as members of the aristocratic warrior class:

"Boar-shapes flashed
Above their cheek-guards; the brightly forged
Work of goldsmiths, watching over
Those stern-faced men".[92]

Boars were sacred to the Vanir god and goddess (Yngvi-)Frey[93] and Freya (who on occasion rode her battle-swine *Hildisvíni* – who had previously been Ottar, a faithful human male worshipper, who she rewarded by making him her boar), as well as to the gods more generally. Boars were respected as totemic guardians in warfare, esteemed as they were for their vicious fighting abilities.[94]

Beowulf himself wears a byrnie, or coat of mail, made by the mythological figure of Weland the Smith. The equivalent figure in Old Norse tradition was Völundr, King of the Elves.[95] The Elves (or at least the Light Elves) were in turn associated with the Vanir, and in particular with Frey, for Frey's home was Alfheim, literally the 'home of the Elves'. Weland/Völundr was a master smith to the gods. Heaney points out that

"In the early medieval context, precious objects are not

inert. They are an extension of the person who owns them, wears them, or made them... [Beowulf's] *stature is thereby enhanced, for Weland is not just a master smith. He also has long been associated with elves, giants and dwarves".*[96]

Danish King Hrothgar is called *"the Danish prince, descendant of Ing".*[97] Tolkien translates this as *"the servants of Ing (the Danes)"*,[98] and later refers to *"the wise lord of the friends of Ing".*[99] Again these appear to be clear surviving references to Hrothgar's people as followers of the Vanir god Yngvi-Frey, conveniently overlooked by the Christian Beowulf poet on the grounds that Ing could be taken to be one of the king's mortal ancestors.

The Danish and English tribes may have been followers of Frey and Freya's Vanir, and the Swedish Geats devotees of Odin's Æsir, but both Vanir and Æsir adherents had in common an understanding of the nature of their gods which differed fundamentally from both earlier southern European (pagan Greek and Roman) views of divinity, and later Christian interpretations. Tolkien discusses the nature of the northern gods as indirectly referred to in Beowulf:

"We may... contrast the 'inhumanness' of the Greek gods... with the 'humanness' of the northern... in Norse... the gods are within time, doomed with their allies to death. Their battle is with the monsters and the outer darkness. They gather heroes for the last defence... When Baldr is slain and goes to Hel he cannot escape thence any more than mortal man... southern gods are more godlike – more lofty, dread, and inscrutable. They are timeless and do not fear death... It is the strength of the northern mythological imagination that it faced the problem [of death], *put the monsters in the centre, gave them victory... and found a potent but terrible solution in naked will and courage... While the older southern imagination has faded forever into literary ornament, the northern has power... to revive its spirit even in our own times. It can work, even as it did work with the Godless Viking, without gods: martial heroism as its own end. But we may remember that the poet of Beowulf saw clearly: the wage of heroism is death".*[100]

As we have seen, for the Christian eternal life might be achieved by surrendering one's individual soul to the one God. The alternative, no matter how heroically fought, is still death... but then for the north European pagan all things must die, even the gods themselves, as the very price (debt) of life. Even Frigg, the grieving mother of the most 'perfect' god Baldr, is wrong to ask all living things to weep in order to bring her dead son back to life – just as she was wrong in the first place to attempt to make him invulnerable and immortal - as Loki teaches her.[101]

In the northern pagan world view, the truly heroic act, whether of human or god, is not selfishly to seek eternal life by giving up one's soul to the one God. On the contrary, it is to die, in order that life itself may continue and others as yet unborn may live, by recycling and reworking individual souls' energies through the goddess Mother Nature's continual re-creation of new life, and new lives. So it is worth restating that the originally pagan Beowulf story ends not with Christian salvation and eternal life in heaven, but with the hero's death. What survives his passing is not Beowulf's individual soul, but something much darker, more creative, and more pagan: his story, which lives on as the collective ever-changing property of subsequent generations:

> "They said that of all the kings upon the earth
> He was the man most gracious and fair-minded,
> Kindest to his people, and keenest to win fame".[102]

Even Tolkien at least partly recognises that this is the true pagan nature of the poem:

> "We must dismiss... from mind the notion that Beowulf is a 'narrative poem', that it tells... a tale sequentially... the poem was not meant to advance... it is essentially a balance, an opposition of ends and beginnings. In its simplest terms it is a contrasted description of two moments in a great life, rising and setting; an elaboration of the ancient and intensely moving contrast between youth and age, first achievement and final death".[103]

Tolkien then does at least grasp the pagan dialectic of continual contradiction and change (the interrelationship of life and death). However by insisting that Beowulf is ultimately not a truly heroic, epic narrative, but something more in the nature of a mourning elegy, he could perhaps be accused of rather misinterpreting the poem. He sees the work's insistence on the tragedy of bereavement,[104] and partially comprehends the poem's pagan view of death as self-sacrificing and heroic, but fails to clarify why this is. Caught within his own Christian world view he sees the individual's death, no matter how valiant, as ultimately pointless and hopeless, when in fact pagans would have understood Beowulf's passing as at least in part a positive event, which facilitated the collective well-being of his people both in immediate terms (illustrated by the successful termination of the threat of the dragon), and through the implication that new generations must now prosper and come to the fore to continue Beowulf's work in the light of his life story.

The Legend of Freawaru and Ingeld

Although the story of Freawaru and Ingeld is briefly referred to in Beowulf, not many details are given. Nevertheless analysis of what we do know of this story probably tells us more than any other source about how the early English perceived key differences between their own pagan world outlook and that of their similarly pagan Danish (later Viking) cousins.

When Beowulf arrives from the land of the Geats (southern Sweden) at King Hrothgar's hall of Heorot in modern day Denmark, the king's daughter Freawaru has already been betrothed to marry Ingeld. Hrothgar and his daughter Freawaru are Danes, but Ingeld is an English Heathobard. As Tolkien explains, *"the stage of the feud that preceded the moment chosen by the poet was a disastrous defeat of the Heathobards by the Danes... It is to settle the bloodfeud which Ingeld has against him that Hrothgar favours the match"*.[105] In other words the Danish king intends to marry his daughter off into a political alliance which he hopes will prevent the surviving English launching a campaign of revenge against him.

The marriage is agreed and Freawaru leaves her father's hall of Heorot to live with Ingeld at his court. As an important princess she is accompanied by her own Danish retinue, including a number of warriors. These give offence and provoke Ingeld's men by turning up at his court wearing swords and other military regalia taken from the dead fathers of the English, killed by the Danes a generation earlier when they invaded and captured the Heathobard original homeland, and built their hall of Heorot there. Quarrels arise, resulting in a young English warrior killing a Dane who was wearing a sword that had belonged to the Englishman's father. Mayhem erupts, and the truce is definitively broken by both sides. Ingeld, despite his love for his new Danish wife, is (at first reluctantly) forced to join in the fighting on the side of his people. The Danes at the English court are killed or flee. Goaded by the reaction of his warriors to the provocations of Freawaru's Danish retinue, Ingeld goes on to lead a more general English rebellion against the Danish king Hrothgar. The English burn Hrothgar's hall of Heorot, but ultimately the Danes are once again victorious, and Ingeld is killed, dying as the last king of the Heathobards. The limited surviving sources do not tell us what happened to Freawaru.

> "Sometimes Hrothgar's daughter distributed
> Ale to older ranks, in order on the benches:
> I heard the company call her Freawaru
> As she made her rounds, presenting men
> With the gem-studded bowl, young bride-to-be
> To the gracious Ingeld, in her gold-trimmed attire.
> The friend of the Shieldings favours her betrothal:
> The guardian of the kingdom sees good in it
> And hopes this woman will heal old wounds
> And grievous feuds.
> But generally the spear
> Is prompt to retaliate when a prince is killed,
> No matter how admirable the bride may be.
> Think how the Heathobards will be bound to feel,
> Their lord, Ingeld, and his loyal thanes,
> When he walks in with that woman to the feast:
> Danes are at the table, being entertained,
> Honoured guests in glittering regalia,
> Burnished ring-mail that was their hosts' birthright,
> Looted when the Heathobards could no longer wield
> Their weapons in the shield-clash, when they went
> down
> With their beloved comrades and forfeited their lives.
> ...a passionate hate
> Will build up in Ingeld, and love for his bride
> Will falter in him as the feud rankles." [106]

This appears to be an incident in age-old, pre-migration, English lore, with the fictional Beowulf story being set in time just before it. Tolkien notes of this episode that *"We can see that it is founded on a pretty extensive story or historical legend, slow-moving, detailed, and with many actors, in the English manner, and not contracted, concentrated and intensely personal in the Norse manner"*.[107]

In historical terms this very early story may be important in reflecting one of the probable key causes of the migration of English tribes to Britain: military pressure from aggressively expanding Scandinavian tribes:

> *"Our story refers to the time of the beginnings of Scandinavian expansion and... reflects the incursion of Danes into Jutland and the peninsula. The Heathobard story depicts their seizure of Seeland, the centre of that world and the seat of its cult. And Seeland has remained ever since the heart of Denmark... It was an attempt to seize the centre of the Anglo-Frisian world, and to conquer it – and it succeeded, and was no doubt a prime factor in the westward migration."* [108]

This was of course but the very beginning of aggressive Scandinavian expansion. The English would be troubled again by Danes three centuries later, well after the migration to Britain, in the form of Viking raids and attacks on English kingdoms across those very years when the Beowulf story was being related in Anglo-Saxon halls, and eventually set down in writing. Tolkien saw this long term Scandinavian expansion as having serious cultural as well as military impacts, and not for the better:

> *"All that relates to the older heroic world has in Norse been overlaid and obscured by the specially Scandinavian sub-heroic period or Viking-age. An age that was in many ways, though later, not an advance but a relapse into violence and barbarism, a triumph of Oðin and the ravens, of bloodshed for its own sake, over the gods of corn and fruitfulness (the Vanir).* [109]

That this particular early north European story is not just the usual heroic and/or tragic adventure built around the bravery of male warriors in combat, but also a love story, is extremely unusual. The marriage between Freawaru and Ingeld may have been arranged to suit diplomatic purposes, but the deeply emotional tragedy in this tale is centred not just on the loss of the originally English Heathobard homeland to invading Danes, with all the loss of life that that military defeat involved, but also the personal inner conflict of the English leader Ingeld, who the Danes force to choose between his love for Freawaru and his devotion to his own people. Without English Ingeld's personal love for his Danish bride there would not be the same dramatic narrative tension. As Tolkien puts it:

> *"We have here that very rare thing in ancient northern legend (and almost unique in what survives in ancient*

English): a love story." [110]

What survives of the story does not explain how Freawaru and Ingeld met and fell in love. Tolkien surmises that there may have been an embassy from the victorious Danish court to the English inviting Ingeld to Heorot under some form of safe conduct pass, enabling him to meet Freawaru, perhaps at *"a feast in which the beautiful princess captivated Ingeld's heart."* [111]

However the pair came to love each other, the Beowulf poet tells us that, despite the marriage, the Heathobard-Danish truce will in any case break down:

> *"Ingeld must suddenly have taken up the feud again and made a descent on Hrothgar, that Heorot was destroyed by fire, but that nonetheless the Heathobards were utterly defeated. Ingeld must have been slain. What was the fate of the hapless Freawaru we do not know."* [112]

Although the Beowulf poet's chronology puts the Freawaru and Ingeld story immediately after the events of Beowulf's stay at Heorot, it seems that Freawaru and Ingeld's tale is in fact the older story, going back to the time when Seeland and its surrounding area had been home to English rather than Danish tribes. The English tribes, including the Heathobards defeated in war by invading Danes (originally known as Scyldings or Shieldings), were followers of the Vanir fertility gods. After their conquest of Heorot It seems that the Danish Scyldings too began to associate themselves with the Vanir, probably in order to secure their position as in-comers by attempting to appease the gods so long venerated there. This went so far that, just like English King Alfred the Great centuries later (see chapter 2), King Hrothgar of the Danes was also held to have added the ancient legendary figure of Scyld Scefing (Shield Sheafing, or Shef) into his family tree.

> *"Heorot and its site had in the ancient traditions... a special association with a heathen cult... one connected with the fertility religion that later in Scandinavia was associated with the names Njörd, Frey, Yngvi-Frey. After the Scyldings became masters of this centre* [defeating and driving out the 'English' Heathobard tribe] *we observe the Danes taking on names reminiscent of that cult: Hrothgar is called 'Defence of the clients of Ing'... his daughter is Freawaru, 'Protection of Fréa = Frey'; and what is more, Sceaf and Beow belonging to corn-myth became blended with*

Scyld in Hrothgar's ancestry".[113]

Despite his eventual final defeat at the hands of the Danes, Ingeld seems to have remained a popular and well known English pagan hero well into post-migration and even Christian times. Tolkien quotes the Northumbrian Christian theologian Alcuin, writing in the year 797 – *"close, that is, to the probable date of composition of Beowulf"* [114] – in a letter to Speratus, the Bishop of Lindisfarne:

> *"In the rectory of the monks the words of God should be read; there it is fitting the reader be heard, not the harper, the discourse of the Fathers, not the songs of the pagans. What has Ingeld to do with Christ?"* [115]

Tolkien explains that:

> *"lays concerning him* [Ingeld] *must have been extremely popular for him to be singled out as the typical pagan hero... Alcuin is rebuking monks for listening to native English lays sung to the harp, and for still taking an interest in pagan kings"*.[116]

Why was Ingeld *'singled out as the typical pagan English Hero'*?

- One reason may be the siting of his adventures in the historic and sacred English/Heathobard home of Seeland. *"Heorot seems to have been remembered specially as a centre of pagan worship. We may suspect that this is of importance in the feud and battles that raged around this site, that the feud was indeed a battle for the possession of a sanctuary"*.[117]

- Another may have to do with the post-migration (7th to 10th century) English seeking their roots in their tribes' 6th century or earlier pre-migration homeland: *"We touch in this conflict... on something very old and central to the nearly forgotten history of the Germanic North in heathen times... the whole matter has been confused and distorted by the adoption and 'Danification' of traditions that were not in origin Danish... but belonged to... the Anglo-Frisian peoples"*.[118]

- The Ingeld-Freawaru story also clarified for the post-Christianisation English that their ancestors' paganism had in any case always been independent of and different from that of their current (i.e. 8th to 10th century) Danish and Viking tormentors. Whilst the Viking world outlook was, in English eyes, based purely on the chaotic values of violence, murder, rape, theft, and the use of force, English paganism was held to have constructed an orderly world view based on the rule of law, the legitimation of authority rather than the naked exercising of unsubtle power, the importance of love, consensual relationships, and the value of peace in the promotion of agricultural and cultural wealth.

By the time the Beowulf story was being set down in writing in the ninth or early tenth century CE, the Anglo-Saxon mythological narrative saw bloodthirsty Æsir-worshipping Danish raiders and invaders as the ancient enemies of their own pre-migration ancestors, who were believed to have been followers of the more peaceful Vanir fertility religion. Now again, three centuries later, the successors of those Danish raiders and invaders had followed the Anglo-Saxons across the North Sea to Britain, and once again it was a case of violent, bloodthirsty Danish Vikings attacking the still peace-loving (but now Christian) English. This was the message of the Beowulf poet to the Anglo-Saxon audience.

As followers of the Vanir goddesses and gods, the English Heathobards were *"especially associated with peace"*.[119] Ingeld was the son of Fróda, meaning frith or peace.

> *"In the background of tradition lies the great peace, the Fródafrithr, in which there was corn in plenty, and no war or robbery... so it is said by Snorri Sturluson in Skaldskapamal 43 that in the time of the Fródafrithr no man did harm to another, and there were no thieves, so that a gold ring lay for three years beside the highway on Jalangsheath"*.[120]

What does this ancient English pagan legend of the "Great Peace" mean? Tolkien's view is that

> *"Heathobard tradition must have contained at least two Fródas: one the historical father of their last king Ingeld, and one the remoter (perhaps mythical) ancestor: the Fróda of the Great Peace. The tradition of the Great Peace may be no more than a legendary way of symbolising a powerful rule, in which (say) the Heathobards were leaders of a confederacy with some religious centre; or it may be in origin mythological: a representation of a dynastic ancestor of the god of the cult and of the Golden Age. Both may well be combined"*.[121]

It seems very possible that, just as in the case of the Scyld Scefing legend, this is another instance of the religious preferences of the early English being linked to the development of agriculture and its success in providing food in abundance for those tribes which adopted it. A pre-condition for the achievement of agricultural abundance is the establishment of a reasonably firm degree of peace and security to allow farming of crops and animals to take place unmolested by violent thieves and raiders. The Vanir gods were perceived as promoting peace, fertility, and the practical learning and spiritual wisdom believed to be necessary to achieve success in those areas. And, if necessary, they could give Odin and his more warlike followers as good as they got in military terms too, but for the English and the Vanir the emphasis was always upon peace and fertility.

The legend of the Great Peace is also clearly linked to the feminine qualities of the Vanir. The apparent imposition of peace and the successful banning of violence as a means to settle differences surely hints at possible legitimisation of female/goddess hegemony, and rule through peace-weaving authority rather than by naked force and power. In even admitting this as a possibility the English believed they clearly differentiated themselves from their Viking enemies. In English culture, love and love-stories are legitimated not just for women, but also for men, to a degree not admissible in Scandinavian paganism.

"In Norse the love of Ingeld becomes, in the fierce and brutalised Viking atmosphere, degraded, a sign of softness and wantonness; no man should ever have given way to it and been forgetful of the duty of murder. Not so in English. The love is a good motive, and the strife between it and the call of revenge for a slain father is held to be a genuine tragic conflict – otherwise Ingeld's story would not be heroic at all... the love referred to is passionate love, not mere reverence for queen and consort and the mother of the royal children".[122]

The English legitimisation of love as admissible male (as well as female) motivation is inextricably linked to their Vanir-following origins:

"It is impossible not to be struck by the fact that the pair of lovers: Freawaru and Ingeld, both bear names including a Frey element (Frea and Ing); and that Frey fell hopelessly in love with the daughter of his enemies: Gerdr the daughter of the giant Gymir. Yet this does not prove either Ingeld or Freawaru or their love wholly 'mythical'... such a love is more likely to arise in a people and family whose traditions are of Frey and the

Vanir rather than of Odin the Goth".[123]

Again for the Beowulf poet's Anglo-Saxon Christian audience the message was clear: true heroism consists of fighting for love and peace, including even love between enemies (English and Danes, gods and giants), not in living like Vikings from plunder, rape, murder, and the exploitation of the weak. In the ninth and tenth centuries this was a Christian message, but those Christian Anglo-Saxons were being told that even hundreds of years earlier their own pagan ancestors had lived by a not altogether dissimilar creed. Successful resistance to violent invasion by Odin-worshipping Danes, and overcoming the pain of the chaos and material loss involved in that, would come not by changing to be like the Vikings, but by staying loyal to the orderly code of peace and honour of their ancestors both Christian and pagan.

The Feminine in Beowulf

The Beowulf poem is renowned as a work surviving from the distant 'Dark Ages', commonly perceived as an era of chaotic violence, when power was surely largely in the hands of aggressive and destructive males. Knowledge of Viking violent raids and their joyful killing and sacrificing of enemies to their bloodthirsty gods, led by the patriarchal 'All-father' Odin, hardly leads us to expect much evidence of the valuing of feminine roles in this story originating from pre-Christian Scandinavia. Nevertheless, as shown by the Freawaru and Ingeld story references in Beowulf, the cultural values of English (as distinct from Scandinavian) paganism did also include aspects traditionally considered to be of more feminine interest, such as peace-weaving and love matches.

There is also some evidence within Beowulf of themes involving more general female power and influence. For example Beowulf's mother is ritually praised:

> *"Whoever she was*
> *Who brought forth this flower of manhood,*
> *If she is still alive, that woman can say*
> *That in her labour the Lord of Ages*
> *Bestowed a grace on her."* [124]

Tolkien says of these lines that *"It is possible that the praise of the victor's mother was an old element in the folk-legend of the 'strong man'"*.[125] Yes, but also it seems probable that in the earlier pre-Christian versions of the story, this would have been a goddess (possibly Frigg?) blessing Beowulf's mother, and not the "Lord of Ages".

When King Hrothgar thinks of rewarding Beowulf for the apparent death of Grendel by proclaiming him his son by adoption, Queen Weahltheow (Hrothgar's wife) steps into her role as active peace-weaver. She loudly and publicly demands that, whilst Beowulf must be fairly and generously rewarded, the King should also immediately publicly recognise that it is not Beowulf, but their own children, Hrethic and Hrothmund, who must remain heirs to the kingdom. Until those children are old enough to lead, she says, her nephew Hrothulf should act as regent:

> "Men say that thou wert in mind to take this warrior for thy son... dispose while yet thy mayest of many a reward, and to thy kin after... leave thy people and thy realm... Hrothulf I know well, my nephew fair, that he will in honour cherish these our youths, if thou, dear master of the Scyldings, sooner than he do leave this world." [126]

Remarkably, to keep Beowulf on side, she then gives him, on top of all his other gifts from the King, a golden torque, so fabulous that the poet compares it to the legendary golden necklace of the Brisings, the property of the goddess Freya.[127] Then she tells Beowulf that the price of this generosity is his loyalty to her children, and politely, but also firmly and surely with scarcely veiled threat, reminds him that the Danish thanes and people are loyal to *her* commands:

> "Treat my sons
> with tender care, be strong and kind.
> Here each comrade is true to the other,
> Loyal to lord, loving in spirit.
> The thanes have one purpose, the people are ready
> Having drunk and pledged, the ranks do as I bid". [128]

Tolkien translates the final phrase even more strongly than Heaney, having the Queen command the hero Beowulf *"Do thou as I bid!"* [129] Heaney says of these lines:

> "Queen Weahltheow fulfils the function of a peace-weaver in Danish society in part through the gifts she gives while circulating among the men and offering them supportive words. In this manner she does her best to support her family's interests while dulling the men's murderous propensities".[130]

It is surely significant in terms of the Anglo-Saxon view of female roles that the Beowulf poet is able to speak openly of feminine skills and power sufficient to dull *"men's murderous propensities"*.

Another queen referenced in the poem, is the Queen of the Geats, Hygd (wife of Hygelac, Beowulf's lord). Hygd is praised for her feminine qualities by contrasting her with a legendary despotic Queen Modthryth:

> *"...although Hygd, his queen*
> *Was young, a few short years at court,*
> *Her mind was thoughtful and her manners sure.*
> *Haereth's daughter behaved generously*
> *And stilted nothing when she distributed*
> *Bounty to the Geats...*
> *A queen should weave peace, not punish the innocent*
> *With loss of life for imagined insults"*.[131]

These lines show that a Queen is praised for

- Intelligence
- Thoughtfulness
- Good manners and respect for others
- Generosity - like a king, she too has wealth and the power to choose to whom she distributes it
- Actively weaving peace (not just passively spinning as Tolkien would have it – see the "Fate and Wyrd" section of this chapter above)
- Resisting the misuse of her powers of life and death.

In return for the treasures bestowed on him by King Hrothgar and Queen Weahltheow, Beowulf also gives valuable presents to his own lord's wife, Queen Hygd:

> *"I heard he presented Hygd with a gorget*
> *The priceless torque that the prince's daughter*
> *Weahltheow had given him; and three horses...*
> *The bright necklace would be luminous on Hygd's breast"*.[132]

By surrendering to Hygd the priceless treasure that Weahltheow had given him, Beowulf is publicly demonstrating his continued loyalty to Hygd as his sovereign queen and ruler, and proclaiming that his new-found status of internationally renowned warrior-hero is no threat to her. This seems to have been a wise move, for when Hygd's husband the Geat king Hygelac dies, Hygd has the power and authority to offer the throne to Beowulf, even favouring him over the heir, her own son Heardred:

"There Hygd offered him throne and authority
As lord of the ring-hoard: with Hygelac dead
She had no belief in her son's ability
To defend their homeland..." [133]

Beowulf turned down the offer, remaining loyal to Heardred, until Heardred is eventually killed in battle against the Swedes, after which Beowulf finally agrees to become King of the Geats. There is an implication here that Beowulf, as the hero of this story, acted responsibly and correctly in continuing to support the legitimate authority of Queen Hygd and her son. By submitting to her female sovereignty in this way, he avoids risking internecine killing amongst the Geats, for it would seem likely that if he had agreed to become king prematurely whilst Hygd and Heardred were still alive, although many would have acclaimed him, others might have violently objected, possibly even risking civil war, given *"men's murderous propensities"* as referred to above. The gods, we may take it, in the original pagan version of the story, subsequently rewarded him for his acceptance of Queen Hygd's female authority, by ultimately legitimising his kingship at the appropriate time.

Beowulf – *Key Aspects of Christian, Scandinavian Pagan, and English Pagan Cultures*

The table below summarises key aspects of three world outlooks or cultures evidenced in the Beowulf poem: Christian, Scandinavian pagan, and English pagan.

Christian and Pagan Cultures in Beowulf

Key Aspects	Christian	Scandinavian/ Aesir Pagan	English/ Vanir Pagan
Male Power (military and personal)	Yes	Yes	Yes
Female Power (military and personal)	No	No	Yes
Male Consensual Authority	Yes	Yes	Yes
Female Consensual Authority	No	Yes (subordinate to male)	Yes
Love as Legitimate Authority	Yes	No	Yes
Necessary Organisational Bureaucracy	Yes	No	No
Belief in Fate (as absolute, or Will of God)	Yes	Yes	No
Mortal ability to affect the Wyrd	No	No	Yes
Individual Eternal Life after Death	Yes	No	No

Nine key factors are shown in the table. Of these, only three are common to both English paganism and Christianity, but the coincidence in views between English and Scandinavian paganism is not much greater, with only four factors (positive and negative) being wholly common to both. The interconnection of Christian and Scandinavian viewpoints is more significant, with five factors being held in common, than that between the two forms of paganism.

Both early Anglo-Saxon English Christians (such as the Beowulf poet) and Tolkien in the twentieth century clearly differentiated between English and Scandinavian paganisms. To the extent that they felt any elegiac empathy with the pagan world outlook at all, they identified more with the English version, which they perceived as better comprehending values held to be essential by Christians, such as consensual authority in terms of the public world, and love in terms of the personal.

In terms of the differences between the two forms of paganism, there are four major aspects to this:

- English paganism took a less deterministic view of 'fate', putting greater faith in human ability to have significant impact within the workings of the Wyrd.
- English paganism better recognised the legitimacy of female (as well as male) power and authority, both in terms of human society and the spiritual realm.
- English paganism, whilst recognising a limited role for the exercising of power, including through violence when necessary, gave greater priority to the creation of legitimate and orderly legal authority, rejecting Scandinavian chaotic violence as a viable long term path to material welfare.
- English paganism promoted cultural values of peace, security, and learning in order to prioritise both
  - spiritual health, and
  - agricultural, animal, and human fertility as a more effective route to the achievement of material abundance and prosperity.

Chapter 4 – *The Vanir*

As has already been noted, of the two major groupings of gods known to pre-Christian north-west European pagans, Odin 'All-father's' Æsir were more associated with the Danes and other 'Viking' tribes which remained longer in Scandinavia, whilst the Anglo-Saxon (later English) tribes (Angles, Jutes, Saxons and others) related more to the Vanir. These relationships were never completely exclusive or clear cut, with both groupings of tribes being cognisant of both groupings of gods. Indeed as in the case of Shef/Heimdal (see chapter 2) it was even possible for perceptions of which group particular gods were members of to change over time, and according to particular tribal interests.

In their commentaries on the Beowulf poem (see chapter 3) both Heaney and Tolkien note that the Danes, after conquering the English Heathobard Vanir sanctuary on Seeland and building their hall of Heorot there, sought to appease the fertility gods by acknowledging their importance in that area, even to the extent of recognising the sovereignty of the Vanir as noble ancestors: Danish King Hrothgar is called *"the Danish prince, descendant of Ing"* [134], and *"the wise lord of the friends of Ing"* [135], Ing being Yngvi-Frey, Vanir male fertility god and brother of Freya. Nevertheless by the time the Danes moved westwards again, settling in northern and eastern England three hundred or so years later, it was Odin and the Æsir that they had to abandon in order to be converted to Christianity.

To the Anglo-Saxons Odin was not the Scandinavians' ruling patriarchal warrior and 'All-father', but simply the mysterious dark wanderer Woden, who far from collecting dead warriors for Valhalla, preferred spending his time quietly exploring human doings in Midgard. Even the surviving stories concerning Freya, the powerful magical goddess of the Vanir, are largely concerned with her time spent with the Æsir in Asgard, no doubt because of the very largely Icelandic and Scandinavian sources of those surviving tales.

Nevertheless it is clear that there were key differences in perceptions of the nature of the two groups of gods, and that these distinct qualities made the Æsir more attractive in general terms to Scandinavians, and the Vanir more attractive to Anglo-Saxons. The cultures of both human groupings valued martial prowess, but for the Scandinavians, living to a greater degree from the plunder of war and regular raids on neighbouring tribes, victory in battle was paramount.

For the Anglo-Saxons however, both pre- and post-migration to Britain, material abundance depended more on agriculture and crop and animal fertility, which in turn required a high degree of secure but whenever possible peaceful settlement on the land. For the early English then, it was natural to turn to the Vanir fertility gods and goddesses when divine approval was held to be necessary.

Who are the Vanir?

The Vanir are a north European family of mainly closely related fertility goddesses and gods. Those that can be named from ancient sources are few in number, and can be counted on the fingers of two hands (between eight and ten).* The named and known Vanir however must be part of a more numerous clan, or their largely successful attack on Asgard in the legendary first war of the gods (following Odin's attempted burning to death of the Vanir witch Gullveig) could not have taken place. The close familial relationship of the known Vanir is another factor differentiating them from the Æsir. The Aesir are not a family but a pantheon, including many individuals, with widely varying characteristics – at least twenty-eight (of which fourteen are goddesses) are named and characterised in Old Norse sources.[136]

Nerthus – *Mother Earth*

Nerthus is a female figure associated with peace and the fertility of the land, a Mother Earth figure whose precise identity and role in the Vanir family is somewhat obscured. She is generally accepted as being the mother of Frey and Freya, but the identity of their father remains less certain. He may be Njörd (see below), who might also be Nerthus's brother (sibling marriage being acceptable to the Vanir, though not the Æsir), or it may be that Nerthus and Njörd are female and male aspects of a single transgender, gender-fluid, or hermaphrodite god/dess.

"The earth mother Nerthus... would correspond to the

---

* Slightly more if Freya's daughter (or possibly two daughters), and Frey's aspects as Ing and Frodi are counted separately.

ON [Old Norse] *god Njörd. The change of sex can be explained in various ways... it seems to be perfectly possible that in Nerthus a male and female goddess were worshipped, as is the case in... brother and sister Freyr/Freyja. Another possibility would be that Nerthus was an hermaphrodite deity."* [137]

This view of Njörd as the male counterpart of Nerthus is however not universally accepted – for an alternative interpretation of his role see for example Sheena McGrath's *Njörd and Skadi – A Myth Explored*,[138] which focuses on Njörd's unhappy marriage with the giantess Skadi, rather than his relationship with Nerthus.

In chapter 40 of his Germania [98 CE] the Roman historian Tacitus writes:

"They [the Germanic tribes] are distinguished by a common worship of Nerthus, or Mother Earth. They believe that she interests herself in human affairs and rides among their peoples. In an island of the Ocean stands a sacred grove, and in the grove a consecrated cart, draped with cloth, which none but the priest may touch. The priest perceives the presence of the goddess in this holy of holies and attends her, in deepest reverence, as her cart is drawn by heifers. Then follow days of rejoicing and merry making in every place that she deigns to visit and be entertained. No one goes to war, no one takes up arms; every object of iron is locked away; then, and only then, are peace and quiet known and loved, until the priest again restores the goddess to her temple, when she has had her fill of human company. After that the cart, the cloth and, if you care to believe it, the goddess herself are washed clean in a secluded lake. This service is performed by slaves who are immediately afterwards drowned in the lake. Thus mystery begets terror and pious reluctance to ask what the sight can be that only those doomed to die may see." [139]

Njörd – *Wind and Sea God*

As mentioned above, Njörd is possibly both a brother and sexual partner of Nerthus, and so also the father of Frey and Freya, but whether or not that is the case, he is more definitely reported as having been married – for a time – to someone else: the giantess Skadi. Njörd was associated with the fertility of the sea, and as such was an important god for coastal tribes, a role which fitted in well with his other function as a god of the wind; clearly the two things were related at a time when propulsion at sea required sails and oars. And it was not just an abundance of wind and fish that Njörd could be appealed to for. He was also associated with riches and material abundance more generally, so definitely a good deity to have on your side.

Njörd only ended up married to Skadi as part of a deal to compensate her for the killing of her father Thiazi by the Æsir.

> "Þjazi's daughter, Skaði, took a helmet, a coat of mail, and 'all weapons of war' and travelled to Asgard, the home of the gods. Upon Skaði's arrival, the gods wished to atone for her loss and offered compensation. Skaði provides them with her terms of settlement, and the gods agree that Skaði may choose a husband from among themselves. However, Skaði must choose this husband by looking solely at their feet. Skaði saw a pair of feet that she found particularly attractive and said 'I choose that one; there can be little that is ugly about Baldr.' However, the owner of the feet turned out to be Njorðr. [140]

Njörd's marriage to Skadi though turned out to be neither happy nor long, in fact lasting only twelve nights (though one source makes it eighteen winters, presumably also not that long in the life of a god). The two just did not get along. Njörd wanted to live by the sea and hated Skadi's mountainous rock-giant home, whilst Skadi found the screeching of Njörd's seabirds equally painful. They separated.

> "Skaði wanted to live in the home once owned by her father called Þrymheimr. However, Njorðr wanted to live nearer to the sea. Subsequently, the two made an agreement that they would spend nine nights in Þrymheimr and then the next three nights in Njorðr's sea-side home Nóatún (or nine winters in Þrymheimr and another nine in Nóatún according to the Codex Regius manuscript). However, when Njorðr returned from the mountains to Nóatún, he said:

> > 'Hateful for me are the mountains,
> > I was not long there,

only nine nights.
The howling of the wolves
sounded ugly to me
after the song of the swans.'
Skaði responded:
'Sleep I could not
on the sea beds
for the screeching of the bird.
That gull wakes me
when from the wide sea
he comes each morning.'" [141]

Frey – *God of Human and Agricultural Fertility*

Frey is a son of the Earth goddess Nerthus and (probably – see above) the sea god Njörd. He is also Freya's brother. It is even possible that in very early times the siblings Freya and Frey were, like their parents Nerthus and Njörd, considered to be sexual partners. What is more certain is that Frey was definitely perceived as a god of peace. He was held to be the promoter of the legendary *Peace of Frodi*, which:

> *"manifested in a long series of good harvests which made the farmers prosperous... and such a sense of inner and outer security that nobody even removed a golden ring lying on the heath at Jelling... representative of the belief in the responsibility of the king for good harvests (sacral kingship)... so that the king's reign must be crowned by peace with the god... a phenomenon... also for the cult of Nerthus".* [142]

It is unsurprising that the 'Peace of Frodi' *"manifested in a long series of good harvests"*, for as a god Frey was also held to promote human, animal, and agricultural fertility, for example by providing rainfall for growing crops when needed. His blessings were therefore essential to the prosperity of mankind.

> *"Flateyjarbok tells how a fugitive Icelander... finds protection with a priestess of Frey, who is travelling through the land in a chariot bearing the statue of the god Frey; [he] soon takes the place of the statue; when the priestess becomes pregnant, the people take this as being a good sign. This story... fits in nicely with the*

procession of Nerthus as told by Tacitus and the belief in the power of the Vanir to bring good harvests and fertility..." [143]

According to some sources it is Frey who owns the magical boat *Skidbladnir*,[144] as well as a magical boar called *Gullinbursti*, which pulls his chariot.

> *"The Poetic Edda and Prose Edda attest that it [Skidbladnir] is owned by the god Freyr, while...Heimskringla attributes it to the magic of Odin. Both Heimskringla and the Prose Edda attribute to it the ability to be folded up - as cloth may be - into one's pocket when not needed...*
>
> *"When Loki had Sif's hair, Freyr's ship Skíðblaðnir and Odin's spear Gungnir fashioned by the Sons of Ivaldi, he bet his own head with Brokkr that his brother Eitri... would not have been able to make items to match the quality of those mentioned above. So to make gifts to Freyr, Eitri threw a pig's skin into a furnace as Brokkr worked on the bellows, and together they manufactured the boar Gullinbursti which had bristles in its mane that glowed in the dark... it could run through air and water better than any horse, and it could never become so dark with night or gloom... that there should not be sufficient light where he went."* [145]

Frey is also sometimes known as Yngvi-Frey. However *"The meaning of the name Yngvi is largely unexplained"*.[146] What does seem relatively clear is that the early medieval Swedish royal dynasty called themselves 'Ynglings' in honour of reputed ancestors, whom they liked to trace back right to the god Frey (or Yngvi-Frey) himself. There was also a related Norwegian royal dynasty bearing the same name, which lasted from the 10th to the 14th century. It does seem likely that the term "Yngvi" or "Ingvi" is related to the word "Ing" meaning "son or daughter of", with both the Scandinavian Yngling dynasties and the Germanic Ingaevones tribe possibly identifying themselves as descendants of the god Yngvi-Frey.

Equally, when post-migration Anglo-Saxon leaders were seeking to envisage a united land in Britain, it appears probable that they sought a new, coalescent but traditional collective appellation, and came up with something like "we are all Ynglish" (or English), seeking to sell to their peoples the narrative that "we are all the descendants of Yngvi-Frey; let us come together as one nation and create a united land of our Ing-related peoples - England".

It is also possible that Yngvi-Frey and Frey represent later manifestations of the ancient Germanic god Ingwaz or Ing, with all these aspects of the god Frey having the same characteristics and associations with the promotion of peace and fertility. Similarly the Ing rune ◇ from the Elder Germanic futhark or alphabet (see chapter 6) is linked to both the god Frey and his associations with (especially male) fertility, health, peace, and plenty. Freya Aswynn tells us that:

> "'Son of' is one of the meanings of this rune... in Anglo-Saxon patronymic names were formed by adding –ing after the father's forename... Ing is also a fertility rune. [Ingvi or Yngvi]-Frey, after whom this rune is named, is traditionally portrayed with a large erect phallus, and can be regarded as the northern equivalent of Pan. Nevertheless I regard this rune as a symbol of female fertility, its shape being reminiscent of female genitalia... the phrase 'son of' may equally well be replaced by the phrase 'daughter of'... the Ing rune represents the continuation of the tribal or family hamingja,[†] an excellent rune to use for astral projection". [147]

Freya Aswynn confirms that the Ing rune is named after the male god (Yngvi-)Frey, but then chooses to see that rune "*as a symbol of female fertility, its shape being reminiscent of female genitalia*". It might be better to see the rune ◇ as having associations with both male and female sexual fertility. After all, whatever the shape of the Ing rune, Frey's statue at Uppsala in Sweden was reported to be "*adorned by a mighty phallus*".[148] Furthermore Frey's behaviour (and that of his servant Skírnir carrying out Frey's bidding) as reported in the tale of his wooing of the giantess Gerd, seems to be fairly prototypically male-orientated:

> "*In the Poetic Edda poem Skírnismál, the god Freyr... looked into all worlds. Freyr saw a beautiful girl... [and] became heartsick for [her]. Freyr has a page named Skírnir. Skírnir requests that Freyr give him a horse and Freyr's sword; a [magical] sword which fights [giants]...*

[†] For an explanation of the term 'hamingja' see the next section on Freya immediately following, and the "*Supernatural Women Guardians*" section of chapter 13.

by itself. Under the cover of darkness, Skírnir rides the horse over nations and dew-covered mountains until he reaches Gerðr's hall. Gerðr asks the stranger if he is of the elves, Æsir, or the Vanir, and why he comes alone "over the wild fire" to seek their company. Skírnir responds that he is of none of these groups... [and] offers Gerðr 11 golden apples to gain her favour. Gerðr rejects the apples. Skírnir offers Gerðr a ring that produces eight more gold rings every ninth night. Gerðr responds that she is not interested in the ring, for she shares her father's property, and Gymir has no lack of gold. Skírnir turns to threats; he points out to Gerðr that he holds a sword in his hand, and he threatens to cut her head from her neck unless she agrees. Gerðr refuses; she says that she will not endure the coercion of any man, and says that if Gymir encounters Skírnir then a battle can be expected. Skírnir warns Gerðr that he will strike her with... his wand, that it will tame her to his desires... He carves "thurs" (the runic character thurisaz) on Gerðr and three runes (unnamed) symbolizing lewdness, frenzy, and unbearable desire, and comments that he can rub them off just as he has carved them - if he wishes... Gerðr responds with a welcome to Skírnir and tells him to take a crystal cup containing ancient mead, noting that she thought she would never love one of the Vanir... Gerðr says that they shall meet at a tranquil location... and that after nine nights she will there grant Freyr her love." [149]*

We are also told that as the result of this adventure Frey loses his sword for good (presumably Skírnir gets to keep it), which means that from then on, right up to and including the final battle against the forces of chaos and destruction at the end of the worlds (known as 'Ragnarok' – meaning 'the destiny of the gods') Frey does not have a sword, and that instead he has to fight using antlers! His antlers prove inadequate to the task of defeating the fire giant Surtr ('the black one'), who seeks him out at Ragnarok, and Frey is killed.

Clearly Freud would enjoy analysing Frey. It is easy to suppose that the symbolism in this story is all about male sexual fears, with Frey's sword perhaps representing his phallus and masculine fertility, which he effectively loses by failing to overcome his fear of wooing the woman he desires himself, and instead asking another man to do that for him (which presumably results in Frey being cuckolded as well, as Skírnir keeps the sword?). After that he still experiences the male desire to rut and mate, as symbolised by his antlers, but is unable to do so successfully, as the experience of being cuckolded has made him impotent. After losing his sword (his ability to penetrate females), he no longer qualifies as a 'real' man. Gerd has welcomed Skírnir, the sexually confident male with the sword, with "*a crystal cup containing ancient mead*", yet is still able to disempower Frey by ordering him to wait on one side until she might deign to receive him, god though he is. He has failed as a macho male, and is consequently fit only to die at the hands of the fire giant Surtr, who definitely does still have a living, flame-energy-driven sword at his disposal.

It is also tempting to speculate that there must originally have been more to this story, and that Frey may have formerly been portrayed in a more positive light. It reads now as a partly comic and disparaging tale, of the kind that later Scandinavian Vikings would tell as evidencing their pride in intemperately masculine Æsir behaviour, and their rejection of more gender-balanced Vanir values.

Freya – *Goddess of Love, Death and Magic*

Freya is a daughter of the Earth goddess Nerthus and (probably – see above) the sea god Njörd. She is also Frey's sister and, as also noted above, it is even possible that in very early times the siblings Freya and Frey were, like their parents Nerthus and Njörd, considered to be sexual partners. Certainly, like her brother, she is a deity very strongly associated with fertility. Famed for her fatally attractive beauty she is desired by many, including giants, who attempt to trick or force the Æsir into giving her over to them, but tend to end up dead for their trouble. At the Icelandic All-thing (assembly of the people) in the year 999 CE (one year before Iceland's official submission to Christianity) the Christian skald Hjalti Skeggjason was outlawed for saying "*I don't like barking gods; I consider Freyja to be a bitch*".[150]

Freya's husband Óðr is oddly absent. Freya misses him, and is said to weep tears of gold in her dismay. She searches for Óðr , but in vain. She has at least one daughter by him, named Hnoss, and possibly a second, called Gersimi. Hnoss means 'treasure' or 'precious one', and she is said to be a goddess of sexual desire and lust, while Gersimi's name also means 'riches' or 'valued one'. Consequently 'Gersimi' could be a nickname applied to Hnoss. If however Gersimi is seen as an independent being (a second daughter), then she is reported to be a goddess of beauty.[151]

It is not surprising that Freya is able to weep tears of gold, for she is renowned as a golden goddess, who supposedly lusts after gold for both its beauty and its value. However this aspect of her reported personality should probably be taken with a large pinch of salt, given that the sources for the surviving stories featuring her are, firstly, exclusively from Æsir-devoted Scandinavia in origin and, secondly, were only written down hundreds of years after conversion to Christianity, and so are likely to be doubly unreliable concerning aspects of her personality which some might have reason to denigrate (as in the Skeggjason case mentioned above).

The tale of the *Brisingamen*, a golden necklace of outstanding beauty, is renowned for its portrayal of Freya as someone who not only lusts madly after gold, but is even willing to sell her body multiple times to the ugliest of dwarves in order to gain possession of that adornment, in effect labelling her as a common prostitute. An alternative re-imagining of this story from a more Vanir-friendly point of view is given in chapter 1 of this book – given the title *'The Breeze Necklace'*. It may be that originally, at least for the Vanir following tribes who later became the Anglo-Saxons, Freya's association with gold was less related to precious metal and more to do with a possible role as a sun goddess, appealed to in particular to ripen grain before summer's end. As late as the nineteenth century in Sweden:

> *"Writer Johan Alfred Goth recalled a Sunday in 1880 where men were walking in fields and looking at nearly ripened rye, where Måns in Karryd said: 'Now Freyja is out watching if the rye is ripe'. Along with this, Goth recalls another mention of Freyja in the countryside: 'When as a boy I was visiting the old Proud-Katrina, I was afraid of lightning like all boys in those days. When the sheet lightning flared at the night, Katrina said: "Don't be afraid little child, it is only Freyja who is out making fire with steel and flintstone to see if the rye is ripe. She is kind to people and she is only doing it to be of service, she is not like Thor; he slays both people and livestock, when he is in the mood"... I later heard several old folks talk of the same thing in the same way.'"[152]*

As well as her ownership of the *Brisingamen*, Freya is also renowned for riding a chariot pulled by two cats, accompanied by the boar Hildisvíni, whose name means 'battle-boar', for Freya can also mount and ride into combat this fierce fighting animal when needed. There is a story that Hildisvíni is also really a magically transformed human male named Ottár, who was in fact one of Freya's lovers. It is said that she rewarded him for his devotion to her by transforming him into her boar – boars being sacred and magical beasts of warfare to Germanic tribes such as the Anglo-Saxons (see the *'Anglo-Saxon View of the Gods'* section of chapter 3). Whenever Freya wishes him to become her human lover again, she gives him a magical drink, the 'memory mead' to bring him back to himself; strong evidence of a female-led relationship, just as would be expected of a goddess.[153]

Freya is very strongly associated with magic, especially shamanic witchcraft skills. As mentioned above when Odin attempts to burn the Vanir witch Gullveig to death (he tries it three times but each time she magically survives) Freya launches a war of the Vanir against Odin's Æsir, besieging them inside the walls of their fortress home of Asgard. As part of the eventual peace terms Freya agrees to teach Odin *seidr* – north European shamanic magic, although this knowledge is usually restricted to women. There is a discussion of this in the 'shamanism' section of chapter 13. Freya also has a magical coat of falcon feathers, giving her the power to fly like that bird of prey, able to see in detail what is happening far below her.

Another Vanir-Æsir agreement sees those warriors falling in battle divided equally between Freya and Odin, with Freya getting first choice, and the remainder going to Valhalla to await the final battle of Ragnarok at the end of the worlds. Odin's soldiers are called 'einherjar' (meaning 'those who fight alone'), and are known collectively as 'the army of the dead', for they are slain every day fighting each other in Valhalla, only to be reanimated there every evening, ready to enter combat again by the following dawn.[154]

Freya's warriors however are taken to her 'large and beautiful' hall of Sessrúmnir. There is no record of them having to slay each other on a daily basis as required by Odin of his fighters, and it is tempting to imagine that with Freya being a goddess of lovers, other less violent pleasures might await them there. Certainly Freya is generally valued for, amongst so much else, her protective attributes, being renowned as a powerful female protective spirit:

> *"Freyja is known by a whole series of names… Syr, Vanadís. These names characterise Freyja as a domestic guardian goddess. The name Syr points out that Freyja… is characterised with the attributes of a*

pig... she even rides on a boar".[155]

As already mentioned, boars were seen as sacred animals, and as being particularly valuable as totemic protective images on body armour and helmets. Vanadís means 'Dís of the Vanir', dísir being *"fetch-like women who appear in dreams... the Valkyrie-like guardians of the dead"*. A fetch or *fylgjur* is a person's 'following spirit' or doppelgänger, usually taking the form of a spirit animal or woman, which can become an independent being at death, or transfer to another family member - closely related to the concept of a person's *hamingja* or personified luck.[156] Freya therefore has an aspect allowing her to act as a female protective spirit even to the Vanir gods themselves; she is a leader amongst them. This is discussed further in chapter 13.

Ullr – *A Winter God*

Not a great deal is known about Ullr. It is possible that he is another son of Njörd, but his mother might be Sif, the Æsir wife of the thunder god Thor, which would make him Thor's stepson. [157] There are Ullr place names in both Sweden and Norway associated with those of Frey and Njörd, but *"...even an association with the place names... is not sufficient to allow us with any certainty to count Ullr as one of the Vanir and a god of fertility"*.[158] As a winter god he was said to be renowned as an archer, hunter, skater and skier, and also to be handsome, warlike, and good to call on in duels(!) Ullr's home is called Ydalir, meaning 'valley of the yew trees' – just like Edale in Derbyshire (England).

The Norse used the term 'Ullr's ship' as a kenning (metaphor) for a shield, based on the idea that Ullr used his shield as a ship. This seems to link Ullr to another Vanir story – that of Scyld Scefing (see chapter 2).

Gullveig – *Witch and Seeress*

Gullveig, sometimes called "Heid" (Fame) was a renowned practitioner of the north European shamanic magic called (in Scandinavia) *seidr*. The name Gullveig means "Golden Power" or "Golden Drink/Intoxication". As already stated, Odin's hatred of Gullveig became the immediate origin of the 'first war', the war between the Vanir and the Æsir, following the Æsir 'All-father's' three failed attempts to burn the Vanir witch to death. The Voluspá says:

> "They called her Brightness when she came to their homes,
>
> A witch who could foretell; she knew the skill of wands,
>
> She made magic [seidr] where she could, made magic in a trance;
>
> She was always a delight to a wicked woman." [159]

> "Then [the Sibyl] remembered the first great war in the world,
>
> When they stabbed at Gullveig with spears,
>
> And they burned her in Odin's hall;
>
> Thrice they burned the thrice-born girl,
>
> Often, not once, but still she lived." [160]

Some believe it possible that Gullveig was in fact an aspect of the goddess Freya. After all Freya was renowned for her interest in and association with gold, and Gullveig's name is all to do with gold. It has even been suggested that the burning of Gullveig referred to in the Voluspá was actually a hidden reference to the process of purifying gold, with Freya and Gullveig both representing gold rather than real characters,[161] but there is no evidence for this. The Voluspá verses are very clearly about magic, seidr, and Gullveig as a seeress, not a technical manual on gold refining.

If there is a hidden aspect to the Gullveig story, it is more likely to be to do with the witch's triple nature rather than gold refining. Voluspá is clear that the tale goes back to some very early days indeed, the time before 'the first war' (which given the very warlike nature of both the Æsir and mankind must really be a very long time ago!); the time before Odin's acquisition of the knowledge of seidr. The reference above to the Sibyl remembering the first great war in the world is from verse 21 of Voluspá. Immediately prior to this verse 20 says:

> "From there come maidens, knowing much,
>
> Three from the lake [the spring or well of Urd] that stands under the tree [Yggdrasil]:
>
> 'Destiny' [Urd] they called one, 'Becoming' [Verdandi] the second,
>
> - They carved on wood tablets – 'Shall-be' [Skuld] the third;
>
> Laws they laid down, lives they chose
>
> For the children of mankind, the fates of men." [162]

This verse records the emergence of the three Norns (the weavers of the *Wyrd*, or fate/s), *Urd* (past/foundation), *Verdandi* (present/becoming), and *Skuld* (that which is to come, or 'the debt which must be paid' at the end: ultimately - death). Odin's triple attempt to destroy Gullveig failed, but why did he try three times? Immediately prior to this, existence had – with the appearance of the Norns - become divided into three parts (past, present, and that which still might come about), effectively creating time itself, and hence mortality. Could it be this (then newly developing) tripartite and dialectical character of material existence (see chapter 10 of this book), complete with its restricted life cycles and sentence of mortality on gods and mankind alike, that Odin the power-seeking patriarch was so desperate to destroy?

Kvasir – *The Muse of Poetic Wisdom*

Kvasir could be said to be the most mysterious of the Vanir, for he is both a 'who' and a 'what'. In the *Ynglinga Saga* he is referred to as "the cleverest of the Vanir", and is given up as a hostage to live with the Æsir as part of the peace agreement ending the Æsir-Vanir war. However in *Skáldskaparmál* Kvasir is said to be created by Æsir and Vanir spitting into a bowl. Whether created by spittle or not, Kvasir was then killed by dwarves, and his blood mixed with mead to create the 'Mead of Poetry'.

This, to our ears, strange story of a deity being created by collective spitting into a bowl, could actually have a relatively straightforward basis in reality. In a pre-literate age the 'Mead of Poetry' was the inspiration needed for effective storytelling, and can be said to originate with Kvasir:

> *"Originally Kvasir was probably the name given to the juice which was gained from berries and then fermented (cf. Norwegian kvase, Russian kvas)... the berries were chewed (as a communal practice) and then spat into a vessel – an exact correspondence to the creation of Kvasir in the Germanic myth."* [163]

Heimdal – *Scyld Scefing*

Heimdal is most often referred to as the guardian of Bifrost, the rainbow bridge access to Asgard, home of the Æsir, and is therefore usually assumed to be an Ás himself. However, as set out in chapter two of this book, Viktor Rydberg argues very strongly that Heimdal is actually the same character as Scyld Scefing ('Scef'), and as such was originally one of the Vanir, though perhaps later also accepted as an honourary Ás "by adoption". Heimdal/Shef's primary and key role, he says, was not the later defence of Asgard against the giants, but rather the much earlier spiritual fathering of children with mortal couples, thereby creating human social classes, a process which brought about a certain unity and identity of interests between the Vanir gods and mankind.[164]

What are the Vanir?

Rudolf Simek, in his *Dictionary of Northern Mythology*, defines the Vanir as:

> *"The second Germanic family of gods, the most important being the Æsir... The Vanir are in particular fertility gods who were called upon for good harvests, sun, rain, and good winds, especially by the agricultural population, and... by seafarers and fishermen. The Vanir practiced a form of magic deemed to be ignoble by the Æsir... incest between brothers and sisters was allowed by the Vanir, again in contrast to the Æsir... which could indicate matriarchal conditions amongst the original followers of a Vanir cult... the Vanir are the gods of the farming population, and the Æsir those of the warlike lords and their followers."* [165]

The Vanir then differ from the Æsir gods in a number of ways. Taken together these differences can be so significant as to lead some commentators to class the Vanir as a separate type of being altogether.

In the northern realms the following beings may be identified:

- Æsir (gods and goddesses) – warlike, aristocratic, patriarchal, respectable, orderly.
- Vanir (goddesses and gods) – peaceful, productive, magical, anti-chaotic, matriarchal or gender-balanced, sexually aware.
- Light Elves – fair faced, associated with nature, fertility, and the Vanir (their ruler is Frey).
- Dark Elves/Dwarves – ugly, subterranean, skilled

miners/metalworkers, cunning.

- Frost/Fire/Rock Giants – powerful, primal, chaotic/destructive, related to Aesir, can be attractive but ultimately seen by the Æsir as enemies.
- Monsters – chaotic/destructive, powerful, amoral, varied in form: dragons, serpents etc.
- Mankind – mortal and short-lived, quarrelsome, innovative, forever making demands (of each other and the gods).

Sheena McGrath says in *Njörd and Skadi – A Myth Explored*, that

> *"Snorri makes the Vanir's sexual arrangements and their magic distinguishing characteristics. The Aesir practice neither seidr nor sibling marriage... Loki calls Freyja a 'witch'... This fits... the general uneasiness about, and disapproval of, seidr... women could get away with it, but it was seen as unmanly... so the Vanir... seem to have specialised in the well-being of society, whether granting prosperity or sexual pleasure, while the Æsir seem to have focused on political power, war and magic."* [166]

The Vanir and Æsir different approaches to magic go beyond just seidr.

> *"Freyja and Odin come to the forefront here, being the magic specialists for each group. We know that Freyja taught Odin the magic known as seidr, which was so disgraceful and therefore remains mysterious. Odin had his own forms of magic, such as galdr, and of course he found the runes. This... shows the difference in their magics: a clash between Odin's ability to unfailingly cause death, against Freyja's ability to revive the fallen, so that as fast as Odin kills them, she brings them back. Another possible form of Vanir magic is foreseeing the future, for we are told that Heimdal could see the future as well as any Van."* [167]

To be fair to Odin it should be borne in mind that in leading warriors to their deaths he was not simply engaging in gratuitous killing, but was aiming to bolster the ranks of his own armies of the dead, ready to take on the forces of chaos and destruction at Ragnarok. And while Odin and the Æsir may find it difficult to pass modern day morality tests, the slightly more peaceable Vanir hardly come through with flying colours either: "...*while the Vanir are marked by incest, the Æsir are marked by fratricide*" [168] (a reference to the god

Balder being killed by Hod/Loki).

Even when it comes to influencing the weather, there seem to be key differences between the two tribes of gods. Whilst Frey of the Vanir can be requested to help ensure the fertility of the land through the provision of adequate supplies of both sunshine and rain, Thor of the Æsir may more usefully direct his attention to the active prevention of the famine and disease that it was feared might come from potential crop damage wreaked by storms. Amongst the Vanir, only Freya's fertility-related interests are in no way linked to the weather:

> "Frey controls sun and rain, 'and through them the bounty of the earth'... Thor was also frequently invoked for good crops, but with a different spin: 'Thor they say presides over the air, which governs thunder and lightning, the winds and rains... If plague and famine threaten, a libation is poured to... Thor' (Adam of Bremen)... The Vanir... seem to have been more about good weather; Freyja [alone] doesn't seem to have any connection to weather... Freyja comes to the fore... as the northern version of those fierce Middle Eastern goddesses such as Ishtar and Anat. We are told that she delights in love songs, and that it is good to pray to her for love. Loki... accuses her of having slept with all the gods and alfs [elves]." [169]

At a time when most wealth was generated by farming, the Vanir link with the agricultural fertility of land and animals also gave rise to them being associated with monetary riches: "Both Njörd and Freyr were called wealth-giving gods. Frey was invoked for peace and abundance... Freyja weeps tears that turn to gold, and her daughter is named Hnoss, 'Treasure'" (but see the section on Freya earlier in this chapter for a discussion of the nature of Freya's association with gold). The Æsir on the other hand were not wealth-generation specialists.

When considering the reasons for these significant association differences between Vanir and Æsir, it seems likely that they reflect the underlying material reality of the two groups' respective social evolution patterns.

Vanir society revolves around an abundance created through physical and mental labour, including everything from farming the land and animals, to the development and deployment of magical knowledge and skills, which together facilitate successful sexual union and fertility, and the generation of new life cycles (of land, animals, goddesses and gods, women and men).

Æsir society on the other hand appears to be fundamentally organised around structured hierarchies designed to allow a male warrior aristocracy to monopolise power, which may then be used to control and extract previously accumulated wealth from others, often obtained through military means (pillage and warfare). This route to the acquisition of material abundance inevitably creates high levels of ongoing security issues, leading to the male warrior aristocracy becoming ever more specialised, dominant, and independent of the interests the tribe as a whole. Warfare becomes a lauded end in itself, rather than just a regrettable but necessary consumption of resources to defend against potential external aggression.

> *"The differences between the two groups, and the war between them, have been explained in two ways. First, the historical school sees the war as reflecting a real conflict between two groups. This idea has faded away, although the new matriarchy theory of Old Europe versus patriarchal invaders has given it some new life... the other school follows Dumézil's theory that the war between the gods reflects the tension between the producer class (and their deities), and the warrior and aristocratic classes. The Vanir, as fertility deities, would have represented the producers, and the Æsir, whose chief gods are Thor and Odin, the other two..."* [170]

Dumézil was a twentieth century philologist who died in 1986. His analysis of early north European societies, with the interests of the working producer class generating priorities different from those of the warrior/aristocratic classes, seems essentially correct, as does his identification of the Vanir with the working producer class, and the Æsir with the warrior and aristocratic classes. It is worth noting though that in the twenty-first century there are proponents of "matriarchy theory" who believe that:

> *"Dumézil's scheme... should be emended into a fourfold one. The fourth section would be ruled by the goddess who, as Dumézil himself stated, symbolises the three separate functions of the masculine gods, assuming and reconciling all three. Rather than being the deity of any one section of the community, she is the 'deity of the entire people'"* [171]

Whether Dumézil's class contradictions could ever really be effectively reconciled by "the goddess" or anyone else remains open for debate. Whilst it is true that the Æsir are as patriarchal as the warrior/aristocratic class functions they are associated with, the same is demonstrably not true of the Vanir. The Vanir are most clearly not all "masculine gods", and even the associations of the male Vanir such as Njörd and Frey hardly fit in only with warrior/aristocracy roles (remember Frey losing his sword – see above); they are much more identified with working class producer functions.

In fact if any of the Vanir are to be associated with a warrior role, then it is surely fierce Freya, the very womanly but also militant goddess. Freya is no insipid "reconciler" of rulers and the productive working class, nor even of the sexes. She promotes her own interests as a powerful female, for example honouring but taming and controlling her human warrior lover Ottár whom she magically transforms into her boar, allowing her to ride him (no doubt in more ways than one). Her function as a Vanir goddess is not to reconcile all classes in society, but rather to operate as a divine advocate of the essential fertility-based requirements of the working producer class, whether woman, man, goddess, or god. Vanir and Æsir developed separately out of necessarily conflicting aspects of existence, which cannot be un-invented or ever fully 'reconciled', but only cyclically transformed through dialectical material processes – see the analysis and comparison of Greek idealist neoplatonism and north European materialist philosophy in chapter 11.

The close identification of Freya and the Vanir in general with the working producer class – so different from the equally close identification of the Æsir with the warrior aristocracy – goes back a long way. As discussed in chapter 2, Viktor Rydberg argues that Shef (Scyld Scefing) was sent by the Vanir as a young child to mankind in general, and to the tribes then living in southern Sweden in particular (the Vanir-following predecessors of peoples later to become the Anglo-Saxons, the early English), to grow up as both a god and a man, and to teach his mortal benefactors the skills of productive work necessary to promote agricultural and material abundance.

In much the same vein Sheena McGrath highlights the Vanir role in the positive and inclusive promotion of peace, fertility, pluralism, and diversity in relations between gods, giants, peoples, races, and female and male, contrasting that with the very different, much more exclusive Æsir roles:

> "...the Vanir operate as a bridge between the infield and
> outfield (Midgard – Utgard), and perhaps hark back to
> a period when this division was less sharp. That would

explain why two of the Vanir men are married to giantesses... the opposition between alliance and war, marriage and death, is also represented in the relations between the myth of Balder and the myth of the marriage of Njörd and Skadi. The relation between Vanir and giants was one of compensation and marriage, very different from the relations between Æsir and jotnar [giants] ... [where] we see a clear pattern of rules about who can marry whom. In this view, the Æsir are on top, the jotnar on bottom, and the Vanir are 'the filling in this uneasy sandwich'." [172]

McGrath sees the Æsir as having made a conscious decision to separate themselves from their blood relatives the giants, forbidding (unlike the Vanir) intermarriage, as a response to the Aesir's perceived self-interest in maintaining a homeland (fortress Asgard) as pure and orderly, uncorrupted by chaotic influences.

"...the Vanir... occupy a strange position, passively inculpated in the murder of Thiazi,[‡] but apart enough that they can marry giant women, which the Æsir will not or cannot do. Perhaps because they are not blood relations of the jotunns, their relationship with them can be less fraught with complications and bad feelings." [173]

"...the difference between the gods and the giants isn't so much that they're of different natures as that the gods made a conscious decision to be different... the murder of Ymir... set out to create an ordered world, unlike the chaos the giants lived in. After that there was no going back. The gods didn't create a world out of nothing, the way that Jahweh did; they killed a giant [Ymir]... and made a world from his body parts, thus literally creating a cosmic order from chaos." [174]

McGrath's emphasis on the importance the Æsir's distinguishing tendency of separating themselves off from constructive interaction with other beings is supported by Stephen Pollington in his book *The Elder Gods*, when he says that

---

[‡] Thiazi – a giant, the father of Skadi, killed in eagle form by the Æsir in revenge for his having forced Loki to kidnap the goddess Idun and her golden apples of immortality (see chapter 6).

> *"the Æsir are belligerent gods of war and magic, while the Vanir are defensive gods and goddesses of prosperity and sensual pleasure... Dumézil sees the Æsir as connected to individuality (separation), and the Vanir to relationality (assimilation). The Vanir thrive by being willing to accept and accommodate the Other, whereas the Æsir separate themselves from the Other, usually by killing it. The Vanir are able to regenerate wealth, knowledge, and military success; the only answer for the Æsir would be to isolate themselves, to reduce their social contact."* [175]

Fertility of Earth (and Sea) – but not Sky?

This is not to claim though that, unlike the Æsir, the Vanir always acted more in line with twenty-first century morality norms. As already set out earlier in this chapter Frey's pursuit of the giantess Gerd, for example, is distinctly morally dubious (sending his servant to threaten and blackmail Gerd into submission). However, as is typical of tales involving the Vanir, this story does at least allow the presentation of difficult and contradictory concerns, openly recording the less than perfect impulses of even the gods themselves. Frey, for example, is acknowledged as an individual (and very imperfect) being - rather than an archetype.

There is a popular view of fertility gods that they consist largely of 'Mother Earth' figures, made fertile through a "sacred marriage" with a 'Sky Father' god: [176]

> *"The ritual marriage of sky and earth has been a popular* interpretation [of the Gerd-Freyr myth] *doubtless because scholars... are the product of one religion, Christianity, which involves a sky-god in whom they, perhaps, no longer wholly believe, and of a second, Darwinism, which involves a procreative Earth, Terra Mater."* [177]

'All-father' Odin of the Æsir is often seen as a sky father figure, with the goddess Jord as earth, but this model does not seem to work with the Vanir. In the story of Frey and Gerd the giantess for instance:

> *"most treatments... have tended to assume that Gerd was... the fallow earth waiting to be fertilised, they didn't concern themselves with what the 'earth' felt*

about it... what we are talking about here is essentially
rape. It's not like the earth is getting any choice in the
matter... unlike... the Sumerian Inanna... [Gerd] doesn't
get to pick her lovers... [but] Freyr is the Veraldagud,
the world-god, not a sky-god like Odin, Tyr and Thor,
and Gerd is not the earth-goddess, but a giantess... This
must be the only fertility myth of sky and earth in which
the earth doesn't want to know, and is essentially
blackmailed into giving up her autonomy... Gerd is the
negative, since she does not want to be with Freyr... she
makes it clear she has been browbeaten into it. Skadi [§]*,*
at the positive pole, states very clearly that she wants
an Ase husband, and not just any Ase, but Baldr... what
women do want... is sovereignty, rule over themselves."
178

The Vanir (and Loki) –
as the Inspirational Gods of Creative Narratives

The pre-Christian early English were largely illiterate, but hardly lacking in creative imagination or storytelling skills. Those north European pagan stories which have come down to us survived because they were written down hundreds of years after the conversion to Christianity, but analysis of the tales told in sources such as the Eddas and Beowulf can still throw some light on pre-Christian thinking and ways of looking at the worlds. Stories of the gods survived for centuries even before the development of literate societies in northern Europe, no doubt changing slightly each time a purely oral rendering was given to a feast hall or other audience.

These narratives survived for so long even prior to being set down in writing because they were valued not just for their entertainment value, but also for their authoritative 'truths' which listeners could engage with as their own precisely because those truths were never absolute, but forever flexible and adaptable to changing circumstances over the years and across half a continent. Beowulf, for example,

---

[§] Skadi the giantess is offered the choice of a husband by the gods as compensation for the killing of her father Thiazi (but has to choose without seeing their faces, and ends up with Njord, although wanting Balder). They subsequently divorce.

contains a certain Christian gloss, but also retains some evidence of fundamental personal and collective values, and aspects of a cosmological outlook, going back centuries to pagan times. It seems likely that both consciously and subconsciously listeners could identify, to varying degrees, with those principles.

With the advent of Christianity the divine realm became remote, monolithic, celestial, static, unchallengeable, and beyond mortal comprehension. Before then the multiple worlds of the gods and mankind were known to be tangible, contradictory, several, varied, perplexing and stimulating. The gods were far from perfect; any part they might have played in the creation of worlds was recognised as having been flawed: *"People had a rather different view of godhood back then, which could accommodate weaknesses and foibles as well as strengths."* [179]

Stories from pagan times could rarely be classed as straightforward parables. At one level they were likely to function as pure entertainment, often appealing to the baser aspects of people's appetites (e.g. episodes of dramatic violence and unalloyed sexual desire). But often they would also contain other, deeper levels of meaning, though these were apt to be both partly obscured and debateable.

"There are aspects of the Njörd-Skadi myth which are clearly about nature, but... if that was all it was... it would be no more than a primitive tale of little interest. It has to have some resonance in human emotions and behaviour before it's of any worth. In other words, a myth needs to be a good story first." [180]

When the Vanir send Scyld Scefing to Midgard with a mission to teach, his lessons are not just to do with agricultural fertility and the military skills necessary to defend that material abundance, but also concern cultural issues,[181] such as storytelling knowledge and techniques, believed to be as necessary to nourish the spirit and soul as a good harvest is to feed the body. Who knows but that such knowledge might one day even permit escape from Ragnarok and the end of the world:

"...that Njörd will return home at Ragnarok is one of the biggest teases in Norse myth... this could possibly mean that only the world of the Æsir is destroyed − that the Vanir survive, along with their home." [182]

But whether the Vanir (and their followers?) might actually escape Ragnarok remains unknown; the future cannot be predicted with certainty, because 'fate' is never inevitable, but subject to the ever-changing multiple interactions of the Wyrd. It is this uncertainty which allows for narrative suspense and hope in both stories and people's lives. Vanir and especially the Æsir would agree that giving narrative purpose to both fiction and individuals' existence requires a well configured and ordered structure, but beyond this true life also needs a more chaotic and uncertain spark: enter Loki –

> "The Norse myths wouldn't be much without Loki. He stirs things up, he makes things happen… Loki was a poet's god, the engine for stories. Or, as Michael Chabon describes him: 'god of the endlessly complicating nature of plot, of storytelling itself… the Eddas: a book whose subtitle might have been 'How Loki Ruined the World and Made it Worth Talking About'." [183]

Loki, the Norse trickster god, is "described as the son of… Laufey… presumably a giantess" [184], and as such his relationship with the Æsir is bound to be ambiguous to say the least. For now it may be sufficient to note his role as being that of a necessary but uncomfortable irritant; for a full discussion of Loki's character and functions, see chapter 13.

Spitting Out the Runes

One of the ways in which runes are magical is that they can be used to communicate words and meanings, and hence facilitate storytelling – see chapter 7. However even before the use of runes and the advent of partially literate societies it seems that oral storytelling was popular, as evidenced by the Kvasir myth as recounted above ("Kvasir was probably the name given to the juice which was gained from berries and then fermented… the berries were chewed (as a communal practice) and then spat into a vessel – an exact correspondence to the creation of Kvasir in the Germanic myth").[185]

This suggests that in northern myth, storytelling, which was originally oral, not literary, in form (often told in poetic verse), was seen as being closely linked to wisdom. Kvasir was renowned as one "so wise that no-one was able to ask him questions to which he did not know the answer; he travelled widely throughout the world, teaching folk wisdom".[186] The creative mead of poetry was conceived through the productive mingling of Vanir and Æsir qualities, leading to the achievement of peace between individuals and peoples – a process helped along by the imbibing of alcoholic refreshment!

Storytelling and Kvasir's 'Mead of Poetry' drive home the wisdom messages of the myths by relating them to individual characters people can understand and relate to, and enable such wisdom to survive by being passed on - from person to person, and generation to generation. Mortals are able to engage with the stories because they feature beings like themselves whose character and behaviour is flawed, with even the gods (Vanir and Æsir) demonstrating *"weaknesses and foibles as well as strengths"*.[187]

Storytelling is about showing mortals, gods, and giants as individuals, each with free will, the freedom to get things wrong and make mistakes, but also the freedom to transcend any restrictive characteristics inherited with collective type (mortal, god, giant), and therefore... the ability to learn, change, and develop through interaction with 'the other' – up to and including intermarriage. It is this interaction with 'the other', the bridging role between races, between infield and outfield (Midgard and Utgard, mankind and monsters) that the Vanir specialise in, and which the drinking of Kvasir's storytelling mead allows us all to learn from.

The Vanir – *Interceding Survivors*

The Vanir are all about the maintenance of peace, particularly as an essential condition for the orderly maintenance of the productive fertility of land, animals, mankind, and gods. The intermediate and independent position of the Vanir between the Æsir and the giants helps them relate to all life forms, as do their magical *seidr* skills, which enable them to travel peacefully between the worlds.

This Vanir role finds its mirror image in Loki. Like the Vanir, Loki enjoys (or suffers from) an intermediate and independent position between the Æsir and the giants, as he himself comes of giant stock but lives with and is brought up by the Æsir. Whilst the Vanir promote an ordered and controlled form of fertility through peace and calm, Loki promotes chaotic fertility by stirring things up.

The Æsir long ago declared their incompatibility with the giants, having created an ordered cosmos through the killing of the chaos giant Ymir. Since then the Æsir have followed a policy of controlled and orderly but separate development, fully aware that this ultimately makes them irreconcilable with the forces of chaos. The Æsir seek safety behind the walls of Asgard, isolated from the chaotic worlds of Utgard, but know that ultimately this will destroy them.

The Vanir on the other hand, although they approve of and engage with the Æsir's defence of the rule of law and order**, do not seek separate development, but maintain some level of relations with the chaos giants, up to and including inter-marriage.

Meanwhile Loki flits back and forth, wavering between Æsir, Vanir and giants, but will ultimately fail to integrate with the forces of order, and end up being instrumental in the destruction of the Æsir.

The fate of the Vanir is less certain. Their story has not yet ended. When Ragnarok happens and Asgard and the Æsir are destroyed by the forces of chaos, the Vanir might yet survive. Unlike Loki they do not live on by switching sides, but neither do they isolate and trap themselves behind encircling stone walls. Instead Njörd (and all the Vanir?) might yet return to fertile Vanaheim, and perhaps tell stories of legendary, heroic, defiant, but long since vanished, Asgard?

** It is interesting to note the contrasting views of law and order derived from pagan polytheistic understanding of the worlds on the one hand (which might be summed up as 'allowable unless forbidden' and therefore 'innocent until proven guilty'), and monotheistic understanding on the other ['forbidden unless allowed by God' and therefore 'guilty from birth' (original sin)]. As Stephen Pollington expresses it: *"Anglo-Saxon society took as its precept in law a presumption of innocence, and in (Christian) religion a presumption of guilt"* [Pollington, The Elder Gods (see Bibliography), p.450].

Chapter 5 – *Æsir Heroes: Thor and Tyr*

As we have seen when the final battle comes, the Æsir will go down fighting to the bitter end. The degree to which this can be seen as tragic or heroic probably depends on analysis of the character of those doomed to die. The leader of the Æsir, 'All-father' Odin, possesses a complex nature, aspects of which are decidedly unpleasant and self-centred, for example his *"eager passion for using sex and deception in the pursuit of his aims"* and the fact that *"faithfulness at any level is not a feature of Odin's actions"*. [188]

> *"Even in Hávamál itself, which is largely dedicated to a celebration of a number of his [Odin's] aspects, the question is posed as to how anyone can trust him. His long-suffering wife Frigg... is frequently deserted in a string of sexual peccadilloes with a variety of female creatures, notably giantesses."* [189]

This lack of personal morality on Odin's part is made all the worse by his apparent hypocrisy. A Vanir-like emphasis on sexual freedoms for himself might be more forgivable if Odin did not condemn libertine behaviour in others (such as Loki), and were he to refrain from choosing declared enemies from amongst the giantesses to seduce and rape (as in the case of Rindr*).

There is even evidence of significant tensions between Odin 'All-father' and his own, much more well-meaning son, Thor. In *Hárbardsljód* for example:

> *"Odin taunts and frustrates Thor at every turn, and clearly regards his own domain as essentially more*

---

* *"In Book III of the Gesta Danorum, written by Saxo Grammaticus around the early 13th century.... Rindr is the daughter of the King of the Ruthenians... Odin went to the Ruthenians... There he was twice turned down by Rindr. He then wrote runes on a piece of bark and touched her with it, causing her to go mad, and disguised himself as a medicine woman called Wecha, who was allowed to see her. Finally she fell ill; the disguised Odin then said he had medicine with which to cure her but that it would cause a violent reaction. On Odin's advice, the king tied Rindr to her bed, and Odin proceeded to rape her. Óðinn's rape of Rindr is [also] described in Sigurðardrápa... denoting Óðinn's magical rape of Rindr with the verb síða. This suggests that... the magic known as seiðr was integral to Óðinn's raping of Rindr."* [https://en.wikipedia.org/wiki/Rindr]

aristocratic than Thor's plebeian constituency." [190]

It should also be remembered of course that Odin did also possess some more positive aspects to his character, for example he was renowned for his knowledge and wisdom, being able to use both runes and seidr, though even that skill was generally regarded as unmanly. Above all he was supreme in battle, though ultimately even his combat skills come to naught at Ragnarok when the wolf Fenrir, Loki's child, seeking vengeance, destroys him.

It is difficult then to regard Odin as truly heroic, or his eventual demise as authentically tragic. Certainly the rape victim Rindr cannot have mourned his passing. However the Æsir were all individuals with complex and developing characters, and there are at least two candidates from amongst them who, whilst still having some weaknesses, may perhaps more fairly claim the title of "hero" – Thor, and the original warrior god of justice, Tyr.

Thor – *Working Class Hero?*

It is widely accepted that Thor is a bit of a commoner amongst the gods, unlike Odin who is seen as the favourite of the traditional Nordic warrior aristocratic elite. Ellis Davidson for example says of Thor:

> *"Thor's realm is very different from that of Odin. His*
> *cult was not an aristocratic one, and indeed a taunt*
> *made against him in one of the Edda poems was*
> *that while Odin received kings who fell in battle,*
> *Odin got the thralls".* [191]

So was Thor the god of the thralls and, by extension, could he also be called the god of the 'lower' class workers of more modern times?

Thor's most potent and widely known symbol is his magical hammer *Mjöllnir*, and he is married to Sif, she of the famous golden hair which was cut off by Loki and had to be magically replanted, causing her to be identified as a corn harvest goddess. The implement traditionally used to cut corn at harvest time is of course the sickle. Put these two tools together, and what do you get? The answer is the hammer and sickle, the archetypal Communist Party and workers' emblem of the twentieth century. Is it possible that there is any connection at all between Thor and Sif as workers' gods, and Lenin's chosen symbolism?

The official reason the communists chose the hammer and sickle as their emblem is that it symbolises the unity of the two great revolutionary classes, the industrial proletariat and the landless peasantry. This alliance was viewed as particularly important in Russia by Lenin because the relative backwardness of his country's economy meant that no revolution based on "the masses" could hope to succeed if it ignored the peasantry. It seems highly unlikely that there could have been any open, conscious decision on behalf of the communists to appeal to some latent, residual faith in the power of Thor and Sif, despite the well-known Viking settlement of parts of what is now Russia, but then again the coincidence of these symbols does seem remarkable, and who can say that some subconscious folk memory did not play a role here?

It may be objected that communism was primarily a Russian phenomenon rather than a Germanic one, but it should not be forgotten that until 1917 Lenin and most revolutionary socialists regarded Germany, with its highly developed economy and mass left wing workers' party as the inspiration and best hope for a socialist revolution. And after all, whilst the sickle may be a fairly obvious and meaningful way of identifying with the peasant, why choose the hammer to represent the industrial worker? Yes, hammers were a common tool in the metal-working industries, but proletarians could be found labouring in a vast range of occupations, so why the hammer?

It might be suspected that the answer lies in the additional, probably subconscious, role of the hammer symbol as a token of male virility. The early communists wished to forge a new world, but their social conditioning led them to appeal primarily to the leading role of male workers to bring this change about. Hence the textile industry, for example, despite being one of the greatest mass employers of the industrial workforce, would not be viewed as an appropriate supplier of proletarian symbolism (weaving being historically a feminine pursuit), but the hard-edged, macho environment of the metalworker would. If this is true then it does provide a tenuous link between communist symbolism and Thor, because Thor's hammer too played a phallic role.[192]

Thor - *God of Thralls?*

The modern-day author, Freya Aswynn, confidently asserts Thor's role as the workers' god. *"Thor is the special patron of those who work the land, the farmers and peasants"*, she tells us.

> *"Thor's hammer symbolises the male power of fertilising and generating life in the Earth... There is a class difference between Odin and Thor. Odin was regarded in the Viking age as the god of the ruling classes. Thor is the patron of the working classes, the yeomen as well as the thralls. His hammer has been taken by the Socialists as a symbol of the workers. Thor's wife Sif is the Northern corn-goddess... she might therefore be associated with a sickle. It is to Thor that the Thralls go after death. Thor is the protector of the ordinary hard-working fellow. Even the slaves came under Thor's protection".[193]*

Hardly any wonder that Thor was so popular then, for he was both protector of the vast majority of the population, and defender of that perennial Northern favourite, the underdog!

Being protector of such a wide range of people however, could be said to limit the usefulness of any attempt to identify Thor as a workers' god. The thralls certainly may have borne a passing resemblance to the twentieth century wage-labourer, in that both in effect sold their labour-power in return only for the bare means of subsistence, without being significant independent owners of property. But what about the 'yeomen farmers' which Freya Aswynn refers to? Surely they resemble more the property-owning middle-classes of today than a communist view of the working class? After all, these independent Northern homesteaders were relatively well off in material terms, very unlike the thralls, as Crossley-Holland explains:

> *"The serfs had a bad time of it. They were manual labourers and they were never free. Thrall and his wife Thir and their nineteen children would have lived in a single stinking hut, made with timber or with turf and clay, shared with such animals as they possessed.... No patron god guarded the lives of these most luckless members of the community".[194]*

So who is right, Aswynn or Crossley-Holland? Was Thor really the god of the thralls, or did they, as Crossley-Holland claims, have to make do without any god to protect them? The evidence is inconclusive. The point about the quotation from Ellis Davidson at the beginning of this section, saying that "Thor got the Thralls", is precisely that this accusation is, as she points out, a taunt. Being a taunt, it might or might not be true. The reference is to *The Lay of Habard*, in which Thor, returning to Asgard from his travels, must cross over a deep sound. There is a ferryman, who is Odin in disguise, who refuses to ferry Thor across the sound, instead taunting the weary god, apparently out of sheer unprovoked malice. Odin, after deceitfully telling Thor that his mother is dead and his wife Sif in the very act of being unfaithful to him even as they speak, adds insult to injury by shouting at him: *"After they've fallen in the fight... the nobly born journey to Odin. But Thor, he caters for a great gang of thralls"*.[195]

Thor doesn't actually deny this. Indeed his reply, although ambiguous, has a democratic sounding edge to it which might lead to the conclusion that it is perhaps Aswynn who is correct. *"I see how even handed you'd be in your gifts of men to the gods"*, says Thor.[196] Is Thor saying that Odin is mistaken not to value the services of all men, even thralls?

Whether or not Thor was god of the thralls, he certainly was a favourite of the social grouping which was the most numerous in pre-Christian Northern societies: the independent 'yeoman-farmer'. These individuals were property owners to various degrees, and lived a life unrecognisable to most thralls:

> *"The great majority of the Norsemen however undoubtedly belonged to the peasant class whose patron was Thor. They were smallholders and freemen... they lived in two or more buildings – a pair of parallel long-houses sometimes supplemented by a barn or two, making a three or even four-sided complex with a court-yard in the middle".* [197]

The diet of these freemen was healthy and varied, including wholemeal rye bread, fish, lamb, goat, calf, pig, cheese, butter, cream, apples, berries, nuts, vegetables, beer, mead and (amongst the wealthier) even wine. These people were clearly of a higher social class than the thralls in their "single, stinking hut". Lenin would surely have rejected them as 'kulaks', i.e. rich, property-owning peasants, with much more to lose than just their chains, who could not be expected to side with wage-dependent landless labourers and industrial workers.

If Odin were to meet Thor at that ferry crossing today, he might taunt our honest hero with being merely the god of the middle-classes! Given our modern-day society's continuing worship of violence and those warrior abilities associated by the Norse exclusively with the aristocracy, this accusation would surely be just as wounding to Thor today as the 'All-father's' original allegation that working class wage-slaves were his only constituency.

Red Thor

Oddly enough there is one further symbol linking Thor to the revolutionary working class, namely the colour red. The flag of communism was of course pure red, that of the Soviet Union the hammer and sickle on a red background, and in the twentieth century even the British Labour Party was still singing *"The People's Flag is deepest red"* at Party Conference every year, even if only Tony Benn, dinosaur relic of an earlier era, actually believed in the symbolism of that martyr's blood-stained banner any more. And Thor is of course known as "Red Thor", though admittedly not because of any known allegiance to the Socialist Workers Party, but because of his famous red beard, and possibly his reputation for "seeing red", that is losing his temper on a divine scale.

Just as Lenin's, Stalin's and Trotsky's Red Armies battled the hated "Whites" (the counter-revolutionaries) in Russia's civil war of the early 1920s, so in the Viking age *"...the battle was one of Red Thor against the White Christ"*.[198] In the 10th as in the 20th century these colours were powerful symbols as well as simple identifiers of causes. To be called "red" was to be viewed as fierce, strong-willed, hot-tempered and battle-mighty – so much so in fact that some Germanic warriors even dyed their hair red as a sign of ferocity.[199] Christians saw white as a symbol of fairness, but heathens saw this colour as a sign of cowardice, a meaning which has somehow survived into modern times (witness for example the white feathers handed out to reluctant volunteers by English women during the First World War).

Thor may not be only a workers' god, but Red Thor is certainly still "the common man's patron".[200] He concerns himself with the defence of not just Asgard but also Midgard against the chaotic forces, and in his role as Thunder God is not feared as a destructive force, but loved as a one-man (or one-god) defence force, ever alert to fighting off marauding ice-giants.

> *"In Germany, where the eastern storms are always cold and blighting, while the western bring warm rains and mild weather, Thor was supposed to journey always from west to east, to wage war against the evil spirits which would have fain*

> *enveloped the country in impenetrable veils of mist*
> *and have bound it in icy fetters".*[201]

Furthermore Thor's colour of red is ultimately symbolic of a power greater than ferocity and rage, namely love.

> *"Brides invariably wore red, Thor's favourite colour,*
> *which was considered emblematical of love, and for*
> *the same reason betrothal rings in the North were*
> *almost always set with a red stone".*[202]

In the end Red Thor *"cares for the land and the people"* [203] much more than he does any single social class, and we should all remember that without him *"there would be a terrible throng of giants; and there would be no men in Midgard".*[204]

Tyr – *Warrior God of Justice*

Thor may have been recorded as Odin's son, but in many ways he seems to take more after another, more ancient Germanic warrior god: Tyr, or Tíw as he was known to the Anglo-Saxons. Unlike the 'All-father', Tyr was not just a god of war and victory at any cost, but a deity dedicated to just causes. Thor could be deemed a hero because, despite some shortcomings such as his quick temper and the relative slowness of his wits, he was honest, straightforward, loyal, brave, and prepared to sacrifice himself defending others.

Tyr is a very similar character, and also usually more quick witted than Thor, though at times his straightforward honesty could leave him open to being deceived by others, for example by Odin in the incident which led to him losing his hand (see the 'Tyr and the Binding of Fenrir' storytelling below). It is thought that he had once been the pre-eminent god of war in the Germanic pantheon, but that in Viking age Scandinavia his position was substantially usurped by the more devious Odin. Crossley-Holland suggests that the story of Tyr's involvement in the binding of Fenrir *"was known in northern Europe for between one and two thousand years before Snorri Sturluson included it in his Prose Edda."* [205]

Like Woden (Wednesday), Thor (Thursday), and Freya (Friday), the English thought Tyr or Tíw renowned enough to have a day of the week named after him (Tuesday). His character was considered sufficiently important for his name to be given to the letter 't' rune [↑] in all three major runic alphabets (the Anglo-Saxon, Elder Germanic, and Icelandic/Norwegian 'futharks' – see chapter 7). This runic upright arrow was held to signify courage and battle readiness.

> *"Sigdrifumál... teaches that one puts victory runes on to a sword by carving Tyr twice, and in Migration Age runic inscriptions (also on bracteates) the T-rune frequently appears as a sign of magical significance."* [206]

In Old Norse a wrist was called a 'wolf-joint'. The Tale of Tyr and the Wolf Fenrir explains why.

Fourth Storytelling – *Tyr and the Binding of Fenrir*

Being of giant rather than Æsir blood, Loki was never fully trusted by the gods as he grew to maturity in Asgard. He was both intelligent and sensitive but - correctly discerning the wariness and doubt of those he grew up amongst - Loki, like many a mortal youth in his position, reacted badly. Part of him strove to meet Æsir expectations. This was the part of his character which led him to marry the honest and faithful Ása Sigyn. Another part of Loki though grew ever more resentful of the way many of the Æsir looked down on him, and vowed that as they denied him their love and respect, so then he would prove them correct by making a study of cunning and deception. After all, he told himself, if such qualities were good enough for Odin, his supposed mentor and guide, then they were good enough for him. This was the part of him that took the giantess Angrboda as his lover.

With Angrboda Loki had three children. True to the giants' genetic inheritance of the most destructive and chaotic bloodlines, these children were not alike in form, but only in their strength and powers of desolation. The first born took the shape of a wolf and was named Fenrir. The second child grew to become a giant serpent, given the name Jörmungand. The third was a girl. By her the parents at first felt blessed. They called her Hel, meaning the bright, shining one, but as she grew only her upper body remained attractively luminous; below the waist her flesh decayed and turned to a putrefying dark green.

As Angrboda's and Loki's offspring grew and all could see what they had become, Odin decreed that they must be banished, or at least imprisoned, for the sake of the safety of all the Æsir. He ordered the unfortunate Jörmungand thrown into the deepest ocean, but there the giant snake did not perish but breathed salt water and grew and grew, until eventually this now sea serpent encircled the world. She is able to bite the tip of her own tail, ready to crush, constrict and shake the deepest roots of the cosmos when Ragnarok comes.

Hel was banished by Odin to become the queen of the 'non-heroic' dead – all those who did not die in battle, weapon in hand. These he condemned to be blinded at first by Hel's half-luminous beauty, leading them to leave the lands of the living, only then to fade and finally die in frozen Helheim, the ice-bright realm of this goddess of the deceased.

Angrboda and Loki were outraged by this treatment of their two younger children, and secretly swore revenge on Odin. One day, when the forces of chaotic destruction grow strong enough, they vowed to each other, they would fight at their children's side to destroy fortress Asgard and the treacherous Æsir. Though their vows of vengeance remained secret, Odin could hardly fail to perceive Angrboda's and Loki's unhappiness at his actions, nor to note their powerful potential to foment trouble for him, so in his treatment of their third and eldest child, Fenrir the wolf, he thought it wise to adopt a more moderate stance.

Whilst still young Fenrir seemed much like any other wolf, and not that great a threat, so Odin allowed him to live, subject to the demand that he reside in Asgard where the Æsir could keep an eye on him. Angrboda and Loki straight away agreed to this proposal, thankful for the relative leniency of the decision. However as Fenrir grew it became clear that this was no ordinary wolf. As his long legs, strong muscles, and powerful jaws and teeth got ever bigger, so the gods became ever warier. Most steered as clear as they could of Fenrir. Only Tyr, the warrior god of justice who was renowned as the bravest of all the Æsir, had no fear of Fenrir, and continued to talk quite happily to the giant wolf and treat him well.

Odin though, grew afraid. Alone amongst the male Æsir he was wont to use magic to talk to the Norns and demand knowledge of what was to come. They told him that he was a fool, for at Ragnarok the wolf would destroy him. The time had come, Odin decided, for him to renege on his promise, and break his word about Fenrir's security amongst the Æsir. At the very least Fenrir must be bound, made helpless and defenceless, so that at the slightest sign of the coming of the end of the worlds, he could be slain. There was though a problem: who would be brave enough to bind Fenrir in the first place, and how could the gods be sure of the strength of the binding? For if Fenrir were bound but then escaped, he would surely crush the gods in his mighty jaws.

Odin took council with the gods – all except Tyr, for the god of justice was both Fenrir's friend and just too honest to be allowed to know of the trickery and deception which Odin suspected might be necessary. The Æsir agreed to their leader's proposal, including a suggestion from the 'All-father' that they should deceive Fenrir into allowing them to test the security of his bonds. This they did by taunting the wolf. *"Look at this chain of iron, mighty Fenrir,"* they told him. *"Even you with your mighty muscles could not escape if this were wrapped around you!"*

Fenrir laughed and told them to try it. They did, and sure enough as soon as the giant wolf flexed his limbs the links of the chain flew apart, and Fenrir rolled over and over in celebration of his strength. A little later the gods attempted the trick again, this time with a new chain of metal twice as strong as the first one. Fenrir looked at them with suspicion, doubting their motivation, but they goaded him with allegations of cowardice, until in the end he agreed to let them tie him down once more. This time he struggled and at first his bonds did not break, but then Fenrir remembered the unjust fates of his sisters Jörmungand and Hel at Odin's hand. He breathed more deeply, resentment at his siblings' betrayal driving new determination into his limbs, and again he succeeded in breaking free.

In desperation the gods again took council, and decided to ask the dark elves, the dwarves, for assistance. They were made to pay heavily in gold, yet Odin thought it would be worth it. When the dwarven device was delivered though, the Æsir were shocked, for this was no chain, but appeared to be a mere ribbon, apparently of no great power at all. *"What,"* demanded Odin, *"is this? What is it made of, that you imagine it will bind so powerful a wolf?"*

The dark elf who had delivered the dwarven strip of cloth explained. *"This is no ordinary material. It may look frail, but it is constructed from qualities that no creature may sever. It is made from the sound a cat makes when it moves, the roots of a mountain, and air breathed by fish. But best of all, it consists of a word, for it has a name. It is dubbed 'Gleipnir', and it is the magic of words that may bind all beings."*

As before the Æsir again dared Fenrir to try his strength. The wolf scoffed and refused to fall into the trap, for so he suspected it might be. *"You can trust us,"* Odin lied, *"it's only a ribbon. Yes, it's supposed to be strangely strong, but if you really can't break it, we'll cut it for you and let you go."*

Still Fenrir was too wise to trust Odin, so the 'All-father' finally sent for Tyr. He explained that the gods were "having fun" with the wolf, and told Tyr to place his hand in Fenrir's mouth as a guarantee that nothing bad would happen. Tyr and Fenrir trusted each other, and so both complied. With Tyr's hand between his jaws, Fenrir permitted himself to be bound tightly in the long ribbon, which was wrapped tightly around him, binding his limbs to his body. Gleipnir's magic proved too powerful for even the giant wolf to overcome. The ribbon painfully constricted his chest until he was howling helplessly in his anguish and rage. Of course Odin broke his word to the wolf and refused to release him. Fenrir's howling caused his jaws to clamp shut, and Tyr's hand was torn from his wrist. Ever after Tyr remained one-handed. But at Ragnarok, the Norns know, the wolf will finally break free, and Tyr's friend will swallow not Odin's hand, but his whole being.

Tyr – *Honest Sky God of War, Wisdom, and Justice*

Despite laying himself open to the deception of others, Tyr's straightforwardness was generally reckoned to qualify him as a good and wise councillor, making him *"the Germanic god of the sky, war and council"*.[207] Snorri Sturluson said of him that *"A man who does not flinch and surpasses others is said to be 'as brave as Tyr'. He was so clever that a clever man is called 'as wise as Tyr'."* [208]

Only Tyr does not fear the wolf. Wolves may be deadly, and need to kill prey to survive, but they do not pretend otherwise. Like Tyr their motivations are straightforward; they do not seek to deceive. At the end of the worlds not only will the giant wolf Fenrir kill Odin, but two other wolves will swallow the sun and the moon. Tyr himself will die fighting another wolf-hound, called Garm, and so be granted an honest and honourable death. Like Thor, Tyr will die as a hero, having deceived neither enemies nor friends.

Chapter 6 – *Apples of Immortality*

It would be a mistake to believe that north European pre-Christian cosmologies (or *Weltanschauungen* – ways of looking at the worlds) developed in complete isolation from the rest of the world, especially the rest of Europe. Just as Anglo-Saxon Vanir-orientated cosmology is closely linked to (but still significantly different from) its neighbouring Scandinavian Æsir-based world view, so links can be found between north and south (in this context largely Greek and Roman) European philosophical viewpoints, and indeed also connections going back even further to very early Middle Eastern pagan beliefs. Sometimes these connections involve positive similarities, but on other occasions those links can demonstrate opposed ways of thinking, for example in the case of the negation of Greek 'idealist' philosophies by Germanic 'materialist' thinking. This is reviewed in more detail in chapters 10 ("Inanna to Freya") and especially 11 ("Hecate").

Greek and Roman civilisations, and north European tribal cultures, all used storytelling for entertainment purposes, with their stories inevitably also reflecting questions of collective identity and history, as well as underlying belief systems and vital cosmological issues. One such key issue concerns perspectives on death, possible further life after death, and immortality. It is remarkable that versions of one such story came to be told thousands of years ago in both the Greek Mediterranean world and in northern Europe: the tale of legendary apples, the consumption of which could grant forms of immortality – a rather more positive valuation of this fruit than the Old Testament tale of Adam and Eve's apple taken from the Tree of Knowledge, the biting of which resulted in God denying mankind immortal life in the Garden of Eden, condemning them and all their subsequent descendants to experience death and possible damnation (although also with some possibility of eternal life and salvation for those who would submit to him).

According to the north European account, the gods of Asgard – Odin, Frigg, Thor, and Loki amongst others – were able to maintain their youth by eating golden apples, which were looked after by the goddess Idun (or Iduna). Should the supply of apples fail, the gods would grow old, lose their strength, and eventually die.

The Greek understanding of immortality was rather different. The gods were unchanging and immortal by their very nature. However Greek myths too told of the existence of mysterious apples, also golden, and also able to provide eternal life, not in this case to the already immortal gods, but to any hero brave and resourceful enough to find and eat them. In Greek myth these apples were said to grow in a distant garden, located at the extreme western (or possibly northern!) edge of the known Greek world, where they were looked after by nymphs known as the Hesperides.

The Hesperides were the nymphs of the sunset. It was usually thought that there were three Hesperides, although some sources name four or seven. The Garden of the Hesperides belonged to the goddess Hera. Not trusting the Hesperides to guard the apple trees on their own, Hera also placed there a hundred headed dragon, called Ladon, who never slept.

The Trojan War

One of these golden apples, taken from the Garden of the Hesperides, played a key role in what must surely be one of the best known stories of all time: that of the Trojan War. Eris, Greek goddess of strife, managed to steal an apple from the garden. She inscribed on it the words "For the fairest", and threw it amidst the goddesses attending a wedding she had not been invited to. Three goddesses, Aphrodite, Athena, and Hera, argued that the apple was theirs, as they were surely the most beautiful. They first asked Zeus, king off the Greek gods, to judge, but he wisely refused to get involved. Instead a simple mortal shepherd named Paris was instructed to choose. All three goddesses attempted to bribe him. Aphrodite won by promising to give him Helen, the most beautiful woman in the world, to be his wife. However Helen was already married to Menelaus, King of Sparta. Aphrodite then arranged for Paris the shepherd to be to be revealed as Alexander, a prince of Troy, and for Helen to be willingly abducted to Troy by Paris/Alexander, thus triggering the Trojan War.[209]

The Labours of Hercules

The Twelve Labours of Hercules (also referred to as Heracles) were tasks that this mythical hero was told to complete by King Eurystheus. The goddess Hera (owner of the Garden of the Hesperides and their golden apples of immortality) loathed Hercules - for he was a living example of her husband's infidelities. She drove the hero mad, making him kill his wife Megara and their children. When Hercules realised what he had done, he deeply regretted it, and went to the Oracle at Delphi to ask for penance. There, he was told to serve Eurystheus, king of Tiryns, for twelve years. If he completed all the tasks he would be given, he would become immortal. One of the final tasks was to steal golden apples from the Garden of the Hesperides.

Hercules first managed to capture the Old Man of the Sea, a shape-shifting sea deity, in order to discover the exact location of the garden. There are two versions of how Hercules then managed to acquire the apples. One version has it that he reached the Garden, where he killed Ladon, the dragon guardian, and took the apples.

According to another version, he came across Atlas, the Titan god who was condemned to hold the heavens on his shoulders. Atlas was also the father of the Hesperide nymphs, and thus had access to the garden at any time. Hercules persuaded Atlas to change places for a while, so that Atlas could fetch some of the apples. Atlas agreed and indeed took some of the apples. However, on his return, Atlas decided he did not want to take the heavens back on his shoulders. So Hercules tricked him. Hercules agreed to keep the heavens, but claimed he needed to adjust his cloak first. Atlas agreed to take the heavens back momentarily, but then Hercules walked away - taking the apples with him.[210]

Idun and the Apples of Immortality

Idun (old Norse, Iðunn which derived from ið 'again' and unna 'to love,') was the personification of spring, the goddess of youth, and like, Bragi, a skald. Few surviving texts refer to Idun, so her background is quite mysterious, but she does appear in several myths. The most notable explains why the gods never grow old, and how they almost lost that source of life and eternal youth, which is described in the skaldic poem Haustlöng and retold in the Prose Edda.[211]

Idun never left her enchanted garden where only she could pick the apples that held the secret of everlasting youth. However when the giant Thiazi captured Loki, in order to obtain his release Loki agreed to help the giant capture Idun by leading her away from her garden. Loki did this by telling Idun that he had come across a wonderful tree outside her home, suggesting that this tree bore fruit even more marvellous than the golden apples which Idun looked after, and asking her to accompany him to take a look at it. This she did, only to be kidnapped by Thiazi, who had been lying in wait for her.

Without the rejuvenating quality of the apples, the gods began to age and weaken. The ninth century poem Haustlöng tells how:

> *"He of Hymir's kin* [the giant Thiazi] *demanded*
> *that the rouser of tales* [Loki],
> *mad with pain* [inflicted by Thiazi],
> *bring him the maid*
> *who knew the Aesir's old-age cure* [Idun].
> *Brisingamen's thief* [Loki]
> *Got the gods' lady* [Idun].
> *to the rock-Nidud's* [giant's] *court,*
> *to Brunnakr's Bench.*
> *The bright-shield-dwellers* [giants] *were not sorry*
> *After this had taken place,*
> *Since from the south*
> *Idun was now among the giants.*
> *All Yngvi-Frey's kin,*
> *At the Thing* [Assembly], *were old and gray –*
> *ugly-looking in their form...* [212]

It is interesting that the poem refers to both the Æsir and Yngvi-Frey of the Vanir. It seems plain that both groups of gods were considered to be dependent upon Idun and her apples for their ability to remain young and strong beyond their years. Unfortunately we are told nothing of Idun's character by either Haustlöng or Snorri. Sheena McGrath says that

> *"Idunn is portrayed* [as] *a passive victim throughout, passed from gods to giants to gods... She has the traditional female role: victim and pretext... I think that the feminine aspects of this myth make people uncomfortable, and that's why Idunn's part in it tends to get glossed over... The myth does show the gods as vulnerable, perhaps more vulnerable than any time except Ragnarok, aging and facing their deaths. Also, it (possibly) shows one of the goddesses becoming the sexual partner of a giant – a possibility the Aesir refuse to contemplate. This could help to explain the reluctance of Scandinavian poets and writers to dwell on this myth."* [213]

Idun is often thought of as being one of the Æsir – she is after all married to the Ás Bragi, god of poetry and storytelling (itself a source of a different form of immortality) - and as a female of that divine patriarchal clan, is presented as lacking the dramatic feminine agency of the Vanir such as Freya. However there is one source which names her as an elf (see the section of this chapter "From Inanna to Idun" below), which would associate her with the Vanir (Frey being king of the light elves), and Simek says of her: *"If Idun was indeed venerated as a goddess in pagan times, she would belong to the fertility goddesses* [the Vanir] *because of her apples".*[214]

In any case, whether elf, Van or Ása, Idun is granted only a passive role in the surviving version of this story, and Loki, in assisting her kidnapping by the ancient forces of chaos, the giants, appears to have completed the disempowerment of the feminine amongst the Æsir. Prior to her kidnapping the gods of Asgard had disregarded Idun as an individual in her own right, but had valued her function as the supreme carer of their vitality, youth, and health. When the feminine principle of collective caring for others is permitted to be dismissed entirely, through the loss of the apples' protectress, the gods approach death. They cannot survive without the feminine, as represented by Idun.

Loki realises that he has to redeem himself, for before they perish of old age the gods will destroy him for what he has done, unless he can somehow recover the situation. To avoid catastrophe he must make good his error and reinstate the feminine power of caring for the wellbeing of others, symbolised by the need to get Idun back from the giants, so that she will be free once again to care for the apples of eternal youth. Therefore he appeals to a stronger feminine power which does have the agency, strength, and ability to save him: Freya of the Vanir. She agrees to lend him her magical cloak of feathers, enabling Loki to transform himself into a falcon to rescue Idun.

Loki then flew to Thiazi's stronghold and, finding Idun momentarily alone, turned her into a nut, clasped her in his falcon's beak, and fled back to Asgard. When shortly afterwards Thiazi returned to find Idun gone, he changed himself into an eagle and chased furiously after Loki. The gods though were ready for this and had built a pyre in Asgard. After a sudden stop by falcon Loki after gliding over the pyre, the gods lit their bonfire just as the closely pursuing Thiazi arrived, only to fly straight into the newly raging flames. Thiazi's eagle feathers caught fire. He fell, and the gods killed him. With Idun safely returned, the gods regained their youth and their strength.[215] Loki's role in this story, and what it tells us about his character, is analysed in more detail in chapter 12, which also contains a fuller version of the tale presented in the form of a storytelling. This chapter deals with Idun's role in the story as guardian goddess of the golden apples.

Apples and Fertility in Northern Myth

English scholar Hilda Ellis Davidson links apples to religious practices in Germanic paganism. She points out that buckets of apples were found in the 9th-century Oseberg ship burial site in Norway, and that fruit and nuts (Iðunn having been described as being transformed into a nut in Skáldskaparmál) have been found in the early graves of the Germanic peoples in England and elsewhere on the continent of Europe. This, she says, may well have had symbolic significance, with nuts still being a recognized symbol of fertility in Southwest England and elsewhere.

Davidson notes a wider connection between apples and the Vanir, as a group of gods primarily associated with fertility, citing the instance of the eleven "golden apples" being given to woo the beautiful Gerðr by Skírnir, who was acting as messenger for the Vanir god Freyr. She also notes a further connection between fertility and apples in Norse mythology. In chapter 2 of the Volsunga saga the goddess Frigg sends King Rerir an apple after he prays to Odin for a child. Frigg's messenger (in the guise of a crow) drops the apple in his lap as he sits atop a burial mound. Rerir's wife's consumption of the apple results in a six-year pregnancy and the caesarean section birth of their son - the hero Völsung.

Davidson also points out the "strange" phrase "apples of Hel" used in an 11th-century poem by the skald Þórbjörn Brúnason. She states this may imply that apples were thought of by the skald as the food of the dead.

From Inanna to Idun

German pagan folk band Faun's album *Eden* (2011) is themed around the concepts of immortality and paradise. The album's extensive supporting notes make wide-ranging reference to the goddess Iduna (Idun), and begin by quoting the poem *Hrafnagaldr Óðins*, ("Odin's raven-spell"), an Icelandic poem in the style of the Poetic Edda:

In the dales dwells
*the prescient * Dís [†]*
From Yggdrasil's [‡]
Ash sunk down,
Of Elven race [§]
Idun by name
The youngest of Ivaldi's [216]
elder children. [217]

The album notes continue:

> *"In many countries the apple was both the symbol of*
> *love and fertility, and the symbol of eternal life. For*
> *Babylonians it was Ishtar [Inanna] who was*
> *worshipped with the symbol of apples, for the*
> *Greeks it was Aphrodite, for the Romans it was*
> *Pomona, and for the Germanic peoples it was Iduna.*
> *Almost identical myths can be found in most*
> *different cultures, e.g. the Golden Apples of the*
> *Hesperides [in] Greek mythology."*

It is surely no coincidence that all the divinities quoted here for their association with apples as a symbol of fertility and eternal life – Inanna (Ishtar), Aphrodite, Pomona, Iduna, and of course Hera, are all goddesses; perhaps a gentle indication that true immortality is contained in birth/life/death cycles involving generations of children, rather than everlasting survival of the individual? The evolution of the understanding of key goddesses from the earliest Middle Eastern histories to later north European pantheons is considered further in chapter 10 ("Inanna to Freya").

The Faun *Eden* album notes to their song *Golden Apples* continue:

> *"The word Eden derives from the Sumerian Adana,*
> *which means 'garden' or 'green plain'. The story of*

---

* prescient = prophetic, seeing, revelatory, psychic; suggesting a priestess/ shamanic/seidr role for this elven goddess?

† Dís – female supernatural being, especially Vanir goddesses (Freya is Vanadís) [Andy Orchard, Dictionary of Norse Myth and Legend, London 1997]

‡ Yggdrasil – the ash tree of life, supporting the nine worlds

§ Not only is Idun "of Elven race", but Frey too is 'King of the Elves' (Light Elves), suggesting perhaps that all the Vanir are divine aspects of the light elves, i.e. are the goddesses and gods of the elves.

*the Garden of Eden is much older than the bible...
On Sumerian seals which date back to 3500 BCE one
can already find a story of a tree, a goddess, and a
snake who gives the fruit of life to a male visitor.
The attributes of a sinful temptress were not given
to the snake until much later, with Christianity. In
many other cultures the snake represents the force
of life which enables rebirth through the shedding of
one's skin. This power of life is bound [limited] by
transience and time, but is still immortal.
Incidentally only in Christian tradition are the ideas
of the Fall of Man, and the woman as sinner, to be
found...*

*"Joseph Campbell, one of the most famous
mythologists, traces this to the Hebrew entry into
Canaan, located in modern day Syria, and the
submission of the conquered nation. The
Canaanites' main divinity was a goddess who had
an alliance with a snake. She was rejected by the
Hebrews because they were committed to one male
god. This is why Campbell interprets the story of the
Garden of Eden as the historical rejection of a
mother goddess."*

The role of the snake as an early symbol of immortality is worth
noting although it is not one of those story elements which made it
across the alps from the Middle East by way of the Mediterranean
(except as a faint memory in the biblical Adam and Eve legend). The
Canaanites' goddess's "alliance with a snake" tells us something of
how they perceived immortality: the snake was seen as renewing itself
through the periodic shedding of its skin, from which, each time, a
new individual appeared to emerge. This is again surely evidence of an
understanding of immortality as a birth/life/death cycle involving
generations of children, rather than the Greek conception of individual
gods/souls living forever.

The north European sense of immortality – Idun's version of the
golden apples tale – is closer to the Canaanites' "alliance with a
snake", than it is to the Greek gods' vision of eternal life. Even the Æsir
are ultimately mortal, doomed to die as they are at Ragnarok, no
matter how many magical apples they eat, but they also have, like us,
some limited form of immortality through their children. This
immortality is collective, not individual. It is the ongoing

life/birth/death cycle of a tribe or people, not one single being – but it is real and material, not an imagined 'ideal'. The real golden apples of immortality, for both gods and mankind, are our children.

In this sense, the biting of the apple and Adam and Eve's resultant expulsion from the Garden of Eden can actually be seen as a good thing. This was realised in the early fifteenth century by the (presumably at least superficially Christian) anonymous English composer of the song *Adam Lay Ybounden*[**], which includes these verses:

> *"Adam lay ybounden*
> *Bounden in a bond*
> *Four thousand winter,*
> *Thought he not too long.*
> *And all was for an apple,*
> *An apple that he tok,*
> *As clerkes finden*
> *Wreten in here book.*
> *Never had the apple taken,*
> *The apple taken ben,*
> *Ne hadde never our lady,*
> *A ben Hevene Quen."*

For the creator of Adam Lay Ybounden, the central tenets of Christianity are subverted: it is no longer one male God of All that is celebrated, but instead "Our Lady the Queen of Heaven". It is as if suddenly, almost from nowhere, Inanna the ancient Sumerian goddess and Queen of Heaven is back, after "four thousand" years! This dating would clearly refer to a time well before Christianity, something which the 15th century composer of the song must have been fully aware of, apparently using this time frame to deliberately emphasise his/her message.

The male principle too is still celebrated, but now the emphasis is upon *mortal* man. Adam, instead of being condemned for accepting Eve's gift of the apple and the supposed 'curse' of mortality that comes with it, is now praised for doing so. He, and she, have done not wrong, but right. He has waited four thousand years, according to the song, to find again his Queen of Heaven, but the time has not been too long, for now She is back. And this has been made possible by his

---

[**] Adam Lay Ybounden – a 15th century song also included on Faun's *Eden* album.

acceptance of Eve's gift: the apple, the fruit of the tree of knowledge. If the apple had never been taken, 'Our Lady' could not have returned as 'Heaven's Queen'.

The composer of these lyrics, instead of mourning the loss of the Garden of Eden, the loss of paradise, seems to be celebrating an escape from spiritual thraldom. What a good thing that Adam took the apple, is what s/he is saying. Why?

- Because now we have knowledge of good and evil, we can do something about it, and progress, however imperfectly.
- Because now we have knowledge of our individual mortality, we can learn how best to live with that reality.
- Because as we now have knowledge of female and male, we can celebrate difference, gender and sex; we can acclaim not unity and monism, but differentiation and diversity, rejoicing in our ongoing survival not as individual beings, but through our and others' children, grandchildren, and succeeding generations.

For the composer of the lyrics to *Adam Lay Ybounden* it is almost as if the old pagan, north European understanding of mortality and immortality had never been interrupted by a thousand years of Christian dogma being preached from Rome and the Mediterranean, with its insistence on such concepts as individual eternal life in a heavenly paradise being everyone's desired objective. For the Church this could be achieved only through submission to the one God's gift of 'salvation' – granted to those individuals found to be judged and deserving to escape the default fate of 'sinners': everlasting pain in the flames of the Christian Hell.

For such a thing to be possible – to be able to look back over ten centuries to celebrate a very different way of seeing the worlds - someone, somewhere, through the ages, must have been telling stories.

Chapter 7 – *The Runes*

Mention twenty-first century Nordic (or "Northern Tradition") paganism to people and there is a good chance that – if it means anything to them at all – they will bring to mind modern day use of runes for divination or, in crude terms, "fortune telling". The runes however are about a lot more than just divination. In fact it is possible to look at runes as having meaning on at least nine levels (see *The Anglo-Saxon Rune Poem – Meanings* section of this chapter below). But first: what exactly are the runes?

The runes are an alphabet consisting of 24 (Elder Germanic), 33 (Anglo-Saxon) or 16 (Norwegian and Icelandic) angular letters, clearly intended to be carved on wood or stone, rather than being written long hand in ink on parchment or vellum. The Germanic and Scandinavian societies which used runes were originally pagan and almost wholly illiterate prior to the gradual introduction of Christianity. Consequently pre-Christian runic inscriptions tended to be brief, and were sometimes seen as magical.

Unlike modern alphabets each individual letter signified not just a sound (or several sounds), but a meaning (or several meanings). Combining modern letters together produces words, and therefore meanings. Combining runes does the same thing, but not just through words and their meanings. Runes can be placed next to each other (like letters) to produce words. But they can for example also be amalgamated, bound together, perhaps one on top of another, to produce magical 'bind-runes', aimed not just at communication, but at production of a practical impact, such as warding or healing.

Runes are also well known as being used in divination. For divination purposes a limited number of runes (often on individual pieces of wood or stone) are usually allowed to be combined in a random sequence (e.g. by being dropped gently on to a table, or taken blindly from a bag one at a time). The interaction of individual rune meanings may then be interpreted by a rune-reader, using personal inspiration and knowledge as much as traditional individual rune associations. See the *Magic and Divination* section of this chapter below for a discussion of pre-Christian Germanic and Anglo-Saxon divination practices.

The three runic alphabets (known as futharks after the first few runes 'f', 'u', 'th', 'a', 'r', and 'k') and their traditional associated meanings are shown in the "Rune Meanings" tables at the end of this chapter. These traditional meanings are largely derived from three centuries-old poems: the Anglo-Saxon, Icelandic and Norwegian rune poems. It is remarkable that the most popular runic alphabet today is the "Elder Germanic" twenty-four rune futhark, yet unlike the Anglo-Saxon and Norwegian rune sets, there is no "Elder Germanic" rune poem. Consequently most of the traditional meanings most commonly now associated with the Elder Germanic twenty-four rune futhark actually come from the Anglo-Saxon rune poem. This does make sense, for as can be seen in the tables, the Anglo-Saxon and Elder Germanic rune sets are quite similar, although the Anglo-Saxon set has more than twenty-four runes (shown here as thirty-three, although there was also some regional variation). There is also some commonality with the Icelandic/Norwegian rune set (also known as the "Younger" futhark) – although the Icelandic/Norwegian version has only sixteen runes.

It is believed that changes in the use and number of individual runes reflected changes in spoken language, so for example Anglo-Saxon Old English developed out of a Proto-Germanic language and, owing to increased complexity of language sounds, needed to develop more runes to facilitate the representation of those sounds more accurately in written form. In Iceland and Norway things went the other way. The variety of sounds being used in everyday spoken language declined over time, and so a number of runes fell out of use.

Where did the Runes come from?

Before letters and alphabets, including runic ones, there were visual representations, or art, which could sometimes be simplified into symbols. Jim Paul says:

> "Before the appearance of runes, the predominant symbols in northern Europe were Neolithic icons, appearing as rock carvings, representations of animals, objects, human beings, and gods... Some of the runes resemble these older symbols and seem to share their identities. In this way, the runes represent an intermediate step, standing between that [visual] Neolithic understanding and the new learning, which arrived in the form of Roman letters and Christian doctrine." [218]

There are various speculative theories about the precise origin of the individual shapes and symbols used in the Elder Germanic rune set, but it seems probable that there is no single source. Some of the runes appear similar to Latin letters in shape (e.g. the runes for the letters B, M, R, S, and T (again - see the tables at the end of this chapter), but others are quite different, leading some to see the old north Italian Etruscan alphabet as the most likely origin:

> "The runes may have come to the north... as remnants of the Etruscan alphabet, which was used in Etruria until the 2nd century B.C. when Rome conquered that sub-alpine land... brought to the north first, perhaps, by Etruscan traders." [219]

Magic and Divination

It is often assumed that pre-Christian Germanic, Scandinavian and English (Anglo-Saxon) tribes associated their runic alphabets with powerful magic, in particular divination. For example Jim Paul says:

> "Before England was England, the people who would bring English to that island lived in tribes in the vast original forest that covered the European continent. They worshipped the gods in the forms of nature. The runes were their mystical signs... letters with magical power, cast in lots for divination...Their original function was to link the natural and the supernatural, the earth and the gods. In the older Germanic societies, families and tribes cast runes often, divining these symbols to learn what Fate held in store." [220]

Others however have less faith in our ancestors' everyday reliance on magic, believing that what evidence is available of pre-Christian practices and beliefs does not support such a view. Bill Griffiths, of respected academic publisher Anglo-Saxon Books, says that:

> "There is no reason to doubt that the appeal of runes... was essentially practical... it cannot be satisfactory to put the magical associations first." [221]

Stephen Pollington (also published by Anglo-Saxon books) explained this more fully when he pointed out that:

> "Norse tradition ascribes the discovery (not invention) of the runes to Óðinn after a nine-day period of sacrifice on the World Tree. This episode has strong shamanic dimensions, and the runes gained are a useful tool, but

they are not in themselves magical in the way that, for example, Mjölnir is; the runes offer a route to wisdom, similar to the mind-altering mead. Nor is the image of the suffering god an imitation of Christ – Óðinn is a devious, wilful, deceitful god with a hidden personal agenda, whereas the conventional Christ figure is selfless." [222]

The source most often quoted in favour of the view that rune-casting was an established practice amongst pagan Germanic tribes is Roman historian Tacitus, whose book *Germania* was written around the year 98 CE. However as Tylluan Penry has pointed out, although Tacitus does mention divination practices, he does not specifically mention runes being used in this way.

"We have little information about whether the Anglo-Saxons used the runes for divination... It is tempting to hark back to Tacitus and his account of the Germanic tribes... yet nowhere in this passage is there any mention of runes:

'They cut off a branch of a nut-bearing tree, and slice it in to strips; these they mark with different signs and throw them completely at random on to a white cloth. Then the priest... or the father of the family... offers a prayer to the gods... and reads their meaning...'" [223]

What the "different signs" were that Tacitus saw being inscribed on to strips of wood we do not know. They might have been runes, but if so Tacitus does not mention that fact. However common sense suggests that this argument is rather academic and ultimately perhaps not very meaningful. Everybody agrees that runes did exist for some purpose or purposes, and were used. It may well be that their primary, everyday use was "essentially practical", i.e. they were used as letters to form words and brief phrases. This view sees runes being used as a script much like our own modern day alphabet, with the implication that, just like our modern day use of letters, their use was originally intended to be for relatively straightforward communication purposes, which were not perceived as also having additional divinatory or other magical functions.

Nevertheless even today language, even everyday, practical language, can make things happen 'as if by magic'. Using a lever to lift a heavy weight is a practical, physical effect. Using words to achieve the same effect – by persuading someone else to carry out that task – also sees that heavy weight lifted, but without the speaker (or writer) moving a muscle. Similarly, advertising goods often results in increased sales without any direct contact between seller and purchasers. Belief matters, and perceptions matter, because they can have practical, physical effects. Wearing a protective amulet, perhaps in the form of a bind rune, can increase the wearer's self-belief and public self-confidence. This can in turn have the real practical effect of making it less likely that criminals will see them as weak and easy prey, meaning that the amulet has worked and actually provided real physical (magical?) protection.

Language, words, and most especially writing, have never just been about the practical, physical, everyday world in its simplest forms. The whole point of writing something down is to engage in an (at least initially) non-physical, non-practical process, whether that be passively recording an event for some degree of posterity, or more actively seeking to communicate something designed to have an effect, perhaps indirectly by persuading others to think differently about something. Words, whether spoken or written, can reasonably be seen as magical – they make things happen, but indirectly, without any immediate, physical, cause and effect process (no physical lever shifting a heavy weight).

It is hardly surprising then that an inevitable thirst for knowledge, a need to know what might happen, can lead to people seeking to derive meaning from the apparent magic of written words, and even those individual signs, letters or runes that make up those written words. It does not really matter whether the Germanic tribes that Tacitus witnessed practicing divination were using the twenty-four "Elder Germanic" rune set, or some completely unknown set of signs. No doubt the use of particular individual runes and signs will have varied over time and geographic area anyway, as proved by the existence of the linked but separate Anglo-Saxon, Elder Germanic, and Icelandic/Norwegian rune sets. The important point is that whichever futhark is used, each rune might be interpreted not just through its phonetic value, but also through a range of associated meanings, which could in turn be seen as making divination and other more active forms of magic a practical possibility.

The Three Poems – *Why Poems*?

The additional meanings historically associated with individual runes have come down to us through the three rune poems: Anglo-Saxon, Icelandic and Norwegian. Each poem gives very brief information about each rune in its own futhark. Although these poems recorded accepted meanings as at the time when each poem was written down, it seems very likely that prior to this meanings may have changed over time. In particular some of the verses have clearly been modified to reflect conversion to Christianity. The Anglo-Saxon rune poem as it is known today is thought to date back to the eighth or ninth century, whilst the recorded versions of the Icelandic and Norwegian poems (relating to the "Younger" futhark) are thought to originate only from the thirteenth to fifteenth centuries.

> *"Each poem differs in poetic verse, but they contain numerous parallels between one another. Further, the poems provide references to figures from Norse paganism and Anglo-Saxon paganism, the latter included alongside Christian references."* [224]

But why compose the poems in the first place?

> *"The rune poems have been theorized as having been mnemonic devices that allowed the user to remember the order and names of each letter of the alphabet and may have been a catalogue of important cultural information, memorably arranged; comparable with the Old English sayings, Gnomic poetry, and Old Norse poetry of wisdom and learning."* [225]

The Icelandic and Norwegian Rune Poems

Both the Icelandic and Norwegian poems consist of sixteen stanzas or verses each, as both refer to the sixteen rune "younger futhark" (meaning the less ancient alphabet or set of runes). The Icelandic and Norwegian rune poems are almost identical with regard to the meanings of the runes, though the verses vary somewhat. Of the sixteen rune verses in each of the Icelandic and Norwegian poems, only two differ significantly in meaning (runes 2 and 4 are, respectively, "rain shower" and "a god" in Icelandic, but "metallic dross" and "estuary" in Norwegian). The remaining fourteen runes have the same meanings in both the Icelandic and Norwegian poems, though the descriptive verses differ. For example, rune 7 "Hail":

Icelandic

"Cold grain

And shower of sleet

And sickness of serpents." [226]

Norwegian

"Hail is the coldest of grain

Christ created the world of old." [227]

It is generally accepted that the Icelandic and Norwegian 'younger futhark' evolved out of the "Elder Germanic" rune set, changing and becoming simplified in line with changes in spoken language – as various sounds gradually ceased to be commonly used, so the need for 24 or more rune sounds was reduced to 16.

It is important to remember also that these poems have been translated, and that different translators rarely produce identical translations, especially of poetry. Differences in translation are not necessarily restricted to the choice of particular vocabulary either – sometimes the very meaning of the verse can appear to vary with the translation. Examples of how translations can differ, depending on the translators' interpretations, will be looked at in a discussion of the Anglo-Saxon rune poem below.

The Anglo-Saxon Rune Poem – *Original Sources and History*

The Old English (Anglo-Saxon) Rune Poem as recorded was likely composed in the 8th or 9th century and was preserved in a 10th-century manuscript housed at the Cotton library in London. In 1731, the manuscript was lost in a fire. However, the poem had been copied by George Hickes in 1705, and his copy has formed the basis of all later editions.

Hickes recorded the poem in prose, divided the prose into 29 stanzas, and placed a copper plate engraved with runic characters on the left-hand margin so that each rune stands immediately in front of the stanza where it belongs. Two more runes are given at the foot of the column: cweorð and an unnamed rune (calc) which are not in the poem itself. A second copper plate appears across the foot of the page and contains two more runes: stan and gar.[228] Cweorð, calc, stan and gar are shown in the table at the end of this chapter, making 33 Anglo-Saxon runes in total, but there are only rune poem verses with meanings for the first twenty-nine.

The Anglo-Saxon Rune Poem – *Translations*

An example has already been given, using the Icelandic and Norwegian rune poems, of different verses being used to describe the same rune. The Icelandic verse for the rune 'hail' makes no mention of Christianity, whilst the Norwegian verse for the same rune says *"Christ created the world of old"*. The Anglo-Saxon rune poem verse for the 'hail' rune, like the Icelandic, makes no mention of Christ or Christianity, but like the Icelandic verse is simply based on hail as a phenomenon of the weather. However, despite this, the Anglo-Saxon verse is different again from not only the Norwegian verse but also the Icelandic one:

Icelandic
"Cold grain
And shower of sleet
And sickness of serpents."

English
"Hail is the whitest of grain;
It is whirled from the vault of heaven
And is tossed about by gusts of wind
And then it melts into water." [229]

The variation in the interpretation of the nature of hail does not end here either, for all modern, readable versions of the poems must be in translation, from Old Norse or Old English. This leaves plenty of scope for translators to interpret the originals in what, at times, can appear to be quite different ways. Other translations of the English (Anglo-Saxon) verse for the hail rune include:

"Wind tossed, twisting
Out of heaven, the white grains
Of hail turn to water later."
[Jim Paul]

"Hail is the most brilliant of grains,
Spinning out of the airy heavens
Tossed upon the wind,
Thereafter turning to water."
[Tylluan Pendry]

"Hail is whitest of corn,
From heaven's height it whirls,
Winds blow it,
It becomes water after."
[Stephen Pollington]

In the case of hail the differences in interpretation are minor, but it is worth bearing in mind, when any one claims a particular meaning for a particular rune, that not only might there be up to three different original poetic verses (Icelandic, Norwegian, and English) attached to that rune, but there are always also issues of translation to be taken into account.

The Anglo-Saxon Rune Poem – *Meanings*

Meaning can be attributed to the runes and rune poems on at least nine different levels:
1. As a single-rune, stand-alone, sound and/or letter.
2. As a single-rune, sound or letter, forming part of a word, and part of a text.
3. As a single-rune, stand-alone, superficial meaning, as described in a rune poem verse.
4. As a single-rune, simple, stand-alone, magical quality.
5. As part of a multi-rune combination, involving more complex and changeable magical qualities, in interaction with a limited number of other runes.
6. As part of a multi-rune, divinatory system.
7. As part of a multi-rune, whole futhark (e.g. 24 rune Elder Germanic futhark) guide to northern cosmology.
8. As part of a multi-rune, whole futhark guide to personal spiritual development and esoteric meaning.
9. As part of a multi-rune, whole futhark guide to the roles of the gods and mankind's relationship with them.

In order to better understand what is meant by these nine different levels of meaning, it may help to work through a specific example. To keep it simple (at least to start with!) a sample analysis of the runic equivalent of a single rune may be useful, and such is presented here for the letter 'k' - for the first four levels of meaning as described above.

A different symbol is used to represent the 'k' sound in each of the three rune sets, but the sound is the same across all three.

[Elder Germanic]   [Anglo-Saxon]   [Younger Futhark}

Meaning - Level One

At the first level (as a single-rune, stand-alone, sound or letter) this is the rune for the modern English letter "k", making the sound "k" or "c" as in c_a_t = cat

Meaning - Level Two

At the second level (as a single-rune, sound or letter, forming part of a word, and part of a text), this single rune can, as with modern alphabet letters, when placed adjacent to other single runes/letters, signify a word with a meaning, so for example:

c a t = cat
and
< ᚠ ↑ = cat (Elder Germanic script)
Most archaeological rune finds are at this simple level. For example early English swords found in rivers might bear runes which when translated are found to mean things like "Harold made me".

Meaning - Level Three

At the third level (as a single-rune, stand-alone, superficial meaning, as described in a rune poem verse), this rune has a name. In the English rune poem the name for this rune is "Cen" or "Ken" ("Kenaz" in Proto-Germanic). Dictionary definitions of this now archaic English word "ken" are all to do with knowing and knowledge[*], e.g.

Noun
1. Knowledge, understanding, or cognizance; mental perception: an idea beyond one's ken.
2. Range of sight or vision.

Verb (used with object), kenned or kent, kenning
3. To know, have knowledge of or about, or be acquainted with (a person or thing), to understand or perceive (an idea or situation).
4. (Scots Law): to acknowledge as heir; recognize by a judicial act.
5. (Archaic): to see; descry; recognize.
6. (British Dialect Archaic): to declare, acknowledge, or

---

[*] Definitions are from www.dictionary.com

confess (something), to teach, direct, or guide (someone).
Verb (used without object), kenned or kent, kenning
  7. British Dialect: to have knowledge of something, to understand.

The Anglo-Saxon rune poem verse for this rune "Cen" says:
> "By its flame the living know the torch,
> Its brightness illuminating
> Life inside, where we rest."
> *[trans. Jim Paul]*

Jim Paul says of this verse:
> *"Images of light suggest metaphors, though this description of the torch seems naturalistic enough. The note of luxury here – of the nobles at their ease in torch light – recalls the small graces of that age, when work and sleep, day and vast night, were all that might be expected."* [231]

So, even at only the third level of simple, superficial meaning, possible differences of interpretation soon become apparent. Is "Cen" simply a flickering torch, as per Jim Paul, or is it "knowledge" and light in a much broader sense? Given the dictionary definitions of "ken", and the fact that in modern day languages such as German and Dutch "kennen" is still the basic word for "to know", it may be suggested that this rune was and is about, even at the superficial level, much more than just flickering torchlight.

Meaning - Level Four

At the fourth level (as a single-rune, simple, stand-alone, magical quality) this rune is certainly described by, for example, Freya Aswynn, as being about more than just knowing and knowledge. It is also:
> *"to be able to... kunst, which can be translated as 'art' or 'craft' and to which the English word 'cunning' corresponds. Kenaz indicates the ability to seek, gain, apply and recognise. It also indicates the learning and teaching process."* [232]

So this single rune, even on a stand-alone basis, without being combined in any way with other runes, can be interpreted as having multiple potential magical facets, many to do with seeking knowledge, and achieving and applying learning. However Aswynn then goes on:
> *"The primary aspect of Kenaz is the torch, that is, the torch of knowledge which is to be passed on to the next*

generation of kin or cyn *(both of these words are of Anglo-Saxon origin and related to Kenaz)... The Old English word Cyning is also related to Kenaz. Cyning meant king – the royal folk referred to in the Anglo-Saxon rune poem".* [233]

But who are these *"royal folk referred to in the Anglo-Saxon rune poem"*? Jim Paul's translation did not mention any "royal folk"!

"By its flame the living know the torch,
Its brightness illuminating
Life inside, where we rest."
[trans. Jim Paul]

However most translations of the same verse do mention them, e.g.

"The torch is known to every living man by its
pale, bright flame;
It always burns where princes sit within." [234]

Aswynn explains further:

"The king, according to esoteric tradition, had to be a descendent of Woden... Viewed in a more contemporary manner, the 'royalty' referred to in the rune poem may very well have a more spiritual meaning, referring to the initiates who are the descendants of Woden and who carry aloft the torch of enlightenment by virtue of their esoteric knowledge. Kenaz represents the light within..." [235]

And in terms of this rune's magical uses and associations, she continues:

"The magical uses of this rune are quite varied. The most obvious use is the gaining of knowledge, by which is meant occult knowledge. In divination, Kenaz can be used to investigate the deeper background of problems encountered in a reading... Kenaz can function... as a guiding torch when one wishes to explore the unknown territories of the inner realms. It can be used as a weapon to expel any unwanted influences, just as light expels darkness... another aspect of Kenaz is the exposure of hidden, unknown, or unacknowledged aspects of the self, or of one's own or someone else's hidden motives... The Kenaz rune can be used as an astral doorway – as a symbol which can be projected through 'the veil'... it will guide us safely back, for travelling into the underworld can be dangerous..." [236]

Clearly there are those, such as Freya Aswynn, who see much more in the Ken or Kenaz rune than Jim Paul's simple explanation that its meaning is all to do with welcome torchlight at the end of a busy day for those who were well off enough to be able to enjoy such luxury. Of course Freya Aswynn could also no doubt be challenged on the grounds that there is no direct evidence in the rune poem verse of any Anglo-Saxon interest in, for example, astral doorways. But the whole point here is that the attachment of different levels of meaning to the runes, going well beyond the simply phonetic, clearly invites further creative exploration by individuals, using the runes as a common starting point, but also being prepared to go beyond that and use them as tools to delve into deeper mysteries. This is surely part of the joy and purpose of poetry after all: every reader of a poem may interpret it differently, but in ways that are correct and useful for them as individuals, building on the common base of words accessible to all. Poetry reading, and rune reading, becomes a two-way process – even without the further complications deriving from translation issues.

Meaning - Level Five

For meanings at level five and beyond it is necessary to look not just at a single rune, but at combinations of multiple runes, or whole futharks.

At the fifth level (as part of a multi-rune combination, involving more complex and changeable magical qualities), the magical impact of this and of any rune will depend upon how and with which other rune/s it is combined. Consequently, as the potential effects are virtually unlimited, it is really only possible to give an example of how this works. Most commonly, runes are combined together for magical workings in the form of "bind runes", often shown as two, three or more runes superimposed on top of each other, in order to produce a certain effect. The example shown in the picture uses the Elder Germanic rune forms.

In this simple bind rune only two runes are used.

- Χ is the rune Gebo or Gifu (the letter G) meaning a gift, and
- ᚨ is Ansuz or Os (the letter A) meaning a god, muse, or mouth (inspired speech).

When combined together the Anglo-Saxons took this sign to mean "Good Luck", or literally "I give luck", as in:

A "Good Luck" Bindrune [Image: Lynne Harling]

- "I give" (= X the Gifu rune, standing for the letter G, and the first letter of the word *Gibu* meaning "give")
- "Luck" (= ᚨ the Ansuz rune, standing for the letter A, and the first letter of the word *Auja* meaning "luck").

An illustration of this "Good Luck" bind rune, carved into tree bark, with the Ansuz rune [ᚨ] overlaying the Gebo rune [X], is shown above.

As Bernard King explains:

"Another example, illustrating both initials standing for words, and the use of a bind rune, is the combination of the two words Gibu *and* Auja... *Together the two mean "[I] give [good] luck", and the initials bound into one symbol have been found on various objects in this form, as well as written out in full."* [238]

Meaning - Level Six

At the sixth level (as part of a multi-rune, divinatory system), runes may be used as a tool to increase awareness and assist understanding for oneself and others. Usually this would involve making use of a multi-rune combination, most often using between three and nine runes selected at random, and set out in a particular order. 'Reading the runes' for divination purposes then involves a rune-reader interpreting the runes in a process not unlike a Tarot card reading. The Rune reader will refer to

- the meanings of the individual runes appearing in the reading, based on the traditional rune poem verses, interpretations by others (e.g. published authors), context (e.g. specific relationship to a specific question being asked), and personal experience and past use of the runes.
- The order in which the randomly selected runes appear, and the sequencing relationship between them.
- Her or his understanding of the question being asked, and knowledge of the person asking the question.
- Most importantly – the rune reader's personal intuition and individual interpretation regarding the message/s the runes are giving.

A sample rune reading – using just three runes (for simplicity) – might look something like this:-

Three runes, selected at random by the questioner, are turned face up:

< ᚠ ↑

At the first level these runes spell: c a t

Which at the second level gives us "cat" !

Whatever the question was – perhaps the answer is a cat.

Perhaps the question was: who ate the mouse?

However, unless the question being asked really was "Who ate the mouse?", in order to truly divine the meaning of this rune sequence, a rune reader is more likely to refer to the third, fourth and fifth level meanings, i.e.

- Level 3 - the 'simple' meaning of each *individual* rune - as given for example in the rune poems
- Level 4 – the more esoteric, magical meaning of each *individual* rune, obtained both from referencing published works (e.g. Freya Aswynn's *Leaves of Yggdrasil*), and the use of personal knowledge, experience, and intuition
- Level 5 – a personal interpretation of the relationship and interaction between the three runes.

So: [level 3]

< = Cen or Kenaz = light, knowledge, torch

ᚠ = Ass or Ansuz = a god/dess, mouth, inspired speech

↑ = Tyr or Teiwaz = courage, battle.

In a three-rune reading it might be helpful to see the position of three runes as working rather like the Norns (weavers of fate) – past (Urd), present (Verdandi), and what still might be done (Skuld). Note: in north European cosmology Skuld is not "the future" or "fate" but that which still might or should be done, or "the debt that must be paid" – the future remains always ultimately undetermined as it is subject to the constant changing patterns of interaction between all things in the Wyrd. For discussion on the nature of the pagan Germanic concept of the Wyrd see, for example, the works of Brian Bates.[239]

Referring to the English rune poem, the rune reader might say:

Your first rune is Cen (Kenaz), which tells us about the basis of things as they already stand. It says:

[rune 6]

"The torch is known to every living man by its pale, bright flame;
it always burns where princes sit within.

Your second rune is Ass (Ansuz), which tells us about what is happening now. It says:

[rune 4]

"The mouth is the source of all language,
a pillar of wisdom and a comfort to wise men,
a blessing and a joy to every knight."

Your third rune is Tiw (Tyr), which tells us about what might still or must be done. It says:

[rune 17]

"Tiw is a guiding star; well does it keep faith with princes;

it is ever on its course over the mists of night and never fails."

It is then up to the rune reader to develop the level 3 meanings as given by the rune poem into level 4 and 5 meanings which might actually answer whatever question has been asked. The result might be something like this:

"The runes are telling us that you already have the knowledge you need to solve this issue. You have already undertaken valuable learning in the past, and this knowledge has already been burning brightly within you for some time now... *[the Cen rune]*

"What is happening now is that you have reached a critical point when the passive knowledge and learning you already have needs to be used actively – spoken out loud! The time has now come when you should no longer be keeping your knowledge and learning to yourself, but sharing it, opening your mouth and imparting the wisdom of your experiences to others... *[Ass]*

"In order to achieve this, what you should consider doing next, is to gather up your courage and freely enter into the battle ahead. When you openly and actively try to pass on your wisdom and knowledge to others, this will generate opposition in some quarters, and you must be prepared to fight to get your points across. It is right that you should do this, and Tyr the god of justice will stand by you and support you in your battle, meaning that, as long as you gather up your courage, your fight is most likely to be successful. In any case, right is on your side." *[Tyr]*

Or... you could just say that the answer is c a t = cat ☺

Meaning - Level Seven

At the seventh level a full set of runes, or an entire runic alphabet, or futhark (e.g. the 24 rune Elder Germanic futhark) can be used as a guide to north European pre-Christian cosmology (by which is meant a *"philosophy dealing with the origin and general structure of the universe, with its parts, elements, and laws, and especially with such of its characteristics as space, time, causality, and freedom"*).[240] For the runes to be used in this way, they must be studied as a full set, with the emphasis being on learning from the relationship of each rune to its predecessor and successor – the runes which come before and after each individual rune. In this way the runes can be seen as telling a story which develops from rune to rune.

In order to help make sense of the story being told, the 24 rune Elder Germanic futhark can be conveniently divided into three sets of eight runes each, with each set being known as an "aett" (plural "aettir"). Commentators such as Freya Aswynn have linked the aettir to northern mythological cosmology as set out in particular in the *Völuspá* (The Völva or Seeress's Prophecy).

The first aett is said to describe the plane of creation. The first rune
> *"Fehu represents the primordial fire of Muspelheim, and Uruz* [the second rune] *represents the eternal ice of Nifelheim... the conflict between fire and frost originated all that exists. The two opposing forces met in the Ginnungagap, the abyss* [the void]. *The first being to be created was a cosmic cow, Audhumla, which is the first feminine creative principle in Nature and therefore the first incarnation of the Mother Goddess... From the same matter the giant Ymir was subsequently formed... evoked by the* [third] *Thurisaz rune (Thurs means "giant")..."* [241]

The second aett is described by Aswynn as continuing the history of the nine worlds, relating each of the second set of eight runes to such major events as the triple burning of the witch Gullveig, the 'first war' between the Aesir and the Vanir gods, the creation of time and the Norns, culminating in the last of the runes in this aett, Sowulu or Sol, the sun — *"which symbolises the return of consciousness in evolution"*. [242]

The third aett, says Aswynn, *"gives an overview of the human condition...*[examining] *the changes and development of human evolution under the guidance of the gods through Ragnarok and beyond"*. [243]

There is more extensive discussion of north European pre-Christian cosmology in chapter 11 of this book on Hecate, though not based on analysis of the runes, but on a comparison of Germanic 'materialist' and Greek neo-Platonic 'idealist' philosophies. Analysing all twenty-four runes in the Elder Germanic futhark in sufficient detail to be able to tell the full story of Germanic cosmology as expressed in the runes would take up more space than can be made available in this publication without omitting discussion of other important aspects of Anglo-Saxon paganism, but a good starting point for anyone wishing to undertake that task would be Aswynn's *Leaves of Yggdrasil* book (see this book's bibliography).

Meaning - Level Eight

At the eighth level, a full set of runes, or futhark, can again be used as a guide, this time to personal spiritual development and esoteric meaning rather than northern cosmology. Once again, the emphasis is on learning from the relationship of each rune to its predecessor and successor – the runes which come before and after each individual rune – and from studying the aettir (three sets of eight runes).

Again the starting point can be the rune poems. Whilst that starting point might be the same for everyone, and the major facets and basic meanings of each rune, and each step along the journey, will therefore appear superficially similar, in reality the details of every individual's journey will necessarily be different, and will require careful, multi-level storytelling and interpretation.

In terms of personal rather than cosmological development, the first three runes for example, Fehu (ᚠ), Uruz (ᚢ), and Thurisaz (ᚦ), would most likely still be interpreted as demonstrating the same fundamental qualities as in cosmological analysis. Fehu and Uruz would still represent the conflicting forces of fire and ice, energy and stasis, but now as encountered within a single person. If the internal contradictions within that person can be productively resolved, by allowing them to come into creative conflict with each other, then a first, very basic step can be taken on the long road towards the development of higher consciousness and self-awareness - though at this early stage still in a primitive, perhaps relatively dull and clumsy, and even painful 'giant' Thurisaz form.

More specifically this might be expressed along the lines of:
- The first rune, Fehu, tells us that our most fundamental (and feminine, no matter whether we are female or male) felt need is survival, and that this requires material security – in part expressed through wealth. As the Anglo-Saxon rune poem[244] says:
    "Wealth is a comfort to all men;
    yet must every man bestow it freely,
    if he wish to gain honour in the sight of the Lord."
- The second rune, Uruz, recognises that our will to survive, which drives us to seek material security, will develop a concomitant basic need in each of us to

establish our own (male, again irrespective of our actual sex) strength and ability to defend ourselves and protect our self-interest. The poem expresses this as:

> "The aurochs is proud and has great horns;
> it is a very savage beast and fights with its horns;
> a great ranger of the moors,
> it is a creature of mettle."

The first two runes, though both are necessarily part of each of us, are also in conflict with each other within us.

- Fehu, the need to generate material security, including new wealth, is female, active, energetic, requires action, and needs an environment in which change and development are possible. Yet too much energy, like fire, risks burning up those resources, and even self-destruction.
- Uruz on the other hand is passive, strong but stolid, inflexible, male, defensive, static, all about avoiding sudden change, and like ice, liable to shatter if hit too hard or subjected to too sudden or great a shock.

In each of us the need to actively achieve greater material security in order to survive, conflicts with our need to remain passive and defensive in order to maintain our strength, again in order to survive.

A resolution (or at least an initial, partial resolution, subject always to an ongoing need to continue exploring further development through the rest of the futhark) can be achieved in the third rune, Thurisaz. The details of how resolution is achieved will be different in every case, but the rune poems tell us that pain will be unavoidable. Any attempt to ignore the necessary inner conflict and so avoid pain will prevent personal progress, and will not work. The Anglo-Saxon rune poem says:

> "The thorn is exceedingly sharp,
> an evil thing for any knight to touch,
> uncommonly severe on all who sit among them."

This example has been limited to a short analysis of the first three runes in the futhark, but the relationship pattern shown here can also be used in further personal development orientated studies of subsequent runes. In this model progression is fundamentally triplicate and dialectical, i.e. each rune is analysed not alone but as one of a set of three, with the first two evidencing needs which appear to contradict each other, with that contradiction only being resolvable through progression to a higher stage indicated by the third rune (thesis, antithesis, and synthesis). It should be noted that the resolution and synthesis found in the third rune can never be perfect or absolute (absolute perfection does not exist except as a negative, nothingness, the void or Ginnungagap between fire and ice); the personal development story continues as long as life itself.

Meaning - Level Nine

At the ninth level too, a full set of runes, or futhark, can be used as a guide, this time to explore the domains of the gods. This essentially means moving beyond personal self-development and self-regard (necessary as that is), to the allocation of priority to others, both as individuals and in the form of collective social entities (e.g. family, friendship circles, and tribe), expressed through study of higher beings, their roles, their stories, and their realms.

As with levels seven (cosmology) and eight (personal development) the study of level nine meanings can be aided by looking at the twenty-four rune Elder Germanic futhark in terms of its aettir (sets of eight runes). The first aett can be referred to as Freya's aett (Nacht Engel [245]), and is said to be concerned with the cycle of life [246] or the plane of creation [247]. The second (Heimdal's aett) is about the forces of nature and the history of the worlds, and is associated with the Norns, Gullveig, and Scyld Scefing (Heimdal). The third aett is Tyr's aett and can be used to illustrate human spirituality and learning from the gods.

As with levels seven and eight there is not space here in a single chapter to describe in detail all twenty-four runes in terms of their deity aspects, but a very brief description of the first three runes in each aett in terms of the roles of the gods, and the relationship between them, may be used as a starting point for further study. The first rune in Freya's aett is Fehu (fee) - ᚠ. This is one of Freya's runes, for it refers to primal, creative, fiery, female energy. The second rune is Uruz (Aurochs) – ᚢ, and is associated with both Thor and Urd. This is a rune of solid ice, unconscious male strength and stolid power (Thor) and origins (Urd). The third rune of this aett is Thurisaz (Thorn) - ᚦ, which is a rune again associated with Thor, but now this is Thor after he has come into contact with Freya, and consequently developed a little beyond his original self: ice has been superseded by wild fire; his power is still subconscious, but is no longer only static, but chaotic and uncontrolled, expanding into forms such as sexual libido. This is the beginning of, or at least a precursor to, character development. The gods are not always the same. They change and develop, responding to contact with others, just as we need to.

The first rune in Heimdal's aett is Hagalaz (Hail) – ᚺ which, as the first rune in this aett, is again associated with the Norn Urd, but also with the elemental powers of the Vanir witch Gullveig and the goddess Hel. All three are female, and at this stage of development very much to do with feminine, unconscious, dark power, including dark witchcraft, and destructive force as a catalyst for change. The second rune in this aett is Nauthiz (Need) – ᚾ . This rune is closely linked to Skuld, the Norn who expresses what is as yet undone and still needs to be done ('the debt that must be paid'), as well as to Gullveig (again), and to Loki and his 'need-fire'.[†] The third rune is Isa (Ice) - | , linked to the Norn Verdandi, Gullveig (for the third and final time), and the goddess Rind – she who was raped by the god Odin who disguised himself in women's clothing in order to gain private access to her. *"This disguise… enables him to rape Rind, deceived and threatened with madness and illness by Odin… disguised as a healing woman called Vecha".*[248] Unsurprisingly then this rune too is associated with the Dark Goddess, and more specifically a need for material protection, spirit crushed and crystallised into matter, and resultant self-centred materialism.

The first three runes of Heimdal's aett are all linked to the triplicate, fundamental and as yet unmet needs of Gullveig, which are to do with change, the overcoming of stasis. Gullveig's first encounter is with Urd, the Norn of the unalterable past – any attempt to interact with Urd to produce transformation generates only negative, destructive impacts. Next Gullveig encounters Skuld, but this meeting too is negative, for although Skuld can help Gullveig identify what needs to be done, those actions as yet remain uncompleted, and therefore ineffective. Gullveig's third ill-met companion is Rind, who has had transformation forced upon her, having been raped by Odin, and who has understandably reacted by defensively retreating into

---

[†] *"Need-fire, or Wild-fire (German: Notfeuer), is a term used in folklore to denote… kindling the sacrificial fire; the need- or wild-fire is made by the friction of one piece of wood on another, or of a rope upon a stake. Need-fire is a practice of shepherd peoples to ward off disease from their herds and flocks. It is kindled on occasions of special distress, particularly at the outbreak of a murrain, and the cattle are driven through it."*
[https://en.wikipedia.org/wiki/Need-fire]

herself. Verdandi, the Norn of the present, is with Rind, but Rind remains, at this stage, frozen in the present. Unable to look forwards, she remains disempowered and incapable of initiating positive, outgoing interaction with others.

Looking at just the first three runes of Heimdal's aett can seem unremittingly negative, so it is worth mentioning that more positive encounters occur in the remainder of the aett. There is insufficient space here to go into detail, but subsequent meetings are largely with the Vanir gods of positive, fertile, growth and transformation: Freya, Frey, Ull, Heimdal (Shef), Njörd and Nerthus, as well as the Áas god Woden (not the same as Odin). These encounters show that positive change is possible but that it is best facilitated by interaction with other beings, the lack of which (being concerned only with the self and looking inwards, valuable as that can be at level eight) results in inescapable and ultimately self-destructive inertia.

Tyr's aett begins – of course – with the rune Tyr (Tyr the god of Justice) ↑ . There are no other deities associated with this rune. Tyr is a character renowned for his sense of justice, interest in law and order, fairness, oaths, and contracts, and is associated with male fertility. He is also a god of battle and war but, unlike Odin, fights not for love of violent combat and death, but for a good cause. The second rune in this aett is Berkana ᛒ (birch), which is linked to three female deities: Berchta (Alpine goddess of spinning and weaving), Frigg (wife of Odin), and Holda (Frau Holle – Old Mother Frost). This is a very feminine rune, being associated with gestation, birth, motherhood, children (especially the protection and nurturing of abandoned children), and creativity. The aett's third rune is Ehwaz ᛗ (horse). This is a very special rune, for horse deities and man-horse deities play a special role in early Anglo-Saxon lore (see the *The Abstract Art of Shamanism* section of chapter 13). Freya and Frey both have links to the Ehwaz rune, as do the legendary Anglo-Saxon figures Hengest (stallion) and Horsa (horse or mare).[‡] Its associations include co-operation, partnership, and marriage: it is the synthesis of the male Tyr and female Berkana runes.

After Freya's aett has shown us that, like us, the gods are constantly changing and developing individual characters (not archetypes), and Heimdal's aett has stressed that successful character development depends on looking outwards and interaction with other

---

[‡] For discussion of Hengest and Horsa see chapter 12.

beings, Tyr's aett illuminates the fact that the development and growth needs of all living creatures require us to relate to each other in multiple ways, including relationships between the sexes, between mankind and the gods, and between mankind and animals (horses and other animals also have sacred roles to play). The realms of the gods are complex, diverse, imperfect, and ever evolving, and their changing nature is as subject to the interaction of all the elements of the Wyrd as are we in Middle Earth.

Conclusion

The rune poems tell us that the early English saw the runes as much more than simple alphabet letters. The existence of explanatory verses for each rune makes it clear that letters, words, written and encoded speech, and communication in general, were all seen as having mystical and magical qualities which can serve as guides to learning which go far beyond the superficial meanings of words. The poems indicate that runes can be used as tools to access knowledge systems ranging from the mundane to the magical, from divinatory skills to cosmological concerns, and from matters of personal spirituality to the realms of the gods.

This chapter can serve only as a very brief introduction to the full potentialities of the runes and the rewards available from their study. It is recommended that anyone interested in following up with further work on this subject should both refer to the works of authors such as Freya Aswynn (see the bibliography), and engage directly with working with runes themselves.

The Elder Germanic Futhark

	Elder Germanic			
	Sound	Rune	Name	Meaning *(P. Jennings)* [1]
1	**f**	ᚠ	Fehu	Cattle, wealth
2	**u**	ᚢ	Uruz	Aurochs, Strength
3	**th**	ᚦ	Thurisaz	Giant, obstacle, attack
4	**a**	ᚨ	Ansuz	God, mouth
5	**r**	ᚱ	Raido	Wagon, travel
6	**k**	ᚲ	Kenaz	Torch, light, knowledge
7	g	ᚷ	Gebo	Gift, sex
8	w/v	ᚹ	Wunjo	Joy, good news
9	h	ᚺ	Hagalaz	Hail, bad weather, air
10	n	ᚾ	Nauthiz	Need, distress
11	i	ᛁ	Isa	Ice, stasis
12	j	ᛃ	Jera	Year, harvest, fruitful
13	y	ᛇ	Eiwaz	Yew, bow, earth
14	p	ᛈ	Pertho	Birth, dice cup
15	z	ᛉ	Algiz	Protection, elk
16	s	ᛊ	Sowulo	Sun, heat
17	t	ᛏ	Teiwaz	Tyr, courage, battle
18	b	ᛒ	Berkana	Birch, healing, woman
19	e	ᛖ	Ehwaz	Horses, adventure
20	m	ᛗ	Mannuz	Man, mankind
21	l	ᛚ	Laguz	Water, leek
22	ng	ᛜ	Inguz	Ing (the god)
23	o	ᛟ	Othila	Home, land, tribe
24	d	ᛞ	Dagaz	Day, balance

[1] Pete Jennings, The Norse Tradition, Abbingdon 1998, p.34

The Runes

The Younger (Icelandic/Norwegian) Futhark

	Younger (Icelandic/Norwegian)			
	Sound	Rune	Name	Meaning *(Icelandic)* [2]
1	**f**	ᚠ	Fe	Wealth
2	**u**	ᚢ	UruR	Rain Shower
3	**th**	ᚦ	Thurs	Giant
4	**a**	ᚬ	Ass	God
5	**r**	ᚱ	Reidh	Riding
6	**k**	ᚴ	Kaun	Ulcer
7	h	ᚼ	Hagall	Hail, sleet
8	n	ᚾ	Nuadh(r)	Constraint, difficulty
9	i	ᛁ	Is	Ice
10	j	ᛅ	Ar	Year, harvest, fruitful
11	s	ᛋ	Sol	Sun
12	t	ᛏ	Tyr	Tyr
13	b	ᛒ	Bjarkan	Birch
14	m	ᛘ	Madr	Man
15	l	ᛚ	Logr	Water, lake, sea
16	y	ᛦ	Yr	Yew, bow

[2] https://en.wikipedia.org/wiki/Rune_Poems

The Anglo-Saxon Futhark

	Anglo-Saxon			
	Sound	Rune	Name	Meaning *(J. Paul)* [3]
1	**f**	Ⱶ	Feoh	Wealth, Money
2	**u**	ᚢ	Ur	Aurochs, Strength
3	**th**	ᚦ	Thorn	Thorn, pain
4	**a**	ᚩ	Os	Mouth, the muse
5	**r**	ᚱ	Rad	Riding
6	**k**	ᚳ	Cen	Torch, light
7	g	ᚷ	Gifu	Gift, exchange
8	w/v	ᚹ	Wynn	Joy
9	h	ᚻ	Haegl	Hail
10	n	ᚾ	Nyd	Need
11	i	ᛁ	Is	Ice
12	j	ᛄ	Ger	Year
13	y	ᛇ	Eoh	Yew
14	p	ᛈ	Peorth	Dice cup, merriment
15	z	ᛉ	Eolhx	Elksedge, blade
16	s	ᛋ	Sigil	Sun, sail, amulet
17	t	ᛏ	Tir	Tyr, courage, battle
18	b	ᛒ	Beorc	Birch, healing, woman
19	e	ᛖ	Eh	Horses, adventure
20	m	ᛗ	Man	Man, mankind
21	l	ᛚ	Lagu	Water, leek
22	ng	ᛝ	Ing	Ing (the god)
23	oe	ᛟ	Ethel	Home, land, tribe
24	d	ᛞ	Daeg	Day
25	a	ᚪ	Ac	Oak
26	ae	ᚫ	Aesc	Ash Tree
27	y	ᚣ	Yr	Yew, bow
28	ea	ᛠ	Ear	Earth, the grave
29	k	ᛡ	Ior	World Serpent
30	cw	ᛢ	Cweordh	Flames
31	c	ᛣ	Calc	Offering cup
32	st	ᛥ	Stan	Stone, obstacle
33	g	ᚸ	Gar	Spear, Gungnir

[3] Jim Paul, The Rune Poem, San Francisco 1996 (runes 1-28).
The poem does not cover runes 29-33. Meanings 29-33:
http://www.therunesite.com/keyword/gar/ [Northumbrian]

Chapter 8 –
Trees in Anglo-Saxon England

Trees were clearly one of the most noticeable and significant aspects of the landscape and environment in pre-Christian England. Pagan English tribes only arrived in Britain after about 450 CE, but the lands from which they had come in northern Europe (modern day Denmark, Holland, north-west Germany and, before that, southern Sweden) were also extensively forested. When the Angles, Saxons, Jutes and associated tribes settled in the east and south of Britain from the fifth century, they brought with them a pre-formed world view which understood trees as being absolutely central and key to life, and indeed all existence. Trees were a vital part of early English cosmology and belief systems.

For the English (as also for many other early pagan peoples) trees were symbols of life itself, and more than this, were even felt to actually embody fundamental existential energies and life forces:

> *"Life, death and rebirth – these are all aspects of the symbolism linked to the tree... their roots and branches evoked an image of a link between sky and Underworld; their longevity represented continuity and wisdom; the seasonal behaviour of the deciduous trees gave rise to a cyclical symbolism, an allegory of life, death and rebirth... Early European traditions envisaged a World , called in Norse mythology 'the ash tree Yggdrasil'... The World Tree linked the underworld to the heavens, the gods to mankind,* [and] *the dead to the living – it was the backbone of all the worlds..."* [249]

Tree Spirits

Yggdrasil is discussed further in the section *Yggdrasil – The Tree of the Worlds* below, but before reviewing the role of this most sacred of all trees it is worth considering the perception of trees by pre-Christian pagans more generally. Firstly it is significant that trees, or at least some individual trees, were believed to possess spirits, rather like animals and human beings. This belief was widespread, and far from restricted to northern Europe. In many cultures tree spirits were said to be young female entities, often connected to ancient fertility and tree worship lore. The status of these tree deities varied quite widely - from that of a local fairy/ghost/sprite or nymph, to that of a goddess.[250] The best known are probably the dryads of ancient Greek legend. *Drys* signifies "oak" in Greek, and dryads were originally the nymphs of oak trees, but the term later came to be used for all tree nymphs. They were normally considered to be very shy creatures – except around Artemis, the Greek goddess of the hunt, forests, the moon, and archery, who was known to be a friend to most nymphs.[251]

There are two main types of tree spirit in Greek mythology: dryads and hamadryads. Dryads were often depicted in myth and art accompanied - or being pursued by – their male counterparts, the satyrs.[252] Male satyrs could pursue dryads because dryads are not bound to their tree – they live near a particular tree, but not within it. Hamadryads on the other hand live within, and as part of, the tree itself.[253] Some viewed tree spirits as minor but still immortal deities, but others believed that dryads, and in particular hamadryads, were mortal, and that their lives were tied to the trees they protected. When a tree reached the end of its life, its dryad or hamadryad died as well.

Stories of tree spirits in north European and other mythologies are less well historically attested to. The Oak and Holly Kings written about by Robert Graves in his book *The White Goddess* for example, and claimed by Graves to be an ancient Celtic concept, are accepted by many commentators today as having been more a reflection of Graves' wishful thinking than genuinely ancient.[254] However one north European example of a tree deity which is historically better attested to is Hyldemoer:

> *"In Denmark, the Hyldemoer ("Elder-mother") or Hyldequinde ("Elder-woman") is a spirit like a wood-nymph or dryad that lives in the elder tree. The spirit is said to haunt or torment people who build from elder wood unless they ask permission first."* [255]

In particular, Scandinavian folklore reveals that Hyldemoer especially dislikes her trees being chopped down to make cradles or cribs. It is said that if you put a baby to sleep in an elder wood cradle, Hyldemoer will come along and pull at the innocent babe's legs until it shrieks![256] This seems to reflect the north European perceived requirement to respect and conciliate the natural environment. Treat the great goddess Mother Nature fairly, and she will be generous.

"We need the gifts of the Vanir [land fertility goddesses and gods] every day in order to survive... the doctrine of exchange teaches that we must balance what we take from the earth with what we give in return." [257]

This 'doctrine of exchange' is fundamental to the pagan world view, not only in terms of trees and Mother Earth, but also in terms of humanity's relationships with the gods themselves:

"There had to be reciprocity: the gods and ancestors must be given their dues in order to maintain friendship. A kinsman who only takes and never gives in return is not a worthy individual. The monotheistic idea of the essential worthlessness of man, needing salvation from the creator in order to justify an intrinsically valueless life, has no place in this scheme." [258]

Breathing Trees

Unlike Graves' Oak and Holly Kings, the 'doctrine of exchange', as for pagans applicable to our relationship with the earth, and with trees, is not just down to wishful thinking. Whether trees have spirits or not, they certainly breathe, and without them we would be very short of breath. As BBC science correspondent Luis Villazon explains,[259] trees release oxygen when they use energy from sunlight, making glucose from carbon dioxide and water. Like all plants, trees also use oxygen - but they produce more oxygen than they use up; otherwise there would be no net gain in growth. A tree's photosynthesis process takes 6 molecules of CO_2 to produce one molecule of glucose, with 6 molecules of oxygen being released as a by-product. A glucose molecule contains 6 carbon atoms, so that is a net gain of one molecule of oxygen for every atom of carbon (growth) added to the tree. The bigger the tree, and the more trees growing, the more oxygen for us to breathe.

A mature sycamore tree, for example, might be around 12 metres tall and weigh two tonnes. If it grows by 5% in a year, it will produce around 100 kilogrammes (kg) of wood, of which 38 kg will be carbon (absorbed from CO_2 in the air). Allowing for the relative molecular weights of oxygen and carbon, this equates to 100 kg of oxygen per tree per year.

A human being breathes about 9.5 tonnes of air in a year, but oxygen only makes up about 23 percent of that air, by mass, and we only extract a little over a third of the oxygen from each breath. That works out to a total of about 740 kg of oxygen per year - seven or eight trees' worth. If we allow for the fact that trees account for 28% of world oxygen production (with 70% coming from phytoplankton in the seas[260]), then every human being on the planet needs two fully mature living trees to survive. Pagan veneration of trees, it seems, was not mistaken.

Trees and Imagery

It is hard to overstate the importance of imagery in the collective human consciousness. Widely accepted beliefs create the capacity to achieve through collective effort; the wielding of power is dependent upon freely given authority. This was dramatically demonstrated in the year 9 CE when the previously unstoppable expansion of the Roman Empire was brought to a halt by Germanic tribes facing the superior, advanced military might of the legions... partly because the Germans were convinced that they had their sacred trees on their side:

> *"Environmental imagery could prove to be a frighteningly potent political force. In AD 5 a Roman army, 18,000 strong, advanced to ravage villages between the Elbe and the Rhine. However four years later* [in AD 9] *at Teutoburgerwald* ["Teutonic Forest"] *in Saxony the Roman Ninth Legion was lured into a wood-girt defile and massacred. Ten years after that Tacitus described the whitened bones that marked the places where men had fought or fled, the litter of weapons, the bones of horses, and the skulls set on poles. Worse still, the Eagles had been lost. The great wooded expanses had allowed the Germanic tribes to maintain their identity, and spared them the humiliation and 'civilising' influences that had been the fate of occupied territories."* [261]

The Germanic victory of the Teutonic Forest campaign changed history. It drew a line through the trees that limited forever the expansion of the Roman Empire. Almost everywhere else the Romans were victorious, but the north European forests and their tribal inhabitants remained unconquered, and consequently free to maintain pagan polytheistic beliefs for several centuries after the formal Christianisation of Rome in 312 CE. Consequently when Angles, Saxons, Jutes, and others migrated to settle in Britain (and later create England) from the mid-fifth century onwards, they were still pagan. It is no exaggeration to say that their freedom of belief was directly linked to their understanding of the importance of trees and the "great wooded expanses", a convincing example of the validity of the 'doctrine of exchange' with Mother Earth in general, and trees and forests in particular.

Trees and Blood Sacrifice

In north European pre-Christian mythology the gods and other major entities (frost giants, rock giants, fire giants, light elves, and dark elves) were held to inhabit their own worlds, with each of nine worlds being supported in the branches of the Tree of the Worlds, Yggdrasil (see below). However it was also possible to travel between the worlds. The Vanir for example sent Scyld Scefing (Shef/Heimdal) as a child from their world of Vanaheim to mankind's realm of Middle Earth (Midgard), to be brought up and live his life here. It was well known that the gods, Æsir as well as Vanir, sometimes took an interest in events happening in this world (witness Odin's concern to collect battle-dead warriors for Valhalla). Consequently it was believed to be wise to take steps to stay on the right side of such powerful entities. The making of sacrifices was thought to be a good way to do this, including, at least in very early pre-migration times, the offering of blood sacrifices.

The nature and prevalence of blood sacrifices probably varied significantly over time, reflecting developments in tribal social structures associated with the growth of kingship:

> "Strabo and Tacitus in the 1st c. AD both mention sacrifices in lakes (e.g. the Nerthus cult), while later writers such as Procopius in the 6th c. refer only to hanging from trees. It may be possible to connect this change in ritual (from lake-drowning to tree-hanging) to a popular move away from the earthbound Vanir towards the celestial Æsir, which would be reflected in the political move from kinship-based chiefdom to a proto-state or kingdom. A change in ritual might

indeed reflect the abandonment of large, collective ceremonies to a situation where the headman (lord or king) could sacrifice on behalf of the community." [262]

Whether carried out collectively or on a people's behalf by their lord or king, sacrifice was always about a perceived need to communicate effectively with the gods. Where then might sacrifices best be made, in terms both of the facilitation of effective communication with the divine and, importantly, its being witnessed to be so? Certainly by the migration (fifth century CE onwards) and Viking periods (late eighth century onwards) the answer came to be: in sacred groves, for woodlands were believed to be favoured as homes from home by Æsir and Vanir visiting this world. As well as (or because of) sylvan groves being perceived as dwelling places of the gods, trees also came to be associated with the practice of blood sacrifice:

"Some early peoples practised divination and/or blood sacrifice in sacred groves... To keep the practice in perspective it must be realised that it was seldom carried out as simple blood lust: sacrificial victims might act as 'messengers'... eventually it was more usual to propitiate the gods with animal sacrifice. Germanic tribes... practiced divination and human sacrifice in holy groves... in the gateway to the underworld of spirits that was unlocked by ritual. The druid priests of the Celtic peoples too, practiced divination by blood sacrifice within oak groves." [263]

Not only were groves held to be dwelling places of the gods, but individual trees could come to be associated with rituals considered a necessary acknowledgment of the existential structure of the worlds. In particular, specific trees could be honoured as symbolising the Tree of the Worlds. This certainly appears to have been the case at the pagan religious centre at Uppsala in Sweden, where some of the predecessors of what later became the English tribes are thought to have lived in pre-migration times:

"Individual real trees could partake of this sanctity and might symbolise the World Tree... Uppsala in central Sweden... is said to have been the political, religious and economic centre... of the Yngling dynasty [proposed by some as a possible source of the term 'English'] *whose kings were also leaders in the cult of Freyr, the Norse god of fertility... the site of* 'a most splendid temple'... *and next to it a grove in which...*

sacrifices would be made every ninth year 'of every living thing that is male, they offer nine heads, and with the blood with which it is customary to placate gods... The bodies they hang in the sacred grove that adjoins the temple. Even dogs and horses hang there with men.'" [264]

There is no evidence that human blood sacrifice was still being practised as late as the fifth century CE when the migration of Germanic tribes to Britain began. Given the abhorrence of pagan practices chronicled by Christians in England, it seems certain that had such ritual still been being practised in the post-migration period, Christian monks would have recorded and publicised it in order to demonise their theological enemies.

Distasteful as the notion of blood sacrifice must seem to many now, it should be borne in mind that this may have been more about the dedication to the divine of those who would have died in any case, rather than the wilful ending of lives out of malice, or a belief that the gods might simply demand such a thing. In the very early (pre-migration) era, this could have applied to the hanging of (specifically male) bodies from trees, whether these might be enemy warriors killed or captured in battle, or local criminals condemned to die for serious crimes such as murder. In later (but still pre-Christian) times animal rather than human sacrifice would have been practised, but using animals which would in any case have been killed for food.

It should probably also be allowed that committed Christian evangelists such as Adam of Bremen (quoted above) are hardly likely to have recorded events at Uppsala or elsewhere in an entirely objective manner. Their concern was to denigrate paganism and pagan practices, and promote their sacred cause of conversion to Christianity in order to 'save souls', not to engage in a scientifically neutral assessment of non-Christian ritual.

The Tree of the Worlds

Yggdrasil is the tree which holds and nourishes the nine worlds. Central to these worlds is Midgard, the Middle World (Tolkien's Middle Earth, or our own world). Just as trees in our world nourish the air with oxygen, so Yggdrasíl the mother tree feeds each of the nine worlds with their different essential energy requirements.

Freya Aswynn explains[265] that Midgard is granted the energies of time, change, and the seasons, culminating in life, death, and birth, marked by the rune ᚼ ('j' - Jera). The moderate, temperate, variable energies which allow life in Midgard, are generated by the interaction of two other nearby worlds of elemental extremes: Nifelheim, the land of freezing mists and ice, marked by the 'n' rune (ᚾ - Nyd), and Muspelheim, the land of fire and flame, marked by the 'd' rune (ᛞ - Dagaz).

Below Midgard is Hel. This is not the Christian Hell of everlasting torture by fire, but the cold land of the goddess Hel, designated by the rune ᚺ ('h' - Hagalaz). Her realm is where those who die on land of old age or illness go (death at sea takes you to the sea-goddess Rán). Close by lie both Jötenheim, the land of the Ice-giants, elemental forces of nature whose rune is | ('i' - Isa), and Svartalfheim, the land of the underground dwelling Dark Elves. Their rune is ᛇ ('y' - Eiwaz).

Above Midgard, higher in Yggdrasíl's branches, there are two worlds linked by the energies of love, fertility, creativity, and growth. The first is Vanaheim, home to the Vanir fertility gods. The Vanaheim rune is ◇ ('ng' - Ing). The second is Lightalfheim, where the Light Elves live, whose rune is ᛋ ('s' - Sol). Both these worlds are ruled by Frey, the male fertility god, and his sister Freya, the mistress of both love and battle.

Finally, at the apex of the tree, at the end of a rainbow bridge guarded by the god Heimdal, there may be found Asgard, the fortress home of the Æsir gods. This is where Odin's Valhalla is located – the destination of half of those dying in battle (the other half being chosen by Freya as director of the divine Valkyrie female warriors). Asgard's rune is ᚷ ('g' - Gifu).

While Yggdrasíl lives, all nine worlds, from the freezing lower levels to the fertile upper realms, are supported in her branches. Yet just as life-giving trees are uprooted in Midgard, so Yggdrasíl herself is threatened. In Nifelheim there lives the dragon Nídhögg; he gnaws away continually at the worlds' tree's roots, thereby threatening not just Yggdrasíl, but all life held in her branches. Just as we in Midgard undermine our own survival by attacking trees, so the dragon Nídhögg's actions threaten even his own existence, for if Yggdrasíl falls, so does Nifelheim, and so does Nídhögg.

Other inhabitants of Yggdrasil are said to include a "very knowledgeable"[266] eagle who roosts in the very top branches, accompanied by a hawk called Vedrfölnir, and the squirrel Ratatosk whose task it is to carry insulting messages between the eagle and the dragon Nídhögg at the base of the tree. There are also four stags said to wander about the branches nibbling on the foliage. Fortunately for the stags Yggdrasil is said to be evergreen, constantly fed as the tree is by the nourishing waters of the springs beneath her base, a process which seems to obviate the need to lose leaves in Autumn and Winter, despite being named most often as an ash tree.

The meaning of the name Yggdrasil, though the subject of some discussion, is usually given as "Odin's Horse":

> "because the gallows can be understood as the horse
> of the hanged; the tree would, according to this, be
> Odin's gallows on which he hung during his self-
> sacrifice... recorded in the famous passage in
> Hávamál 138-141 where it says:
> I know I hung on the wind-swept tree
> For nine nights in all,
> Wounded by a spear, and dedicated to Odin,
> Given myself to myself,
> On the tree, of which nobody knows
> From which root it grows.
> With nothing to eat and nothing to drink,
> I bent my head down,
> And groaning took up the runes,
> And fell down thereafter." [267]

According to this popular interpretation Odin gained his knowledge of the runes and mastery of their magical use through his 'sacrifice of himself' by hanging "wounded by a spear" from the world tree for an extended period of time. However this seems remarkably reminiscent of Christ's reported protracted suffering hanging from a cross, leading to suspicion that the runes' story may be a late addition to Scandinavian Æsir-related mythologising after contact with Christianity. Alternative suggestions to "Odin's Horse" for the meaning of Yggdrasil include "Yew-pillar" (leading to some naming the tree as a yew rather than an ash), and "tree of terror" as a metaphor for the gallows (unrelated to Odin). [268]

In any case there seems to be a contradiction between understanding Yggdrasil as the nurturing Tree of the Worlds, which holds and supports all nine known realms of gods, mankind, and other beings in her branches, and the idea that such a sacred tree would be named after a single act of self-inflicted violence by Æsir 'All-father' Odin. Being patriarch of the gods of Asgard is no doubt a role of great importance but Odin, whether or not he mastered the magic of the runes by hanging himself, is only an individual being, whereas the Tree of the Worlds supports all forms of ever evolving life. The full complexity of the Wyrd would exist without Odin, but perhaps not without Yggdrasil.

The Wyrd exists independently of the will and actions of Odin and all deities, mankind, and all mortal beings. The personified energies which do have some impact on the complex workings and interactions of the Wyrd are the three Norns: Urd, Verdandi and Skuld. Each has her own role. Urd expresses that which has already come about (the past, or *synthesis*). Verdandi is concerned with that which is still changing (the present, or still contradictory *antithesis*). Skuld considers that which still might be – not 'the future', which remains always only possibility and undetermined - but viable impending options (or possible *theses* to facilitate 'the debt which must be paid', i.e. which take pre-existing and still developing realities into account).*

The Norns then are primal energies more fundamental to all forms of existence than any deity. And who or what nourishes them? Urd, Verdandi and Skuld live sheltered under the boughs of the Tree of the Worlds, tending a nearby well or springs, whose pure waters nourish the tree.

> *"The tree itself was not eternal but underwent constant regeneration. Three maids, known as the Norns... sprinkled water daily from the spring of Urd over the ash to prevent its limbs from withering (i.e. keep it 'evergreen'), but the tree constantly suffered more*

---

* This way of understanding dialectical transformation emphasises the early pagan view of change and time as being almost circular, or at least cyclical (repeated according to periodic or seasonal rhythms, but potentially at a higher or lower level), rather than lineal. Modern (i.e. 19th century and later, from Hegel and Feuerbach to Lenin) thinkers have tended to see change in terms of 1) thesis, and 2) antithesis, leading through mutual interaction to 3) [future] synthesis. This forward looking but linear model is rather stood on its head by envisioning the past (Urd) as synthesis, the still evolving present (Verdandi) as contradiction and antithesis, and that which is still to come about (Skuld) as possible resolutions or theses (plural and uncertain). The modern 'scientific' view tends to see change as progressive, improving, linear, rational, and able to be modelled and predicted (culminating in synthesis). The pre-Christian, pagan view tends to see change as cyclical, and at least partly chaotic and unpredictable (culminating in theses – possibilities).

than men can know, its limbs... eaten by a goat and a hart, its roots gnawed by the serpent Nídhögg... From its branches fell the dews that would, in turn, replenish the well: all power coming from beneath the tree but constantly folded back into its base in a continuous cycle of activity... drawn into a past which remains the driving power of the present." [269]

The true esoteric wisdom of Yggdrasil as Tree of the Worlds then might be thought to be little to do with seizing the magic and power of the runes after all, whatever Odin may have imagined, and be rather more related to the pagan 'doctrine of exchange' with Mother Earth in general, and trees and forests in particular - facilitated by the Norns' feminine gifts of time, life cycles, and mortality. Ultimately even Yggdrasil herself must perish, and all the nine worlds with her (remember Ragnarok), yet even catastrophe on this scale cannot be absolute or eternal. Odin and the Æsir may go down fighting, vanquished by the forces of chaos, but something will survive and new worlds will be born. Material reality cannot countenance a total void or vacuum; Njörd, Nerthus and the Vanir (or perhaps at least their children and future generations) may survive into new eras, and as their and Scyld Scefing's offspring, Embla and Ask (Elm and Ash, woman and man, new children born of trees) they will one post-Ragnarok day again experience arboreal birth.

Conflicting Pagan and Christian Views of Trees

The advent of Christianity brought with it an enforced requirement to understand all of existence as being subject to a single all-powerful God, which in turn implied that that God's faithful servants should perceive all of nature as being, through the 'Will of God', subject to, and exploitable by, mankind:

"When paganism prevailed, the link between people and nature was closer and more accommodating. There was no Christian mythology concerning a God-given dominion over natural resources. Instead people considered themselves to be within Nature and to be inhabiting a world where everything was permeated by spirituality... Pagan beliefs were characterised by the indivisibility of the natural world, the subsuming of individuality into the stream of life, a low-profile

> regard for property rights, and the existence of meaningful relationships between humans and the trees, beasts, water bodies and landforms that constituted the context of their lives... Christianity however came to be associated with control, hierarchies, and a code of values that elevated humans far above the contents of their context, and saw all other creatures as being subservient and provided merely for human use." [270]

If there is only one God, then his (and throughout most of history monotheism has been closely tied to patriarchy, with the one God being presented as male) will is law, unmoderated by other deities, spirits, or spiritual beings of any kind. The new hierarchies which convinced themselves that they were the earthly expression of that single divine will, whether churches, emperors, or kings, perceived all other world views as wrongful threats to their position and power. Merely to think freely and differently made you an enemy who must recant or be destroyed. People who continued to value the living spirits of trees for example, were held to be denying the single truth of the one God, and thereby threatening to undermine the power and position of that single God's chosen representatives on Earth. To be perceived as venerating trees, instead of exploiting them as part of God's dominion, was to be perceived as promoting evil.

> "Tree worship was a potent force in Europe at the beginning of the first millennium CE... it was often thought that the trees themselves had souls or, at the very least, were inhabited by spirits. Christianity abhorred such beliefs... 'Ye shall utterly destroy all the places wherein the nations... served their gods... under every green tree' (Deuteronomy 12.2). The association of trees with prophecy, or even with healing power, had to be interpreted as evil." [271]

Christians interpreted 'God's Will' as requiring the eradication of 'evil' such as the recognition of other gods or spirits, including those associated with trees. Christian Saint Boniface, for example, who was born in Crediton in Devon in Anglo-Saxon England, became a leading figure in the Anglo-Saxon Christian mission to convert Germanic pagan parts of the Frankish Empire during the 8th century. This mission apparently required him to destroy trees because of their associations with paganism:

> "Oaks symbolised the old pagan practices and St.

Boniface, who strove to convert the pagans, was represented with his foot resting on an oak just as an Edwardian big game hunter might pose to show his dominion over a slain lion." [272]

The Christian Tree of Life

"In the bible... among the trees standing in the Garden of Eden, planted there by God... [is] the tree in a two-fold form... the Tree of Life and the Tree of Knowledge of Good and Evil... It was the fruit of the latter that Adam and Eve were forbidden to eat, but which they tasted after Eve had been lured to do so by the serpent. They thus... gained the ability to distinguish between good and evil. Is there a hint here that Adam had partaken of a forbidden faith, represented by the ancient symbol of the serpent, and encouraged by woman (perhaps the embodiment of an earlier matriarchal faith)?" [273]

Whether or not Adam and Eve had a pre-history as secret goddess worshippers, their male biblical God proved decidedly unforgiving. Just as in Christian Anglo-Saxon England, any slight misstep (honouring a tree; eating an apple) incurred severe punishment (see below). Adam's biting of an apple, the bible informs us, was enough to bring down the wrath of God on the whole of humanity for evermore:

"Humanity was thus destined, as a punishment, to a life of sorrow and travail followed by death... Adam and Eve had to be cast out of Eden... with death the final destiny before a descent to the darkest realms of fire... the Tree of Knowledge became... 'the death-bringing tree'... the living tree as a feature of delight was thus to be replaced by the dead tree, in the form of the cross... The replacement of real sacred trees by a Christian cross seems to have been a deliberate way of replacing the old non-Christian beliefs." [274]

Given the Christian abhorrence of any deity (arboreal or otherwise) being recognised as existing independently, outside of their single God's dominion, it is unsurprising that the Christian perception of their own *'Tree of Life'* should be based around the transformation of a living tree firstly into a *'death-bringing tree'*, and then into a *'dead tree, in the form of the cross'.* The very existence of trees with independent living spirits seems to have been perceived by the church as a threat to its hearts and minds campaign aimed at eliminating diversity of thought and belief. In Anglo-Saxon England, as much as anywhere else within its empire, the Church appears to have taken this biblical disciplinary lesson to heart:

> *"They also replaced trees at the sides of roads, especially in Northumbria [†], although the ornamented stone crosses of eighth-century Northumbria continued to be decked with foliage, jewels, and hung with garments like pagan trees. Some were even soaked with blood, a familiar association with necromancy, but changed here to represent the blood of Christ."* [275]

The English Church attempted to replace the earlier pagan Anglo-Saxon love of living trees with obedience to the Will of God, as represented through the dead wood of the cross. However the surviving literary evidence suggests that at least some later Anglo-Saxons continued to venerate living trees, thereby rendering them worthy recipients of Christian condemnation and punishment.

Christian Punishment of Tree Veneration

It is remarkable that long after Christianity was imposed as the obligatory and single permissible belief system across Anglo-Saxon England (a gradual process starting with the kingdom of Kent in 597 CE, and ending with Sussex in 680 CE), the Christian church still found it necessary to implement punishments for those falling by the pagan wayside, including some apparently still insisting on venerating trees. For example at the beginning of the eleventh century Bishop Wulfstan of Worcester still found it necessary to require the punishment of pagan practices honouring trees and springs:

> *"The 'Penitentials'... compiled by Bishop Wulfstan after he obtained the See of Worcester in 1002, suggest that pagan practices may have been 'resurgent under Danish influence':* 'Punish those who dedicate offerings... to trees, or to springs ... let [them] fast for

---

[†] Anglo-Saxon Northumbria covered all the English land east of the Pennines from present day South Yorkshire to the (then not yet fixed) Scottish border.

three years on bread and water...' [276]

It might be expected that the informal survival of Anglo-Saxon pagan tree veneration would be restricted to the lower social classes, as the aristocracy had much to gain from the worship of hierarchy and power promoted by the Christian church, but even in the very limited surviving written sources still available to us, hints that this was not necessarily so can be found:

> *"The 'Northumbrian Priests' Law', possibly composed by Archbishop Ælfric Puttoc (1023-51) appears to recognise that ancient sacred places had not been entirely eradicated by the mid-eleventh century:*
>
>> 'If there is on anyone's land a sanctuary around a stone or a tree or a well or any such nonsense, he who made it is then to pay... a fine, half to Christ and half to the lord of the estate. And if the lord of the estate will not help in the punishment, then Christ and the kings are to have the compensation'
>
> *....Heathen practices were not restricted to the peasantry, for this same law orders a fine for* 'any heathen practice, either by sacrifice or divination', [and] *if the perpetrator is a king's thegn he should pay* '10 half-marks, half to Christ, half to the king.'" [277]

Conclusion – *The Centrality of Trees in the Pagan World View*

Trees were without doubt one of the most significant aspects of the north European environment in the pre-Christian age. As such it is hardly surprising that they formed a vital part of early English tribal peoples' cosmology and belief systems. Tribal inhabitants of almost impenetrable north European forests were able to remain independent of the Roman Empire, and consequently (thanks to the trees) free to maintain pagan polytheistic beliefs for several centuries after the Christianisation of Rome.

Wooded groves were perceived as dwelling places of the gods, and as such, could be seen as sacred places facilitating communication with deities, through sacrifices and rituals. Individual trees in such groves could also be seen as symbolic of the Tree of the Worlds, Yggdrasil, or even as embodying some of Yggdrasil's energies. As it was known that the web-weaving, life-determining Norns lived sheltered under the boughs of the Tree of the Worlds, sacred groves would also have constituted optimal spaces for divination rituals.

So central to the pagan world view were trees that they came to be perceived not just as providing shelter for the gods in the form of holy wooded groves, but also as a vital part of the divine themselves. Permanent pagan temples of the kind found in southern Europe and the Middle East were not to be found in Germanic and Nordic Europe. Instead those desiring contact with the gods could seek it both in forest glades, and in the divine, erect form of the tree trunk itself. Vertical wooden poles or posts could play various such roles, whether in terms of communication, veneration, or protection.

> "The term áss is used not only of a 'god' but also of a block of wood, a pole, beam or post in Norse. This ties in very closely with the testimony of Tacitus who states that the Germani of his day had no temples but were accustomed to worship in a woodland grove – where doubtless the images of the gods were set up in the form of wooden posts carved with appropriate images... Links to a phallus cult have been proposed, but perhaps more fruitful is the association with the World Tree as sustainer of life...
>
> "The post is called by Woodard an 'unboundary', meaning that it denotes an extent in space but does not fix its limit. Rather, the column denotes the vertical boundary, but not the horizontal. It is, therefore, a columna mundi, a post supporting the sky... The Old Saxon term for this pillar or post was Hirminsuul (or Irminsul). The element irmin- means 'vast, great'... while sul is a word for 'column' or 'post'... This 'column which sustains everything' has an obvious reference in the Norse Askr yggdrasils which is also a support for the universe and for all life." [278]

Just as Yggdrasil shelters the Norns, so the Norns nurture Yggdrasil, a fundamental example of the pagan 'doctrine of exchange'. Early English (and other) pagan tribes viewed human beings as part of Mother Nature's diversity, and recognised tree spirits as independent living entities. In line with the 'doctrine of exchange' world view, Mother Nature and her trees and forests protected and nurtured human beings, and people in turn respected and reverenced them.

The advent of patriarchal, hierarchical monotheism in England, as elsewhere, devalued Nature, which came to be seen as merely part of God's dominion, available to be exploited and consumed. Christianity replaced the pagan veneration of living trees with that of the dead wood of the cross. Yet, despite the arboreally negative impact of the Church, the Anglo-Saxon love of living trees survived for some, as evidenced - even hundreds of years after formal 'conversion' - by the recording of punishments thought to be necessary to chasten those of all social ranks still making offerings to trees.

Chapter 9 – *Freya*

Anglo-Saxon paganism was very much marked by the diversity of its vision of both the cosmos in general and the specific North European pantheon of goddesses, gods, and other beings and spirits, from frost giants to trees. A crucial part of this diversity was the recognition of the individuality of different entities, who were perceived not as archetypes but as living, often self-contradictory, ever changing and developing personalities. Stories were told to illustrate the lives of these marvellous but strange creatures, their adventures, and the challenges and tensions they had to face. Inevitably though, some characters became better known than others. Storytelling audiences were no doubt most enraptured by the histories and individual personalities that people could most easily relate to their own lives, whether exemplary models such as the strong, protective, magical, and feminine figure of the 'great goddess' Freya, or much more dubious characters such as the eternal trouble-maker Loki.

'Freya' (or Freyja) means 'lady', and some commentators have understood this to mean that she was seen as 'the Lady', a supreme or great goddess whose standing was on a distinctively higher level. Britt-Mari Näsström called her definitive 1995 Lund University publication "Freyja – the Great Goddess of the North"[279], and argues that this is indeed the case. It is not that Freya was the only goddess, or entirely unique; she was not the 'One Goddess' or 'Goddess' in the way that monotheists speak of the 'One God' or simply 'God'. She was neither perfect nor all-powerful, but she was complex, multi-faceted, and problem-solving, which made her believable, capable, and lovable, rather as ordinary mortals strive to be, if nevertheless operating on a somewhat higher level:

> "A great goddess is... distinguished from other female deities by her complex of characteristics and by holding a dominating position in the pantheon. Her cult is widespread; she is worshipped by both men and women and she usually bears many bynames...
>
> "The Great Goddess... appears as a counterpart to that phenomenon which the history of religion refers to as a High God. A typology of her most prevalent characteristics can be read in the following way:

She is autonomous.
She decides fate.
She is associated with earth,
but can appear as a sky-goddess.
She is connected with the moon,
only rarely with the sun.
Her ambiguous character comprises
both good and evil..." [280]

Whether Freya's character can ever be described as truly evil is surely doubtful, unless perhaps her sexual autonomy is perceived as a terrifying threat, as in the 'original' Sörla þáttr version of the story of the Brisingamen[281] in which she 'sells' her body four times out of supposed greed for gold (but see also my rewritten version *The Breeze Necklace* in chapter 1 of this book, and the discussion of the Brisingamen story at the end of this chapter). Nor should Freya surely be seen as being more associated with the moon (masculine in Germanic languages and early culture) than the sun (feminine). However she is definitely *"distinguished... by her complex of characteristics"*. Hilda Ellis Davidson, for example, portrays her as a "Mistress of Animals" (both wild and domesticated), "Mistress of the Grain", "Mistress of Distaff and Loom", "Mistress of the Household" (including the birth and nurturing of children), and "Mistress of Life and Death" (including healing).[282] In an earlier book[283] the same author also discusses Freya's important role as a mistress of the shamanic magic of *seidr*, used to facilitate the female functions of sooth-sayer and communication with spirits able to travel between the worlds. All in all Freya definitely does hold *"a dominating position in the pantheon"* and rewards study of her multiple characteristics.

Socio-Cultural Context

Although it is clear that Freya was always seen as an extremely important goddess, it must also be borne in mind, as ever, that the available written sources of information about her, as with all aspects of pre-Christian north European belief systems, are largely late (e.g. 13th Century, post-Christianisation), and partial (in both senses, i.e. firstly incomplete, and secondly also biased in the sense that they have been recorded by scribes required to be 'non-believers', unsympathic to pagan ways of looking at the worlds).

This is particularly problematic for the interpretation of goddess roles. Not only were authors/recorders most often inherently patriarchal Christian monks, but the pre-Christian stories, histories, and poems they set down in writing mainly reflected the late pagan period - which was itself also inherently patriarchal. Reading between the storytelling lines however does sometimes allow us to glimpse a possibility that earlier pre-Christian 'English' tribes had a broader, more gender balanced (even possibly originally matriarchal) understanding of the common north European pantheon.

Late (8th to 10th century) Scandinavian 'Viking' paganism clearly largely reflected male warrior and warfare-based values (linked to the acquisition of power derived from the establishment and expansion of kingdoms). However early (5th to 7th century) English tribal paganism may have also reflected the fertility-based values of settled, relatively peaceful, agricultural societies, in which authority would have been derived from competences in both female and male roles. One story which seems never to have lost its ancient portrayal of powerful female roles is *Hyndla's Lay*, a tale which is retold below. In order to see deeper into the underlying messages implicit in Hyndla's Lay, it is useful first to consider its cosmological context (the pagan world view it reflects).

Freya - *and the North European Weltanschauung*

In order to better understand Freya within the broader context of the pre-Christian north European way of looking at the worlds it is worth briefly reiterating some of the most fundamental principles of pagan cosmology.

- In the beginning... there is no beginning (or end). There is always: Something and Nothing.
  - o 'Nothing' is the void, the negative, 'no thing', *Ginnungagap* – the 'yawning void'.
  - o 'Something' is the positive, some thing and potentially any thing, but even at its most simple, plural and diverse, i.e. not one but at least two - different - things:
    - Fire and Ice, heat and cold, change and stasis.
    - Fire is active, always changing, never still, both energetic and destructive, and feminine. She is the sun, and she is energy, warmth, creation, birth, life, and death.
    - Ice is static, apparently unchanging, frozen,

solid, and masculine. He is the moon, cold and still.

- However... he can be melted by the warmth of his female partner, the sun, and be wonderfully changed by her - to become (jointly with her) life-sustaining water. Fire and ice are expressions of the two most basic forms of being, of realities beyond the 'yawning void' of nothingness and unbeing – but they are contradictory forms.

- Fire can never become ice, and ice can never become fire. Their contradictions, the tensions between them, are complex, ever changing, and both creative and destructive. Old forms of being are continually destroyed and new ones created, but even the new forms of being are themselves always dynamic, both internally and externally contradictory, never perfect, and subject to both growth and decay.[*]

The cycle of being, and the life cycle, are cycles of continual change: of creation, birth, growth, decay, and death. The alternative to this is the void: unbeing, nothingness, the *Ginnungagap*, which avoids change and is perfect, but at the price of every thing ceasing to exist, the loss of creation and being. Not for nothing does the Hindu Rig Veda say *"Crawl to your Mother Earth. She will save you from the Void."* [284]

Everything that does exist is constantly changing from one moment to the next, and is therefore by definition imperfect, but part of material reality. The attainment of perfection, if it were actually possible, would be the attainment of non-existence, of unreality. The nanosecond it were obtained, it would cease to exist.

For fire and ice to exist, they must be different not only from the void of nothingness, but also from each other, for if the two most basic forms of existence were to become absolutely identical, they

---

[*] Fire and Ice – in the pagan dialectic female fire is the *thesis*, male ice the *antithesis*, and the outcome of their mutual interaction (parturition) is the *synthesis*, a cyclical process of initially increasing (but also potentially decaying) complexity, with all factors directly or indirectly linked through the web of the Wyrd.

would become one, a perfect unity, and instantaneously unreal, non-existent. Reality, existence, requires differentiation; it is necessarily plural and diverse.

Given the necessarily contradictory nature of reality then, the imperfection and constant change of all things, it comes as no surprise to discover that the life stories of the gods too are subject to change, even when written down. The myths as recorded rarely tell a single, consistent story. They often disagree with each other, or at least present alternative versions of tales of divinities and their worlds. Stories have always evolved, especially in pre-literate, oral societies. In paganism there is no single, perfect, supposedly never-changing 'Word of God', no bible. And with a complex character like the goddess Freya, her stories were always going to be ever developing.

Freya, as we have seen, has been described as a "Great Goddess", one who is *"distinguished from other female deities by her complex of characteristics and by holding a dominating position in the pantheon."* [285] But how does she come to enjoy such richness of character? Why is she in such a dominant position in the pantheon? This will be reviewed more fully below in terms of her function in the north European pagan cosmos, but prior to that a greater understanding of Freya's popularity with both women and men might be assisted by following an example of her reported adventures. This story is known as *Hyndla's Lay*.[286] The version presented here has been rewritten from the fourteenth century version, which had no doubt itself evolved and changed over preceding centuries.

Fifth Storytelling – *Hyndla's Lay*

Gods and giants have never been exactly renowned for being the closest of friends. The Æsir in particular were well known for having declared all giants to be way beyond the pale. The very fortress walls of Asgard were reported to have been constructed largely to deter unwanted visits from rough mannered and definitely socially unacceptable *Jötnar*. Admittedly the Vanir were said to be a little more understanding of social differences, but when Freya unexpectedly turned up early one morning to pay a call on the giantess Hyndla in her cave, it was still something of a surprise.

"Hyndla," Freya shouted from the dark cave's entrance, "Are you at home?" All that came by way of response was a deep subterranean rumbling sound. This might have worried some. Could it perhaps have been a warning of a dangerous earth tremor? But Freya knew that what she was hearing was only the giantess snoring. Giants are not early risers, and tend to get tetchy if disturbed much before lunchtime.

Freya however was nothing if not persistent. She had arrived riding her famous battle-boar Hildisvíni. Now she dismounted and peered into the gloomy cave. "Hyndla," she shouted again, "It's me, Freya. Wake up! I need your help." A noise reminiscent of heavy millstones grinding against one another erupted from the depths. Hyndla, it seemed, might be stirring. "I'll make it worth your while," Freya continued, now trying to make her voice sound warm, friendly, and encouraging.

Eventually the giantess, looking somewhat the worse for wear, staggered clumsily out into the light. "What in all of Jötenheim do you want Freya?" she asked. "Since when have we been on visiting terms?"

Freya took a deep breath, determined to remain winning and polite. "Look, it's about Thor," she explained. "I know you fancy him, picture of masculinity that he is. Of course we both know he'd never normally even deign to look at a giantess; he'd be too worried about his precious reputation for one thing. But I can help you gain his favour... if you'll just do me a small service in return of course?"

Hyndla snorted loudly in disgust. "Freya," she exclaimed, "Thor's never even going to glance at an old giantess like me! It's all right for you, with your looks and your seductive ways, taming men and getting them eating out of your hand. It'll never be like that for me. And Thor's an Áas, he hates giants, and he'll run a mile as soon as he sees me, or crack my skull open with his hammer!"

"Not if I put a spell on him he won't!" said Freya. "He won't even know what's happening to him. All he'll be able to think about in your magically enhanced presence will be how to get himself into your welcoming bed. Believe me, I can do these things."

Hyndla gazed darkly at the goddess. "Well it's obvious that you can bend males to your will Freya," she sighed, looking at Hildisvíni. "I've heard all about your wonderful battle boar, and now I can see him with my own eyes. It's true what they say isn't it: he's really your latest lover, the man called Ottár, isn't he! He's enjoyed being ridden by you in bed... and now you're riding him everywhere, taking him around with you, disguised by your witchcraft." The giantess paused her scolding for a few seconds, but then asked Freya: "Where's your husband Óðr by the way? I haven't seen *him* around for quite some time."

Freya struggled to control her temper, but she needed something specific from this rough-hewn, coarse, and disrespectful creature, and was determined to keep on her good side until she got it. Nevertheless she was not about to give public confirmation of the enchanting games she and her lovers enjoyed playing. "Of course it's not Ottár," Freya said, as calmly as she could manage. "See for yourself, look at how his boar's bristles glow with light, allowing him to travel and carry me even in the dark. It's Hildisvíni. I don't sleep with boars!"

"That's not what I heard," Hyndla shot back, with surprising speed for a giantess. "And ugly little dwarves? I heard you had four of them, one after the other." For a moment Freya was speechless, but then Hyndla appeared to get bored with insulting the love goddess, as curiosity got the better of her. "Anyway, what was it you wanted of me?" she asked, sounding a little puzzled. "I can't imagine what an old giantess like me could possibly do for you."

"You've been around a long time Hyndla," Freya explained to her. "You've seen a lot, many generations of men in fact. Your memory is long, and you've witnessed a lot. I've never really paid much attention to doings in Midgard myself, but now my friend Ottár needs my help."

At the mention of Ottár's name Hyndla laughed out loud and gestured rudely at Hildisvíni. Freya ignored her and pressed on. "Ottár, who is currently in Asgard visiting Odin and the Æsir," she lied, "has always been good and loyal. He's forever making sacrifices to me, reddening his altar with ox blood in my name, and now it's my turn to help him. He's always been respectful. He's a good man."

"Good in bed, you mean," Hyndla interrupted. Freya could not help but scowl at the giantess, but bit her tongue. "There's a dispute between Ottár and a rival of his by the name of Angantyr," she continued, keeping her voice as level as she could manage. "The two of them have agreed to let Odin be the judge as to which of them has the nobler ancestry and therefore the greater claim to lead their people. Odin has summoned both Ottár and Angantyr to appear before him in Asgard. They have to prove their knowledge of their ancestors by reciting before the gods the names of their forebears as far back as they can go. Odin will judge the relative nobility of the families involved, but those who Ottár or Angantyr fail to name won't be counted as legitimate ancestors."

"And where do I come in then?" Hyndla asked, staring thoughtfully at Hildisvíni.

"It's dead easy Hyndla," Freya told her. "Like I said, you've been around a long time, many generations of men in fact, and unlike me, you've been paying attention. While I've been busy chasing around the worlds in my chariot, or flying around as a falcon, you've been quietly and patiently observing. You know what's been going on, and what the histories of men are. All I need you to do is to recite Ottár's noble ancestry to me, so that I can teach it to Ottár, and he can be judged the winner by Odin."

"And in return...?"

"In return I'll snap my fingers in front of Thor's eyes... and he'll do whatever you want him to," Freya told Hyndla. "You can have him for a day or however long it takes you to exhaust his physical abilities. He's pretty virile, I expect you can make him last quite a while?"

"I'm not going to Asgard," Hyndla responded. "It's too risky. You'll have to bring Thor out here to me. Oh, and I'll recite Ottár's ancestry alright Freya, but instead of telling it to you, why don't I just speak it directly into Ottár's ears" she added, staring hard at the goddess's pet battle boar.

Freya stayed silent, so Hyndla approached Hildisvíni, gave him a meaningful look, and began to chant hypnotically. She recited Ottár's honourable lineage at length, going back many generations, and including kings, dragon-slayers, and even some who long ago had themselves been counted amongst the gods. "Ottár, you fool," she called him, over and over again, as she listed each ancestor.

When it was done at last Freya could not resist a satisfied smirk. She just had one last small demand to make of Hyndla. "Great!" the goddess exclaimed. "Now Hyndla, if you could just give Ottár, I mean Hildisvíni, a good draught of your famous 'memory mead' so that we can all be sure he'll be able to remember everything perfectly when in Odin's rather intimidating presence, Angantyr won't stand a chance."

But now the giantess suddenly exploded with anger. "Who in Hel's name do you think you are Freya?" she demanded. "That was never part of the deal. My 'memory mead' is mine, and not for mere men! Go and get me Thor, now! And let's see if Ottár's man enough to remember what I've taught him!"

Hyndla though had made a mistake. Freya had already got most of what she wanted from her, and no longer needed to be gentle. Before the giantess knew what was happening, she found herself surrounded by fierce, leaping blue flames. A circlet of fiery pain danced in the air around her, and then slowly began to tighten its burning noose around Hyndla's body. Faced with impending destruction at magic-wielding Freya's hands, Hyndla gave in. "Alright noble one," she spat at Freya.

"Here's a draught of my memory beer for your Ottár. But know this, I've poisoned it! It'll bring your precious lover to a very bad end!" Freya laughed with joy at her victory over Hyndla. "You're speaking nonsense Hyndla," she exclaimed. "You're an ugly old hag who is full of nothing but empty threats, bitterness and rancour. You could have had fun with Thor, but not anymore." The goddess ran her fingers lovingly down her wild boar's back to bring him pleasure. "When I get my way with Odin and the Æsir," she continued quietly to herself, Ottár will be drinking nothing but the finest mead. My Ottár will be recognised as truly more noble than Angantyr, and be named leader of his people."

Hyndla's Lay – *Commentary*

Kevin Crossley-Holland comments that Hyndla's story confirms that Freya is indeed a goddess of multiple roles:

> *"This myth displays Freyja as goddess of fertility (the promiscuity with which Hyndla taunts her is echoed elsewhere)... , goddess of war (Hildisvíni, the name of her boar – actually Ottár in disguise – literally means 'battle-boar'), and goddess of witchcraft (raising flames around the giantess)"* [287]

He also explains that the theme of ancestry recognition, and its ability to confer and legitimise authority on those seeking power, was of key importance in tribal societies:

> *"The matter of lineage is invariably of immense importance to any leader in a tribal society (think of the litanies in the Old Testament) and it was customary for a pagan North-West European king to claim divine descent. The early pages of the Anglo-Saxon Chronicle, for example, contain genealogies of kings who traced their line back to Bældæg (Balder) and Woden (Odin)."* [288]

H. R. Ellis Davidson speculates that references to Ottár's boar disguise might have had an origin in real Anglo-Saxon magical practice, and that this would evidence a further role of Freya, as a goddess of protection:

> *"When we are told that Freyja's worshipper, Ottár the Simple, disguised himself as a boar, this might be explained by the donning of a boar-mask by the*

priest of the Vanir, who thus claimed inspiration and protection from the deity. Although the Vanir were not gods of battle, the protection they offered would no doubt extend into times of war, and it is noticeable that both Tacitus and Beowulf stress the protective power of the emblem." [289]

The boar as a protective emblem (and possibly amulet?) has also been found on Anglo-Saxon armour, such as the famous Benty Grange helmet on display in Sheffield's Weston Park Museum.

What is perhaps most remarkable about this story which clearly originates from a pre-Christian age is its portrayal of powerful females, in particular of course the goddess Freya. In this tale it is the female characters who are active, whilst the males are passive:

- Freya nurtures and protects her male lover Ottár, but Ottár remains passive, in animal form, without even the magic of speech. He must literally carry Freya on his back for the whole story.
- Supporting, and apparently making love with Freya, is the reward allowed to Ottár the mortal man for his loyalty, dedication, and extensive sacrifices to the goddess.
- Freya is seen to be able to choose her lovers, and disregard her absent husband in this important matter.[†]
- Freya is seen to be manipulating and outsmarting both Odin and her lover's male rival, Angantyr.
- Freya is powerful – she knows and uses magic.
- Hyndla may be a monstrous, old giantess, but in this story she is nevertheless outclassed only by the goddess Freya. Hyndla's specialist knowledge of nobility and ancestry constitutes a rare and valuable ability, and in her "memory mead" she possesses a magical item so powerful that she is envied by the gods themselves.
- The male characters are largely off-stage. Thor, Odin, and Angantyr are discussed but never actually appear. The same applies to Freya's husband, Óðr.

Freya is very much the character both most active and most dominant in this story. Odin the divine patriarch will judge in his own

---

[†] "Njörd raised his voice in defence of the goddesses and against Loki. '*A woman lies with her husband or lover or both. Does it really matter much in the end?*'" [Loki's Flyting, in Crossley-Holland, ibid. p.165]

realm – i.e. between two men (Ottár and Angantyr), and no doubt considers himself to be the all-powerful male leader and 'All-father' of the gods, yet in reality his decision is being taken for him by Freya. By the end of the story Odin's decision, though not yet taken, is not in any doubt. He will decide in favour of Freya's beloved Ottár, because Freya is effectively dominating and controlling the actions and beliefs of all the other characters in the story.

Freya's will is effective in its implementation because she exercises her skills and power intelligently, in multiple forms, distinguishing in her approach (in both words and actions) between individuals she wishes to influence. This is not the exercising of naked power, bluntly battering foes into submission. She is not Odin on the battlefield, consistently bludgeoning declared 'enemies' one and all in an undifferentiated manner, though that too remains an option for her. In her encounter with Hyndla, Freya initially relies on persuasion, seeking consent through an appeal for personal solidarity (she needs Hyndla's help, she says), flattery ("unlike me, you've been paying attention"), cajolery ("It's dead easy Hyndla"), and the promise of reward, i.e. manly Thor in her bed. Only when Hyndla nevertheless eventually rebels and is clearly no longer open to being reasoned with, does Freya resort to coercion and the threat of physical pain to be inflicted by the feminine element of fire.

Freya's varied abilities flicker like active flames into being, burning fiercely one minute, only to die down and be replaced by a differently coloured fire the next, but throughout the story she is never still, but always active. This contrasts sharply with the male characters. Odin remains passively oblivious, offstage in Asgard, unaware that his decision is already being taken for him. Thor ultimately remains uninvolved, but only by decision of Freya; had she involved him he would have unknowingly acted against his usual will and become passively enchanted by Freya's magic. Angantyr also remains offstage and completely unaware of what is going on; his fate is being decided for him, and he is powerless to oppose it.

In cosmological terms then Freya is the epitome of active, female fire. Her energies erupt in conflagrations of various sorts, but are always directed by her consciousness or will. This is not uncontrolled wild fire, not Loki (see chapter 12). This is surely the 'great goddess' Freya's most important of many roles: she is an example of the divine embodiment of active, elemental fire. As such she can defy the void, Ginnungagap, and maintain the active balance needed to underpin all of material reality. However according to the fundamental north

European pagan world view, she cannot achieve that on her own. She is fire, but ice is also needed, and she cannot also be ice herself, for ice and fire are ultimately irreconcilable, contradictory elements. They can interact together, and become creative, as her warmth melts static ice, and 'he' takes on the life-sustaining, feminine characteristics of flowing water, but they nevertheless remain separate elements. So, if Freya is (amongst many other things) an embodiment of elemental fire, who, in her worlds and in her stories, embodies elemental ice? The answer is surely Óðr, her husband. Óðr is missing, and Freya misses him. She is said to have searched for him, and to have wept tears of red gold because of her inability to find him, despite travelling across many lands.[290] It is said that during these extensive journeys she became known to many peoples and hence acquired her many names. Her search is, once again, a positive action, whilst Óðr's mysterious absence is a very negative quality. She is quintessentially female. Óðr is surely quintessentially male. He is unchanging (because not present). He is the cold and distant moon, a pale and shadowy memory. Freya is the sun, her warmth and light generating growth and illuminating emergent life on earth. She nurtures her child, Hnoss (also called Gersimi)[291], the daughter she had with her husband Óðr. Clearly Freya had melted Óðr's frozen heart, and got warmer blood running in his icy veins, at least for a while! But though Freya and Óðr, fire and ice, came together and interacted sufficiently creatively to produce a daughter, these two ultimately drifted apart again, for they remain different and paradoxical. They can never be just a single, unitary, perfect whole; only the void (nothingness) is perfect.

It may be that Freya's relationship with Óðr is also an expression of gender complexity and the necessarily contradictory nature of individual being, for:

> "The word Óðr is cognate with Old English wod
> [which relates to a kind of mental excitement,
> intoxication, rage, fury, exultation – any kind of
> inspired, ecstatic or trance-like state]... The search
> for Óðr is therefore a pursuit of inspiration and life-
> force. Freyja may have had to draw Óðr out of the
> realm of the dead... Óðr may represent Freyja's
> spirit-self, her separable soul, which is traditionally
> of the opposite sex in shamanic societies." [292]

Freya - *and the Brisingamen Necklace*

There is a version (rewritten by this author) of the Brisingamen Necklace story given in chapter 1 of this book, where it is renamed as *The Breeze Necklace*. In the most complete surviving early written version of the story however, to be found in the Sörla þáttr section of the late fourteenth century *Flateyjarbók*, the emphasis is rather different. Sörla þáttr records that the golden necklace was forged by four dwarves, and that Freya spent a night with each of them in order to obtain it. Loki had spied on Freya, and informed Odin of what she had done. Odin then forced Loki to steal the necklace from Freya, which he did by entering her bedroom in the shape of an insect. Freya was asleep, wearing the necklace, and initially Loki could not get at the clasp without waking her, so (as an insect) he stung her, causing her to move in her sleep. He then stole the necklace and gave it, as ordered, to Odin. When Freya awoke she discovered what had happened, and demanded that Odin return her property. He refused to do so unless she provoked an everlasting war between two mortal kings for him, which she did.

In the Sörla þáttr account, Freya is presented as behaving dishonourably in selling her body four times for greed of gold, or at least that is the way that Odin sees it. He is angry and feels justified in bending her to his will, forcing her into provoking eternal deadly violence between men, apparently as a punishment for her perceived disreputable behaviour. The implication is that Freya would not have done this of her own volition, but that once again her insatiable greed for gold leads her to commit wretched acts.

Unsurprisingly it is this version of the Brisingamen tale which became best known and most widely associated with Freya in Christian times, showing the pagan 'great goddess' in a generally accepted bad light as it does. Given that this is the case, it is worth analysing this notorious rendering of Freya's character to examine whether the tale nevertheless leaves us any clues about pre-Christian views of Freya.

The word Brisingamen means "the necklace ['amen'] of the Brisings". Who the Brisings might have been is not known, although Brísing is "Possibly the name of a dwarf in the poem Haustlǫng",[293] so perhaps they were dwarves (dark elves) who were originally presented as the makers of the necklace, before the story was subsequently changed to show Freya discovering it newly forged by a different set of dwarves. It is also not absolutely certain that 'amen' is being used here as 'necklace' either; it could perhaps be taken to signify a 'girdle'. In any case H. R. Ellis Davidson points out that:

> "A necklace is something which is associated with the mother goddess from earliest times. Figurines wearing necklaces found in the Mediterranean area date back as far as 3000 BC, and small female figures wearing them have survived from the Bronze Age in Denmark, and are thought to represent a female deity. Students of Freud will recognise the significance of a necklace for a fertility goddess... It illustrates the familiar tendency to represent the sexual parts of the body by others higher up, and by ornaments worn on these." [294]

To add to the uncertainty, *Brísingr* is also Old Norse for 'flame', so this could be the "flaming necklace" (or girdle). Looking back to the surely more authentically ancient and pagan story of Hyndla's Lay, this association with flames is doubtlessly significant, for Freya, as we have seen, was fundamentally associated with the element of fire, including being able to use fire magic and the conjuring of flames.

There is no doubt that the key aspect of the Sörla þáttr version of the Brisingamen story is the recounting of Freya's 'sleeping around' with the four dwarves. The fourteenth century Christian monks who set this down in writing presumably saw this as typically unacceptable pagan behaviour in a female, which could only undermine her claim to be perceived as holy in any way. Back in pagan times however, things might have been seen rather differently, particularly amongst early, less patriarchal, followers of the Vanir. The Van god Njörd for example, he who is possibly Freya's father (see chapter 4), does not seem too worried by the idea of women or goddesses, including possibly his own daughter, enjoying multiple sexual partners:

> "Njörd raised his voice in defence of the goddesses and against Loki. 'A woman lies with her husband or lover or both. Does it really matter much in the end?'" [295]

Amongst her multiple other roles Freya was a goddess of love and fertility, so having multiple sexual partners may have been seen as no bad thing. Audiences for such stories would after all be aware that life-long monogamy in human societies is hardly universal. In such a context a golden necklace (or girdle), associated also with the hot, flaming, and passionate energies of fire, may have been perceived as marking a celebration of Freya's divinity, rather than as any kind of criticism. The goddess's alleged greed for gold may actually have previously been presented as a keenness to provide and spread the life-giving fertility of the sun's golden rays, perhaps symbolised in a priestess's golden adornment. After all Freya had no need to lust after what for others might be normally unobtainable metallic riches, given that it was known that she could cry tears of gold. Perhaps these 'tears of gold' were a symbolic representation of the sun's light rays rather than actual metal, but if so then the goddess's desire for the golden necklace was surely also equally symbolic of positive, life-nurturing factors.

Conclusion – *Freya the Great Goddess*

Freya may be a 'great goddess' but she is also an individual, with a complicated personality, as is the case with all the north European goddesses and gods. She is not a simple archetype or representation of specific aspects of the human condition, such as love, beauty, magic, battle, or death. One of the most important aspects of her complex personality is that she is able to function as an embodiment of the elemental feminine energy of fire. As such she needs to interact, both creatively and destructively, with embodiments of the masculine elemental strength of ice, such as her husband Óðr.

As with all individuals the multiple and diverse aspects of Freya's personality will be perceived differently at various times, by different people, and according to changing circumstances. Some will see her as being on balance a positive force, whilst to others with a different mindset[‡] she will seem to be negative, or even an evil influence. In any case, again like all the north European goddesses and gods, Freya's character is not static but changes and develops. Like us she is part of many stories, making diverse journeys through her life, and through others' lives as well.

Freya is deeply emotional. She is a driven individual, who responds impulsively to her own and others' needs. According to the best-known version of one story, her desire for the Brisingamen necklace impels her to apparently rash action, risking Odin's anger and

---

[‡] Such as the Christian skald Hjalti Skeggjason, outlawed in Iceland in the year 999 CE for saying *"I don't like barking gods; I consider Freyja to be a bitch"* (Simek, ibid. p.90)

punishment. But even at the superficial, physical level, her relationship with Ottár seems just as much motivated by affection and love for him as by sexual lust.

Freya feels the need to develop herself, which drives her to seek out interactions with external factors in a search to help make herself more complete. In the late versions of the stories told about her these factors are superficially represented as material lusts, whether for gold as wealth, magic as power, sexual love and beauty as physical satisfaction, or the selection of the dead as a shamanic ability. However a careful reading of the stories can expose contradictions which suggest that the superficial presentation of Freya's lusts, needs and desires as being purely selfish and materialistic, is deeply inadequate. For example her reputed greed for gold as ornament and wealth (the Brisingamen necklace) does not make sense for a lady who can cry tears of that same precious metal.

For Freya then the more fundamental attractions of the necklace must lie in other qualities that it contains, possibly related to factors such as:

- The energies contained in its rare and skilled manufacture, which are apparently not inherent in Freya, or at least not to the extent she would like.
- The mysterious form and art of the necklace and the patterns incised into it, which could perhaps indicate gateways to knowledge on a level which the goddess feels she did not previously have access to.
- The completion of rich, fertilising journeys through the worlds, bringing the light and warmth of the fiery-golden sun to the dark earth, melting ice and snow to produce life-giving water, whilst using air through speech and storytelling to consolidate that knowledge in others as much as in herself.

Similarly Freya's reputed obsession with sexual love, as in the case of her affair with her mortal lover, Ottár, can be understood simply on a superficial physical and material level, or possibly also interpreted in other ways. For example, the repeated stress in the story on the magical importance of the wild boar, and its inter-relationship with humanity (Ottár is both a man and a magically transfigured boar) perhaps hints at transformational ways of understanding both mankind's relationship with animals, and relationships between the sexes:

- The boar is by definition wild and free, not a farm-raised pig. The story appears to indicate, in a way that would have been easily understood by pre-Christian north European audiences, that animals can be seen, if allowed their freedom and independence of mankind, as potentially magically protective of women and men.

- For the entire length of the Hyndla story it is Freya the female who is in control of the relationship with her chosen male lover. She transforms and rides him, not he her. Having achieved this she then feels a need to reward him by recognising the dignity of that role (for example by giving him magically enhanced bristles which light the way at night), and protecting him from those (for example, Hyndla) who would disparage it. At the very least this appears to make a case for female autonomy in decision-making in partner relationships, with the goddess's personal feminine hegemony benefitting both male and female. This was no doubt anathema to both the patriarchal Christian church and Odin-worshipping Scandinavian Vikings, but seems to have been more acceptable to earlier Vanir-following pagan tribal cultures.

What ultimately makes Freya truly great are her multiple abilities to promote change and positive development in others as well as herself. As an embodiment of fundamental female fire energies, she can act as a catalyst capable of interacting with incarnations of the essential male energies of frost and ice to produce new iterations of birth/life/death cycles – new generations. In doing so she keeps us safe from the perfect unreality of the void (Ginnungagap).

Chapter 10 – From Inanna to Freya

As a multi-aspected 'great goddess', Freya does not stand alone. The earliest recorded such goddess is surely Sumerian Inanna. Some of her stories have come down to us inscribed on clay tablets dating from around four thousand years ago. Remarkably there are some distinct similarities between Inanna and Freya, enough to make it worthwhile considering whether those similarities might amount to connections of some kind, either direct or indirect. Initially such an idea might seem absurd, given that the two goddesses are separated by huge distances of both a temporal and geographic nature. However it is generally accepted that there are substantiated cases of the veneration of some specific deities spanning cultures despite this involving huge distances in both time and territory. In such cases the deity may be renamed in the younger culture, but still be held to exhibit substantially the same multiple personality aspects as in earlier cultures. There are far too many known interconnections between numerous goddesses and gods for them all to be reviewed here, but it is possible to look at half a dozen major goddesses with generally accepted common features, and consider to what extent, if any, Freya might be connected to them.

Aspects evidenced by both Inanna and Freya include strong associations with:

- Love
- Sex
- Fertility
- War/combat
- Death
- Magical knowledge
- Female sovereign power.

In addition to these common traits or areas of activity and responsibility, both goddesses even share certain symbols in common, such as:

- Large felines – Inanna is often depicted in the company of, or even riding, lions or other large cats, while Freya's chariot is drawn by large cats.
- Birds of Prey – Inanna is shown in ancient images as being accompanied by birds of prey, while Freya has a magical cloak of falcon feathers which allows the wearer to fly as a falcon.

- Ability to Fly – whilst Freya could don her cloak of feathers to fly, Inanna too was often shown with her own set of wings, and even as having a bird's talons for feet.

Of course it could be argued that at root these shared traits and similarities of character might merely reflect fundamental needs common to all of humanity throughout history. Women and men are, for example, surely always going to be interested in unavoidable issues to do with sex, war, and death. However this might not explain a common fondness for large felines and birds of prey. So might it really be possible that Inanna and Freya could effectively be the same goddess, or are all the similarities down to underlying societal factors shared by both the civilised city states of ancient Sumeria, and the relatively primitive Germanic tribes of 'Dark Age' northern Europe?

From Inanna to Freya – *Possible Routes of Travel*

In order to review potential connections between Inanna and Freya it is helpful to trace and consider links (or the lack of them) already known to exist between several goddesses, specifically:

Goddess	Culture	Approximate Peak Veneration Dates
Inanna/Ishtar	Sumerian/Semitic	4500-1750? BCE
Astarte	Phoenician	1000-200 BCE
Isis	Egyptian	1570 BCE – 529 CE
Aphrodite	Greek	1500 BCE – 500 CE
Freya	North European	? BCE – 1000 CE

To deal with the question of geographic distance first, it has been generally accepted that, certainly within and around the margins of the Roman Empire, it was quite usual for specific deities to be recognised in lands thousands of miles apart, albeit subject to some degree of local flexibility and adaptation:

> "The Mediterranean pantheons were always seen as flexible... Egyptian gods and goddesses were similar to Greek ones, and Roman deities were similar to Celtic and German ones. This was due to a number of reasons: the goal of integrating conquered

*peoples... a belief that gods were universal and thus
should obviously find different expressions and
names in different places; and the probability that
some of these gods came from the same ancient
roots and were therefore... variations of the same
gods...*

*"...the Romans absorbed the Greek religion... the
earlier Roman gods were seen to be simply different
names for the Greek gods... the Greeks accepted this
development – they had performed a similar
process on the gods of other nations for
generations..."* [296]

An excellent example of this geographic fluidity in the worship of
specific goddesses is the last surviving pagan Roman shrine still to be
found in exactly its original location. This is not in, or anywhere near,
Rome itself, but at Chester in England:

*"As 'Minerva', the cult of Athena was exported across
the sprawling Roman Empire, including Britain and
Germany... one exceptional relic of Athena's far-
flung cult... survives to this day: Minerva's shrine in
Chester, England. This stone carving of the goddess
is worked into a wall... in Chester, and miraculously
survived centuries of hostile Christianity...
weathered but intact to the present day... It is the
last surviving Roman pagan shrine in its original
location in the world..."* [297]

Such strong evidence of the long-distance travel of devotion to
individual deities does not in itself indicate that Freya and Inanna are
in fact one and the same, just because they evidence similar
personalities and are linked by common symbols. However it is
accepted that some of the goddesses on the list above were
substantially the same deity, though with different names being used
in different regions and cultures.

The closest such identification is between Inanna and Ishtar, which
has been held to be proved not only by their many common
characteristics, but also by the fact that Ishtar was unique (and
uniquely Sumerian/Inanna-like) amongst Mesopotamian deities in
having wings and being able to fly:

*"Ištar is conspicuously unusual, because ancient
Mesopotamian iconography does not know any
other case in which such a prominent deity is*

> portrayed as winged... the winged feature of
> Inanna/Iŝtar, the most prominent goddess of
> Mesopotamia, infiltrated gradually into the
> peripheral regions... The protective function of
> Iŝtar's wings is also clearly stated by her in one of
> the Neo-Assyrian oracles given to Esarhaddon, the
> Assyrian king:
> 'I am your father and mother.
> Between my wings
> I have brought you up.'" [298]

Inanna/Ishtar (or Iŝtar) is also accepted as being substantially the same as the Phoenician goddess Astarte, and Greek Aphrodite:

> "Inanna is the ancient Sumerian goddess of love,
> sensuality, fertility, procreation, and... war. She later
> became identified by... Assyrians as the goddess
> Ishtar, and further with... Phoenician Astarte, and
> Greek Aphrodite, among many others. She was also
> seen as the bright star of the morning and evening,
> and identified with the Roman goddess Venus." [299]

The case for seeing Astarte and Aphrodite as heirs to (or substantially the same as) Inanna/Ishtar will be looked at in more detail later in this chapter, but in order to consider that more effectively it is first necessary to take a closer look at the character of Inanna herself.

Inanna – *Goddess of Fertility and Female Agency*

Inanna's surviving stories make it very plain that she was an independent ruler, ultimately – despite all kinds of difficulties and adventures of the most extreme kind – powerfully in charge of both herself and others, including her relationships with males, and in particular her husband, King Dumuzi. What is truly outstanding about these stories is that they provide a surprisingly detailed life of Inanna as a goddess and an individual being, complete (rather like Freya's stories) with complex character development, including (arguably) not just her actions and roles, but her motivations, and even emotional and spiritual involvements.

Her key roles included that of guaranteeing the fertility of the land through the type of sacred marriage or *hieros gamos* also known in other, later, cultures:

"The Sacred Marriage of Inanna and Dumuzi was central to the fertility of the land and was re-enacted at important festivals by the king and a priestess having sexual intercourse." [300]

However the stories of Inanna's relationship with Dumuzi make it plain that this sacred marriage was anything but straightforward. Firstly:

"Inanna is always depicted as a young woman, never as mother or faithful wife, who is fully aware of her feminine power and confronts life boldly without fear of how she will be perceived by others, especially by men." [301]

Secondly, Dumuzi also has problems with the marriage, which as a result goes through a stepped decline. In the story of *'The Courtship of Inanna and Dumuzi'*:

"The love of Inanna and Dumuzi divides into three sections. In the first section, the young woman, Inanna, still belongs to her family. Her brother guides her... In the second section, the lovers embark. The world of the senses so explodes about them... that they are oblivious of everything but each other... Inanna sings... 'He sweetens me always'... [In] the third section.... The 'always' ends... Change is the human condition... As Dumuzi takes on the role of father and king, he asks Inanna to set him free, for he cannot be her exclusive paramour, making love to her 'fifty times', and also serve in the manifold ways demanded of him as King of Sumer... The courtship has come full circle... The two are together, yet separate." [302]

As can be easily imagined, Inanna was not altogether happy with this development. Given that Inanna's sovereignty is necessary for the success of the 'sacred marriage', Dumuzi's sexual and spiritual separation of himself from the goddess seems rather short-sighted, even in terms of his own (and his people's) self-interest:

"The marriage of the goddess Inanna to the king was of essential importance... it was by this religious ritual that Inanna, Queen of Heaven, would take the earth-king into the 'sweetness of her holy loins', and by her cosmic powers ensure the king's powers of leadership and fertility. Yet Inanna, the Goddess of

*Love, does not offer her favours freely. Not only
must she be properly approached with sweet words
and gifts, but she must be properly and amply
loved."* [303]

What happens when Inanna is not "properly approached with
sweet words and gifts, [and] properly and amply loved" is explained in
another story, *'The Descent of Inanna'*, in which the goddess sinks into
a deep depression. She is described as abandoning her role of Queen
of Heaven and Earth, and descending instead into the Underworld,
where not Inanna but bitter Ereshkigal is queen, a goddess

*"...full of rage, greed, and desperate loneliness. In
many ways, Ereshkigal is the other, neglected side
of Inanna..."* [304]

In the Underworld Inanna has to pass through seven gates, at each
of which she has to surrender vital aspects of her identity as a queen,
a powerful priestess, and even as simply a living woman. As she loses
more and more of herself, Inanna is dying. In desperation Enki, the
Sumerian god of wisdom, tries to save Inanna. He is able to recognise
the dark, shadow side of the feminine as it is now being expressed in
both Inanna and Ereshkigal, and so:

"he creates... creatures [called kurgarra and galatur]
*with the artistic and empathetic talent of being
professional mourners, capable of mirroring the
lonely queen's emotions."* [305]

When Ereshkigal cries out her pain, the newly created kurgarra and
galatur cry with her. Discovering that other beings are expressing
empathy with her, Ereshkigal, Dark Queen of the Underworld, is able
at last to look outwards, beyond herself, and identify with others. As a
result she is able for the first time to agree that one of the dead
(Inanna) may return from the Underworld to the realm of the living.
The kurgarra and galatur sprinkle "food of life" and "water of life" on
Inanna's lifeless body,[306] but to be able to rise from the 'land of no
return' Inanna must be prepared to be replaced by another in
Ereshkigal's realm of the dead, and to this end her homecoming must
be accompanied by "gruesome demons", who will see to it that
another suffers death in Inanna's place.[307]

When Inanna re-enters the surface world of Sumeria, she is
distraught to discover that her husband, Dumuzi, has scarcely cared
about her absence:

*"Yet the King of Sumer goes on with life as if nothing
had happened, as if the Queen of Heaven and Earth*

had not disappeared, as if his own wife were safe and secure... Dumuzi... clings to his new role of kingship and refuses to acknowledge the ties of feeling and love that once bound him to his wife..." [308]

Outraged and distressed, Inanna curses her husband, unleashes Ereshkigal's demons, and topples him from his throne in the land of the living; now it is Dumuzi's turn to die and descend into the harsh Underworld and meet Ereshkigal. He tries to flee but is hunted down by the demons, found cowering in a sheep fold, and killed. [309]

Faced with the loneliness and emotional pain of the dead, Dumuzi at last begins to comprehend the feminine need (in both males and females) to love and be loved. Knowing that he has alienated Inanna, Dumuzi now asks for feminine compassion from another source, his own sister Geshtinanna:

"...the heart of the shepherd king is filled with tears. The ruling king, who once sat so proudly on his noble throne, permitting himself little compassion towards others, now is overwhelmed by his own feelings and vulnerability... Therefore he turns to the feminine wisdom of his younger sister... The compassionate Geshtinanna... The depth of Geshtinanna's grief leads her to offer her life to share her brother's death." [310]

Geshtinanna appeals to Inanna on her brother's behalf. Inanna, having had time to calm down a bit, realises that she has allowed the dark side of herself to destroy the man she has loved, and agrees to a compromise with Geshtinanna:

"...having returned from the underworld charged with her own dark, ruthless powers, the widowed Inanna grieves because she has... destroyed the bridegroom and husband she loves... Inanna... blesses Dumuzi and Geshtinanna with eternal life and death. The loving sister is given her request: she will... share his fate... Half the year the goddess Inanna and the king Dumuzi will be united; and half the year they will be separated. For half the year, Dumuzi will actively rule over Sumer. He will join Inanna on the sacred marriage bed... But then as the seasons change and the harvest passes, Dumuzi will enter a period of inactivity... He will surrender his worldly powers..." [311]

During Dumuzi's half-yearly periods of inactivity, stasis, Inanna is in effect allowing him to once again be his original, male, cold and unchanging self: in north European terms he is the ice and frost of winter. This is how he was before Inanna interacted with him in their marriage, the fiery energy of which (coming from her) positively transformed but also eventually exhausted him, burned him out. After his fertile period of being able to engender growth and promote new life (the result of his interaction with Inanna), he must now be allowed to rest. Inanna had not previously understood this, that her fiery, female energy could eventually prove too much for Dumuzi. Unlike her he simply could not make love 'fifty times' in quick succession. Nor, without her help, could he understand his own and her needs to give and receive emotional and spiritual love. But now both Dumuzi and Inanna have learned to balance their own light and dark sides by allowing room for the appreciation of their differences, their weaknesses and strengths.

Inanna's introduction of the pattern of the seasons to the world, with fertile summer being followed by dormant winter every half year, does not mean that Dumuzi is being periodically abandoned by Inanna. Dumuzi remains bound to Inanna throughout the year and the years:

> "...although Dumuzi seems to be separated from Inanna six months of the year, he is actually wed to her all year, for in the winter as he rests with Ereshkigal, he is staying with the dark, instinctual side of Inanna... not only is he to 'know' the love goddess, he is to 'know' the Goddess of Death as well." [312]

By promoting an ongoing pattern of constant change and development Inanna has, through her introduction of the seasons of summer and winter, allowed Dumuzi to rest and recuperate periodically, in order that she and he may lovingly reunite in sacred marriage on an annual basis. In doing this she has again acted as the fiery, energetic, female initiator, able to positively disrupt Dumuzi's static male power, melting his will so that the two of them may together promote the fertility of the land and people of Sumer. She has done this before, prior to her descent into Ereshkigal's Underworld. But now that she has learned from Ereshkigal that love and the regeneration of life in the middle world require not just the fiery heat and light of the feminine summer, but also death and the icy darkness of the male winter, her catalytic energy is working at a higher, celestial level:

"At this moment at the end of the story, when Inanna acts as divine ordainer, she shifts from active participant in her life story to constellated divinity... By giving Dumuzi eternal life half the year, Inanna changes the cosmic pattern. Love... budding, blooming, and dying – is henceforth guaranteed, by being linked to the seasons, as an annual renewal. The king who enters the underworld once a year will emerge every six months renewed in feminine wisdom and inner strength." [313]

Inanna - *and the North European World View*

It is striking that stories such as *'The Courtship of Inanna and Dumuzi'* and *'The Descent of Inanna'* as summarised above can easily be read as fitting in very well indeed with basic pre-Christian 'north European' cosmology. The early Sumerian pagan worldview expressed through these narratives stresses that continuing existence very much depends upon the interaction of fundamental, contradictory forces (light and darkness, fiery summer heat and winter ice, female creative energy and male stolidity). Equally, the goddesses and gods of Sumeria are every bit as much troubled and imperfect individuals as are the members of the north European pantheon. The simple monotheistic concept of divine perfection is nowhere to be found in either Sumeria or early pagan northern Europe. And in neither culture are the gods perceived as immortal. Death must have her place, in order that new life may be brought about through the changing seasons and life cycles.

Just as the Sumerian and pagan north European basic worldviews seem to be remarkably similar, so too do the characters and life stories of the goddesses Inanna and Freya. Both marry but have troubled relationships with their husbands. Freya's Óðr has disappeared from her life altogether, whilst Inanna's Dumuzi goes cold on her, and must eventually be granted half-yearly breaks from the passionate side of the relationship. Both goddesses take additional lovers. Inanna's are not featured in the two stories reviewed above, but in the *'The Epic of Gilgamesh'* (featuring Inanna in her Babylonian guise of Ishtar):

"When she tries to seduce Gilgamesh, he lists her

> *many other lovers who have all met with bad ends*
> *at her hands."* [314]

Other characteristics which the two goddesses have in common have already been listed at the start of this chapter [both are associated with large felines, birds of prey, the ability to fly, love, sex, fertility, war and combat, death (and what happens thereafter), magical knowledge and power, and female sovereignty].

The patriarchy inherent in both Christian and later pagan Viking societies limited respect for Freya as a dominant, sovereign 'great goddess', and similarly as time passed in Sumeria and Babylon Inanna's status too was eroded by male rulers whose drive for power increasingly came to include a desire to dominate and control women's social roles as much as those of men.

Inevitably the power of men to control women's reproductive rights became a central area of contention. The increasing demotion of goddesses in Sumerian and Babylonian society, and their replacement by male gods, must have tended to undermine the previously perceived need for a King's legitimacy to be established through his 'sacred marriage' with the Queen of Heaven and Earth, as symbolised and re-enacted through sexual intercourse with the High Priestess of Inanna's temple. It is interesting to note that so fundamental is this male drive to control and restrict women's independent sexual and reproductive rights that even in the twenty-first century male attempts to rewrite Inanna's history in forms more acceptable to patriarchal ideology are still being made. Eiko Matsushima for example (writing in 2014) says of Inanna's sacred marriage role that:

> *'Sacred Marriage'... Greek hieros gamos... has now*
> *come to be seen as outdated... Though she [Inanna]*
> *is a goddess of sexual love, she is connected with*
> *extramarital sex. I know of no mythology that*
> *defines her as a mother goddess. Thus the theory of*
> *the fertility pattern cannot explain the raison d'être*
> *of the ritual... marriage in general has much to do*
> *with family, i.e. a fixed relationship between two*
> *persons... but Inanna/Iŝtar stands far from the*
> *purpose of a marriage. Her ceremony was a ritual of*
> *sexual love, but not a marriage in the proper*
> *sense.... many scholars now doubt that a marriage*
> *rite involving human intercourse took place in*
> *Sumer... Is it too fantastic to imagine a love ritual*

> *with a statue of the King, the incarnation of Dumuzi, and a statue of Inanna, finely costumed and decorated with jewellery, playing the roles?"* [315]

This statement appears to completely misunderstand the nature of the sacred marriage. It was not about *"a fixed relationship between two persons"* designed to produce a nuclear family. It was about a King physically, spiritually, and no doubt emotionally acknowledging, through a sacred sexual act, the 'great goddess' of his people and land in order to promote the collective vitality and fertility of both. This did not place Inanna *"far from the purpose of a marriage"*. On the contrary, it facilitated the marriage of people and land. By blessing that collective partnership with the fertility of crops and animals which would allow the King's people to thrive, Inanna also promoted the fertility of individual marriages between women and men.

Eiko Matsushima may wish to believe that the concept of sacred marriage is outdated, but to jump to the conclusion, apparently on the basis of wishful thinking rather than any actual evidence, that no physical sexual intercourse ever took place between King and High Priestess, and that instead what was being referred to as 'sacred marriage' was actually some kind of love/fertility ritual being played out between "finely costumed" statues, is surely absurd. Such polite play-acting between puppets would most likely have been perceived as ineffectual compared to real sexual intercourse between the goddess Inanna (through her High Priestess) and her earthly King.

Whilst the idea of sacred marriage being relegated to the realms of pantomime puppet statues may be too extreme, we can still speculate that the importance of such beliefs must nevertheless have declined alongside the downgrading of goddesses in later Sumerian and Babylonian society, evidenced in particular by the replacement of goddesses by male gods during the reign of King Hammurabi of Babylon (1792-1750 BCE)[316]. However this did not lead to the immediate abandonment of Inanna as Queen of Heaven and Earth. In fact a trend for the recognition and veneration of Inanna to expand through rising cultures in a general north westerly direction was already beginning. From Sumerian cities such as Lagash near the Persian Gulf (modern day south-eastern Iraq), the reverence of Inanna had spread to Babylonia (central Iraq), where she was known as Ishtar, and from there subsequently also to the rising Assyrian Empire, which came to occupy much of modern day Iraq, Syria, south-eastern Turkey, Lebanon, Israel, Jordan, and Egypt, though Ishtar was popular mainly in the northern parts of that empire.

"Inanna continued as a powerful and popular goddess until the decline of the prestige of female deities during the reign of Hammurabi which... coincides with women's loss of status and rights in society... In Sumerian culture women were regarded as equals... however... under the reign of... King Hammurabi of Babylon (1792-1750 BCE) goddesses were increasingly replaced by gods. Inanna kept her position and prestige through her adoption by the Assyrian empire as Ishtar, goddess of war and sex..." [317]

The Assyrian Empire included the great trading land of Phoenicia (roughly modern-day Lebanon, on the eastern most coast of the Mediterranean), and here the goddess Astarte was worshipped.

Astarte – *Goddess of the Phoenicians*

Just as Ishtar was very closely associated with Inanna, so Astarte was associated with Ishtar, with whom she had many characteristics in common. She was known quite widely, for variants of the name "Astarte" can be found in the Phoenician, Hebrew, Egyptian and even the Etruscan language. [318] Etruscan was a pre-Roman language used in northern Italy, and is thought to be one of the sources of the symbols or letters used in the Elder Germanic runic futhark (see chapter 7). It would seem logical to assume that if knowledge of Etruscan runes or letters spread north of the Alps into areas inhabited by Germanic tribes, then knowledge of deities such as Astarte might also have spread that far, though perhaps (as elsewhere) subject to name changes in local languages. Knowledge of Astarte herself certainly spread out from the Middle East into central Mediterranean areas and beyond, carried westwards by Phoenician traders from cities such as Tyre, Sidon and Beirut.

" *'Athart* [Phoenician for Astarte] *was always connected with the evening star,* [and] *...with Ishtar, her apparent female counterpart in Mesopotamia...* [319] *the goddess's primary character involves pugnacity, manifest in the hunt and in battle... This... comports closely with Ishtar's title as 'lady of battle and war'.* [320]
"'Ashtartu is a warrior'... 'Ashtartu is power'... She is

also famous as one of the West Semitic war-
goddesses in New Kingdom Egypt. She is called
'furious and tempestuous'...[321]
"...the lioness [is]... the emblem of... the warrior
goddess, Astarte." [322]

Astarte's associations with the evening star (Venus) and lions both link her to Inanna and Ishtar. The Phoenicians were so successful in their trading ventures, and so devoted to Astarte (or 'Athart), that she became even more popular in the first millennium BCE than she had been in the second millennium BCE. Johanna H. Stuckey, University Professor Emerita, York University, says of Astarte:

> *"Devotion to Astarte was prolonged by the*
> *Phoenicians... From cities such as Byblos, Tyre, and*
> *Sidon, they set forth by sea on long trading*
> *expeditions, and, venturing far into the western*
> *Mediterranean, they even reached Cornwall in*
> *England. Wherever they went, they established*
> *trading posts and founded colonies... Of course they*
> *took their deities with them. Hence, Astarte became*
> *much more important in the first millennium BCE*
> *than she had been in the second millennium BCE. In*
> *Cyprus, where the Phoenicians arrived in the ninth*
> *century BCE, they built temples to Astarte, and it*
> *was in Cyprus that she was first identified with*
> *Greek Aphrodite."* [323]

Astarte as Greek Aphrodite will be looked at later in this chapter. Her transformation into Aphrodite when taken west by the Phoenicians to Cyprus reminds us that, like Inanna/Ishtar and Freya, Astarte's qualities of *"pugnacity, manifest in the hunt and in battle"* (see above) were very much combined with another role as *"A deity of fertility and sexuality".*[324] Furthermore, again like Inanna/Ishtar and Freya, Astarte also had protective qualities and magical skills. In particular:

> *"Astarte is regarded as a curative goddess and*
> *invoked in an incantation for neutralisation of*
> *poisons in so-called magical spells. It is highly*
> *plausible that the supposedly miraculous healing of*
> *Amenhotep III from severe health problems after he*
> *received the cult figure of Ishtar (Mesopotamian*
> *Astarte) from the ruler of Mitanni influenced the*
> *Egyptians and consequently made them trust and*

> *count on Astarte for their own prosperity, health*
> *and stability."* [325]

Finally in terms of qualities which Astarte shares with Inanna, Ishtar, and Freya, it is worth noting that in New Kingdom Egypt, amongst other epithets, she was known by the appellation "Mistress of all the Gods"[326], which is undoubtedly reminiscent of the 'great goddess' concept (Queen of Heaven and Earth) also applied to her predecessors.

Astarte - *and Patriarchal Monotheism*

In the first millennium BCE Middle Eastern and Mediterranean cults of Astarte may have been strengthening and growing significantly in both popularity and range compared to the previous millennium, but in doing so they came to be confronted by a new and powerful enemy. To a degree the threat came from an old source: patriarchy - but this time the intolerance and absolutism of patriarchy was reaching a new extreme in the unyielding and inflexible form of monotheism.

This happened as, after the 9th century BCE, the strong Phoenician cult of Astarte expanded south into Israel. There, people with a polytheistic background came up against Yahwism, the monotheistic cult of the god Yahweh, who was held by his followers to encompass all aspects of divine power within himself. Archaeological evidence suggests that, just as the Christian authorities more than a thousand years later incorporated the demoted Irish goddess Brigid into their church as a saint, so the worshippers of Yahweh at first found it necessary to attempt to assimilate Astarte, but in this case eventually discovered the goddess of fertility and the One God of everything to be irreconcilable. During the eighth and seventh centuries BCE:

> *"Judean Pillar Figurines (JPFs)...* [were] *religious*
> *archaeological artefacts unique to Iron Age Judah...*
> *likely... related to the cult of the 'Queen of Heaven',*
> *a particular kind of Astarte or Ishtar cult introduced*
> *in the latter half of the Judahite kingdom...* [327]
> *Probably such figurines were meant to make it*
> *easier for people with a polytheistic background to*
> *accept Yahwism, and to show a monotheistic god*
> *who encompassed all aspects of divine power...*
> *however... the transcendent nature of Yahweh came*

*to be no longer sufficiently shown by a 're-reading'
of previous cult elements. Thus, the policy for
monotheistic Yahwism was altered to exclude all the
polytheistic elements..."* [328]

The relegation of feminine power to a position of subservience
within monotheistic, patriarchal Yahwism is also evidenced by changes
in depictions of the 'Tree of Life' discovered in the same geographic
area, covering the period 1200 BCE to about 750 BCE:

*"A similar phenomenon can also be observed in the
'tree of life' iconography... a naked woman or a
'tree of life' was often engraved between ibexes as
an expression of a fertility goddess... but after Iron
Age I [1200-1000 BCE],* the female figure
completely disappeared. During Iron Age IIA [1000-
750(?) BCE], the 'tree of life' also faded away, and
only ibexes are left... the 'tree of life' on the Iron Age
III-C seals... is not related to a goddess but rather to
a male god... understood to parallel the situation in
which the concept of fertility was abstracted and
absorbed into Yahweh's attributes...."* [329]

It seems likely that the patriarchal followers of Yahweh found the
gender challenges emanating from the Queen of Heaven and Earth to
be simply too destabilising of their own belief system to be tolerated
even as a controlled and managed sub-component of would be all-
embracing monotheism. One of the reasons for this, apart from the
ever-present irreconcilability of patriarchy and independent female
power, might have been the unacceptability of another aspect of
Astarte's cult: gender fluidity and divine hermaphroditism.

During the first millennium BCE the followers of Astarte (in her
various local guises) were definitely swimming against the patriarchal
tide, and in more ways than one. Firstly, the trend in the Middle East
and eastern Mediterranean at the time was for goddesses to be
downgraded or abandoned in favour of male deities:

"Most ancient Near Eastern kingdoms worshipped

---

* *"The Iron Age is divided into two subsections, Iron I and Iron II. Iron I (1200-
1000) illustrates both continuity and discontinuity with the previous Late
Bronze Age. There is no definitive cultural break... Iron II (1000-550)
witnessed the rise of the states of Judah and Israel in the tenth-ninth
century."* [https://www.bu.edu/anep/Ir.html]

> patron gods. Astarte and Asherah of Tyre, and
> Ishtar of Nineveh and Arbela... are notable
> exceptions... in general, coastal urban centres on
> the islands of Cyprus, Rhodes, and Crete adopt a
> goddess as their patron deity. Phoenician worship of
> the goddess Astarte as a city patron follows the
> Ishtar tradition..." [330]

Secondly, the success of the Astarte cult was not simply a passive anomaly, which might have been tolerable to surrounding patriarchal cultures, but an active challenge and ideological defiance of male hegemony. Astarte-following male rulers were perceived as promoting the subversion of an otherwise presumed masculine exclusive right to rule by publicly submitting to the goddess through becoming a priest in her service:

> "While horned crowns are generally worn by male
> deities... Astarte placed upon her own head a bull's
> head as an emblem of kingship..." [331]

> "The 9th century BCE King Ithobaal of Tyre served as
> 'priest of Astarte' (887 BCE)... Sidon had its own
> temple to Astarte... Inscriptions on late 6th century
> and early 5th century BCE sarcophagi... identify
> royalty as priests and priestess of Astarte." [332]

Thirdly the clear definition of gender roles required by patriarchal ideology was subverted by the teachings of Astarte's followers, who at times appeared to openly tolerate or even actively promote homosexuality and forms of gender inversion from cross-dressing to hermaphroditism. In this too Astarte seems to have been a true heir of Inanna/Ishtar:

> "Hermaphrodite figures were not uncommon...
> Ishtar... is often said to 'turn a man into a woman
> and a woman into a man'. The gender of... priests
> who served Ishtar, is also described ambiguously,
> and it is reported that they had sexual intercourse
> with men, and that there was a ritual in which they
> wore women's clothes; this again suggests the dual
> character of Ishtar... Rivkah Harris thus argued that
> he/she was a being who broke down binary
> oppositions... There are also some archaeological
> artefacts that depict Astarte as an hermaphrodite...
> examples that clearly show female breasts and a
> beard... Almost no other goddess except for Ishtar,

*Astarte, and the 'Queen of Heaven' can reflect such
duality."* [333]

The association of fertility cults with greater tolerance of
homosexuality and the acceptance of greater fluidity and variance in
gender roles, alongside the rejection of such tolerance by more
patriarchal cults, was to be witnessed again a thousand years later in
pre-Christian Anglo-Saxon England, with the Vanir-following English
tribes proving to be more tolerant of such practices than both the
Æsir-worshipping Scandinavian pagans and later English Christians.
This is discussed further in chapter 12 "Loki and Dissent".

Isis – a True Egyptian?

Isis is another goddess associated with birds of prey, like Inanna,
(to be specific: falcons, just like Freya), and felines (again just like
Inanna and Freya). However, the cult of Isis spread far and wide from
Egypt, and inevitably came to be seen differently in different lands:

*"In Egypt the cat was sacred to Bastet but in the Isis
cult outside Egypt it was considered a sacred animal
of Isis... the Greeks and Romans assumed that the cat
symbolism belonged to Isis. They also associated the
cat with the moon, unlike the Egyptians who viewed
it as a solar animal. As they saw Isis as a moon
goddess this was a further link with the cat."* [334]

The common association with falcons and cats does not of course
in itself establish any direct link between Isis and Inanna or Freya. In
the case of the Queen of Heaven and Earth in her various
manifestations, as in that of Freya, being able to grow wings and take
on the form of a bird of prey seems to have mainly been about
acquiring an ability to fly, as and when circumstances demanded.
However in the case of Isis the uses that wings may be put to seem to
be rather more vital and varied:

*"As deities were commonly perceived to reside in the
sky, contact could be established with them through
flight. Birds flew between earth and sky, and so
were ideal messengers and symbols... The falcon is
the most frequently depicted bird throughout
Egyptian history... the kestrel is a type of falcon... in
particular associated with Isis..."* [335]

"The protective aspects of wings suggest a feminine

force... Birds use their wings to shelter their young...
Goddesses in both human and cobra form often
have wings to emphasise their protective aspects...
Hovering was also seen as a protective action...
Wings and feathers were believed to create air to
allow the deceased to breathe again... Isis hovers
over the mummy of Osiris in the form of a kestrel or
falcon." [336]

There is no evidence that either Inanna or Freya (or Astarte) took on avian form in order to hover and create air through the beating of their wings to "allow the deceased to breathe again".

Isis also differs from Inanna/Astarte/Freya in other important ways. In particular Isis was considered to be the divine mother and protector of the ruling pharaoh, not the earthly male ruler's wife in the manner of Inanna and Dumuzi. She did not embody a sacred marriage between the female earth and a male king. She was not primarily concerned with the fertility of land and people, but did have a more detailed and extensive role to play in matters of life after death:

"Despite some superficial overlapping associations
(falcons and cats), Isis is an independent goddess,
unrelated to the Inanna/Ishtar/Aphrodite lineage.
Whilst the latter were heavily linked to love, sex,
and fertility, but not motherhood, Isis stands out in
her role as divine mother: "Isis... was considered the
divine mother of the pharaoh." [337]

"Isis was a major goddess in ancient Egyptian religion
whose worship spread throughout the Greco-Roman
world. Isis was first mentioned in the Old Kingdom
(c. 2686–2181 BCE) as one of the main characters of
the Osiris myth, in which she resurrects her slain
husband, the divine king Osiris, and produces and
protects his heir, Horus. She was believed to help
the dead enter the afterlife as she had helped Osiris,
and she was considered the divine mother of the
pharaoh, who was likened to Horus." [338]

The conclusion must be then that despite some superficially similar symbolism, Isis was an ancient and independent Egyptian goddess who was not yet another local incarnation of Inanna. Like Inanna her cult did spread out far and wide beyond its original homeland, and in both cases this partly reflected adoption and incorporation by Greek and (later) Roman cultures (see the section on Aphrodite in this chapter below), but nevertheless Isis always had been, and remained, an independent, original, authentically Egyptian goddess in her own right.

> "It is fair to ask whether Isis was originally an Egyptian goddess or one... from Libya or the Near East. There does not seem to be any evidence to support this... so we can assume that Isis is a true Egyptian." [339]

> "The Greeks certainly changed, or reinterpreted, Isis to align her with their own needs and perceptions... It was the Hellenised Isis not the Egyptian Isis who went on to conquer the Mediterranean world and compete with Christianity." [340]

It is true that the cult of Astarte did have a presence in Egypt concomitant with that of Isis, her arrival there having been facilitated by the incorporation of Egypt into the Assyrian Empire (circa 677-663 BCE[341]), but of course Isis had been worshipped in Egypt for at least two thousand years before that event. It seems that despite the rise of patriarchy in the second and particularly the first millennium BCE, the cultural roots of both Isis and Inanna (in her many subsequent incarnations) were so ancient and deeply rooted that the reverence of both 'great goddesses' was initially able not just to survive the patriarchal ideological advance, but actually to expand to new lands, in both cases in western and northern directions across the Mediterranean.

Aphrodite – *the Greek Stories*

Before looking at the question of how the Greeks interpreted the qualities of the 'great goddess' Inanna/Ishtar/Astarte as expressed in Aphrodite, it is worth briefly summarising some of the main stories told about her in Greece, in order to see her better in her new context. The first thing to be said about the Aphrodite myths that have come down to us, is that they do not all tell the same story, and can contradict each other, even about who she (and her family) is:

> "Hesiod says Aphrodite arose from the foam that gathered around the genitals of Uranus. They just happened to be floating in the sea - after his son Cronus castrated his father. The poet known as

Homer calls Aphrodite the daughter of Zeus and Dione [an early Mother Earth figure]. She is also described as the daughter of Oceanus and Tethys (both Titans). If Aphrodite is the cast-offspring of Uranus, she is of the same generation as Zeus' parents. If she is the daughter of the Titans, she is Zeus' cousin. Aphrodite was called Venus by the Romans - as in the famous Venus de Milo statue."[342]

Aphrodite possessed a magical girdle which was so beautiful that when worn its splendour was also reflected in the face of the wearer, enabling them to attract and enchant anyone they desired. It is tempting to speculate that this legend might even be the original source of Freya's Brisingamen story (perhaps via Astarte's Etruscan route as mentioned above). As explained in chapter 9, the term 'amen' is most often translated as 'necklace' but could also mean 'girdle'. The Brising-amen too was of course said to possess such unearthly beauty that even the goddess Freya found it irresistible. A magical ability to make its wearer equally irresistible might be a more convincing account of its charm than merely calling it 'golden'.

"Aphrodite's girdle was as beautiful as its wearer, and it was said to embody the unrelenting force of love itself. The gods often asked Aphrodite to borrow her girdle, or asked her to use it to inspire love in the merest of mortals they took their fancy to, and Aphrodite rarely refused them. The girdle made mortals frail to the charms of the gods, and simply seeing Aphrodite wearing it was often enough to ensnare immortal hearts as well. All except Zeus's that is. He never slept with the goddess of love, but chose to live in constant temptation instead." [343]

It comes as no surprise to learn that Aphrodite, as the Greek goddess of love and beauty, had an interesting and varied love life. In the story of her marriage Zeus featured as her father rather than as the only male god somehow just about able to resist the temptations offered by the goddess in her wondrous girdle. As her father, Zeus took it upon himself to find his daughter a husband (this was patriarchal Greece after all), and arranged her betrothal to Hephaestus, the blacksmith god, who was said to be both ugly and lame, though good with fire, volcanoes, and metal-working:

"but laughter-loving Aphrodite found Hephaestus

> *repugnant… It was Ares, the formidable god of war,*
> *who caused her to cuckold poor Hephaestus…*
> *'…they lay together in the house of Hephaestus*
> *secretly; and Ares gave her many gifts, and shamed*
> *the bed of the lord Hephaestus.'"* [344]

Hephaestus got to hear about Aphrodite's disloyalty, and determined to publicly humiliate her in the presence of every available god and goddess. To do this he used his supreme metalworking skills to make a net, the threads of which were so fine that they were invisible, yet so strong as to be unbreakable. This net he suspended above his marital bed. That night whilst Ares and his wife were preoccupied making love with one another, Hephaestus crept silently back into his bedroom and slipped the knots holding up the net. The metallic mesh entangled Aphrodite and Ares inextricably together; there was no escape.

> *"When the sun rose again, Hephaestus… called to his*
> *father [in-law], Zeus, to bring all the gods and*
> *goddesses… [to] look upon his wife's shame and*
> *that of Ares, now bound hopelessly together. All the*
> *gods came from Mount Olympus and made the land*
> *tremble with their laughter at the guilty pair. But*
> *the goddesses abstained, either out of propriety or*
> *disgust… Hephaestus told Zeus that he wanted him*
> *to return the betrothal gifts… but Zeus said he*
> *would pay nothing to a fool who would make public*
> *his wife's infidelity."* [345]

In the end Hephaestus let the lovers go free, for he was still in love with Aphrodite and could not bear the thought of harming her. Ares fled back to his homeland of Thrace, whilst Aphrodite did the same, in her case going back to Cyprus, at least for a while. However in the longer term her public shaming did nothing to restrict Aphrodite's sexual adventures. In fact she went on to have four children by Ares, handing each baby after their birth to her cuckolded husband Hephaestus to hold. The children were named Phobos ('fear'), Deimos ('terror'), Harmonia, and Eros (the male god of love and sex – in other myths Aphrodite has Eros by either Zeus or Hermes the messenger god, but never by husband Hephaestus).

Aphrodite also had affairs with both Poseidon, the god of the sea, and Hermes, and bore three more children to them, including double-gendered Hermaphroditus (to Hermes). In every case Hephaestus knew all about it, but always ultimately forgave Aphrodite because, despite her disregard of him, he always remained in love with his wife. Though a goddess who possessed a magical girdle that made her irresistibly attractive, Aphrodite could still betray a certain lack of self-confidence. This was demonstrated in what must surely be the most famous story involving her: that of the Trojan War, the origin of which was said to have much to do with Aphrodite's need to be recognised as the most beautiful of all the goddesses.

All of the gods - except Eris, the goddess of discord - had been invited to a wedding. Eris was not invited owing to her habit of instigating strife and conflict. This proved not to be a wise move however, for in revenge Eris dropped a golden 'Apple of Discord' into the party. The golden apple was inscribed with the words "To the Fairest". The goddesses Hera (goddess of marriage, and wife of Zeus), Athena (another daughter of Zeus, and powerful goddess of virginity), and Aphrodite (not known for virginity), disagreed very loudly as to who was the fairest. The three goddesses asked Zeus to judge between them, but he was reluctant to do so, and instead appointed a shepherd, who turned out to really be Paris, Prince of Troy. The goddesses offered Paris various bribes, but he eventually picked Aphrodite, whose bribe had been to promise him the most beautiful woman in the world: Helen, wife of Menelaus, King of Sparta. Helen ran off with Paris, as promised, but at the price of 10 years of war between the Greek states and Troy.

These stories give us a good idea of how the Greeks saw Aphrodite. The emphasis is very much on the goddess as a deity of love and sexual prowess, rather than as also a promoter of skills in combat and warfare as had been the case with Inanna/Ishtar and Astarte. However these military attributes were not altogether forgotten:

> "The connection between Astarte-Ishtar and Aphrodite goes even further. Aside from sharing the same 'Heavenly' name, both goddesses were worshipped with incense altars and sacrifices of doves, something that was unique to Aphrodite in ancient Greek religion. Astarte-Ishtar was a warrior goddess too, and Aphrodite, when depicted wearing armour, was also believed to bestow victory on those she favoured." [346]

Nevertheless the Greeks clearly highlighted Aphrodite's connections with matters of love, beauty, and sex over military matters. Some modern-day researchers have even named Aphrodite as a goddess of prostitutes, explaining that this is yet another manifestation of the goddess as a Greek version of Inanna/Ishtar/Astarte:

> "The final similarity... is their part in prostitution. Astarte-Ishtar was the goddess of the 'Hetaerae', whom historians today usually define as 'companions' or 'courtesans'... distinguished from the more mundane 'Pornai' by the fact that the Hetaerae were well educated and often reserved their service for a select and smaller group of clients, with whom they had longer term relationships. Some scholars believe that Aphrodite was also a patroness of the Hetaerae, further... evidence of a direct connection between her and the Phoenician Astarte-Ishtar." [347]

Aphrodite – *Inanna Disempowered?*

As already noted above, "*in Cyprus, where the Phoenicians arrived in the ninth century BCE, they built temples to Astarte, and it was in Cyprus that she was first identified with Greek Aphrodite.*"[348] The Greeks may have adopted Phoenician Astarte (and through her Inanna/Ishtar) as their own in the form of Aphrodite, but female power and sovereignty was always a difficult issue for patriarchal Greek culture, and there is no doubt that in needing to understand Aphrodite in their own terms Greek men found it easier to accept some of Astarte's qualities than they did others. The qualities they could readily accept were to do with Aphrodite's functioning as a goddess of female beauty, love, and (more controversially for some Greeks) sexuality.

> "The idea that Aphrodite was originally an Eastern goddess appropriated by the ancient Greeks at the onset of their great cultural revolutions of the Archaic Period (ca. 8th century BCE) is one that has been corroborated by modern and ancient historians alike... most scholars today believe that ancient Greek worship of her is most closely tied to the ancient Phoenician goddess of love Ishtar-Astarte..." [349]

> "Plato expressed disgust at the idea that his gods

> *would debase themselves in the adulterous,*
> *murderous, and mischievous ways they were said to*
> *have in their myths. However... the rest of the*
> *populace didn't seem to have much of a*
> *problem...* "[350]

It seems that although male patriarchal thinkers such as Plato were disgusted by Aphrodite, the common people felt themselves able to identify more easily with the goddess. Nevertheless the Greek male elite were never going to give up their masculine absolutist ideological hegemony that easily. They might not have been able to dissuade the mass of the population from their empathy with Aphrodite, but they could still use their own storytelling to limit the damage to patriarchy as best they could:

> *"No extreme mental exertion need be employed to*
> *see the hand of the ancient Greek patriarchy in*
> *giving Aphrodite a father in the form of Zeus..."* [351]

Zeus, rather like 'All-father' Odin, embodies pure male 'head of the family' authority and power. In making Zeus the father of Aphrodite it seems likely that Greek patriarchy was not only attempting to manage her perceived chaotic wildness through a restatement of paternal power, but also seeking to overcome her recognised foreignness by incorporating her into the Greek family model:

> *"Without this parentage Aphrodite appears unwieldy,*
> *an elemental force who represents an image of*
> *'woman' that didn't fit with the ancient Greek idea*
> *of what a daughter, wife, and mother should be...*
>
> *"This 'foreignness' was not just a patriarchal*
> *projection however. The ancient Greeks often*
> *referred to Aphrodite... as a 'foreign' deity that was*
> *brought into Greek culture at an 'earlier date'. The*
> *historian Herodotus... makes this explicit:*
>
>> *'...they came on their way to the city*
>> *of Ascalon in Syria... a few... plundered the*
>> *temple of Heavenly Aphrodite. This*
>> *temple... is the oldest of all the temples of*
>> *the goddess, for the temple in Cyprus was*
>> *founded from it... and the temple on*
>> *Cythera was founded by Phoenicians*
>> *from... Syria'.* " [352]

This view of Aphrodite as foreign in origin is key to understanding the Greek male elite's view of her as disreputable, dangerous, and even dishonourable. Essentially they saw her as something 'other', from outside, an 'un-Greek' bad influence that would be best minimised if at all possible. The elite, including Plato and his successors, were unable to dismiss Aphrodite altogether, but they were able to emphasise through storytelling and myth making what they saw as her more disreputable functions (the more superficial aspects of sexual relationships) at the expense of those facets of her personality which they might have had no option but to recognise as noble in their own terms: associations with warfare and military skills.

The concept of Aphrodite as an armoured goddess of victory came to be very much de-emphasised, whilst tales of her repeated humiliation of the cuckolded male god Hephaestus proved much more acceptable. It seems likely that the loss of the war goddess role is connected to Aphrodite's 'foreign' and 'liberated' nature. As a male dominated culture the Greeks had a male god of war and frenzy: Ares, who had probably been around well before Astarte/Aphrodite's incorporation into the Greek pantheon. Given the Greek patriarchal way of looking at the worlds, it is hardly surprising that when it came to recounting the story of the repeated cuckolding of Hephaestus, it was Ares who was chosen as the epitome of the virile alpha male. It was he who would put the sexually independent Aphrodite back in her correct place by making her pregnant, and thereby implicitly emotionally and practically dependent on male authority. Hephaestus on the other hand was mocked by the storytellers for his 'unmanly' quality of putting love first, over and above his personal male sovereignty, whilst Ares was admired for his physical, non-romantic qualities, both sexual and military.

The Greeks did acknowledge one goddess as having a specific warfare-related skill: Athena – goddess of wisdom, for she was thought able to sometimes advise on battle strategy and tactics. And the goddess Nike was allowed to be seen running around after a battle awarding victory garlands to heroic males, but Athena and Nike's roles were strictly limited to indirect, non-combat-role assistance, and the praising of victorious male warriors. Ancient Greece remained the patriarchal culture *par excellence*, much more so than some neighbouring cultures (e.g. 'Amazon' nomadic tribes with female horse-riding warriors).[353] However the Queen of Heaven and Earth's multiple functions were never entirely forgotten even in her personification as Aphrodite – hence the continuing memory of her as an armour-wearing goddess of victory, a militant stance with which Inanna, Ishtar, Astarte, and Freya herself could all also associate themselves.

In matters of love and sexuality too, Aphrodite's appetites were much deeper, complex, and fundamental than Plato and his followers were ever capable of understanding. They condemned the goddess for her allegedly superficial, fun-loving, mischievous, and adulterous behaviour, but could not comprehend that there was a lot more to it than that. Goddesses of love are not usually well known for being monogamous, nor for limiting their interests in matters of divine and human sexuality to the purely heterosexual, or for limiting their understanding of love and gender to just the simple dualist wife-husband relationship. Some important Greek opinion-formers found the complexity of Aphrodite's sexual roles to be unacceptable as any kind of a model for moral human behaviour, but as the true heiress of Inanna and Astarte it was never going to be possible for the Greeks to completely avoid facing up to more complicated issues of sexuality and gender as personified in Aphrodite:

> "...[Aphrodite's] *night with Hermes produced the double-sexed child Hermaphroditus... Aphrodite's prior incarnation, Ishtar-Astarte, was actually a dual goddess-god... Aphrodite inspires men, women, and beasts to 'obey their higher nature', so to her belong the genitalia of all... whilst she was most certainly a goddess whose duty pertained very much to women, the affairs of the heart are undiscerning of gender. Love is not a duty or a role; it is the 'higher nature' that is the driving force behind the cosmos, whether for procreation or not... Aphrodite would appear to be the catalyst of all life in the universe."* [354]

The appreciation of Aphrodite as a 'great goddess' not just of sexuality and gender, but of the 'higher nature' of love itself, making her "the catalyst of all life in the universe", once again confirms the essential, fundamental nature of this goddess (whether known as Inanna or by subsequent names) as being that of primal female energy itself. She represents the elemental feminine energy of fire, which must interact with the male strength of solid ice to produce fertile reality and life generating flowing water, which in its ever-changing form is the negation of the void, of empty oblivion.

Unfortunately even great thinkers such as the Greek philosopher Plato and his successors could allow themselves to be wilfully blinded to the essential dialectical and sexual nature of reality in all its necessary complexity, simply as a result of their desire to keep things comprehensible, orderly, manageable, controllable, and ultimately subject to their own male drive for personal power. This is discussed further in chapter 11 "Hekate – Materialism and Idealism".

Freya – *Inanna of the North?*

On the face of it Freya's characteristics (as discussed in chapter 9) do appear to be remarkably similar to those of Inanna and inheritors of Inanna's mantel such as Ishtar, Astarte, and Aphrodite. In fact if anything Freya could be said to be closer to Inanna than Aphrodite, or at least closer than the Greek male elite's conception of Aphrodite. The question of a possible Middle Eastern origin for Freya has been considered by a range of commentators for at least a century, without any firm, definitive conclusion becoming widely accepted one way or the other.

Britt-Mari Näsström[355] briefly reviews the work of some earlier researchers who have looked at Freya's possible Middle Eastern connections, and is generally dismissive of that "oriental hypothesis", whether related to Cybele, Isis, or Inanna (the three goddesses she compares Freya to). She admits that the Phrygian[†] Cybele[‡] appears superficially similar, in that she too was a fertility goddess who rode in a chariot drawn by large cats (lions, in Cybele's case), but then goes on to say that:

[†] "Phrygia... was a kingdom in the west central part of Anatolia, in what is now Asian Turkey... Stories of the heroic age of Greek mythology tell of several legendary Phrygian kings:
- Gordias, whose Gordian Knot would later be cut by Alexander the Great
- Midas, who turned whatever he touched to gold
- Mygdon, who warred with the Amazons"
  [https://en.wikipedia.org/wiki/Phrygia]

[‡] "Cybele... is Phrygia's only known goddess, and was probably its state deity. Her Phrygian cult was adopted and adapted by Greek colonists of Asia Minor and spread to mainland Greece and its more distant western colonies around the 6th century BC. ...her most celebrated Greek rites and processions show her as an essentially foreign, exotic mystery-goddess who arrives in a lion-drawn chariot to the accompaniment of wild music, wine, and a disorderly, ecstatic following."
  [https://en.wikipedia.org/wiki/Cybele]

> *"This is in point of fact the only resemblance between*
> *these two goddesses; but references to an affinity*
> *between Freyja and Cybele still appear in virtually*
> *every work about the old Norse religion. These*
> *"parallels" are due to sheer ignorance about the*
> *characteristics of Cybele."* [356]

Näsström states that Cybele rose to prominence when she was successfully invoked by the Roman people to save them from invasion by Hannibal in the second Punic War, after which *"her cult increased in popularity and was disseminated to the provinces, where remains of her sanctuaries have been found in both Gaul and Germany".* [357] This actually sounds like quite good evidence that Cybele could indeed have become known to Germanic tribes as a protective goddess of both fertility and war. Näsström also considers the story of Óðr's absence, and explains that the tale of the end of Attis, Cybele's husband, is quite different. In fact she says that there are a number of different versions in the myths, but in all cases Cybele is mourning her husband's death, not searching for him as Freya does for Óðr.

> *"In other myths Attis kills himself in different ways,*
> *usually by castrating himself, an action ritually*
> *repeated by his priests during the ceremonies of the*
> *Vernal Equinox... this wake ends in exhilaration, and*
> *the following day is called Hilaria.*§*"* [358]

Näsström then goes on to consider possible parallels with Isis and Inanna, but again largely restricts her analysis to contrasting Freya's search for Óðr with these two goddesses' respective involvement with the dead, concluding that there is no significant link between the three.

Commentators such as Näsström then generally reject any idea that Freya might be considered the Inanna of northern Europe, mainly on the basis that they do not see sufficient similarity in the associated myths. However it can be argued firstly that there is actually more correspondence between the stories of the two goddesses, even at a superficial level, than is being admitted to by Näsström and others, and secondly that a rationale can be constructed showing that superficial readings of the myths in any case miss the point; it is the fundamental identity of the most basic nature of these two goddesses

---

§ *Hilaria*: joyful or merry day [Latin: *hilaris* - cheerful, merry, gay, joyful, genial, glad (google translate)]

that raises the possibility of commonality.

After all, despite being arguably rather weak compared to those of Freya, Aphrodite's links to Inanna are apparently acceptable to academia, because they are evidenced through archaeology and ancient written sources. Aphrodite, as perceived by patriarchal Greeks, inherits Inanna's major aspects as a goddess of love and sex, and gains a new (male-given?) emphasis on beauty, but she largely loses Inanna's associations with combat, war, and political power. Aphrodite's magical abilities too seem to be restricted to the area of sexual enchantment, whilst Inanna's[**] and Freya's are rather broader. Aphrodite's fertility associations are largely limited to the narrow concerns of individuals (personal love and sex), whereas Inanna's connections with fertility are much broader, concerning not just individuals but Mother Nature and life generally, including human community, animal, agricultural, and cosmic regeneration cycles, in turn leading into issues of queen/kingship and political power.

Furthermore it is not just large cats and birds of prey that Inanna and Freya have in common. It is the combination of combat and warlike associations with issues including what happens to the dead, love, sex, fertility, and magic, all in a single powerful goddess, that make Inanna and Freya so alike. And those are just the superficial similarities.

But before concluding by summarising the deeper, more fundamental, and even cosmological nature of the two goddesses, it is also worth briefly reviewing more practical issues which might or might not allow for even indirect knowledge of Inanna to extend to northern Europe.

- **Geographical distance** - does not seem to be an obstacle. Even in ancient times, veneration of Inanna/Astarte expanded long distances westwards from Sumeria into the western and central Mediterranean areas. Knowledge of Astarte was said to have reached Etruria in northern Italy, from where some of the Elder Germanic runic symbols are believed to have crossed the Alps northwards, suggesting that this would also be possible for mythological tales of deities. Similarly it is known that popularity of the originally Phrygian goddess Cybele extended westwards from Asia

---

[**] *"In some myths she (Inanna) is the daughter of Enki, the god of wisdom, fresh water, and magic"* [https://www.ancient.eu/Inanna/]

Minor to Rome, and subsequently northwards into Germany.

- **Cultural and language barriers** - do not appear to be an obstacle. Even in ancient times the imperatives of power, trade, and war, brought contacts, both peaceful and violent, between peoples of widely differing cultures and languages. In addition to the well evidenced journeying of Inanna-like goddesses from Sumeria westwards to Syria, Phoenicia, and Cyprus, and from there to Greece and Rome (in the forms of Astarte, Aphrodite, and Venus), the Romans were well known both for taking their homeland deities with them to the ends of the then known earth, and for then encouraging local communities to adopt those deities, sometimes with local variations in name and characteristics. The shrine to Minerva in Chester, England, stands as a good witness of this process.

Given then that there do not seem to be any insuperable practical obstacles to the popularity of an Inanna-like goddess travelling thousands of miles across the centuries, there still remains the question of whether this did actually happen, or whether the long list of similarities between Freya and Inanna could have come about independently. It seems logical that similar social conditions and levels of cultural and economic development might lead to analogous cosmological speculation and similarities in pantheons. However, though this may well also be a factor, the fact remains that there are strong hints in northern mythology of a direct awareness of Mediterranean goddess stories. Freya's necklace or girdle strongly echoes Aphrodite's magical golden girdle, and Idun's golden apples of immortality surely have too much in common with those found in the Greek Garden of the Hesperides[359] to be mere coincidence.

It does seem possible that stories of the Inanna-successor goddesses Astarte and Aphrodite could well have reached Germanic tribes in both early pre-Roman (Etruscan) and Imperial Roman times. Had such stories not fitted in well with local north European tribal culture, they would probably not have survived very long. But given what we know of ancient Germanic culture, with women bearing weapons, sometimes fighting in battles, and being perceived as powerful magic users, it is surely not impossible for the 'great goddess' Freya to have been both venerated independently in Germania as a powerful goddess of love, war and magic (well before contact with the Roman Empire), and for later contact with tales of Astarte to have led to their being applied also to Freya.

Finally, having already reviewed the long list of similarities in terms of possessions and personality between Inanna and Freya (from large cats and birds of prey to associations with matters of love, sex, fertility, war and combat, death and the afterlife, magical knowledge and power, female sovereignty, and the ability to fly – summarised in a table at the end of this chapter), more fundamental, divine and cosmological factors should not be overlooked either. If Inanna's and Freya's stories are considered in the context of not just what they tell us about the actions, adventures, and personality traits of those two goddesses as individuals, but in terms of implicit ancient Sumerian and early pagan north European world outlooks, then remarkable similarities in cosmological understanding can be found.

Inanna's impact on the worlds – both upper and under - is eventually transformed from the quantitative (involving herself and individuals) to the qualitative (transforming collective life-enabling cycles at the level of whole worlds). Wolkstein and Kramer express this as Inanna acting *"as divine ordainer, she shifts from active participant in her life story to constellated divinity..."*[360] Having returned from the Underworld and gained personal knowledge of the dark side of femininity, Inanna is able to come to an accommodation with her husband Dumuzi, whom she has experienced as embodying both light and dark aspects of masculinity. She grants him 'eternal' life by allowing him to rest in the frozen male stasis of winter and the Underworld for half of every year, in order that he may regenerate and fulfil his active, growth and new life promoting role in the upper world by re-partnering with her each summer.

In achieving this, which makes life possible for all through the establishment of constant change in the form of the birth/life/death cycle, Inanna acts as the divine feminine, the spark of fiery female energy which interacts positively with the initially frozen stasis of the masculine to produce flowing water: ever-changing, fertile, and life-sustaining. In doing this she has truly become a multi-aspected 'great goddess'.

Freya too is recognisable as a multi-aspected 'great goddess', though her stories may not be as openly cosmological as Inanna's descent into, and return from, the Underworld. Inanna's stories were set down 'in clay' at a time well before the total dominance of monotheistic patriarchy, whereas Freya's tales are known to us only through the no doubt distorting mirror of the coming of Christianity, and the passing of centuries before being put down in writing.

Nevertheless Freya is a Van goddess not just of sexuality but of all forms of fertility, of female sovereignty, of magic and spellcasting, of combat and warfare, and of death and the afterlife. She is the rune Fehu [ᚠ] – the first rune of the futhark, the elemental female energy of fire, the initiator. Just as Dumuzi fails Inanna, so Óðr goes missing for Freya, but just as Dumuzi is also subsequently redeemed by Inanna, so Freya's lover Ottár is transformed by her, thereby allowing him to fulfil a positive, supportive, male role. And just as Inanna facilitates the annual strengthening of the summer sun, so Freya's alleged 'lust for gold' in the form of the Brisingamen necklace/girdle might be better interpreted (as discussed in chapter 9) as a keenness to proliferate the life-giving fertility of the sun's golden rays, perhaps symbolised in a priestess's golden adornment.

The argument about whether Freya, Astarte, Aphrodite, and Inanna are really all representations of the same goddess, or at least have a common origin (in Sumerian Inanna), depending on how many possessions and personality traits can be counted as genuinely similar in all cases, might itself be thought a bit superficial and academic if contextualised by these more cosmological commonalties.

Freya's characteristics as a multi-aspected, independently powerful Van, can be said to stem from an earlier non-patriarchal age, pre-dating the warrior society of the Odinic Vikings. Inanna's female sovereignty likewise clearly originates from a time before the relative demise of goddesses under the patriarchal King Hammurabi of Babylon in the early second millennium BCE. It is highly unlikely that the Sumerians were ever in contact with early or pre-second millennium Germania, so Freya and Inanna were certainly originally independent manifestations of divine female sovereignty. However at the same time they were both aspects of that fiery, elemental, feminine energy which, by interacting with masculine strength and stolidity, maintains material reality and keeps as all from the void. Freya and Inanna may be separate individual goddesses, but if so, they are still both fighting on the same side. Their stories reflect the same ultimate reality and meld into one another.

'Great Goddess' Aspects and Associations (1)

Goddess Name	Culture	Approximate Dates	Major Aspects
Inanna	Sumerian	4500-1750? BCE	Love Sex Fertility Combat War Political Power
Ishtar	Akkadian East Semitic Babylonian Assyrian	4500-1750? BCE	Love Sex Fertility Combat War Political Power
Astarte	Phoenician Egyptian Canaanite Hebrew West Semitic	1000-200 BCE	Love Sex Fertility Combat War Political Power
Isis	Egyptian Greek Roman Mediterranean	1570 BCE – 529 CE	Magic Resurrection Political Power Divine Mother
Aphrodite	Greek Roman (Venus)	1500 BCE – 500 CE	Love Sex Fertility ~~Combat~~ ~~War~~ ~~Political Power~~ Magic
Freya	Germanic Scandinavian Anglo-Saxon	? BCE – 1000 CE	Love Sex Fertility Combat War ~~Political Power~~ Magic

'Great Goddess' Aspects and Associations (2)

Goddess Name	Associations	Comments	Key
Inanna	Lions/ large cats Morning Star Evening Star *(Eight-pointed Star)* Doves/Birds	Widely accepted to be the same goddess as Ishtar	
Ishtar	Lions/ large cats Morning Star Evening Star *(Eight-pointed Star)* Doves/Birds	Widely accepted to be the same goddess as Inanna	
Astarte	Lions/ large cats Morning Star Evening Star *(Star in a Circle)* Doves/Birds	Widely accepted as being substantially the same goddess as Inanna/Ishtar (with some limited local variation)	'~~Strike-through~~' text = original goddess aspects later reduced or eliminated in more heavily patriarchal cultures.
Isis	Throne/Royalty Falcon/Kestrel Flight/wings Ankh Papyrus Staff Cats *(outside Egypt)*	An independent, originally Egyptian, goddess - <u>not</u> related to Inanna/Ishtar/ Astarte	
Aphrodite	Golden Apples Magical Girdle Morning Star Evening Star Doves/Birds Pomegranates The Sea	Widely interpreted as having evolved from Astarte, but with the female power/combat/war role minimised or eliminated by Greek Patriarchy	
Freya	Golden Necklace/Girdle Large cats Falcon Flight/wings Boars/pigs	No known evidence of any direct archaeological or literary connection with any Middle Eastern or Mediterranean goddess	

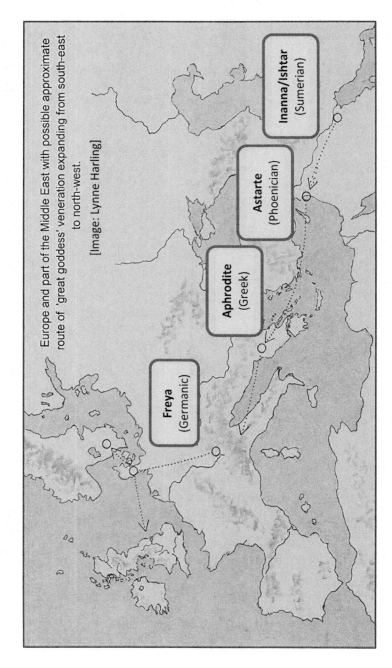

Europe and part of the Middle East with possible approximate route of 'great goddess' veneration expanding from south-east to north-west.

[Image: Lynne Harling]

Inanna/Ishtar (Sumerian)

Astarte (Phoenician)

Aphrodite (Greek)

Freya (Germanic)

Chapter 11 – *Hecate:*
Materialism and Idealism

It might at first seem strange to find a discussion of the Greek goddess Hecate (also spelt 'Hekate') in a book about Anglo-Saxon paganism, but just as comprehension of the Anglo-Saxon 'great goddess' Freya can be assisted by an examination of possible links back across thousands of miles and many centuries to ancient Sumeria's Inanna, so too the Anglo-Saxon pre-Christian world outlook may be usefully reviewed in the context of philosophical contradictions first expressed in literary form in ancient Greece, contradictions which were themselves vividly articulated within changing Greek perceptions of one of their most important and complex goddesses: Hecate.

The popularity of the goddess Hecate can be evidenced in Greece and greater Greece (Magna Graecia – including Greek colonies in Sicily, southern Italy etc.) over a period of more than two thousand years, from about 1600 BCE to the arrival of Christianity as a state-sponsored religion, and the outlawing of paganism in the late 4th century CE – see the "Hecate in Pagan Greece – Timeline" table at the end of this chapter.

During these two thousand years the perception of Hecate's roles changed very significantly. In particular, from the 4th century BCE onwards, the older polytheistic pagan worldview came to be increasingly replaced by Platonic and Neoplatonic philosophies, which served as precursors of Christianity. These philosophies are summarised and compared to the north European pagan world outlook in the table "Platonic Idealism and North European Materialism" at the end of this chapter.

During the last eight hundred years of this two-thousand-year period, Hecate continued to be seen by the common people as an important guardian of crossroads, thresholds, and disembodied souls, and to be associated with witchcraft and magic. However for the higher social classes, those who formed a literate minority, and who received an education in philosophy, mathematics and other subjects, Hecate came to be seen very differently. For many of them she became the 'Cosmic Soul', a sort of female subdivision of a single, all-powerful, male creator-god, partially prefiguring the Holy Spirit of Christianity.

Later still, over the last 400 years of the period (the first four centuries CE) she came to be understood – again predominantly by the educated higher social classes – as *Hecate Soteira*, or 'Hecate Saviour', a female Christ-like figure whose primary role was now thought to be the redemption of souls in a manner closely resembling Christian salvation: facilitating unification of individual souls with a single, all-powerful, male creator-god, through absorption within the Cosmic Soul.

This chapter seeks to analyse changing perceptions of Hecate, and the underlying philosophies which gave rise to those changes, in order to illustrate the polytheistic pagan world outlook (both Greek and Anglo-Saxon) as clearly as possible, by contrasting that essentially materialistic outlook on life with Greek Platonic idealism. This is important to any review of early English paganism, because Platonic idealism functioned as the ideological precursor of the Christian monotheism that eventually became the ruling religion in England, largely replacing the pluralistic heathenism indigenous to northern Europe. Better understanding 'anti-paganism' should also assist comprehension of paganism itself.

Hecate in pre-Platonic Greece
– Keyholder Goddess of Crossroads and Thresholds

It seems likely that Hecate's earliest role was as a guardian goddess of travellers. In ancient times travel was often an uncertain and risk-laden adventure. Roads could be poor and possibly infested with thieves and potential murderers, especially in remoter areas. In such circumstances travellers would seek the reassurance of Hecate's motherly protection. Small offerings to Hecate would be made upon departure, and at key points on the journey.

Key points on the journey would often be crossroads – worryingly liminal places where a wrong decision might result in getting lost, potentially dramatically increasing the chances of disaster, whether this be attack by robbers, injury through accidents, snake or scorpion bites, or loss of essentials such as pack animals or food. Hence Hecate came to be particularly associated in travellers' minds with crossroads.

There was however a lot more to being a goddess of crossroads than giving good directions to travellers and ensuring that they made it to their destinations safely, without falling into the hands of thieves, or being killed.

Pre-platonic Greeks (Plato died in 348 BCE), believed that when a person died their body decayed away, but that their soul survived. After death, disembodied souls would attempt to make their way to the Underworld – known as Hades. Safe arrival at Hades however was far from guaranteed. The soul's journey after death was a dangerous one, which could – just like any above-ground, earthly journey by living people – benefit from the blessings of a protector goddess of travellers.

Hence Hecate also came to be seen as a guardian goddess of disembodied souls. Unfortunately even her best efforts were not always successful, and sometimes unwise individuals even failed to make the necessary offerings to her. These individual disembodied souls failed to make it to the relative comfort of Hades – and were condemned to remain stuck in the no-man's land between the Underworld and the earth above, in the form of miserable ghosts and malignant phantoms.

The Greeks believed that newly disembodied souls at first found their new bodiless status rather confusing and hard to deal with (especially those who had died suddenly, unexpectedly, or as children). Consequently they would often pause in doubt on their way to Hades, seeking the correct direction. Their route between the worlds usually went via those most liminal and uncertain of places: crossroads, and here they paused to consider their way. Those souls who had sufficiently honoured the gods, and in particular Hecate, would stand a good chance of being able to move on and successfully reach the Underworld, perhaps guided there by the goddess herself. Others however would eventually lose their way entirely and, ultimately losing all hope, become embittered and spend eternity as spiteful ghosts haunting the crossroads they had failed to escape from.

The crossroad ghosts were perceived as being a particularly serious threat to the living. These resentful phantoms hated the warm blood of those still alive, and would haunt you and drive you insane if they could. Those they succeeded in driving into insanity would in turn also become ghosts when they died, being unfit to populate Hades. Therefore it was necessary for the living to honour Hecate because

a)   She offered protection against earthly dangers such as thieves and murderers
b)   She offered protection against the hauntings of malevolent ghosts, particularly at crossroads, and
c)   She offered protection and guidance to the souls of the recently dead as they journeyed to Hades.

Hecate's role as guardian of crossroads also expanded to cover other forms of liminal threshold, especially entrances and doorways, particularly at temples. Supplicants visiting the temples of many different gods and goddesses, coming to seek their favour, might often pause at the entrance, finding there a small shrine to Hecate, the protectoress of entrance ways. There they would first make a small initial offering, in order to enhance the chances of their request being successful, irrespective of whichever goddess or god it might be whose favours they would be seeking once they got over the threshold and entered the temple.

Similarly, Hecate's role as guardian of entrances and doorways led to her becoming associated with keys. She held the keys, not just literally to the doors to temples and other important buildings, but often also the key to a successful outcome to a traveller's journey. Hecate was the keyholder – the key to successful outcomes and safe arrival, whether that might be the next town down the road, a prayer received favourably by the gods, or, after death, entrance in to Hades itself.

Hecate in pre-Platonic Greece
– Goddess of Witchcraft, Magic, Ghosts and Necromancy

Archaeological evidence seems to show that in pre-Platonic ancient Greece magic was most commonly used to curse your enemies, with love spells also being popular, but ranking a poor second compared to imposing painful afflictions on people magicians, or their clients, had fallen out with.

Placing a curse on someone was obviously a malevolent activity, so the Greeks deduced that the most effective way to curse an enemy must be to enlist the assistance of those very embittered, malevolent beings who were always only too keen on carrying out evil deeds: the disembodied souls or ghosts who had failed to make it to Hades. It was thought that the more experienced and powerful ghosts, who had been stuck between the worlds the longest, could travel back to earth, not as fully reincarnated human beings, but as bodiless, haunting phantoms. These more powerful ghosts were known as daemones.

In order to curse a living enemy a magician would write an incantation on a stone or clay tablet, and place it either in a grave, or at a crossroads where disembodied souls were believed to be lingering. Some of these tablets survived the centuries to be rediscovered by archaeologists from the nineteenth century CE onwards. The incantation on the curse tablet would most often invoke both the daemones themselves, who would be needed to do the practical work of implementing the curse, and a chthonic god or goddess thought to be capable of controlling these evil spirits – most often Hecate. After placing a curse tablet in a grave or burying it at a crossroads, the magician would invoke a lingering dead soul to carry the message of malediction to the daemones or chthonic deities believed to be capable of enforcing the curse.

> *"Disembodied souls or daemones were the magician's tools; their ability to travel between the worlds enabled them to make good his requests [and] their unsettled status put them at his mercy. But ultimately they were still under the control of Hekate. To obtain a soul or daemon's help – to make magic work – required her co-operation."* [427]

It was Hecate's role as leader of the daemones and disembodied souls that led to her connection with witchcraft.[*] The seer in Seneca's *Oedipus*, intent on calling up shades, declares that he has succeeded as soon as he hears Hekate's dogs[†] bark. Before the emergence of

---

[*] Witchcraft: Who is Hecate in Shakespeare's play *Macbeth*?

"Hecate is the goddess of witchcraft, and one can view her as the ruler of the Three Witches. In Act 3, Scene 5, Hecate appears before the Witches and demands to know why she has been excluded from their meetings with Macbeth. She tells them Macbeth will be back to know his destiny and she proclaims that he will see apparitions that will, 'by the strength of their illusion' lead him to conclude that he is safe. She plays an important role in the play because of the lines she utters at the end of the scene: 'And you all know, security/ Is mortals' chiefest enemy.' She reveals in these lines that Macbeth's belief that he is untouchable will ultimately result in his downfall."
[http://www.shakespeare-online.com/faq/macbethfaq/hecate.html]

[†] Hekate's dogs: *"The dog (or more specifically, bitch) is the animal most commonly associated with Hecate, sometimes as a three-headed dog, and black dogs were once sacrificed to her in purification rituals. She was also believed to manifest herself as a dog, and the sound of barking dogs was often seen as the first sign of her approach. She is also often depicted with snakes."*
[https://witchcraftandwitches.com/witchcraft/witches-hecate/]

Theurgy[‡] (from Platonic times onwards) magicians, as explained above, would often seek the help of chthonic daemones and disembodied souls; magic was then largely a chthonic art. As a result, in popular thought and literature Hecate gradually came to be represented as being ever more horrific, in part owing to the increasingly ghastly and threatening character of the daemones she led. She came to be seen as a goddess of chthonic, horrific, witchcraft, the deity you appealed to when necromancy and hauntings were required.

Hecate in pre-Platonic Greece – *The Abduction of Persephone*

Hecate, as a chthonic goddess, plays a part in the Greek myth of the abduction of Persephone, daughter of the grain goddess Demeter – unsurprisingly, as the story has much to do with the Underworld. This tale to some extent covers the same ground as Sumerian Inanna's descent from the upper world, although whereas Inanna initially leaves her husband Dumuzi alive and ruling as a king on earth whilst she sinks into the realm of the dead, Persephone is forcibly abducted and carried off to the Underworld by its ruler, Hades. Nevertheless in both cases the eventual outcome is broadly the same: the fertility of each goddess is restricted to just part of every year. In Persephone's case she must agree to spend part of each year in the barren realm of the dead, the Underworld, but in return is allowed to be present for the rest of the year on earth, accordingly promoting an annual summer season of growth and abundance after each unproductive winter period. In Inanna's case the infertile winter months are marked by the seasonal loss of her husband King Dumuzi to the Underworld.

> *"Hades, Lord of the Underworld, falls in love with the maiden daughter of Demeter, the Kore* [virgin] *(Persephone). Knowing that Demeter would not give*

[‡] Theurgy: in the ancient Greek context not just *"the working of a divine or supernatural agency in human affairs"* [dictionary.com], but rather the use of magical ritual to attempt to influence the gods, and in particular to induce them to aid the magicians' (or their supplicants') development of their souls in line with the neo-Platonic perceived need of individuals to aspire to incorporation within the Cosmic Soul (see *Hecate in post-Platonic Greater Greece* later in this chapter).

her consent... Hades successfully kidnaps Persephone, taking her into his kingdom to become his wife and queen. The Grain Goddess Demeter is distraught over the disappearance of her daughter, and takes to wandering the earth... Finally, on the 10ᵗʰ day, Demeter speaks to Hekate:

> '...Hekate, with a torch in her hands, met her, and spoke to her and told her news: 'Queenly Demeter, bringer of the seasons and giver of good gifts, what god of heaven or what mortal man has rapt away Persephone and pierced with sorrow your dear heart?'

"Hekate then accompanies Demeter to Helios [the sun god], *who tells her that her daughter is with Hades. Hermes, the messenger god, travels to Hades and returns Persephone to her mother. However Hades had persuaded Persephone to eat a pomegranate seed, and as a result, she has to return to Hades for a third of every year. On her return, Hekate embraces Persephone and becomes her companion and guide 'from that time', being both her preceder and her follower... By being both in front of and behind Persephone, Hekate takes the roles of both protector and guide of the Queen of Hades..."* [428]

If Hecate is both a guide and a protectress of Persephone as the guardian of the seasons, including the summer season of fertility, the growth of crops, and the production of grain for bread and beer, then Hecate is not just a chthonic goddess of the crossroads leading to the barren, dead Underworld, or of witchcraft, magic, necromancy and ghosts. She also plays a key role in facilitating seasonal fertility, abundance, and continuing life, no doubt through her function as a guardian of the liminal, facilitating the crossing of thresholds, including even those cyclical and temporal ones between the linked realms of life and death, a divine function necessary because without the one the other would be impossible. Hecate's multi-faceted roles then are anything but purely negative, having more to do with a necessary balancing of negative and positive elements.

Hecate in pre-Platonic Greece – *Hecate's Triple Form*

The earlier forms of Hecate all show her as single bodied, but from the fourth century BCE onwards images of Hecate in triple-form became popular, although single bodied depictions of the goddess also continued to be used. As a Triple Goddess Hecate is usually shown as three women, all of the same age, often standing side by side, or back to back – sometimes around a central pillar.

There is no widely accepted explanation as to why this additional triple form became popular. What does seem clear is that Hecate's triple form is not an early example of the modern-day Maiden-Mother-Crone (MMC) concept. Sorita d'Este has commented that Hecate's genuinely ancient association with witchcraft has led some 21st century authors to see her, mistakenly, as a crone:

> "Robert Graves is the likely source which popularised the concept of Hekate as a Crone in his 'Greek Myths', where he wrote that: 'Core, Persephone, and Hecate were, clearly, the Goddess Triad as Maiden, Nymph and Crone'... Crowley and Graves... evoked the witch stereotype when they were describing Hekate. They encouraged their readers to believe that witches were old women with crooked noses, living on the edges of society..." [429]

d'Este argues that if it should be considered necessary to look for a maiden/mother/crone (MMC) pattern in myths concerning Hecate then the role of maiden suits Hecate much better than that of crone, for she is the guide and protectress of Persephone as the mother figure, who *"when she returns to the earth... brings with her the tide of Spring, new life is born, and the crops flourish".*[430] The crone would then be Demeter, for although Demeter *"is the grain mother... in the absence of her daughter life withers and the crops fail. She brings winter and barrenness to the earth."* [431] Having said this though d'Este then goes on to assert that in any case the very nature of the Greek gods is fundamentally irreconcilable with the MMC concept because:

> "The ancient and immortal gods are all old, without exception. They are ancient, and both age and ageing are simply not relevant to them... Deities... who are as pervading as Hekate will not fit into a human model. Age, as linked to the phases of life, is an immaterial element through which to understand an eternal, ageless deity." [432]

This however is at least debatable. It is true that unlike the Anglo-Saxon gods who would die of old age were it not for the goddess Idun's apples, and who could also be killed (like Balder), and who were believed to be doomed to perish in the last battle at the end of the world (Ragnarok), the Greek gods were thought to be not just long lived, but truly immortal. In that sense the concept of a crone goddess might seem odd, yet Persephone is Demeter's daughter, so youth, maidenhood, adulthood, and motherhood, all do seem to be age and maturity related concepts which can be applied even to the Greek deities. And of course the definition of 'crone' is not limited only to old-age; it is also often to do with wisdom acquired through time, again a concept which might be thought applicable even to the Greek goddesses, though they do not physically wither with the years.

> "The word Crone is derived from the old word for
> crown, suggesting the wisdom that emanates from
> the head like a halo. Her own childbearing days are
> past; she is the wisdom keeper, seer and healer and
> midwife, whose knowledge is sought out to guide
> others during life's hardships and transitions." [433]

As has already been noted however, triple goddess Hecate is usually shown as three women all of the same age, often standing side by side, or back to back. Given that surviving figurines of triple aspected Hecate show three women apparently all of the same still youthful age, it can be argued that the triple form is not meant to illustrate any kind of aging or maturing process, but is rather a recognition of pluralism and negation of monotheism. d'Este prefers the view of triple-form Hecate as three maiden goddesses because she is a polytheist and pluralist, a believer in many independent deities.

> "The Maiden, Mother, Crone (MMC) construct
> proposes that the feminine divine is singular,
> manifesting in many different forms (or aspects).
> Adherents of this construct usually believe that 'all
> Goddesses are one Goddess' and that the Goddess
> manifests with three faces, representing the three
> phases they feel epitomise the life of a woman:
> Maiden, Mother and Crone..." [434]

d'Este is of the view that the MMC concept not only fails adequately to grasp the pre-Platonic pluralist complexity of ancient Greek understanding of divinity but is, if anything, even less relevant to 21st century women than to the ancient Greeks, because:

> "while it is undoubtedly empowering for some

> women, the MMC is restrictive and painful for others. Not all women have a choice in experiencing the MMC phases of life in straight forward and predictable ways, and for them, the MMC can be uncomfortable and problematic. This includes women who have been unable to fulfill their desire to have a child, women who have had their maidenhood taken from them by force, women who decided not to have children (for whatever reason), and women who experience menopause early." [435]

Hecate's triple form then might be an expression of the pluralist nature of divinity, as seen in pre-Platonic terms and very much in line with Anglo-Saxon paganism (further discussion of that relationship follows below in a review of post-Platonic Greek thinking), rather than an MMC-style reflection of the mortal aging process. There is however also another, simpler, possible explanation, which does not contradict the 'statement of pluralism' argument. It is notable that Hecate's triple form originated in Athens, and was first evidenced at a very specific place:

> "The first statue showing Hekate as three-formed stood next to the Temple of Nike on the Parthenon in Athens...
>
>> 'It has generally been recognised that the representation of Hekate in triple form is an Attic invention'...
>
> "The Triangular Shrine, in the Athenian Agora, must be one of Hekate's most impressive shrines in the city, certainly one of the oldest. It is located at the crossroads outside the south-western corner of the ancient Agora[§]..." [436]

It was also initially in Athens that: "Hekate was syncretised with the cult of the goddess Enodia, whose name became a favourite epithet used for Hekate." [437] Enodia means 'the one in the streets', and seems to have been an epithet linked particularly to Hekate's role as a guardian of roads, travellers, and crossroads. The ancient Athenians, it

---

[§] Agora: "a central public space in ancient Greek city-states. The literal meaning of the word is "gathering place" or "assembly". The agora was the centre of the athletic, artistic, spiritual and political life of the city." [Wikipedia]

appears, envisaged crossroads, not as the meeting of four ways, but as the traveller's arrival at three possible routes or options (you were unlikely to want to immediately return the way you came). This might be the mundane origin of Hekate's triple-facing aspect. If sufficiently respected by the traveller, Hekate would reveal her advice about all three options at a crossroads, with each of three faces separately divulging information about each of the three possible routes to be taken.

Either way, whether triple-aspect Hecate was simply about offering three possible ways forward at a crossroads, or constituted a broader statement of the plural nature of divinity, from the mid-fourth century BCE onwards a thousand years and more of Greek pluralist theology began to be increasingly challenged, at least amongst the educated elite, by new hegemonic, increasingly monotheistic thinking. The most influential advocate of this new way of looking at the worlds was the philosopher Plato. Before looking at his and his 'Neoplatonic' successors' cosmological and theological analyses, Greek thinking, both pre- and post-Platonic, can be put into context by being briefly compared to pagan North European understanding of the gods.

North European and Ancient Greek Views of the Gods

The pre-Christian north European view of deity was fundamentally at odds with the ancient Greek view. Northern gods, Vanir and Aesir, must all die, as they are truly mortal. They, like us, must face their end at *Ragnarok*. Even prior to that, they grow old and die, should Idun's golden apples not be available to give them age-outlasting, but still ultimately limited, life spans. The Greeks, on the other hand, thought their gods were truly immortal.

In north European cosmology, the elemental nature of being (Fire, Ice and the *Ginnungagap* void), the most basic existential dialectic, is applicable to every thing, living or inanimate, including the gods. It operates as shown below:

- Stasis: *(the void)*
- Dynamic female **Fire** energy *(thesis)* meets:
  male **Ice** strength *(antithesis)*, resulting in
- Birth: new transformed life *(synthesis)*,
  female and male
- Life and ageing
- Death → stasis

The process is cyclical, or at least recurring: after death the resulting decay of dynamic, energetic change into stasis is not permanent. Stasis will always again be disrupted by the dynamic. The new change-cycle is not always simply cyclical, but may operate at a more developed, higher, more complex level, or at a decayed, lower level.

It is worth noting in passing that the MMC concept actually fits the above dialectical model quite well. Possibly even Hecate could become a crone! After all to become a crone it is clearly not necessary to become a mother first, and nor is attaining the status of crone all about aging. Hopefully it has much to do with the acquisition of wisdom over time, and a willingness to actively share that experience and knowledge for the benefit of others. Even the Greek gods lived through learning experiences which necessarily involved the passing of time.

Hecate in post-Platonic Greece
- Classical and Hellenistic Period Platonism [438]

Plato (428–348 BCE) believed that it is impossible for human beings to perceive truth and reality with complete accuracy (a belief summarised in the term 'sceptical philosophy'). For Plato this was not merely a matter of the inherent limitations of our sense organs and intellectual capacities, but much more fundamentally because he chose to believe that we subsist in a world which consists of a series of imperfect material reflections of true realities. True realities, he asserted, exist only as perfect, mental 'Ideals' or 'Ideas', not material entities. Material entities, including living beings, are, to a degree and in a limited sense only, real, but necessarily imperfect. True ultimate reality exists, for Plato, only as a mental construct in the mind of God.

The material world is real, but less than perfectly real, and always less than the ultimate truth (a belief summarised in the term 'idealist philosophy').*

For Plato, Greek gods and goddesses such as Hecate did not exist, except as false myth. According to his original philosophy (referred to as 'early Platonism') the gods as they are presented in the Greek myths cannot exist, because their characters are imperfect. Gods subject to passions and sufferings must necessarily be false, because for Plato there is only one God, and he is perfect. He is the God of perfect reasoning, whose mind creates everything. He is perfection, existing at the ideal level, not the material, and for Plato less than perfect gods acting in the material world were an impossible contradiction in terms. If they are less than perfect then they are not the one perfect God, and are neither gods in their own right, nor aspects of the one true and perfect God.

Although Plato saw human beings as existing in an always less than truly perfect material world, he also believed that human souls are immortal. For at least a thousand years before Plato, Greeks had believed that after the death of the body the soul could survive and attempt to travel to Hades, the Underworld, where it could live on in a disembodied form. Plato reinterpreted this belief in the potentially immortal soul by claiming that souls not only survive the body's death and live on in Hades, but could also travel back to the material, upper world, and potentially be reborn into new bodies, and subsequently live new mortal lives, i.e. he believed (unlike most of his contemporaries) in reincarnation.

Plato's pupil Xenocrates (395-314 BCE) further developed his master's 'idealist' philosophy, his concern with perfection, and the notion that ultimate truth and reality are incompatible with the material world. In particular Xenocrates asserted that numbers are perfect, that they are Ideals in the Platonic sense. This raised a philosophical issue concerning how 'Ideal' numbers function in our material world, which Xenocrates attempted to resolve by declaring that numbers operate at the level of the 'Soul' as created in the mind of God. He explained that he meant by this not the individual souls of human beings (disembodied or otherwise), but a divine all-embracing

---

* The use of the terms 'Ideals' and 'Ideas' in their Platonic sense as expressions of perfect reality (ultimate truth) originating in the mind of God is indicated in this discussion by the use of the capital letter "I" in both cases.

concept of 'Soul' at the cosmological level, which he called the "Cosmic Soul". This Cosmic Soul, said Xenocrates, uses numbers as Ideal truths created in the mind of God to delineate and shape the physical cosmos, and to create the less than perfect, and therefore only partially real, material world.

For Xenocrates the Cosmic Soul functioned as a kind of interlocutor between the mind of God (containing perfect, ultimate truths) and the imperfect material world. Having developed the concept of such an interlocutor function Xenocrates then went on to attempt a partial reconciliation of Platonic idealist philosophy with the traditional Greek view of the gods, perhaps intending to make Platonism more acceptable to a wider audience. He did this by describing the Cosmic Soul as an emanation of Hecate who, after all, had been widely perceived as having an interlocutor or intermediary function guiding disembodied souls between the worlds.

In this way, despite Plato's rejection of the Greek pantheon as false and unreal (because in Plato's mind gods could not be imperfect), Hecate, alone amongst the gods, lived on even in the minds of idealist Greek Platonists. For them she was transformed from a goddess of witchcraft, thresholds, crossroads and the chthonic, into something akin to the "Holy Ghost" of later Christian belief. For Platonists Hecate was not seen as an individual goddess in her own right, but as a form of the spirit of the one God, a type of holy spirit, which God used to project perfect, Ideal truths such as numbers into His Universe, thereby creating the physical cosmos and our material, imperfect world. This constituted the Platonic explanation of how an imperfect material world could subsist as an emanation of the perfect mind of God.

What Plato's and Xenocrates' ideas clearly demonstrate is that traditional Greek thinking (which they rejected) understood the gods to be real, material beings. They were seen as imperfect, and relatively limited in their abilities. They were very far from infallible, and not all-powerful. They disagreed with each other, sometimes loving and sometimes falling out with their fellow deities. The Greek pantheon was pluralistic and diverse, and therefore necessarily imperfect. In fact in the traditional view that very diversity and imperfection, the contradictions within the pantheon and between the gods, was (contrary to Platonic idealist philosophy) evidence of their reality.

This originally polytheistic Greek traditional understanding of the multiverse and its diverse and pluralistic material realities reflected the lived experiences of the pre-Platonic ancient Greeks: if something can be perceived by your senses, be rationally made sense of, and therefore be conceived of and reacted to in useful, practical ways which remain valid through repeated experiences over time, then it is a part of ever complex material reality. This way of looking at things and understanding the worlds constitutes materialist philosophy. It was rejected by Plato and his Neoplatonist successors (see below). Their idealist philosophy with its vision of a single, perfect, all-powerful, infallible God, and its attempts to incorporate and subsume all of reality within a single universe, a single 'ultimate truth', served as a precursor for later absolutist, monotheistic, Christian thinking.

Pre-Christian Anglo-Saxons, it seems reasonable to assume, would have understood the pre-Platonic Greeks much more easily that the material reality denying Platonists. For pagan Anglo-Saxons too the gods were many, the worlds plural, and reality imperfect, complex, and diverse. They may have felt no need to express it in philosophical terms, as for them it was no doubt simple 'common sense', but Anglo-Saxon cosmology and theology was materialist, not idealist.

Hecate in post-Platonic Greece - *Middle Platonism*

Middle Platonism is the name given to a stage in the development of Platonic philosophy, lasting from about 90 BCE until the development of Neoplatonism under Plotinus in the 3rd century CE. Middle Platonic philosophers were concerned with the problem of evil, and how its existence might be accounted for in a single universe existing only as an Idea in the mind of the perfect one God. Evil, they thought, cannot exist in the true, perfect world of the one God. It can only exist in the imperfect, only partially real, material world. Therefore evil must be an expression of materiality, of matter itself. Matter, for Middle Platonists, was evil; only the truly divine Ideal was not.

Middle Platonism also reversed the earlier Platonic 'sceptical philosophy' (see above), which had stated that it is impossible for human beings to perceive truth - because the material world is but a pale and inaccurate reflection of divine truth. Antiochus of Ascalon (c.125–68 BCE) *"returned to a pronounced dogmatism"*,[439] arguing that it did not make sense to promote belief in a single, perfect, all-powerful, creator god, while at the same time claiming that it is impossible for material beings to know truth. The truth could be known, and the truth was that the material world was truly evil.

Middle Platonists had to recognise that the gods of traditional Greek belief had, several centuries after Plato's death, still not lost all their popularity, especially with the common people, many of whom continued to acknowledge them. So for Plutarch[440] for example the gods of the people were explainable as powers that served the single true deity. God was a transcendent being, operating through divine intermediaries, whether these were called gods or daemones.[441] Plutarch agreed that matter was 'the receptacle of evil', and went on to argue that therefore the Cosmic Soul, as the projection of Hecate which promotes the creation of the material world, must also function as the source of evil:

> *"Some Middle Platonic authors hypothesised the existence of an evil or irrational Cosmic Soul, or of two opposing Cosmic Souls. Plutarch is one of the more notable proponents of this idea."* [442]

As, for the Middle Platonists, true knowledge of evil could after all be known in the material world, so it became the responsibility of human beings to recognise this and acknowledge the one true, perfect God, accepting that they too must be receptors of evil (rather anticipating the later Christian doctrine of 'original sin'). The perceived role of the Cosmic Soul became the insertion of "correct opinion or belief" into individuals, passing to them the knowledge that they must recognise the truth of the necessary hegemony of the one God. This could be done (again this is an idea later taken up by Christianity) by recognising the triplicate nature of the one true God: God himself is "the Father", who self-generates another holy being, which is also part of Himself, the 'Demiurge' (perhaps equivalent to Jesus the son of God in Christianity). These two divine aspects of the triplicate nature of the One God then create the Cosmic Soul (or holy spirit) through their servant Hecate, which functions as the link between the divine and the material. The interaction of the Cosmic Soul with elements of matter facilitates the creation of individual souls, seen as being in part material (and mortal), and in part of divine origin (and immortal).

> *"Soul plays a crucial role in the formation of correct opinion or belief and of knowledge... Plato says that the Father and Demiurge gathered together the... Cosmic Soul and... other, less pure, mortal ingredients... from this mixture were created individual souls – part immortal, part human."* [443]

The view of the Cosmic Soul as a holy spirit which facilitated the creation of individual souls through allowing the combination of matter and spirit was common to both Early and Middle Platonists, as was the viewing of numbers as an expression of perfect, Ideal truth. Middle Platonists also agreed with their earlier forebears about the impossibility of the divine Ideal existing in the material world, which was necessarily at least in part evil, for all matter was evil, in that it was the negation of the Ideals which could exist only in non-material forms in the mind of God.

The key new development for Middle Platonists was that they believed that it must be possible to know truth, or at least religious truth, even for individual souls mired in the evil and materiality of the physical world, for how else were they to aspire to submit themselves to the ultimate Ideal truth within the mind of God?

> "To summarise 'Middle Platonic' views, the Soul
> contained – or was – Number... Ratio and Harmony.
> Number, in turn, was... related to or identified with
> the Ideas. The Ideas... were cast by Soul upon Primal
> Matter, which then became the physical Cosmos...
> the Cosmic Soul was understood as the projection or
> emanation of Hekate." [444]

As has already been noted above in relation to early Platonism, the pagan Anglo-Saxon world view contradicts Greek Platonic idealist philosophy. For Anglo-Saxons the gods were many, the worlds plural, and reality imperfect, complex, and diverse. There were many truths, but no one perfect, ultimate Ideal or truth knowable only in the mind of a single God. For pre-Christian Anglo-Saxons the worlds, whether of the gods or of Middle Earth, were material and real in themselves, existing independently as matter outside of the mind of any god or other entity. In this materialist (as against idealist) way of understanding reality, everything is changing all the time. It is not possible to obtain perfect, absolute truth or knowledge, because it does not exist. To be perfect and Ideal, truth (or any entity) would have to be unchanging, and there is nothing that never changes except for pure nothingness: the void. Everything that is real, whether inanimate or living, is either growing and developing, or decaying and dying. And everything that is real, because it is ever changing, is forever interacting with (potentially) everything else through the web of the Wyrd, a process which in itself promotes yet more change.

Platonists conceived of the 'harmony' of numbers and mathematics as being perfect and unchanging, but in doing so had to acknowledge the immateriality of such a concept, that it could only exist as an Idea or Ideal. For early Anglo-Saxons, perceiving themselves through their senses to be living in material worlds, the Greek Platonic concept of reality would have been seen as the very opposite of the truth: perfect Ideas (numbers or otherwise) would cease to be true or real the very moment they achieved unchanging perfection.

The Greek Platonic view might be described as the male philosophical gaze, seeing only the illusion of stasis (male strength and stolidity un-enlivened by transforming, life-giving, ever-changing, feminine energy). For pagan Anglo-Saxons it would be seen as a failure to appreciate the essential dynamic of the female, ever-changing, repeatedly birthing, multi-verse: the rhythmic pulse and constant change of the (partially chaotic) dialectic replaced by an illusion of the Eternal. The Platonic worldview sees masculinity as the primary existential and creative force: a single, all powerful, Father God. He creates everything, including his son the Demiurge, and the subordinate female Cosmic Soul (Hecate), which He impregnates with 'noetic'[‡] Ideas which then give birth, through the subordinate medium of the Soul, to the physical, material 'hylic'[§] world and its creatures, including mankind.

This Platonic worldview, envisaging a single Universe built on Harmony and the Eternal, can be argued to have functioned as a logical precursor of both monotheism in general, and Christianity in particular. Its emphasis on the perceived necessary autocracy of a single, all-powerful male deity, could logically be said to precede and promote concepts such as absolutism, anti-pluralism, intolerance, and censorship, which might then in turn lead to a conviction which pagan Anglo-Saxons would surely have seen as ultimately negative: the conception of stasis ("the formation of correct opinion or belief") as achievable and desirable.

Hecate in post-Platonic Greece – *Neoplatonism*

Neoplatonism began with Plotinus (204-270 CE), an Egyptian-born Greek who taught philosophy in Alexandria, and later Rome. Neoplatonism does not consist of a single set of ideas so much as a chain of thinkers, ending with the closing of the Platonic Academy in

---

[‡] Noetic: *"of or relating to the mind"* [dictionary.com]

[§] Hylic: *"(from Greek ὕλη (hylē) 'matter') is the opposite of psychic (from Greek ψυχή (psychē) 'soul')"* [https://en.wikipedia.org/wiki/Hylics]

Athens by the Christian Eastern Roman Emperor Saint[**] Justinian I in 529 CE.[445]

Neoplatonic thinkers espoused a range of views, but the two most important were monism, and the concept of the potential salvation of souls. Monism holds that all existing things originate from a single source, which in Neoplatonism is called 'The One', the single true God – hence 'monotheism'. For Neoplatonists not only is there only one true God, but the whole of reality is also singular: there exists only a single thing, the *Uni*-verse. God can and does divide the unified universe into many apparently separate things, but these many things have all been created by the single God, and ultimately exist only at his divine behest.

Neoplatonists generally agreed with Middle Platonists about the triplicate nature of the One God (Father, Demiurge and Cosmic Soul), and about the equivalence of matter and evil, but went on to develop a more detailed analysis of evil. In an even more extreme reversal of the early polytheistic Greek (and pagan Anglo-Saxon) materialist view of the worlds, and a denial of the senses, they defined matter as 'indeterminate' with no real qualities or existence of its own, unlike pure, divine thought or Ideas. Types of matter lacking form and Idea were, for Neoplatonists, evil. Evil was understood as a parasite; it was that unreality which has no existence of its own. For something to truly exist it had to be a creation or emanation of the one God, and therefore by its very nature exist in 'perfect harmony' with Him, as part of the Ideal, or Ideas emanating from Him. The material world, consisting of physical matter, was - because at least partially separated from God - at best an illusory partial existence based on parasitism of the divine, and as such remained ultimately unreal.

A possibility was acknowledged that other types of matter might be perceived as non-evil, if they were potentially capable of form and Idea, but even these were, whilst ever they remained even partially material, 'hylic' as against 'noetic', at best neutral. The evil elements of the material world (those untouched by noetic form) were doomed to ultimate non-existence. However the neutral elements of the material world (those potentially capable of noetic form) had the possibility of salvation (continued eternal existence) through being fully reunited with and within God. The concept of 'salvation' was a key Neoplatonic concept, later of course also taken up by Christians.

[**] Justinian is a saint only in the Eastern Orthodox Church.

For salvation to be achieved - by those 'neutral' elements of the material world potentially capable of noetic form – mediation was required between the celestial divine (God and the Demi-urge) and the material world. Mediation – contact and communication with the celestial divine – was possible because human beings have souls, and individual human souls were not only matter, but had originally been formed from, and could potentially again be reunited with, the single divine Cosmic Soul, itself a key third emanation of the one God. The Middle Platonists' Cosmic Soul now also came to be referred to as the World Soul, emphasising its function as the link needing to be accessed by mortal souls in this world, should they aspire to eternal salvation through reunification with God in the celestial sphere of the Ideal, after the death of the physical body. Access to the World Soul was held to be controlled by Hecate, who could be entreated to grant her favours through the ritual magic of theurgy. As Hecate's role of intermediary between the material and the divine was now believed by the Neoplatonists to extend also to the possible obtaining of salvation, to them she became known as 'Hecate Soteira' or Hecate Saviour.

Neoplatonists believed that for the human soul to achieve salvation it should avoid being content with a disembodied afterlife in Hades or the Underworld. It should instead be aiming higher, literally higher, in fact at traveling through the heavens, via the moon, to celestial reunification within the one God. As well as being everywhere and everything, God was simultaneously located more specifically in the lunar sphere:

> *"Plutarch* [describes]... *The Moon* [as] *the proper element... of souls... for they are, in the end, resolved back into the Moon, just as bodies are resolved back into the earth... First the soul is separated from the body 'in the realm of Demeter' – that is, on the earth; then the soul is separated from the mind 'in the realm of Persephone' – on the Moon... Plutarch seems to regard Persephone and Hekate as different manifestations of a single goddess."* [446]

> *"Hekate, by controlling the crossing of the boundary between humanity and divinity, could either aid the ascent, or force the descent of the soul... the special abilities and goodwill of this goddess were important for those seeking salvation."* [447]

Hecate of course was not seen by Neoplatonists as an independent goddess, but as a creation of God, conceived of either as God's 'holy spirit' (the Cosmic or World Soul itself), or as God's servant whose role it was to act as mediator between the Ideal and the physical domain. As the World Soul she was a spiritual source for the initial configuration of the material world by the Demiurge (the son of God), who also used numbers as tools to shape primal matter. Then once the physical world had been created, because of her role in that process she was able to act as intermediary between the limited reality inherent in the material sphere, and the true Ideal reality of the divine domain.

The Middle Platonists too had understood Hecate in this way, but what was new about Neoplatonic thinking was that it now clearly anticipated Christian concepts of Heaven (above) and Hell (below). The Greeks had originally seen Hades as the appropriate and desirable destination for disembodied souls after the death of the body; to fail to get there was to risk having to spend the afterlife as a miserable ghost. But for Neoplatonists Hades became an undesirable terminus for souls, which should be avoided if at all possible. Instead people should be aiming for salvation of their souls in the form of unification with God in His celestial sphere, to be reached via the moon. Only this, not living on as a disembodied individual soul in Hades, could provide meaningful eternal life.

It was believed that practical steps could be taken to enhance the chances of individual souls managing to avoid sinking down to Hades and instead climbing into the celestial sphere. Such steps included both fervent prayer, and theurgy: the use of magical ritual to attempt to influence the divine sphere, most often by appealing to Hecate as the intermediary between material earth and divine heaven.

> "It was essential to the belief in an absolutely transcendent God that a gulf between divine and human be established, yet also essential that prayers, salvation, and the creative force necessary to enform and ensoul the physical world, be transported across it. It is not difficult to understand then, why the [Neoplatonic] system so greatly exalted Hekate/Soul, who both performed these cosmological roles, and was also... a personal mediator, able to bring the theurgist closer to divinity..." [448]

As Sarah Iles Johnston points out above "It was essential to the belief in an absolutely transcendent God that a gulf between divine and human be established". This was very different from what had gone before. In north European, Anglo-Saxon, and pre-Hellenic-age Greek pagan tradition, the gods were perceived as very human-like. In all their diversity, ultimate frailty, fallibility, and confused morality, they could not be less like the single, all powerful, patriarchal God of either the Christians or the Greek Neoplatonists.

In north European pagan cosmology the gods did not create the worlds, but are part of them. They played no role in gestating the seed of a single male God in any created material reality. They simply are material reality, just like human beings. Reality is not formed, whether from Ideas or anything else. Material reality simply is; constantly changing, both evolving and decaying. This perception of the divine as complex, contradictory, limited, and imperfect, allowed for human identification with the struggle of the gods, not for 'salvation', but for survival and self-reliance, for spiritual independence, and individual and collective freedom. Perfection – 'salvation' through the incorporation of the individual soul within an all embracing 'Cosmic Soul' as part of a transcendent Father God – would have been neither desirable nor possible.

Pagan Anglo-Saxons would not have seen either Greek Neoplatonic Ideas or the later Christian 'Will of God' as ever being capable of impacting on underlying material realities, which would always remain complex and contradictory, generating conflict and decay, but also development and growth. For them the achievement of any form of ultimate 'Harmony' would have been seen as unrealistic, and in any case undesirable, for the only possible conflict-free reality would be nothingness, the void. For pagan materialists, wherever something exists, it is by definition limited to a specific form, and therefore different from other existing things. All things exist in a state of less than total harmony with each other.

This was seen as being as true for the gods, existing in their own material worlds, as it is for human beings in ours. We and the gods were perceived as alike (frail and fallible), and therefore capable of communicating with each other without the need for any intermediary, divine or otherwise. There was no "unbridgeable gulf" between us, because there was no single *absolutely transcendent God*". Any desire to subsume one's soul within such a concept in the hope of 'salvation' would have been seen as a denial of material reality, and therefore doomed to failure.

Conclusion – Hecate: the Evolution of a Goddess

The Hecate of pagan Greater Greece then, was many things. She had many aspects and roles. It is possible to discern how perceptions of her evolved over two millennia, and how different people experienced her in different ways.

> "Hekate... could be the goddess supplicated at the time of the new moon and the new month, the escort at the palace door, and the guide at the crossroads, the conductor to Hades, and the Queen of the souls that never made it there, the key-holder to the higher realms of the cosmos, and the lunar purifier of souls – or all of these things at once. But the concept behind these duties was at heart the same: from early times, Hekate was the deity who could aid men at points of transition, who could help them to cross boundaries, whether they be of a prosaic, everyday nature, of an extraordinary, once in a lifetime nature or, later, of a theurgical nature."
> 449

Some of the changes in Hecate's roles were gradual and incremental: from guardian of travellers to guardian of travelling souls, from single aspected, key-holding guard of entrance ways and thresholds to triple aspected crossroads guide, from protector against malevolent spirits and ghosts, to controller of magical curses and witches' spells. These are the kind of roles likely to have remained most relevant to the mass of the Greek-speaking people for over two thousand years.

From Plato's time onwards however, from about 350 BCE for the last thousand years or so of Greek paganism, a more fundamental, cataclysmic change in the perception of Hecate took place, or at least it did for many educated members of higher social classes, the literate minority. These people ceased to believe in polytheism. For them, goddesses and gods only made sense, if at all, as aspects of a single, all powerful, creator God.

To Early, Middle, and Neoplatonic Greek philosophers and their followers, this God was male. Like the later Christian God, he was held to have created, himself and alone, both his own son (the Demi-urge), and the Holy Spirit or Cosmic Soul which first facilitated the creation of the material world, and then communication and mediation between the material and the divine. Hecate as Cosmic Soul was no longer interpreted as the chthonic goddess of witches and magicians, but inherited instead the role of celestial goddess of theurgists, those alchemists seeking communion with the perfect Harmony of God, so as to attain salvation of their souls: eternal life in God and Heaven.

The change from polytheism to Neoplatonism amongst the Greek educated classes constituted a switch from freedom of belief to monotheism and intolerance of pluralistic belief systems. Those in power developed a need to control not just the actions but also the beliefs of those they ruled over. "Correct opinion" became a necessity, and in 380 CE paganism was banned in what was by now the Eastern Roman Empire, ruled from Greek Byzantium. Three emperors of the divided empire issued the Edict of Thessalonica[450], demanding that all their subjects adhere to a single Catholic ('universal') and Orthodox ('correct') Christianity. Communion with Hecate – in any form – was no longer acceptable.

Unlike the Greeks, largely illiterate pre-Christian northern Europe had no written record of theological or cosmological debate; there was no pagan Anglo-Saxon Plato. For the Greeks indigenous monotheistic philosophy was well established centuries before the arrival of Christianity, although Platonic monotheism never achieved the totalitarian exclusivity eventually attained by rulers recognising the Catholic and Orthodox Christian Church. Until the outlawing of all forms of paganism and alternative belief systems from 380 CE, pluralistic Greek polytheism survived, at least amongst the common people, alongside the Platonism of the educated elite.

When absolutist, patriarchal monotheism came to northern Europe and the Anglo-Saxons over two hundred years after the issuing of the Edict of Thessalonica, it arrived as a foreign belief system which suited the aristocratic Germanic and English rulers. Kingdoms were already developing into larger and ever more rigidly ruled entities. Kingship was becoming more firmly hereditary, and the power of the local Witan (the council of advisors) to appoint or at least confirm a ruler in post was being gradually eroded. The concept of a king ruling by divine right, and of that right being granted by a single and therefore unchallengeable God, no doubt seemed most welcome to power-hungry rulers, keen to maximise their ideological legitimacy and hegemony, especially when that ideological supremacy could be backed up in organisational form through the new (to northern Europe) institution of a powerful Church, which could reach throughout and beyond the land, and touch all social classes within it.

It seems unlikely that many amongst the early English fully

understood the Greek Platonic idealist concepts of salvation and the 'unreality' of the material world, as inherited by what became the Church of Rome, though many do seem to have found the prospect of an eternal afterlife in heaven attractive, especially when told that the only alternative was everlasting, burning pain in the flames of an Underworld populated by demons dedicated to torturing the ungodly. Whatever the limited Idealism of the early English Christian Church and its Greek Platonic inheritance, most Anglo-Saxons seem to have retained a fundamentally materialistic world outlook, choosing to reject monastic withdrawal from the world of the senses in favour of prioritising the cycle of life in the form of family and children. Family and friends, though imperfect, were at least generally knowable and mainly trustworthy. Blind faith in any ultimate, perfect truth, it appears, was better left to the priests. The pagan world outlook never really went away.

Platonic Idealism and North European Materialism
Greek Platonic *Idealism*

Cosmology
In the beginning:
God - male, unique, perfect, unchanging, eternal, ultimate truth, immaterial - pure intellect.
Creation:
Emanations from the mind of God - Son of God (the Demi-urge); Cosmic Soul (Hecate)
Cosmic Soul is intermediate between indivisible (unchanging) existence, and divisible (physical) existence. Within the Soul's structure is the basis of mathematical proportions and harmony.
The First Intellect (God) emits the Ideas. Hecate/Soul transmits them; her womb helps to turn the Ideas into structured matter, it arranges and regulates the previously formless physical world. The Second Intellect (the Demiurge) completes the materialisation of the Ideas.
Hecate/Soul plays a crucial role in the formation of 'correct opinion' or belief, and of knowledge. The Father and the Demiurge gathered together the Cosmic Soul and other, less pure, mortal ingredients; from this mixture were created individual souls – part immortal, part human.

The Worlds
One Universe, consisting of three worlds/spheres: 1. Celestial/lunar - [pure Intellect (male God and son (Demi-urge)] - located beyond the moon 2. Material/physical - Earth, located between the Celestial and Chthonic spheres, contains both less 'real' hylic (matter) and more 'real' noetic (intellectual) elements. 3. Underworld/Hades - upon death souls failing to achieve salvation (rising to the Celestial sphere and communion with God) descend to Hades to await earthly reincarnation. Note: Hecate as Cosmic Soul travels/mediates between all three worlds/spheres.

Nature and Purpose of Existence - the *'meaning of life'*
Salvation of the soul, by: rejection of material unreality (evil), refining of the soul through theuristic/intellectual/philosophical activity, submission to and ultimate communion within God (achievement of Perfection and Harmony).

Platonic Idealism and North European Materialism
North European *Materialism*

Cosmology
In the beginning:
Fire (female energy), Ice (male strength), the void *(ginnungagap)*.

Creation:
Dynamic, moving, dancing fire energy encounters static ice; they react with each other.
The elements (fire and water/ice) procreate and birth living beings: nurturing *Audhumla* (cosmic cow), and *Ymir* (primal giant).
The creative fire/ice dialectic evolves naturally - independently and undirected by any form of ideal/divinity - into multiple complex forms: worlds and beings - goddesses, trees, elves, dwarves, frost giants, rock giants, men, wolves, ravens, rabbits etc.
Opinions and beliefs reflect complex material realities and are diverse - there can be no 'correct opinion'. Knowledge is not 'correct' but ever-changing. All living beings (inc. gods) are mortal. Upon death, energy is naturally reprocessed in the dialectal cycle of existence (souls' surviving in Valhalla or Hel die at *Ragnarok,* after which new worlds evolve).

The Worlds
Unlimited Multiverse
Nine worlds, each home to different beings (e.g. Asgard - the Aesir, Midgard - men).
All nine worlds are material (matter) and real. Thought/intellect reflects physical processes. All worlds reflect a (different) balance between order/chaos.
Upon death souls falling in battle go to Asgard, others to goddess Hel. All will be destroyed with the victory of chaotic forces at *Ragnarok*.
After *Ragnarok* new worlds (and new beings, inc. *Embla/Ask*, Women/Men) will appear/evolve.

Nature and Purpose of Existence - the *'meaning of life'*
Collective re-energising of life by: procreation, achievement of individual self-reliance, voluntary sacrifice (living for family, tribe, humanity), death - facilitating the existential renewal cycle.

Hecate in Pagan Greece - Timeline

Year BCE	Period	Historic Events	Dominant Cosmologies Name	Dominant Cosmologies Aspects	Hecate Aspects	Hecate Roles
1600 1500 1400 1300 1200	Mycenean Greece	First (late Bronze Age) Greek mainland literate civilisation (after early Bronze Age Minoan Crete)	Polytheism	Many gods (as immortal divine individuals) Materialism	Individual goddess	Crossroads Thresholds Keyholder Witchcraft Magic Ghosts Necromancy Single form
1100 1000 900	Greek Dark Ages	Civilisation collapses. Literacy disappears				
800 700 600	Archaic Period	Greek alphabet created. Magna Graecia (south Italy, Sicily etc.) colonised.				
480 348	Classical Period	Persian Invasion of Greece / Death of Plato	Platonism	Idealism One God Scepticism Re-incarnation		As above; Single and Triple form
323 300 200 100	Hellenistic Period	Death of Alexander the Great; Greek power and culture expands into Egypt and Middle East				
CE 31 100 100 200	Roman Empire Greece	Cleopatra/Anthony defeated at Actium	Middle Platonism	Cosmic Soul Numbers	Hecate/Cosmic Soul	Daemons; the Moon; Ensouler
312 330 380	Christianisation	Constantine converts to Christianity; Byzantium capital of Roman Empire; Edict of Thessalonica outlaws Paganism	Neo-platonism > Christianity	Monism (Divine Trinity) Salvation of Souls	Hecate Soteira (saviour)	The Father's Holy Spirit; Theurgist-teacher

Key: Polytheism   Platonism

Chapter 12 - *Loki and Dissent*

It should be admitted straight away that there is almost no direct evidence specifically linking Loki to the Anglo-Saxon pantheon, as distinct from the broader Scandinavian/Germanic paganism as represented in the poetic and prose Edda. However there is also very little evidence marking veneration or acknowledgement of most such deities in England, though it is commonly accepted that, though the names may be different (Thunor instead of Thor, Woden instead of Odin), pre-Christian Anglo-Saxons followed the gods and goddesses of that broad Germanic fellowship and sorority. The evidence for this is relatively scarce but well known from both literary (for example references by Bede) and place-name sources:

> *"The existence of fields and groves dedicated to specific deities is attested by a range of place-names... Feld (field) and Leah (grove) occur several times in combination with gods' names such as Woden, Thunor and Tiw... These sites presumably functioned as places of belief or cult locations where sacred activities might have been carried out."* [451]

Unlike Woden, Thunor and Tiw, evidence of this type for Loki in England is virtually non-existent, although some are willing to speculate:

> *"A fragmentary late 10th-century cross located in St Stephen's Church, Kirkby Stephen, Cumbria, England, features a bound figure with horns and a beard. This figure is sometimes theorized as depicting the bound Loki... A depiction of a similarly horned and round-shouldered figure was discovered in Gainford, County Durham and is now housed in the Durham Cathedral Library... The mid-11th century Gosforth Cross [Cumbria] has been interpreted as featuring... a depiction of a long-haired female kneeling figure holding an object above another prostrate, bound figure. Above and to their left is a knotted serpent. This has been interpreted as Sigyn soothing the bound Loki."* [452]

It is notable however that even this very restricted possible evidence of knowledge of Loki in what is now England, appears to be restricted to northern areas strongly associated with relatively late

Scandinavian influence, rather than earlier pre-Christian Anglo-Saxon paganism. It is also surely significant though that, despite Loki's repeated appearance in various Nordic myths, place-name and other evidence of any Loki cult is just as absent in Scandinavia as it is in England. This perhaps suggests that Loki's (at best) mischievous character defined him as a god unsuited to veneration and cult. Asking for the blessing of a trickster deity on one's family for example, might well have been regarded as a very unwise thing to do.

The lack of direct evidence of acknowledgement of Loki in the Anglo-Saxon literary and topographical landscapes therefore certainly does not prove that he was unknown in pre-Christian England, though perhaps like Thunor, Woden, and Tiw, his name may have been pronounced differently. Given the common appearance and great antiquity of Loki-like trickster deities throughout world mythologies[453] it is hard to believe that Loki (or a similar namesake) was completely unknown to early pagan Anglo-Saxons. As a character of a unique nature within the north European pantheon the importance of Loki's interactions with Æsir and Vanir – it is argued below - can hardly be overstated.

Loki is renowned as the trickster god who, despite being brought up in Asgard by the Æsir, eventually turns against them, and in the end shows his 'true nature' by siding with the forces of chaos in the final battle at the end of the worlds, when he attacks the god Heimdal (he who is also Shef or Shield Sheafing of the early English – see chapter 2), and they both die in the ensuing combat. Before that can happen though, a series of stories relate some of the many adventures from Loki's very complicated life. If there is one thing that is certain about Loki, it is that it is never clear exactly who or what this constantly changing and developing character is, though he always seems to act as a catalyst for radical change.

Loki – *Origin and Families*

Loki comes of a family of frost giants.[454] True to giants' chaotic nature, neither Loki's gender nor his/her sex are fixed. His mother is Laufey, and his father is Farbauti.[455] Laufey means 'island of leaves' and Simek suggests that this could be derived from *lauf-awiaz* 'the one full of leaves', suggesting that she might have been a tree goddess.[456] However Laufey might also mean 'the one who awakens confidence',[457] perhaps suggesting the type of fast-talking persuasive skills her son also cultivates for himself.

As befits someone of giant heritage who is nevertheless brought up in Asgard, the home of the Æsir gods who proclaim themselves the defenders of order and deadly enemies of chaotic frost and rock giants, Loki establishes not just a single family of his own, but produces children with four partners of varying sex and species.[†] This is summarised in the illustration below.

As a male Loki marries Sigyn of the Æsir, and has two sons with her, Narfi and Vali. Despite Loki's many adventures and betrayals Sigyn stays loyal to him. When he is eventually shackled and imprisoned with acidic serpent poison left to drip painfully on to his face, Sigyn stays by his side and catches as much of the poison as she can in a bowl to protect her husband.

Loki also partners Angrboda, a giantess. With her he has three infamous offspring: the goddess Hel (she whose form is half alive and beautiful, and half ghastly in decay and death), the wolf Fenrir (who bites off the god Tyr's hand), and Jörmungand the oceanic serpent whose body encircles the entire world of Middle Earth.

As if this were not enough, in the story of "The Building of Asgard's Wall" (summarised in a storytelling below) Loki shape and sex-changes into a mare and gives birth to Sleipnir, Odin's eight-legged magical stallion, which was so swift as to be uncatchable.

Finally there is also a reference to Loki giving birth to a *"child, thence in the world every ogress sprang"*. [458] It is not clear whether Loki did this with some unnamed (presumably monstrous) male partner, or by a magical process of impregnation when he *"ate from a heart, burned with linden, a half-charred woman's heart he'd found."*[459]

Loki then functions as both god and giant, as both male and female, and can shape-change to become a different creature altogether, such as a horse or a salmon (see the storytelling "The Binding of Loki" in this chapter's section on "Loki's Ultimate Role" below). He has also been associated by Grimm and other scholars with the element of fire, though Simek alleges that *"This is a misrepresentation caused by the similarity of names with the giant Logi, the personification of fire"*. [460] This may be so but nevertheless the association of Loki and fire does seem very appropriate. After all

---

[†] Loki changes sex but, for the sake of simplicity and in line with common practice, male pronouns are usually used to refer to Loki here.

Loki's Families [Image: Lynne Harling]
For full colour Loki image see back cover and
anglosaxonpagans.co.uk

not only is he famously intelligent, quick thinking, and assertive in a most incendiary manner (the rune Kenaz as the burning torch of knowledge and wit springs to mind, as does the eddic poem *Lokasenna* – Loki's 'flyting' or teasing and insulting of the gods based on his knowledge and public 'outing' of their personal weaknesses and foibles), but also his ability to change sex and become female further associates him with fire, for fire is the female element and creative energy, as in the rune Fehu, the first of the futhark.[‡]

Snorri Sturluson, writing in the thirteenth century, said of Loki:

> "Loki is pleasant and handsome in appearance, wicked in character and very changeable in his ways. He had much more than others that kind of intelligence that is called cunning and stratagems for every eventuality. He was always placing the Æsir into the most difficult situations; and often extracted them by his wiles." [464]

In order to study Loki's nature and roles further, it may be useful to look at some of the stories told about him.

Sixth Storytelling – *Loki and the Kidnapping of Idun*

At the time the first events of this tale took place, the gods Odin, Hoenir and Loki were all still living together as good friends in Asgard. The three enjoyed each other's companionship, and one day decided to set off to explore Midgard. They spent a day tramping through the hills and valleys of Middle Earth, which was enjoyable but tiring, and all that walking up hill and down dale made them hungry. Fortunately they found an ox, and quickly decided to kill it and roast the flesh. They gathered wood and lit a great fire, before sitting down to rest and tell each other stories while the meat cooked. Strangely however, despite constantly throwing wood on the flames, the ox flesh remained raw and inedible.

Staring into the sky at the smoke curling uselessly upwards, Hoenir was surprised to see a giant eagle in the distance, gliding towards them on outspread massive wings. Before long the eagle had settled on a tree branch near their fire, looking warily at the orange and yellow flames. On a day such as this, the tired gods were not all that

---

[‡] "*Fehu represents the primordial fire of Muspelheim... the first being to be created was a cosmic cow, Audhumla, which is the first feminine creative principle in nature and therefore the first incarnation of the Mother Goddess.*" Freya Aswynn, *Leaves of Yggdrasil*, St. Paul USA 1990, p.46

shocked when suddenly the bird spoke to them. "You must share the meat with me," it haughtily announced, "or your food will never cook".

The gods looked at each other. Nobody actually spoke out against the idea, so Odin shrugged his shoulders and agreed to the eagle's ultimatum. After that, sure enough, the meat was soon crackling in its fat, and a wonderful smell of roasting food reached all their noses. The eagle then spoke again, this time demanding first choice of its share of the meal. Again Odin, Hoenir and Loki agreed to the demand, glad that now at last they could expect to assuage their hunger.

At that however, to the gods' astonishment and dismay, the giant eagle used its enormous, razor-sharp beak to tear off nearly all the most tender and best quality parts of the roasted ox's body. Odin and Hoenir cried out in fury, whilst Loki angrily grabbed his walking staff and rammed it into the bird's body, intending to force it to fly off before its greed could completely deny them their meal. The hurt and now outraged eagle did indeed fly off, but so quickly that Loki was unable to release the staff from his grasp, although the eagle now had that too in its talons. In a moment of noise and confusion Loki found himself being pulled high into the air, suddenly in danger of falling to his death.

Desperate to avoid being killed, Loki wept and pleaded with the eagle for mercy, at which the soaring bird shook Loki menacingly, stared at him with an evil glint in its eyes, and silently carried him off into the unknown.

After that Odin and Hoenir made their way back to Asgard, wishing they had never made their visit to Midgard, and uncertain as to whether they would ever see Loki again. However a few days later Loki did turn up, looking sheepish and seeming very reluctant to explain what had happened. In fact the giant eagle had carried Loki back to his homeland: Jötenheim, for the eagle had really been a frost giant in disguise. As the price for his release Loki had agreed, unknown of course to anyone else, to yet another demand of the frost giant. This time he wanted not just roasted ox flesh, but that the goddess Idun should be handed over to him, along with her supply of the golden apples of 'eternal' youth.

Having learned to fear the shape-changing frost giant's death threats, Loki felt he had no choice but to trick Idun into leaving Asgard and travelling to Midgard with him. He achieved this by telling her a tall tale about a tree he had supposedly found bearing golden apples, which looked just like her own. As soon as Idun set foot in Midgard, the giant swooped down in his eagle form, and carried the unfortunate goddess off to Jötenheim, boasting that he was really called Thiazi, whilst loudly and openly proclaiming himself to be a frost giant. "Now the gods will grow old," he declared, "whilst I shall remain forever young".

Without the apples the gods did indeed quickly begin to age and even feel the threat of death. Odin summoned a council, which all the gods attended – except of course for Idun, and Loki who in his shame had wisely gone into hiding. The gods deduced from Loki's absence that he must be connected to the source of their problem. Odin ordered Loki's capture, and he was eventually discovered sleeping on Idun's land. Loki was dragged roughly before Odin, who ordered him to get Idun back, on pain of death. The harassed trickster had no choice but to agree to travel to Jötenheim, yet even now he bargained for the goddess Freya to lend him her magical cloak of falcon feathers, so that he might fly between the worlds. "It'll be a lot quicker," he told them, "so you won't age so much!"

It has to be said that Loki could, despite everything, sometimes prove to have luck on his side. When he arrived at Thiazi's home, the giant had gone out fishing with Skadi, his daughter. Quickly Loki worked rune magic to change Idun into a nut, which he then picked up in his falcon claws, before immediately flying off, heading home to Asgard. Before long Thiazi returned and discovered that Idun was missing. Immediately he clothed himself in his eagle skin again, and set out to search for her. Soon he spotted Loki the falcon flying as fast as he could towards Asgard and, guessing what had happened, the eagle sped after the falcon.

Loki arrived at Asgard only just out of reach of the more powerful eagle's claws, but Odin had seen Loki's approach, and had got the gods to light kindling on Asgard's walls. As Thiazi closely chased Loki his eagle wings caught fire, and he plummeted to the ground just inside Asgard's walls, where the gods killed him. Loki returned Freya's falcon feather cloak to her, and changed Idun from the nut back into her goddess form again. Idun happily offered the gods her apples, and their health, strength, and youth began to return to them. Loki had redeemed himself, and was allowed to live, but the gods never forgot that they had all almost died because of him.

Loki's Character – *in the Story of the Kidnapping of Idun*

It is very noticeable that in the tale of the kidnapping of the goddess Idun, whilst Loki's behaviour is appalling, he is also shown to be a weak, vacillating, and passive character. He is not some evil genius directing a heinous plot against the Æsir, but repeatedly himself appears in the role of victim. Firstly he is completely outwitted and physically overwhelmed by the giant Thiazi in his disguise as an eagle, being helplessly carried off to the giant's lair. Then he is bullied by Thiazi into betraying the gods who have nurtured him by arranging the kidnapping of Idun. He tries to disappear and hide away from the anticipated wrath of the gods, only to fail miserably and be dragged before Odin. Once again he is then bullied into reluctant action, this time by the All-Father's death threats. Only at the very last does he partially redeem himself by saving Idun and successfully returning her to Asgard, but even this requires great luck (in that Thiazi has left Idun alone and unguarded), and the agency of others (the loan of Freya's cloak of falcon feathers, and the killing of Thiazi by the Æsir). No doubt the gods looked down on Loki with disgust after this incident, but surely not so much out of fear of Loki, as out of abhorrence of his weaknesses both physical and moral, and his repeated inability to stand up for himself against bullying.

Despite Loki's passivity and victimhood, Crossley-Holland still sees this story as marking an active step in the development of Loki's character in the direction of an ever firmer association with destructive forces:

> "It is probable that Idun was originally one of the Vanir, a goddess of fertility, youth and death. Thus... Loki accuses her [in Lokasenna] of being so wanton (a quality she shares with Freya), that she made love to her brother's murderer... It must be significant too that Idun is turned by Loki in to a nut... fruit and nuts have been found amongst Scandinavian grave goods (to ensure life after death)... Loki is now no longer mere agent provocateur but acts directly contrary to the interests of the gods. Here too we meet Loki as a shape changer again... Loki's debonair use of the falcon skin should not obscure its true purpose, which must have been to carry the goddess's spirit, in her role as shamaness, to the underworld." [465]

Crossley-Holland is surely correct, given Idun's life-promoting qualities, in identifying her as having originally been a fertility goddess and one of the Vanir. Given the very early association of Anglo-Saxon tribes with the Vanir as fertility deities, going all the way back to the pre-migration period (see for example the chapter on Scyld Scefing), it also seems probable that the early English tribes would have known of Idun, and if so then certainly also of this key story of her kidnapping, and Loki's major role in the tale. Again this implied early English knowledge of Loki is speculative rather than firmly evidence based, but does seem to make sense.

Further hints about the development of Loki's character and role are contained in other story details. At first glance it perhaps seems odd that Loki turns Idun into, of all things, a nut. Certainly a nut is small in size, light, and apparently securely portable in a falcon's claws, but it is also presumably not insignificant that a nut is also a seed of life and future growth. Like Idun's apples however, nuts, whilst clearly part of an ongoing fertility cycle, form part of a botanical or vegetal generative process, rather than functioning at the level of divine sexual reproduction. It is tempting to conclude that there is a hint here that even higher life forms such as the gods need a healthy, fertile botanical setting in order to be able to maintain their own health, and that this nurturing botanical environment can be promoted through the use of divine female spirit: Loki donning Freya's falcon feather cloak to carry her spirit to imprisoned Idun.

Certainly Idun does seem to represent a rather passive and decidedly botanical/agricultural aspect of continuing healthy youthfulness. Her own apparent lack of character complexity and development has been lamented by Sheena McGrath, as commented on in chapter 5.

> "Idunn is portrayed [as] a passive victim throughout,
> passed from gods to giants to gods... She has the
> traditional female role: victim and pretext..." [466]

Perhaps though the presentation of Idun's role as passive might not be attributable solely to the patriarchal values of late pagan Scandinavian storytellers, as portrayed by McGrath (see chapter 5 for more detail). It could possibly also reflect an older intuited need for the active agency of female spirit to progress beyond passive (nut-borne) botanical fertility, to the promotion of animal and divine corporeal fertility (Freya's falcon-cloak borne spirit), operating at higher, more developed and more complex physical levels (at least for frost giants, Aesir and Vanir, and presumably also for women and men).

If Loki is able to carry female spirit, at least when he is in Freya's falcon shape-changed form, this may be an early hint of what becomes undeniable in subsequent stories: that Loki is not just a shape-changer but also decidedly transgender – to the extent that he can become fully female and actually give birth (see the storytelling "The Building of Asgard's Wall" below). No wonder then that Loki too *"has the traditional female role"* of victim (of both Thiazi and potentially Odin) in this story.

Finally in relation to the story of the kidnapping of Idun, it is worth asking: in allowing the goddess and her apples to be stolen away by Thiazi, was not Loki signing his own early death warrant? Did he not worry that he too, along with the Æsir and Vanir, would quickly age and die without access to those magical golden apples? It is true that Thiazi is a giant and that Loki too is of giant stock, but it does not appear that Thiazi wants Idun and her apples for the community of giants as a whole, but rather that he lusts for the illusion of eternal life for himself alone. Hence, he keeps Idun as an isolated prisoner, inaccessible to others.

The answer again may lie in less obvious aspects of Loki's singular character. Loki is not a god in the strict sense of being a member of either the Æsir or Vanir clans, but neither is he simply a giant. Rather his nature seems if anything close to being uniquely 'supra-godlike', in that he can do things that even many gods cannot, for example change shape and sex. The gods generally protect and promote order, whilst the giants are perceived as agents of chaos. Order is developmental but structural and necessarily limiting; Chaos is destructive but potentially boundless. At least at this stage in his story Loki never seems to be sure which side he is on; in fact he seems to get pushed around and bullied by agents of both order and chaos. Could it be that Loki's apparent lack of interest in both the gods' and Thiazi's desire to live 'forever', reflects a nature which at its most fundamental actually lies outside the standard gods versus giants and order versus chaos dialectic? It might be that Loki does not worry about the loss of Idun's apples not because he is in any way uniquely immune to the gods' mortality, but because he understands and accepts the necessity of death, unlike Thiazi or the Æsir who all dream of living forever, and are prepared to kill in their struggle for supposed immortality.

Seventh Storytelling – *Loki and the Building of Asgard's Walls*

After Odin had ordered the attempted burning to death of Gullveig, the Vanir wise woman and witch, the Vanir took up arms to defend themselves, and laid siege to the Æsir's walled fortress of Asgard to avenge that failed attack. Despite the Æsir's love of war and pride in their military abilities, the Vanir eventually succeeded in laying waste to Asgard's high, protective fortifications, making much use of their superior magical skills. In desperation Odin sued for peace. Eventually an exchange of hostages was agreed to guarantee the terms of a peace settlement. In line with this agreement Njörd and Frey volunteered to live in Asgard for a time, whilst Hoenir moved to Vanaheim.

After the war was over Asgard's walls remained in ruins for a long time, but one day a stone mason arrived, offering to rebuild them. He said that it was clearly a big job, and that it would probably take about eighteen months. Of course Odin was keen to see his fortress reinstated, but even he had to take a step backwards when the stone mason told him what his price would be: he wanted nothing less than the hand of the goddess Freya in marriage, "Oh, and the sun and the moon as well". Odin stared hard at the stone mason, expecting him to announce laughingly that he had been 'only joking', but it seemed that this was a serious demand.

Of course even Odin felt forced to reject such a ludicrous idea out of hand. But then Loki spoke up, urging the gods to at least discuss the matter in private before publicly rejecting it. Once he had got them out of earshot of the mason, Loki suggested to the gods that they offer him only the six months of winter to rebuild the walls. If he were foolish enough to accept, Loki argued, then they should let him attempt it - confident that there would not be enough time to finish the job. That way the gods would get Asgard's walls at least partially repaired free of charge, and Freya would be safe.

The builder was summoned back. He tried to argue that if he were to be given only the winter to complete his task, then he should be allowed to employ additional workers, but Odin forbade that idea. However Loki then suggested that they should agree to the man's final request: that he at least be allowed to use his own stallion, Svadilfari ["Unlucky Traveller"]. Reluctantly the gods accepted Loki's suggestion.

The mason began his task on the first day of winter, and the gods were amazed at the vast quantities of stone he managed to quarry and shape each day. They even began to suspect that the stone mason must really be a rock giant in disguise. Three days before the end of winter the mason had almost finished. Seeing that her future might be forfeit, Freya wept tears of gold, but the gods could not think of any honest way to back out of their agreement. Finally, with very little time left, Odin threatened Loki with death unless he could think of a way to save Freya.

That evening as the stone mason and his stallion were finishing their work, a mare appeared and trotted up to Svadilfari the stallion, clearly in the mood for love. Svadilfari was enticed to chase the mare, leaving the builder furious and alone. Realising that without his stallion to haul stone the walls would not after all be completed on time, the mason – in his anger – threw off his disguise and revealed himself to be an enemy - a powerful rock giant. Seeing the deception Odin quickly declared the building contract null and void, and summoned Thor, who used his hammer to smash the giant into a thousand pieces.

Many months passed before Loki the shape changer was seen at Asgard again, and when he did return, he was leading a frisky eight-legged colt.

Loki explained that he, Loki, had given birth to the horse, named Sleipnir ["Slippy"]. The colt's father was of course Svadilfari, the giant's stallion. Loki presented his equine offspring to Odin, commenting that the eight-legged animal could outrun all other horses, and even bear its rider from Asgard to the land of the dead and back again. Odin accepted the gift, and in return allowed Loki to return to live in Asgard, despite his over cleverness having almost resulted in the goddess of love having to be surrendered into the solid arms of a bestial rock giant.

Loki's Character – *in the Story of the Building of Asgard's Wall*

At first reading, this story seems relatively simple compared to the tale of the kidnapping of Idun. This time it is just the one Vanir goddess (Freya) who is under threat, not the entire Æsir and Vanir clans, and she is wanted only as a marriage partner, not threatened with becoming a trigger for the onset of old age and the death of all the gods, as Idun had been. Loki's antics seem superficially clever and perhaps even comic. This time he is not deceiving the gods; rather it is they who agree to his proposal that they collude in deceiving the stone mason. Nevertheless it quickly becomes clear that more fundamental contradictions are again in play here. This is no ordinary stone mason, but a representative of the giants, the primitive forces of disorder and chaos who will destroy the carefully constructed order of the gods if they can. Once again the means by which they seek to destroy the gods is through the abduction of a leading goddess who embodies the feminine spirit:

> "The mason demands... Freyja... the foremost goddess of fertility. The giant's intention was... to bring to an end the natural revolution of the seasons and deprive the gods of the possibility of regeneration – and... by taking away the sun and the moon, to consign them to eternal freezing darkness... The gods embody aspects of natural and social order; the giants subvert that order and seek to overthrow it." [467]

The stone mason seeks to trick the gods, but they too are deceiving him. It appears that the supposed upholders of order and honour are no more trustworthy than their enemies, the champions of chaos. The gods then have to be rescued from oblivion by the very trickster whom they view as dishonourable and dishonest: Loki. And Loki's methods for achieving that salvation can hardly have been to the liking of the Æsir:

> "Loki is not only a shape changer... he can change sex, and even bear a child... Bisexuality was not a characteristic that appealed to early Icelanders, and homosexuality was a crime punishable by outlawry. It seems likely that Loki's sexual antics... would have aroused more distaste than amusement." [468]

It might be thought that Loki's actions amount to rather more than mere "sexual antics". He does after all actually change species and sex, and become pregnant, and give birth, and not just to any foal but to one of the wonders of the worlds: Sleipnir, the eight-legged marvel capable not just of outrunning all other horses[**], but even of travelling safely between the realms of the living and the dead. It could be said that through Sleipnir Loki is here acting as a symbol of the

---

[**] It should be noted that horses were perhaps seen as sacred animals by the early English – see chapter 13.

interrelationship of death, fertility, and rebirth. The giant stone mason threatens the gods with the loss of their fertility through the forced surrender of Freya, the goddess of love. Once Freya was no longer there to keep the dynamic female and male cosmic energies of the sun and the moon balanced and in place, the barren stasis of sterility would be all that was left.

Loki's answer is to act outside of accepted, orderly processes. By changing both shape and sex he disrupts the moralities and plans of gods and giants alike. At this point he is perhaps acting to maintain a necessary balance between the forces of order and chaos by subverting their simple dual opposition to each other, through the linking of fertility and death as ongoing interactive processes, rather than totally separate factors. For Loki, death is as much a precursor of life, as life necessarily is of death.

After male Loki has accepted the principle of femininity, the child of Loki's womb, Sleipnir, is capable of existing in both the sun-warmed, feminine, procreative world of the living, and the cold, frozen, moon-shadowed, masculine realm of the dead. Sleipnir is a stallion with all a horse's sacred strength[††], but he also embodies the feminine procreative spirit of rebirth so effectively that, like Freya's predecessor the great goddess Inanna, he can descend to the decayed land of the deceased, experience and learn what that means, and then return to the land of the living.

Loki's 'outsider' changes of sex and species, and his pregnancy and delivery whilst in his changed state, challenge and potentially undermine the lawful, ordered certainties of the gods. Yet - probably against the 'better judgement' of the Æsir - this new challenge to the established, constrained rhythms of seasonal fertility might be positive. It might prevent its potential decline and decay into something itself resembling stasis: fixed, merely cyclical and undeveloping, unchanging patterns of reproduction.

On the positive side, Loki's challenge can provoke new and more developed, more varied forms of reproduction, as demonstrated so effectively by the birth of the magical Sleipnir. This offspring of order- and chaos-defying Loki can journey to the land of the dead, and return alive again – which is more than can be said for example of Frigg's son Balder. As an Ás, the 'perfect', beautiful, male god Balder is ultimately constrained by the laws of the ordered universe and, once dead, must

---

[††] English sacred horses – see chapter 13

remain so, despite his mother's attempts to revivify him. Of course Loki is responsible for Balder's death. The reasons for the irreconcilability of 'perfect' Balder and Loki as the dissident disruptor and enemy of perfection are discussed below in the analysis of the story of the death of Balder.

On the negative side, Loki's challenge surely involves all the uncertainty and risks of disruptive change, including the demise of established forms, and even the potential triumph of darkness and stasis (the very outcome both Loki and the gods are struggling to avoid). Loki's bisexual roles might be a dissident triumph, but whilst in female, equine form, Loki does not dare appear in Odin's ordered realm of Asgard. He ventures a return only after giving birth, when it seems that once more he has become a two-legged male, to that extent complying with the public appearance rules of the home of structure and order. And it should not be forgotten that it was Loki's risk-taking in the first place which almost resulted in the giant's triumph, the implied demise of the gods, and eternal darkness.

This story taught pagan North Europeans that whilst simple reproduction of existing life forms is facilitated through ordered, seasonal, sexual rhythms (the gods, Vanir and Aesir, have sex and children, who grow up to replace their parents), the creation of entirely new energy forms (e.g. Sleipnir) requires disruptive, potentially chaotic magic, involving the erosion of the existing social and even physical order. Loki is capable of this. The gods are not, or prefer to limit themselves to the safety and security of the more ordered, constrained reality of Asgard's walls – yet even Odin himself was prepared to use and benefit from the products of potentially risk-laden disruptive magic (he accepts Loki's gift of Sleipnir). This was always going to be a difficult balancing act for the Æsir and Loki to maintain. From Loki's point of view the failure of 'All-father' Odin and the Æsir to accept the need to change and adapt would ultimately drive him to despair, the killing of Balder, and to play a leading role in the destruction of Asgard at Ragnarok.

Eighth Storytelling – *Loki and the Death of Balder*

The gods revered Frigg's son Balder as the embodiment of physical beauty and perfection. Being held in such high regard, Balder might have been expected to enjoy a good life and be happy, but he became troubled by persistent dreams of his own death. In a desperate attempt to save her son from his feared doom, Frigg travelled the nine worlds demanding that every living being, and even every inanimate element, swear an oath not to harm her son. Everything bowed to Frigg's will. Animals, trees, water, stone, metals, earth, and even illnesses all swore as required.

After this, testing Balder's invulnerability became a sport for the gods. At feasts and drinking sessions they would, for fun, hurl everything from stones to deadly spears at Balder, laughing with joy as all these weapons bounced off him. Of all the gods, only Loki refused to participate. He found that indestructible Balder's perfection angered him.

Loki's anger drove him to attempt to discover some flaw in Balder's protection. He changed himself into the shape of a crone, and in that form went to visit Frigg. In his disguise as an apparently harmless old woman Loki complained to Frigg that he had seen the gods stoning beloved Balder, but Frigg laughed and explained that her son was invulnerable. However, thinking the old woman no threat, Frigg let slip that there was one thing which she had not made swear never to harm her son: mistletoe, which she had thought too young and inoffensive to be worth worrying about.

Immediately Loki dashed off to find an oak tree, and a sprig of mistletoe growing on it. This he took, and sharpened a twig from the mistletoe to make a spear point from it. Returning to the scene of the gods' sport, he was pleased to get there just as Frigg and her second son, blind Hod, were also arriving. Loki gave his sharpened mistletoe twig to the unseeing Hod, Balder's brother, and urged him to join in the fun by hurling it at Balder. Hod obeyed, and Balder fell dead.

Frigg responded to her son's unexpected death by pleading for a volunteer to visit the goddess Hel, queen of the land of the dead, and there offer to pay her any ransom - if only she would return her son Balder to her and the realm of the living. Odin's son Hermod stepped forward, and Odin lent him his magical horse, Sleipnir, to ride to see Hel.

Whilst Hermod was gone, the gods prepared a ship to bear

Balder's body out to sea, there to be set alight. Balder's wife, Nanna, died of a broken heart, and her body was now placed beside Balder's in the funeral pyre ship. Freya arrived for the ceremony in her chariot dawn by cats, leading the female warriors, the Valkyries. Representatives from the elves, dwarves, frost giants, and rock giants also attended. The sea herself sobbed. Balder's horse was sacrificed and its body placed in the ship, along with many valuable treasures, including even Draupnir, Odin's miraculous gold ring, which produced eight more circlets of gold every ninth night. The funeral pyre was lit, blessed by Thor raising his hammer over the vessel and saying the necessary sacred words.

The blazing ship was then allowed to drift out to sea, where it gradually disappeared.

Hermod meanwhile was riding Sleipnir in search of Hel. For nine nights he rode, crossing many rivers, before eventually arriving at Hel's hall of Eljudnir. The gates to Hel's hall were locked, but Sleipnir simply leaped over them. Hermod found his brother Balder sitting in the hall's high seat. In the morning Hel herself appeared. From the waist upwards she was a beautiful, living woman, but she had the rotting legs of a corpse.

Hermod told Hel of Frigg's unimaginable distress at her perfect son's death, and begged the mistress of the deceased to allow Balder to return to Asgard and to life. Hel agreed, subject to one condition only: that Hermod return ahead of him with the message that for this to happen all things must weep tears of true sorrow for Balder's death. Balder sent the magic ring Draupnir back to Odin with Hermod, as a token of his continuing fealty and intention to return. His wife Nanna likewise sent a gold ring back to Asgard for the goddess Fulla.

Upon Hermod's arrival back in Asgard, the gods sent out messengers throughout the nine worlds, imploring all things to weep for Balder. Everything they asked, from stones to metal, from trees to illnesses, from birds to animals, agreed and wept, just as when the spring sun melts ice-rime. However when, after their apparently successful mission, the messengers stepped back through the tall gates of fortress Asgard, they were met by an old giantess, who gave her name as Thokk. She refused to weep for Balder, and so Hel refused to release him after all. The gods could not prove it, but they all felt that Thokk the giantess was surely really Loki in disguise.

Loki's Character – *in the Story of Balder's Death*

Analysis of this story can tend to focus upon comprehension of Balder's character and role rather than Loki's, although the two are clearly presented as dialectical opposites, meaning that any deeper understanding of what is going on must require not only an assessment of both Loki's and Balder's functions in the narrative, but also an exploration of the interaction between them. Kevin Crossley-Holland says:

> "Snorri's image of a passive suffering god... has its origin in the fertility gods of the near east, Tammuz, Attis, Adonis, Baal, and Orpheus... 'Gods of this kind often died in youth, and violently... their death was publicly lamented at festivals held in the Autumn, as if the participants would weep them from the Underworld. Their return, sometimes celebrated in Spring, was the occasion of jubilation. Snorri's picture of Balder was probably influenced, too, by the story of Christ in the Anglo-Saxon poem, The Dream of the Rood:
>> 'Shadows swept across the land,
>> Dark shapes under low-flying clouds.
>> All creation wept,
>> Wailed for the death of the king;
>> Christ was on the cross.'" [469]

This may all be true, but it does not tell us anything about Loki, or the relationship between Loki and Balder, and therefore in the end not very much about Balder either. As a thirteenth century writer, Snorri may well be reflecting images of Christian lamentation, and even harking back to earlier Middle Eastern mythological failed attempts to return from the Underworld, but it is why Frigg fails to revivify Balder, and Loki's key role in that, that is truly illuminating.

Firstly it must be said that the death of Balder is obviously not just another uncomplicated reflection of seasonal fertility and the agricultural year. In fact, if anything, Frigg tries to deny the natural cycle of life and death through her attempts to make Balder perfect, invulnerable, and immortal. Her struggle to bring her son back from the realm of the dead is not an annual, seasonal ritual, but a desperate one-off attempt to defy death entirely, and restore Balder to his manufactured immortality. And of course the rebirth of the god in the Spring just does not happen; Balder remains dead until the end of time.

Secondly it is worth asking why Balder's apparent perfection, invulnerability, and immortality angers Loki so much. It would be easy to assume that this is just Loki being Loki, and once again demonstrating unpleasant characteristics such as envy, lack of empathy, and taking joy in the destruction of others. It is important though that Loki is the single dissident here, the only freethinker, whatever the morality or otherwise of his personal motivation. Everyone and everything else submits to Frigg. Their universal alignment in disciplined rows of publicly demonstrated consent eradicates diversity of opinion.

This amounts to an attempt by Frigg to defy and alter the fundamental operating laws of existence itself: the necessarily ever-changing (because imperfect and unstable) nature of energy, as expressed through the cycle of birth, growth, life, and death - a cycle with which Balder's would-be perfection is irreconcilable. The alternative to the unstable deficiencies of life and death is stasis and perfection. But perfection, stasis, is not life, nor even existence. The only truly perfect thing is unbeing, the unchanging void. Loki may not see himself as virtuous, but objectively it is his apparent meanness of character which preserves diversity and saves the worlds from descent into stasis and unbeing.

A third key point in this story is that Loki chooses to shape change into a crone. Again superficially this choice of disguise might be thought to be just another example of Loki's underhand trickery and cunning: nobody would suspect an apparently harmless old woman of intending to oppose Frigg and condemn Balder. There is surely more to it than this, though. In particular Loki's actions once more raise fundamental issues of sex and gender.

The crone signifies both wisdom and the female principle (the regeneration and creation of new life) in the end phase of life. Loki the crone provides the story with an alternative, more traditional reminder of the female life cycle than that sought by Frigg. Whilst Frigg seeks the achievement of eternal youth and immortality for her child, Loki as a crone wisely reminds us that all living things must die (if they are not simply to cease to be, and thereby to never have been born - as unchanging perfection is irreconcilable with individual, ever variable, flawed, births and lives).

Loki takes female form, rather than that of an old man, because it is the female principle of the life cycle – birth/growth/life/death – that Frigg is attempting to betray. Frigg the mother goddess is the active entity in this story. Her son Balder is but a passive recipient of his mother's bounty. Hod too, as Balder's brother, is passive. He kills Balder, but (misled by Loki) only inadvertently, not actively. Loki is male (at this point), but his male role here is to restate the indispensability of the female life-cycle principle violated by Frigg. In order to do this, and show us the error of this mother goddess's ways, he must himself become female (as Thokk), in order to personify healthy, life-giving, female fertility – ironically, but necessarily, by reminding us of the end of life.

A fourth vital matter is the role of the goddess of the dead. Hel is the very embodiment of the inevitability of death, and its interrelationship with life - from the waist upwards a beautiful, living woman, but from the waist down a rotting corpse. Even so she agrees, against all usual practice, to release Balder back to the realm of the living – though only if all things will weep for him. Why does Hel set this condition? She apparently has the power to release Balder, so if she is really prepared to do so, why not simply let him go; why the condition?

The answer surely is that she is not really able and/or willing to defy the laws of mother nature. She placates the potential wrath of the gods, and the enmity of Frigg, by appearing to give way to their request, but does so in such a way as to negate the possibility of her ever having to comply with Frigg's impossible appeal . Hel knows that Balder is not truly perfect, whatever his mother thinks of him, and that therefore something, somewhere, will feel compelled to refuse Balder their tears. Hence Balder will stay dead, the interactive, dynamic, balancing of life and death across the worlds will be maintained, and Hel will continue to receive the dead into her realm. Death and annihilation will continue, but so too will birth and new life.

Fifthly and finally there is the giantess Thokk, she who refuses to shed tears for Balder. The gods cannot prove that Thokk is really Loki, but apparently nevertheless recognise that it must be him. So Loki has yet again magically shape shifted and changed gender, just as he did to become the crone in his previous approach to Frigg. Why is it necessary for Loki to change sex, and in this case race as well, in order to defy Frigg and the gods? After all, in order to achieve his aim, and appease his anger without getting blamed for it, he had only to disguise himself as anybody else, something he seems capable of doing very effectively, not necessarily change both sex and race.

Again Loki's role appears to be to correct, or at least restate and revalidate, the female life-cycle principle violated by Frigg. In order to do this, and once more show us the error of this mother goddess's ways, he must himself again become female, in order to personify healthy, life-giving, female fertility. This time however his new female form reminds the story's audience not of the end of individual life (as a crone), but of the threat to life itself from the forces of chaos, the frost giants, the traditional enemies of the gods. The giants, as the forces of chaos, will of course eventually bring about the doom of the Æsir in the final battle at the end of the worlds, Ragnarok. So at the conclusion of the story it is no longer an individual's life or death at stake, but the survival of the gods themselves. Frigg, as a mother goddess, in personally seeking the everlasting avoidance of death for her son Balder, risks undermining the ability of all the goddesses, and women, to go on reproducing life.

Loki's Last Acts

The stories of Idun's kidnapping, Asgard's walls, and Balder's death all serve to confirm that there is always more to Loki than meets the eye. He is never just a trickster, and his status as a dissident and outsider is also borne out by further stories involving him.

In "Lokasenna" or 'Loki's Flyting'[‡‡] he insults many of the gods assembled in a feast hall, both Æsir and Vanir, publicly giving away many personal details of their flawed behaviour in front of the divine multitude. Yet again questions of sex and gender come to the fore. When Loki accuses Odin of giving victory in combat to his favourites, even when they constitute the weaker side who should in all fairness lose the battle, Odin attempts to divert attention and undermine Loki's credibility by accusing him of both transsexual acts and homosexual desires:

> "You spent eight winters under the earth,
> As a milking cow and a matron,
> And there you bore babies;
> That signals to me a cock-craver." [470]

Immediately Loki gives as good as he gets, letting it be known that Odin too has engaged in effeminate activity, in his case performing unmanly magic which should only be done by goddesses:

---

‡‡ Flyting – "a contest consisting of the exchange of insults between two parties, often conducted in verse" [https://en.wikipedia.org/wiki/Flyting]

"It's said you played the witch on Samsey,
Beat the drum like a lady-prophet;
In the guise of a wizard you wandered the world:
That signals to me a cock-craver." [471]

Needless to say, such wounding exchanges of insults hardly enhanced the chances of the gods overlooking for very long Loki's strongly suspected role in Balder's death. In the story of "The Binding of Loki" things come to a head. Fearing that the gods are losing all patience with him and are about to inflict a painful revenge, Loki flees Asgard and, trying to put as much distance between himself and the angry gods as possible, ends up in some remote part of Middle Earth. Even here he still fears that he will be tracked down, and so the shape changer takes on the form of a salmon, dives into a fast-flowing river, and takes to swimming in the river's torrent pooling at the base of a powerful waterfall. Here, he hopes, he will be neither seen nor recognised.

For a while Loki was able to survive alone in this manner, but one day a party of gods appeared, following the course of the river upstream, clearly looking for something. As luck would have it, the tired and hungry group settled down by Loki's pool and produced a fishing net. This they stretched across the racing stream of water, with Thor wading across to the far bank, then weighted it with river stones, and began dragging it against the flow.

They caught a salmon. Hauled up on to the bank, Loki was helpless. Out of the water he needed to reveal himself in order to be able to breathe air again. The gods, who had indeed been searching for the being they took to be responsible for Balder's death, gasped half in surprise and half in triumph. They dragged Loki to a cave, and there bound him tightly to a slab of rock with the entrails of his own son. They did not kill him; that would have been too easy on him! Instead they sent for Skadi, the daughter of the giant Thiazi who had kidnapped Idun, only to be led to his death by Loki in falcon form. When she arrived at the cave, she had with her a venomous, hissing snake. This she now fastened inescapably to a rock immediately above Loki's head, from where its acidic poison dripped painfully on to his exposed face. There, the gods explained, Loki must remain in agony until Ragnarok and the end of the worlds.

Only Sigyn, Loki's wife, took pity on him. When told what had happened to her husband she dashed to Midgard and found him suffering terribly. She could not free him, for magic had been used to change their son's binding entrails to immovable rock, but she took a bowl and held it between Loki and the snake to catch the poison. This alleviated much of Loki's pain, though whenever the bowl became full Sigyn had to take it away to empty it, allowing the venom to burn Loki's face again until she could return. When this happens, his pain is so great that his roaring and writhing cause the earth itself to quake.

It is said that in the end the gods' condemnation of Loki to suffer until the end of time will rebound on them, for as Ragnarok approaches the forces of chaos will storm across Midgard, racing to attack and destroy Odin and his Æsir in Asgard. As they pass Loki's cave, its walls of stone will shatter, and Loki will at last break free. Outraged and in anguish from his long years of torture, fixated on revenge, he will join the rampaging chaos armies, rising to play a leading role in the destruction of Asgard. Yet, even in his moment of long delayed triumph, Loki too will fall. He will seek out Heimdal, the guardian of the Rainbow Bridge and watchman of the home of the gods, and challenge him to single combat. Then as Asgard shatters, collapsing before the hurled flames of the fire giants, Heimdal and Loki shall both die on the point of each other's sword.

Loki – *Transgression, Dissent and Diversity*

Loki is very far from perfect, but then that seems to be the whole point about him. He is both unique and 'everyman'. His failings, moral and otherwise, may be awful, yet they mirror and throw light on those of the gods.

He is unique in that he is neither fully god nor wholly giant. He is of giant stock, but brought up in Asgard. He clearly feels himself to be, and acts as, an outsider, and eventually also an outlaw. He is unique, at least in the known stories of the north European gods, in that he is truly transsexual. He is a shape changer who can also fully change sex, a male who can at times become female and bear children. His offspring may be in part monstrous (Fenrir the wolf, Jörmungand the world serpent, and Hel goddess of the Underworld), or wonderous (Sleipnir the eight-legged sacred horse able to travel to Helheim – the world of the dead – and return).

He is a male who is able to bear sacred feminine energy in the shape of Freya's falcon feather cloak, but his ability to change sex is perceived by the Æsir as transgressing acceptable social norms. Odin berates him as a "cock craver". He is conscious of being seen as a transgressor by the gods, but refuses to be silenced. Again and again in Lokasenna (Loki's Flyting) the gods, one after another, order him to be quiet, but again and again Loki publicly and loudly exposes their weaknesses. The gods may have high opinions of themselves, but Loki openly dissents from the usual social niceties governing what can and cannot be said.

He is a male who fails to meet the Æsir's expectations of masculine behaviour, being seen to lack a warrior's necessary physical and moral resolution. Being weak he is bullied by giants (Thiazi) and gods (Odin) alike. At times he tries hard to improve his relationship with the gods (rescuing Idun, getting Asgard's fortress walls half rebuilt for free, saving Freya from an ignominious marriage to a rock giant), but ultimately his need to exercise his wits makes this impossible.

The Æsir see themselves as living by an honest moral code, and as the heroic defenders of order against the raw, chaotic, destructive power of the giants. They encase themselves inside Asgard's fortress walls, which they look to as fixed, physical protection against threats of all kinds, both material and ethical. In so doing they deliberately disregard their own dark side, engaging in a conspiracy of silence about matters deemed unpleasant, such as Odin's practicing of unmasculine magic. Ironically it is only the morally dubious Loki (he who betrayed Idun and all the gods) who cannot accept this hypocrisy.

Loki's own personal ethic requires him to analyse individuals' behaviour and compare it to their individual and collectively proclaimed moral norms. Where there is discrepancy he feels unable to betray his own wits as others do by deliberately ignoring such things and making sure never to speak of them in public. On the contrary the tension between professed and actual behaviours drives him to release the internal pressures arising from such knowledge by playing the role of dissident and speaking out.

Loki suffers for his roles of transgressor of social norms and outspoken dissident. Ultimately he is imprisoned, bound, and tortured at great length. Characters who are otherwise enemies unite against him to achieve this. Skadi the giantess joins the god Thor in their joint objective of inflicting pain on Loki. The justification is Loki's role in the death of Balder. There is no doubt that in tricking Hod, Balder's brother, into causing his death, Loki is indeed morally guilty. It could be argued however that Loki was driven to this by Æsir moral hypocrisy, and that the gods are no better than he is. Frigg's insistence that her son Balder was perfect and that all of existence must acknowledge him as such, as well as swearing never to harm him, but to accept him being made invulnerable and effectively immortal, surely conflicted with reality. Nobody can appear perfect to everybody all the time. Reality is too complex, with too many factors proving irreconcilable (except perhaps through conflict), for that ever to be possible.

Frigg's publicly pronounced view of Balder was surely the ultimate example of the kind of tension between professed and actual reality that Loki's intellectual and moral intelligence made it impossible for him to accept in silence or without challenge. Loki's words in Lokasenna challenged the Æsir to acknowledge dark truths about themselves. In the case of Balder however, words could not be sufficient to set things right by rebalancing perceived reality and truth, because Balder was proclaimed as perfect; there were no known unpleasant truths which could be spoken out loud. Yet, as in reality perfection is not possible, Loki still felt driven, as in Lokasenna, to somehow end the mismatch between reputation and reality. This is what drove him to lead Hod to strike down Balder. It does not excuse him. But neither are the giantess Skadi, or Thor and the other gods who torture Loki (because killing him would have been relatively quick and kind) excused.

Ultimately it is Loki and not the gods of order or the chaotic giants who teach us the importance of diversity. Loki does not deny his misdeeds. When challenged about them he responds not by denial but by counterattack, making it plain that everyone, and not just he, has their dark side. What he does deny is the untruth contained in exclusive, unitary views of what is acceptable. His transgressions undermine totalitarian world views, whether they promote an exclusive emphasis on stability and order at the price of limiting others' freedoms (from Odin's denunciation of alternative, fluid sexualities, to the Æsir obsession with isolating themselves behind fortress walls in order to prevent uncontrolled interactions with multiple others), or at the other extreme stimulate disordered, negatively directed, devastation and destruction (the sacking of Asgard and Midgard, and massacre of their inhabitants, by Loki's own kin, the frost, rock, and fire giants).

Loki's upbringing with the gods teaches him the creative value of structured lives, whilst his giant-kin inheritance imbues him with a dynamic, wild and fiery energy. Whilst the Æsir's dark sides are repressed, hidden, and may not be spoken about, Loki cannot avoid his; it is too important a part of his nature. He struggles to reconcile these conflicting energies within himself, only to discover that in the end there can be no lasting, viable, balancing of order and chaos. The contradiction between them can only be resolved by conflict and combat, and even that can only bring about temporary solutions, which themselves inevitably eventually develop their own contradictions.

Loki's last deed, even as he dies, is to slay Heimdal. Heimdal was the Scandinavian version of Scyld Scefing (Shield Sheafing, or Shef – see chapter 2), the human-god child and later king sent by the Vanir to bless the early (pre-migration) English tribes with fertility of land and body, culture, learning, and skills of all kinds, from crafts to warfare. The Scandinavians knew him only as an Ás rather than a Van. For them he was a much-reduced figure whose once much more vital role as intermediary between gods (Vanir) and mankind was now limited to the guarding of the Æsir rainbow bridge to Asgard. This watchman function was largely concerned with keeping outsiders away, rather than the positive, welcoming connection with the very early English tribes promoted by the Vanir through Shef as their own ambassador on Middle Earth.

Loki, in choosing to match himself in combat against Heimdal, must surely be aware of his opponent's importance and identity as Shef, the shield and guarantor of the fertility of the land and hence the tribes living on it. Driven to destructive, murderous rage by his years of torture in Midgard at the hands of the Æsir and giants (led by Thor and Skadi), he targets Shef of the Vanir knowing that in killing him he can condemn all of mankind to destitution and starvation, should the fire giants allow any to escape their flames. The price will be his own demise, but Loki probably knows this, and might even desire it, conscious not only of the acidic, physical pain of the torture inflicted on him, but also of his failure to reconcile his own chaotic energies with that structured creativity of gods and mankind which his upbringing taught him to desire.

Chapter 13 - *Diversity and Death*

The need to acknowledge a trickster god's role as dissident and transgressor probably fitted in with early English pagan culture more easily than might at first be imagined. It is virtually axiomatic that any truly polytheistic society reflects at least some degree of acceptance of diversity in its basic world view. If there are many gods then there is no single 'Word of God' which must be obeyed at all costs. When the gods do not agree on everything amongst themselves, mortals may more easily forgive dissidence. Combine a basically pluralistic understanding of deities with practical day to day experience of multiple lifestyles, and recognition of diversity becomes just common sense.

Of course the breadth and variety of what may be accepted as lying within social norms will still vary even across different polytheistic cultures. As was noted in the previous chapter it can be demonstrated that Vanir followers such as the early English, who remembered the Van Scyld Scefing being sent to lead them, imbibed a greater tolerance of transgressive behaviour than later Scandinavian worshippers of patriarchal 'All-father' Odin. In *Lokasenna* the Van Njörd makes a plea for greater understanding of female sexual sovereignty for example, whilst Odin the Ás berates Loki for both homosexuality and transsexuality.

More can be discovered about early English tolerance of diverse sexual and gender attitudes and practices from a perhaps unexpected source: the elves. Elves were closely associated with the Vanir and with Frey in particular, who was said to rule in Lightalfheim, the home of the light elves (he was not associated with the dark elves, sometimes called dwarves).

> *"Both Freyr and the elves are also connected with the sun... Freyr is said... to control 'rain, sunshine, and the fruitfulness of the earth', while the sun is several times called 'álfröðöll', 'glory of the elves'."* [472]

Like the Vanir the elves too were linked with fertility concerns. As Roderick Ellis says, *"the association of the elves with fertility is the essential one."* [473] In this both elves and Vanir differed markedly from Odin's Æsir. In *Olaf's Saga Helga* a versa appears to record a woman fearing the wrath of Odin should she be witnessed sacrificing to elves:

> *"Go thou in no further,*
> *'base wretch', the lady said;*

'I fear the wrath of Odin,
For we are heathen people'.
That unattractive lady,
Who drove me from her dwelling,
Curtly, like a wolf, declared she
Held elf-sacrifice within. " [474]

Odin and the Æsir promoted a regulated social order which they intended to be relatively disciplined and intolerant of aberrant behaviour, or at least its open display. Both Vanir and elves were known to be more relaxed about issues of sexual conduct, but it is the early English view of the elves in particular that can give us some insight into diverse and developing Anglo-Saxon understandings of gender.

Gender in Pagan Early England - *What the Elves can tell us*

If we were taught anything at all in school about life in pre-Christian early England, it was probably that these were the years of the dreaded 'Dark Ages' - that chaotic time squeezed between the withdrawal of Roman civilisation from Britain around the year 407 CE, and the gradual rebirthing of social sanity that came only with the gradual conversion to Christian belief from the early 7th century onwards. The 'Dark Ages', we were told, bear that name because not much can be known about those pagan, pre-literate years. However the impression given was that this was a violent, chaotic time, marked by the invasion of Britain by marauding Angle and Saxon tribes; an age when men were (brutal) men, and women just had to put up with it.

More recent academic research however has demonstrated that, at the very least, there was another side to the incoming English tribes; in fact several other sides, as pagan English ways of understanding the worlds changed and evolved over those early centuries and beyond, partly in response to the advance of Christian ideology – for some pagan beliefs did survive the onslaught of the new Roman ecclesiastical invasion – thanks in no small part to the ever present, other-worldly relationships of the early (and later) English with Elves.

It appears that in very early times (covering both the pre-migration and pagan early English periods, so at least up until about the 7th century CE) the Angle and Saxon peoples, who were later to create the single kingdom of England, thought of Elves as being predominantly male, or at least it was the male elves who got all the attention. Not a great shock perhaps? After all, these were the Dark Ages, ruled by patriarchal, violent men. So not a huge surprise then if, even by the standards of those very gloomy times, females and femininity remained invisible and undiscussed?

But these male elves were not seen by the pagan early English as heroic, model warriors, or as anything like their much more macho Scandinavian Viking cousins. In fact English elves were, during this early period, perceived as being charmingly effeminate. As Alaric Hall explains:

> "Early Anglo-Saxon 'ælfe' were prototypically male,
> but... were paradigmatically associated with
> seductive, feminine beauty, and intimately linked
> with 'síden' [magical and shamanic powers], whose
> Scandinavian counterpart 'seidr' could not be
> conducted by men without compromising their
> masculinity and was itself associated with
> seduction."[475]

How could this be? Hall believes that the effeminacy of the elves reflects a 'systematic gender inversion' found in early English mythology. In other words, not only were other-worldly male beings perceived as effeminate, but other-worldly females were seen as having 'masculine' traits. It appears that 1,500 and more years ago the early English were already using pagan mythologies to explore the complexities of relationships between sex and gender, for early Anglo-Saxon effeminate male ælfe (elves) were matched by female but manly, martial, hægtessan ('witches') - perceived as armed and violent women:

> "Weapon-bearing was associated with masculinity,
> and freedom, at profound and ideological levels...
> The fact that... it is women who bear and use
> weapons represents a striking transgression of
> gender norms." [476]

It appears that in the early English pagan worldview, other-worldly beings, whether predominantly male elves or generally female witches, were believed to transgress the gender boundaries normally experienced in everyday life.

The Middle Ages and Beyond

With the passing of the centuries and the ever increasing (but never total) ideological dominance of Christianity in England, perceptions of other-worldly beings and their gender roles evolved in response to mounting pressures on even limited female sovereignty in the 'real' world. Belief in elves and witches continued, but suffered some degradation and erosion, as one result of which gender differentiation between elves and witches was to some extent lost. Elves were no longer perceived as predominantly male, and witches ceased to be differentiated from female elves. Why was this? Hall is clear that it happened in response to increasing Christian disempowerment of women:

> "Christianisation introduced concepts of sin, and associations of sin with sexual behaviour, which had not previously existed in Anglo-Saxon culture, and would both have encouraged the idea of female seductiveness as a spiritual threat to men, and the idea that male sexuality needed to be constrained... We can understand the rise of female ælfe [as] a drive... more rigorously to align sex with gender. Their appearance may relate to the gradual curtailment of women's power and independence."
> [477]

Christianity's undermining of female sovereignty was not at first entirely successful, as the Church's drive to patriarchy was initially limited by traditional Anglo-Saxon cultural values which held women in high esteem:

> "The evidence which has survived from Anglo-Saxon England indicates that women were more nearly the equal companions of their husbands and brothers than at any other period before the modern age... this rough and ready partnership was ended by the Norman Conquest... the teaching of the medieval Church reinforced the subjection which feudal law imposed on all wives." [478]

> "Christianity as interpreted by the fathers of the church developed a full set of theories on the inferiority of women... yet throughout the Anglo-Saxon period they seem to have had little practical effect." [479]

After the Norman Conquest however:

> *"theological concept hardened into cannon law, and cannon law acquired control of much legislation concerning women... practically, the status of women deteriorated."* [480]

The Church in England had attempted to control women's sexuality ever since the arrival from the Middle East of Theodore of Tarsus to be Archbishop of Canterbury in the 7th century, but after 1066 church laws imposing seven years of penitential punishments on any woman "fornicating with heathens" were much more likely to be put into practical effect. Apparently "fornicating with Jews" was even worse – that got you nine years. [481]

Hall nevertheless believes that subversive concepts of female sovereignty did survive the early English period into the Middle Ages and later. In Chaucer's "Wife of Bath's Tale" for example, the Elf-Queen or 'Queen of Fearrie' is the dominant power in her world, including male elves within her dominion:

> *"This female dominance of the other world inverts the usual patterns of rulership in medieval English society. Accordingly, rebels in Kent around 1450 were styling themselves 'servants of the Queen of the Fairies...'"* [482]

...in an attempt to establish an anarchic ideological legitimacy outside everyday societal norms. Similarly the indictment of Andro Man, a healer executed for witchcraft in 1598, reads:

> *"Thou affirms that the elves have shapes like men... and that they are but shadows, yet stronger than men, and that they play and dance as they please; and that the [elf-] Queen is very attractive; that she makes king any who pleases her, and lies with anyone she likes".* [483]

This is a clear example of a belief in other-worldly, subversive, female sexual sovereignty. Female elves were perceived as personally autonomous, able to rule their own bodies, and free to choose and change their sexual partners at will.

An Effeminate Route to Male Power?

It is only in the most recent centuries that the long history of female disempowerment has begun to be reversed. In northern

Europe's Iron Age[*] societies, it is suggested, gender transgression had originally been ideologically important and empowering.[484] Even up until late medieval times *"male experience of liminality or crisis could involve adopting feminine traits"*.[485] An obvious psychological escape route for men suffering spiritual or emotional crises was to cease envisioning themselves as having to comply with standard perceptions of manly constraints and responsibilities, by choosing to see themselves as effeminate.

The individuals whose accounts of such crises have survived were male members of the aristocratic ruling class. It is thought that, despite their attempts to relate to the feminine, they probably remained unable to fully transcend their necessarily male view of existence. Hence they assumed, for example, that women going through sharp personal crises would react the same way high class men did:

> *"and that their liminal moments were accompanied by gender reversal... In liminal space males were seductively beautiful and worked magic, and females bore and used weapons."* [6]

It has been argued that in reality women and other less powerful groups were much less likely to experience personal crises as involving gender reversal, as in practice they did not (unlike powerful male members of the aristocratic class), enjoy anything like the required degree of personal sovereignty to permit such social defiance and transgression. They simply would not be allowed to get away with it, not only in everyday life, but even in storytelling. Hall comments that:

> *"one notes a certain satisfying continuity with ælfe's capacity a millennium before to destabilise the rational, masculine mind"*.[486]

The conclusion seems to be then that even when envisioning effeminate male elves in mythological narratives, early English males of the aristocratic class were in reality far from contemplating any relinquishing of power. Gender inversion concepts may have helped men transcend personal spiritual and emotional crises, but even when viewing male elves apparently adopting feminine traits as part of such a process, men continued to seek power, though in different forms - firstly by claiming the authority to renounce some male constraints

---

[*] The Iron Age in northern Europe lasted from about 500 BCE to 800 CE [Wikipedia]

and responsibilities as and when desired, and secondly by seeking access to traditionally female power sources, especially magical and shamanic síden (seidr) abilities.

Such (self-)deception is perhaps most clearly demonstrated by the 'All-father' male god, he who appeared to temporarily disempower himself by hanging from a tree – but only in order to gain knowledge (power) of the runes; he who, despite being in many respects the very essence of masculinity, sought for himself the feminine magical power of seidr in order, it has been said, that this on occasion cross-dressing god could *"inflict a fever while disguised as a woman* [and healer] *in order to rape Rindr".*[†] As Loki pointed out in Lokasenna, even Odin, usually perceived as the patriarchal, warrior god 'par excellence', would adopt effeminate gender characteristics when it suited his masculine quest for power.

It may then be no bad thing that by the Middle Ages the earlier aristocratic Anglo-Saxon fascination with effeminate male elves had largely evolved into a broader cross-class mythological recognition of a more gender balanced other-world, featuring both female and male elves, and where power at last came to lie not with cross-dressing, effeminate males, but with a genuinely female, genuinely autonomous Fairy Queen, who could freely express her sexual sovereignty by choosing her own male partners.

The Abstract Art of Shamanism

The 'effeminate' magic which Loki accused Odin of practicing had a lot to do with shamanism - interaction with the spirit world by entering into a trance, dream-state, or altered state of consciousness, with the aim of seeking healing (physical or spiritual), asking advice on important matters (for self or others), engaging in prophecy, or soliciting spirits to directly influence events in the waking world. This art was known as 'seidr' in Scandinavia, and 'síden' in Old English, the literal translation being 'to extend, make wide, become wider', i.e. presumably to open oneself up to and/or actually enter into a broader reality. So firmly acknowledged as a feminine art was this that the

---

[†] Hall [see Bibliography] p.148. *"Rindr (English: Rind) is a female goddess in Norse mythology; raped and impregnated by Odin, she gave birth to the avenger of Balder's death: Váli."* [Wikipedia]

practitioner was known as a seeress (or seidkona in Scandinavia) .

> "There is evidence from German antiquity to the High
> Middle Ages that the Germanic peoples believed
> that women had prophetic gifts, and that they quite
> clearly worshipped some women as seeresses. In
> Germania 8 Tacitus records:
>> 'The Germans even believe that there
>> is something sacred and prophetic
>> inherent to women.'" [487]

Small wonder then that Odin's attempts to play the part of a wise woman or witch were not approved of by patriarchal Scandinavians.

The shamanic art may have been held to be inherent in women, but it still had to be learned as an exceptional skill which few actually became proficient at. Mother-daughter teaching doubtless played a key role in passing on skills through the generations, but it has also been suggested that in addition visual art may have been a useful tool employed to this end, and that use of illustration in this way might help explain the development of abstract visual concepts in Anglo-Saxon art.

Mention the term 'abstract art ' to someone these days and they will probably think of "modern art" and the twentieth century gradual move away from figurative painting towards ever more non-representational forms. However abstraction from, and at times codification of, visual structure is nothing new. Just think of all those Celtic, Viking-Scandinavian, and Anglo-Saxon semi-abstract bird and animal patterns, whose curving outlines bend back on themselves and at times almost disappear into completely abstract shapes and designs.

Why were these abstract art forms so popular a thousand and many more years ago? Was it all down to primitive lack of figurative technique as might once have been assumed, or was something else going on? In the twenty-first century it is becoming more widely accepted that such millennia-old designs probably encapsulated a range of meanings. Certainly they demonstrated an appreciation of beauty, as well as human creativity and crafting ability. But beyond this, for those who knew how to look, they could also function as tools used to promote the legitimacy and authority of ruling groups, and even embody wider spiritual narratives.

Hengist and Horsa

An example of this is the Anglo-Saxon myth of Hengist and Horsa, and how it may tie in with the use of abstract double horse figures in early English art. Hengist and Horsa were the legendary mid-fifth century joint leaders of the first Anglo-Saxon invasion of Britain and settlement in Kent, as told for example by Bede in his 'Ecclesiastical History of the English People' (c. 731 CE). 'Hengist' is Old English for 'stallion', and 'Horsa' is usually translated as 'horse' or 'gelding'. Various Anglo-Saxon rulers sought to boost their authority and legitimacy as rulers by claiming Hengist and Horsa as direct ancestors, and through them the god Woden as their peoples' original patriarch.

The archaeologist Chris Fern [488] has suggested [489] in his paper "Horses in Mind" that *"Anglo-Saxon kingdoms and kings claimed their political and genetic legitimacy from twin warhorse-warlord deities"*,[490] most clearly recorded in the mythological history of Hengist and Horsa. These figures were seen as part human, part horse, and part semi-equine god – as represented *"by the 'animal-men' and double-horse motifs found in the animal art of the period"*.[491]

However, relatively clear as this may be, it is additionally suggested that such art also bears more spiritual messages, which have been deliberately made more obscure and even hermetic, their meaning being intended to be restricted to those who could be appropriately entrusted with it. These additional, deeper meanings are said to be shamanistic:

> *"Horse ideologies have been linked to shamanistic beliefs, with the animal viewed as a guardian spirit and mode of transport to the afterlife".* [492]

In a non-literate age, visual art could be a vital ideological and communication tool, but at the same time rulers and priestesses might believe it prudent not to display their key meanings too openly, perhaps in order to avoid personal vulnerability that might potentially arise from openly evidencing shamanistic knowledge. The answer to this dilemma, it is suggested, was abstraction:

> *"The stylisation of Germanic animal art may have been a deliberate strategy, designed to restrict access to its narrative, the interpretation of which brought psychological enlightenment to its 'learned' viewer... its departure from the naturalistic aims of Christian Mediterranean art... may also have been a conscious act, creating an aesthetic that was*

distinctly non-Christian".[493]

It is quite possible that advances made in the interpretation of Anglo-Saxon art to allow for additional hidden meanings to do with shamanism and horses as spirit guides do not go far enough, for the related readings of early English and north European shamanism seem to be rather limited and undifferentiated from twenty-first century general interpretations of the functions of shamanism in many ancient cultures. In particular Fern's 'Horses in Mind' interpretation could be said to be rather restricted and patriarchal in appearing to limit shamanism's functions to those useful to the male warrior aristocracy, despite the extensive evidence that in early northern Europe shamans were predominantly female, and that any male participation in such roles was consistently reviled as unmanly.

Fern chooses to see the double horse motif as representing two stallions fighting, with an imagined figurative image such as that at (a) below...

(a)   Two Horses (Fighting?)
[Image: Lynne Harling]

...being eventually transformed, through several stages, into an actual original Anglo-Saxon abstract image, such as that redrawn at (b) below...

(b) Anglo-Saxon Double Horse Abstract Image
[Redrawing: Lynne Harling]

However if the abstract image really is two stallions fighting each other, they surely cannot be the equine demi-gods Hengist and Horsa. Horsa was not a stallion, but either a mare or a castrated male gelding who would, in either case, not be fighting for females and foals like a stallion. Fern refers to the Hengist/Horsa legend *"establishing the male pairing of stallion and gelding"*.[494] This is not impossible, but it is surely more likely that the pair referenced in abstract image (b) above would be male and female, stallion and mare, particularly if the image has been highly stylised in order to encompass memes related to shamanistic functions which, as we have seen, in early northern Europe were carried out predominantly by women. The abstract image could then be interpreted as representing the coming together of female and male horses, which would surely fit well with the usual emphasis of the Vanir-following early English on fertility and sexual issues, probably here concerning not just human sexuality but broader fertility issues such as that of the land which the sacred horses have brought the tribes to.

Shamanistic practitioners *"appear in the sagas as marginalised figures, and... though respected, are rare."* [495] These rare "marginalised figures" were not aristocratic male warriors but, most commonly, women of non-aristocratic background: *"most of the accounts of seidr or magical practice from the sagas are of women."* [496]

Furthermore the general restriction of shamanistic and magical roles to women applied not just to human society, but to the gods as well. Vanir fertility goddesses such as Freya and female Vanir witches such as Gullveig knew magic, but the more patriarchal Æsir gods generally did not, or at least not the powerful shamanistic kind. Indeed the practicing of seidr was regarded as unmanly and appropriate only to women. As we have seen Odin 'All- father', leader of the Æsir, ever keen to monopolise power, had Gullveig dragged to his hall and there commanded she be burned as a witch – to death. Three times he attempted it, but each time she magically survived. In revenge for the attempted murder of Gullveig, Freya launched the Vanir in a war against Odin's Asgard. As part of the eventual peace terms Freya agreed to teach Odin seidr, but this was very much the exception to the rule; none of the other male gods would risk learning such emasculating practices.

Having said that, it is not impossible that there may also have been a few equally rare and no doubt also similarly marginalised effeminate male shamans. Remembering again Loki's accusations against Odin in Lokasenna, who knows exactly what the 'All-father' might have been up to on the Danish island of Samsey. It is not impossible that the Anglo-Saxon double horse motif could indeed reference a stallion and a gelding, with some shamanistic activity possibly involving behaviour of an effeminate and/or homosexual nature:

> "Many researchers have attempted a theoretical understanding of shamanism as incorporating an ability to move between 'realities' generally considered 'male' or 'female'. The 'third gender' concept... is that
>> 'Socially, the shaman does not belong to either the class of males or to that of females, but to a third class, that of shamans. She indicates that by clothing or ritual observance (taboos)'." [497]

So it seems that even if the two horses in the motif are stallion and gelding, then they are still more likely to have been enjoying sex with each other than fighting as two stallions would. However for the greater part of the Anglo-Saxon population it is probable that the double horse motif reflected heterosexual equine, human, and divine societies, including in some cases a feminine shamanistic ability to move between those worlds, escorted by horse spirit guides, exemplified above all by the legendary figures of Hengist and Horsa. In any case, whether shamanistic activity was hetero- or homosexual, or more gender-fluid, the art of abstraction was being used to hide something from public view, and that would not have been necessary if that 'something' had been only standard and open inter-male rivalry and combat, rather than the feminine (and also possibly effeminate) much more hermetic ability to travel spiritually between the worlds.

The Realms of the Dead

The shamanic ability to travel between the worlds included the power to journey to the land of the dead and to return from there, but what exactly did Anglo-Saxons and other pagan north Europeans envisage as the world of the dead?

Firstly it is again worth remembering that

> *"All through the heathen period belief and thought were shifting and fluid, varying according to local cultures, developing in accordance with particular influences in separate localities."* [498]

It is also worth bearing in mind that the various pagan conceptions of continued survival after death were all very different from later Christian understandings of heaven and hell. For pagans existence both pre- and post-death remained always complex and contradictory, involving positive and negative possibilities, potential joys and possible suffering. The perfect and perpetual happiness of salvation in heaven was not on offer, but neither was the threat of eternal torment in the searing flames of hell. Whatever might be the fate of the deceased, it would certainly not be unchanging or everlasting, for it was known that ultimately all worlds would end, including those of the dead and the gods themselves.

Probably the best known destination of the pre-Christian Scandinavian dead is Valhalla, Odin's feasting hall for the brave, those warriors who died fighting with sword in hand. There they would fight each other every day, coming to life again if slain, ready to truly and finally die engaging the forces of chaos in the eventual final battle of Ragnarok at the end of the worlds, when both Asgard and Midgard would be destroyed. Slightly less well known is the allocation, in the same myths, of half the battle-dead to the warrior goddess Freya. She in fact got first choice of the dead fighters, taking them off to her own hall of Sessrúmnir, while leaving the rest for Odin. However:

> *"Entry into the realm of the gods was to some extent
> at least a matter of aristocratic privilege... for
> people in general this realm of the gods had little
> real interest or significance."* [499]

For the majority of the population, whether Scandinavian farmers and craftsmen more likely to wear Thor's hammer than carry a spear dedicated to Odin, or Angle and Saxon tribes in Britain asking the blessings of Vanir fertility gods on their newly settled lands, any expectations or concerns about what might happen to them after death seem to have been rather more limited in scope. If these dead were to have any continued existence, it was expected to be found not in the realms of the major deities, but either within burial mounds here on earth, or in the more prosaic world of Helheim, the realm of Hel, goddess of the dead. There may also have been a third possibility for some:

> *"Supernatural guardian women... give help to certain
> men through life and... and receive them in their
> abodes after death. They have become linked with...
> the peculiarly Norse notions of hamingja and dís."*
> [500]

The Dead – *and Burial Mounds*

Reports of the alleged doings of the dead down the ages have tended to range mainly from the sensationalist to the horrific, but not exclusively so. Roderick Ellis quotes *"the wonderfully restrained and effective picture of... the good and influential man resting at peace in his grave, and still retaining an interest in the affairs of the living... in Njal's Saga"*:

> "There was a bright moon, with clouds drifting over it from
> time to time. It seemed to them that the howe was open,
> and that Gunnar had turned himself in the howe and
> looked up at the moon. They thought they saw four lights
> burning in the howe, but no shadow anywhere. They saw
> that Gunnar was merry, with a joyful face." [501]

Then as now however it was tales of the unmerry dead which seemed to more readily find attentive audiences. The deceased inhabitants of burial mounds could emerge and prove a terrible threat to the living, particularly if they had been disturbed in their howe, for example by grave robbers seeking grave goods treasure. In such cases the corpse could become reanimated, *"possessed of superhuman strength and unlimited malice"*,[502] and fully able to leave the burial mound. These 'undead' were called *draugar*.‡ Their herculean powers could be ended only by the destruction of their physical bodies. It is notable that these living dead came only from burial mounds:

> *"There is no case... in the sagas of any spirit or 'ghost' returning from a realm of the dead to visit the living. It is from the mound that these draugar come."* [503]

Presumably the dead of Valhalla, Sessrúmnir and Helheim were believed to have become spirits which had progressed beyond the stage of inhabiting bodies, whereas those inside burial mounds were regarded as still being bound by corporeal form, and therefore more able to be active in the physical world. However not every burial mound corpse was thought to be animate at all times. The sign of a dynamic corpse was thought to be fire – 'cold fire' which could be seen by the living flickering around any haunted barrow.

The Dead – *and Helheim*

Hel is not the only northern goddess intimately connected with the human dead, but she is surely reputedly first amongst them in this role.

> *"Freyja is the true Valkyrie, welcoming the dead with wine in the house of the gods... Gefion is attended by all those women who die unmarried... Rán [is] the wife of Ægir, god of the sea... if drowned men attended their own funerals it was looked on as a sign that Rán had received them well."* [504]

To judge by recorded Christian worries, Freya's Valkyrie role was as well known and respected amongst the early English as by Scandinavians, so much so that it survived for centuries after formal Christianisation:

> *"Supernatural 'choosers of the slain' were also known to the Anglo-Saxons. By the tenth century they have*

---

‡ *"Draugar live in their graves, often guarding treasure buried with them in their burial mound. They are animated corpses with a corporeal body, unlike ghosts."* [https://en.wikipedia.org/wiki/Draugr]

> *taken their place amongst the adversaries of the Christian God, and are placed contemptuously by Wulfstan beside witches and criminals; similarly as late as the fourteenth century they are still paired off with witches in the alliterative poem 'Cleanness'".*[505]

Freya receives half the battle-dead, Gefion unmarried women, and Ran those drowned at sea, but these are all very specific functions related only to limited numbers. The goddess most directly relevant to the greatest number is surely Hel, child of Loki, the tortured god of trickery, and Angrboda the giantess, whose very name translates as "the one who brings grief". Hel is a sister to the Midgard Serpent and the wolf Fenris, those two creatures who, along with Loki, will take the side of the forces of Chaos in the final battle at the end of the world and help destroy Asgard and Middle Earth.

North European deities are rarely simple archetypes, but rather complex and often contradictory characters, and Hel is no exception to this pattern. She is the ruler of the world of Helheim (or simply 'Hel'), sometimes referred to in later sources as an Underworld, lying beneath one of the three roots of the World Tree. Helheim is of course not the burning inferno of the Christian envisaged hell; in fact just as 'cold fire' marks the howes of the active dead on earth, so is Helheim also a glacial land of freezing fogs, connected to the icy world of Nifelheim – the land of mists. Despite its freezing nature, Helheim also differs from the Christian hell in not being *"a place of retribution and punishment... Snorri... attempts to make Hel such a place, but his interpretation is likely to be chiefly due to Christian teaching about the after-life."* [506]

Hel's appearance is described as being "morbid and fierce looking",[507] with one half of her body being beautiful, and the other half consisting of decomposing decay, reflecting the interrelated nature of life, death, and constant change.

Hel welcomes all the dead into her halls. She takes those who die of old age and disease, and mothers and children who die during childbirth. She does not discriminate, and welcomes all who perish away from any battlefield.

This information about the nature of Helheim and the goddess Hel herself largely comes from Snorri Sturluson's Edda,[508] and there remains a question about to what degree (if any) pre-Christian north Europeans actually acknowledged this goddess. It is believed that Snorri, witing as a Christian in the 13th century, allowed Christian tradition to influence him in filling in any gaps in his retellings of pagan myths, and that this may be most clearly evident in his descriptions of Hel and Helheim. Simek goes so far as to say that *"On the whole nothing speaks in favour of there being a belief in a goddess Hel in pre-Christian times"*.[509]

Certainly, just as in the case of Loki, there is no evidence specifically identifying Anglo-Saxon acknowledgement of Hel as an important deity. However, also as in the case of Loki, this could simply reflect the fact that in neither Scandinavia nor Britain would it have been thought desirable to dedicate oneself or one's family to following Hel as one might Freya, Thor, Odin, or other more beneficent gods. And if Simek is right, and Helheim was not known in pre-Christian times, then where did Anglo-Saxons believe that their loved ones might go after death?

A possible answer might be that there is in fact no answer – because pagan Anglo-Saxons may not have believed in enduring life after death, or certainly not for all. Roderick Ellis asserts that *"The Norse mind was not particularly interested in the clear-cut conception of another world beyond the grave"*.[510] Warriors falling in battle may have been granted a temporary reprieve from final death in Freya's or Odin's halls, but they too would eventually perish alongside the gods. For pagans all beings were ultimately mortal. Therefore there may have been no need to allocate after-death accommodation for all in Helheim or any other world. *Draugar* may have been thought to survive in their barrows for limited periods in some cases, but even this was only possible while their bodies remained intact and, as already noted above, there is no case in the sagas of any disembodied spirit or 'ghost' returning from another world (Helheim or anywhere else) to visit the living; in fact famously not even Balder could manage such a trick.

Such a relative lack of concern with worlds of the dead would fit in well with the philosophical materialism of north European cosmology (see chapter 11) which rejected the Mediterranean monotheistic obsession with the survival and perfection of individual souls, in favour of the prioritising of life/death/new-life cycles and collective (family, tribe, and land) fertility issues.

The Dead – *and Supernatural Women Guardians*

Having considered whether the dead might go to the halls of Freya,

Odin or Hel, and if so which amongst them might go where – if indeed anywhere – there remains another possible destination for at least some of the dead: the abodes of certain supernatural female guardians who, having nurtured their mortal charges in life, might continue to do so (at least for a while) after death. These unearthly women are most commonly referred to as disír, and appear to be connected with the Vanir, fertility, and in particular the goddess Freya, one of whose titles was Vanadís, or 'the dís of the Vanir', implying that just as disír nurtured individual mortals, so one of Freya's multifarious roles as a 'great goddess' was to care for the Vanir gods.

> "Place-name evidence appears to suggest that the
> disír were linked with fertility... and there seems to
> have been a sacrificial festival known as Dísablót
> that... was celebrated in the Autumn. Elsewhere
> however the disír appear to be associated with the
> dead... Valkyries are described as 'the disír of Odin',
> and in the poem Atlamál, the disír are simply called
> 'dead women'. The situation is complicated still
> further by the fact that the simple noun dís ('lady',
> 'woman'; cf. Old English ídes)... appears in
> descriptions and allusions to many of the female
> deities or Ásynjur as well as to other female
> figures." [511]

It should be said straight away that for the pagan English there would have been no fundamental contradiction between an Autumn Dísablót fertility (harvest?) festival and equally seasonal (Halloween or Samhain-like) associations with the dead. In fact a close awareness of the seasonal and cyclical nature of fertility rhythms would have served to remind people of interconnections between fertility, harvests, death and the dead. Then as now the onset of Autumn would have been regarded as an appropriate time to remember previous generations and deceased ancestors.

The apparent confusion concerning the roles and nature of the disír is lessened when these links between the living and the dead are taken into account, and reduced further if we allow (as stated at the beginning of this chapter's section on "The Realms of the Dead") for the fact that *"All through the heathen period belief and thought were shifting and fluid... developing in accordance with particular influences in separate localities."* [512] The key point about the disír is that they were seen as powerful, other worldly, female entities who played positive, nurturing roles which could extend beyond the death of the individuals they cared for. At certain times and in some places the beings fulfilling these roles were named 'hamingjur' (singular: 'hamingja') and thought of as *"the embodiment of personal or family luck... which... might pass from one family member to another."* [513] At other points in time and place they were recognised as more fully independent supernatural beings, or in some cases even as Vanir goddesses, but ultimately *"the evidence certainly seems to suggest that the guardian Valkyries, the guardian hamingjur of the family, and the guardian dísir are one and the same conception."* [514]

The dísir appear to care for souls on an individual basis, although the hamingjur might be perceived as attaching themselves to families rather than just a single individual. In Norse belief the hamingjur were not the only spiritual being which might be associated with specific individuals. There was also the 'fylgja' (plural: 'fylgjur'). Fylgjur were seen as *"protective spirits... which attach themselves to individuals, often at birth, and remain with them right through to death, when they may transfer their powers to another family member"*.[515] Unlike dísir, fylgjur most often had animal form, and were so closely linked with an individual as to be considered their 'fetch' or doppelgänger. The specific animal form depended on the character and standing of the individual, with *"those of high birth and outstanding character being represented by dignified and noble animals"*.[516]

The death of a person's animal fetch would also be the death of that individual, and vice versa. A person's protective dís however was an independent, autonomous, supernatural being who survived her charge's death:

> *"After his death he is able to enter her abodes, and she then attaches herself to another, often from the same family. She is frequently attended by a company of similar women, generally three or nine in number. She seems to be looked upon as the wife of the man to whom she has joined herself."* [517]

Given that after death a man may enter the abode of his dís, but that she then leaves him for another, what can his entering of her abode actually mean? At the very least it seems to imply that he has become passive, no longer active in life, and so no longer requires female protection. But that would also have been the case had he simply died and been left interred in the earth, or inside his burial mound, so why is it significant that he should "enter her abode", particularly given that she will then leave it to accompany another?

Perhaps this is his final act, and it is an offsetting or balancing act of reparation and restitution. The dís has used her energies to nurture and protect him in life; in dying he chooses to give himself, his own essential energies, to her. To do this, wherever his bodily death has occurred, his soul now elects to die into "her abode", rather than simply fading into the soil or the flames of his funeral pyre. Having then finally fully died, both body and soul, he is no longer there for her to care for, and she will, thanking and respecting her former partner's love for and dedication to her, use her now renewed energies to nurture another.

This may be the ultimate expression of that key pagan doctrine of exchange: a gift for a gift, the return of one's fundamental life energy to the goddesses or dísir who granted it in the first place, the payment of the spiritual debt of individuals to the otherworldly 'mothers' who gave life to them. This is perhaps the most probable explanation of the Norn Skuld's nature as representative not of the 'future' (despite her sisters Urd and Verdandi representing respectively the past and present), but rather 'the debt which must be paid'. Time, and life and lives, for north European pagans, were not perceived as simply linear and individual, but rather as cyclical and collective, with energies being freely but necessarily returned to their sources. Ultimately the individual's life and soul were limited, but collectively, through family and tribe, life energies survived and were regenerated through new generations. As Stephen Pollington explains:

> "The notion of human death as a return of the soul to the gods was current in pre-Christian times... Life is seen as a gift (from the gods) and... has to be returned to those who gave it. These life-givers were the heathen gods, and the collectors of this debt probably included the wælcyrigan.[518] The phrase used to describe the surrender and sharing of a life ended is reconstructed as gast dælan, 'ghost dealing, separation of spirit', which was subject to taboo in Christian times..."[519]

Chapter 14 - *Summary and Conclusions*

Perhaps the major conclusion to be drawn from this exploration of Anglo-Saxon paganism is that, whilst it constituted a world view which was very much part of a broader pre-Christian north European and Germanic *Weltanschauung*, it did differ significantly from the generally much better known later Scandinavian 'Viking' version, despite there being much in common in terms of the pantheon or, more accurately, pantheons (Vanir and Æsir). This is hardly surprising given the passing of the centuries and the different socio-economic contexts which Scandinavian and Anglo-Saxon clans and tribes respectively experienced, with for example Anglo-Saxons being able to enjoy a more settled lifestyle on more extensive and more fertile agricultural areas in southern and eastern Britain than Scandinavians did in mountainous Norway or freezing Iceland.

The early English kingdoms had been formally converted to Christianity by 680 CE, whilst Iceland did not declare itself Christian for another three hundred and twenty years. The Viking raiders, traders, and settlers who came to England over a quarter of a millennium, from the very late eighth to the mid-eleventh centuries, celebrated a militant, warlike ideology which emphasised conquest and victory in battle. The establishment of the "Danelaw" in 886 CE divided England in two, with Danish self-rule extending over the north and east, and Anglo-Saxons continuing to control the south and west.

As part of the peace agreement between Danes and English after battles at Edington and Chippenham (in Wiltshire) in 878 CE, Danish King Guthrum was baptised a Christian, with English King Alfred acting as his godfather.[*] In being required to abandon their militaristic Scandinavian paganism it could be argued that the Danes were at last accepting a non-itinerant lifestyle based on living off the fertility of the naturally rich land of England, instead of their 'get rich quick' schemes based on theft (raiding and plunder-orientated warfare), the blackmailing of entire peoples (through their 'Danegeld' nation-scale protection rackets), and the selling of captured English women and men into slavery.

The abandonment of Odin 'the betrayer' by the Danes in England reflected their new settled status. Bringing up new generations of

---

[*] https://en.wikipedia.org/wiki/Danelaw

Danish children to aspire to become predatory warriors in adulthood was hardly likely to guarantee ongoing prosperity for Danish farms on English soil, but would have invited the burning of crops and harvests in retaliatory wars. An ideology that, formally at least, promoted peace not war was needed, and Alfred and the English Church were most insistent that their own Christianity should provide a common all-England social environment based on avoidance of open warfare, and the rule of law.

For the English themselves, the Anglo-Saxons, this was nothing new. Going right back to pre-Christian and even pre-migration times, Anglo-Saxon paganism had been not Odinist, but Vanir based. For the 'proto-English' Anglo-Saxon tribes their earliest legends, such as that of Scyld Scefing (Shield Sheafing or Shef), had emphasised the blessings of the gods very much in terms of fertility, whether agricultural, socio-cultural (everything from crafting to storytelling), or human sexual activity. Military abilities too were acknowledged as having an important role, but the emphasis was on a defensive ability to protect the rich lives and food sources stemming from a settled agricultural lifestyle, not on aggressive warfare as a means to enrichment.

The gods of pagan Anglo-Saxons were the gods of the general Germanic pantheon, just as were those of the Scandinavians, but the way those gods were seen, and no doubt the stories which were told about them, evolved over time and in accordance with changing socio-economic conditions. Prior to the migration to Britain the Angle tribes had lived in southern Denmark, apparently in agricultural communities with deep roots in the land. There they had followed the Vanir gods, associated as those deities were with the promotion of fertility, whether of the soil, farmed animals, or human beings in terms of both the development of skills (from handicrafts to epic poetry recital) and sexuality. It seems that clan and family decisions to migrate, from the mid-fifth century on, to what later became England, were likely to have been motivated by a range of factors, possibly including military defeat by the Danes in Jutland, but also a developing knowledge of the richness of the land and climate in eastern Britain following some limited very early Saxon migration to (initially) Kent, as well as subsequent family connections stretching across the North Sea.

Prior to migration the major Angle settlement of Seeland in what is now Denmark seems to have been a renowned Vanir religious centre and sanctuary, so renowned in fact that when taken over by invading Danes following victory in war over the Angles, and their expulsion or voluntary migration in large part to Britain, even the Æsir-following Danes felt it wise to continue, at least for a generation or two, public veneration of Vanir deities in that place (as discussed in chapter 3 on Beowulf). It might even be worth speculating that such inter-tribal contact and warfare might well have played a role in the original generation of the story of the "first war" been the two tribes of gods, Æsir and Vanir. However that might be, when the Danes came to attack the English again four centuries on, this time in Britain, it was once again Odin to whom they appealed for military victory.

The English on the other hand, had they retained their own Vanir based version of Germanic paganism into the ninth century CE, would almost certainly have been asking not Odin, or even Woden the wanderer, to aid them in the military defence of their land, but Freya, the 'great goddess' not only of love but also of battle – she whom even Scandinavians recognised as being entitled to half those killed in war. Again, it is tempting to speculate: perhaps in Viking eyes Freya got to choose her half of the deceased first because the dead she received would be those from the tribes who followed her (Angle and Saxon), whilst Odin would then take his own dead Viking followers to Valhalla.

If the Scandinavian dead went to meet their patriarch 'All-father' Odin in Asgard, whilst after death the early English went instead to the hall of their 'great goddess' Freya, then that would certainly be in line with the more gender balanced pantheon of the pre-Christian Anglo-Saxons. The Vanir goddesses were known, by Anglo-Saxon and Scandinavian peoples alike, to be greater in status, power, and sovereignty than their Æsir equivalents. The difference was that whilst the Angles and Saxons accepted the sovereignty of both goddesses and gods, patriarchal Scandinavian Odinists revered what they perceived to be exclusively masculine qualities above all others.

Freya for example had great feminine magical powers, abilities which were looked down upon, and even cursed as 'evil' witchcraft, by Æsir-worshipping Vikings, whilst being celebrated by Freya-worshippers. Gullveig became famous as the Vanir 'witch' whom Odin attempted to burn to death, envious as he was of her magical powers, seeking to destroy her if (as he then thought) he could not have them for himself. And Idun, the goddess of the golden apples of long-lasting life - her gifts and powers too, it is now commonly accepted, were originally those of the Vanir.

In summary then it can be said that Anglo-Saxon paganism differed from its better known Scandinavian equivalent in its emphasis on the primary importance of fertility related issues, whether of land, animals or people, and that this was necessarily reflected in a more gender balanced appreciation of both female and male divine principles: of the celebration of both goddesses and gods. The emphasis on fertility stemmed from a settled lifestyle which looked to the abundance of the land to provide collective nourishment for all, rather than relying on the appropriation of wealth from others through sheer individual strength in physical combat. The practice of living on an ongoing, settled basis, through a cyclical and reciprocal exchange of gifts of fertility with the land, permitted the early Anglo-Saxons, they believed, also to develop in cultural terms, allowing the promotion of both practical crafting skills and more esoteric talents, from storytelling to magical, divinatory, and shamanic abilities. All this, the Anglo-Saxons believed, came to them originally as gifts from the Vanir, subsequently developed by themselves in harmony with those goddesses and gods.

Freya – *and the Feminine*

Freya was the primary, multi-aspected, 'great goddess' of the pre-Christian Anglo-Saxons, but she was never just 'Goddess' alone, or a female version of the Christian One God. She remained a vital part of the Vanir family of gods, interacting in multiple positive ways with both other deities and other beings. It is very probable that the surviving versions of stories concerning Freya do not do her justice in terms of her elemental status, powers, or achievements, for they have clearly been coloured by succeeding centuries of both Scandinavian pagan patriarchy and subsequent Christian demotion of the feminine, both divine and material. Hence the negative moral judgement implied in the 14th century Sörla þáttr[520] version of the tale of the Brisingamen, in which 'All-father' Odin is outraged by the goddess's autonomous sexuality.[†]

Freya may have been looked to as a goddess of many skills and powers in areas such as love, war, agricultural fertility, spinning and weaving, healing, and shamanic magic, but – perhaps at first sight somewhat ironically for a goddess of fertility – she was never

---

[†] See the very readable modern version of the Brisingamen story in: *The Penguin Book of Norse Myths,* Kevin Crossley-Holland, London 1982.

particularly associated with motherhood, despite being a mother herself. Anglo-Saxon women and men did not look to Freya as a divine mother figure, to be appealed to when they felt themselves in need of a mother's love and care. Freya was perceived very much as an adult goddess, with adult concerns, such as sexual love. She did have roles in the nurturing and protection of families, but they were very much adult roles, including those of provider (promoting fertility of the land and hence harvests), and female warrior. As such her protective roles tended to be broader than just the immediately familial, impacting more at the level of a whole clan or tribe. In their perception of Freya as an adult goddess fulfilling adult functions at a whole community level, it seems that Anglo-Saxons saw in Freya a feminine deity who was able to express the vitality of female roles going well beyond procreation and the nurturing of young children. Women (and goddesses) were not envisaged as being confined to the home, but were expected and encouraged to perform a wide range of responsible tasks, as valued and effective adult members of a wider community.

The emphasis on Freya's broader, community-wide, collective impact, fits well with her even more fundamental bearing on the fortunes of whole peoples and indeed the cosmos itself. In early Germanic culture the element of fire was feminine, and the 'great goddess' can be seen also to contain within herself an expression of that element. In Freya fire is a positive feminine initiator. She is a goddess of the sun, its light, warmth, and generative capacity. In Germanic culture (and the modern-day German language) the sun is female. Freya's fire is not wildfire as in Loki, who having been originally male fails to control this element which he desires for its damaging power. Whilst Loki attempts to use flame for his own, ultimately destructive ends, Freya directs this elemental expression of the energetic feminine into a measured, productive, exchange with the static masculine element of ice. In Freya, for early Anglo-Saxons, the feminine was not negative and passive, awaiting male stimulation in order to become fruitful, but active and positive, able to choose if and when to engage with the masculine. The result of such interaction could be procreative, though often neither pain nor contradiction free.[‡]

[‡] This female generative process can be codified in runes. The first rune of the futhark, Fehu (Freya's 'f' rune ᚠ), interacts with the second rune (the static

The erosion of Freya's 'great goddess' status by patriarchal forces even before the conversion of north European societies to Christianity appears to mirror a cyclical process that has been happening since the dawn of recorded history in Sumeria over five thousand years ago.[§] Similarities in different peoples' perceptions of important goddesses across the miles and millennia, from Sumerian Inanna to Phoenician Astarte and Greek Aphrodite, strongly suggest close connections between them, connections that are in many cases widely accepted as proven. Northern Europe's Freya however is an exception. Despite her exhibiting many characteristics in common with the likes of Astarte and Aphrodite, she is not usually considered in terms of any historical or wider geographic relationships outside central and north western Europe.

It is likely that the recognition of great goddesses down the centuries reflects a fundamental need common to all human societies to acknowledge, value, and celebrate the feminine alongside masculine aspects of cultural development, and that the repeated and continual unbalancing of such essential gender related social structures by patriarchal pressures will consistently and necessarily result in countervailing feminist tendencies coming to the fore. In that sense it hardly matters whether or not Germanic and early Anglo-Saxon perceptions of Freya were, at least in part, directly influenced by other cultures' discernment of great goddesses, or of a single great goddess who bore various names (Inanna, Ishtar, Astarte, and Aphrodite amongst other possibilities). Nevertheless it is interesting to note that such a connection cannot be dismissed as impossible. Astarte came to be revered by the Etruscans in northern Italy, and it seems that some of the runes of the Elder German futhark may have come from that same area; if writing and letters travelled north of the Alps, then perhaps too did some acquaintance with aspects of devotion to a 'great goddess'.

Whether or not this is the case, it must also be recognised that

---

masculine 'u' of Uruz ᚢ), the result of which is the (often painful) generation of energy, as expressed in the third rune ('th' or Thurisaz [Thorn] ᚦ).

[§] *"The Sumerian invention of cuneiform* [writing on clay tablets] - *a Latin term literally meaning 'wedge-shaped' - dates to sometime around 3400 B.C."* [https://www.history.com/news/9-things-you-may-not-know-about-the-ancient-sumerians]

Freya, however and to whatever large or small degree her followers may have been affected by Middle Eastern and Mediterranean influences, is substantially an indigenous goddess of the North. Germanic peoples needed her life-giving function as a goddess of the sun's warming and golden light rays to help ensure the fertility of their fields and animals. In Scandinavia particularly her early sexual freedom and sovereignty came to be increasingly disregarded or actively challenged by power-seeking male warrior-aristocrat worshippers of 'All-father' Odin, in a process which repeated the experience of Inanna in ancient Sumeria, which had seen the downgrading of goddesses over an extended period, reaching a peak in the reign of King Hammurabi of Babylon (1792-1750 BCE).

Prior to the arrival of Christianity in what became England however, and to some extent even thereafter, the veneration of the powerful and sovereign feminine which had been such an essential element in the honouring of Freya, was not forgotten. Historians consistently report that right up to the destruction of Anglo-Saxon rule in England following the Norman French invasion in 1066 CE, *"The evidence which has survived from Anglo-Saxon England indicates that women were more nearly the equal companions of their husbands and brothers than at any other period before the modern age".*[521] The survival of such relatively gender balanced values over many centuries, despite the increasing incursion of patriarchal principles from both pagan (Viking) and Christian sources, surely confirms the historic importance of the 'great goddess' Freya in Anglo-Saxon England.

Living in the Material World

What is real? The development of ways of looking at the world (or worlds) has much to do with attempts to answer this question. It is usually assumed that for animals what is real is that which their senses allow them to perceive. This may also be true of very young children, but for older children and adult human beings the question can be less easy to answer. Of course our physical senses always remain key to our comprehension of ourselves and our environment, but our mental ability to interpret physical sensations, combined with a capacity to creatively imagine possibilities which have not been directly experienced, together make it difficult to satisfy ourselves that anyone can ever know everything that is real, or indeed even recognise what is real and what is not. Nevertheless evolution has imbued us with a drive to survive, as part of which we continually attempt to improve our understanding of the worlds we live in, and accordingly our ways of looking at those worlds continue to change and develop.

Certainly from Sumerian times onwards, and possibly from a lot earlier than that, people have been aware of the limitations of our physical senses, and that not even the combined information our brains receive from sight, hearing, touch, taste and a sense of smell can fully inform us, at all times, of everything that is happening around us. Even when our five physical senses are as fully functional as they possibly can be, and remain unimpaired by illness or old age, still they have their limitations (we cannot, for example, see behind us). Consequently we have come to realise that the quality of our lives, and our survival chances, can be enhanced by exercising our power to move beyond simply accepting information provided by our physical senses to the envisaging of additional possibilities.

This necessary envisioning of additional possibilities has given us a will to explore and explain our physical environment, driving us to discover with our own eyes both what lies beyond the next hill, and how and why that hill got to be there, in that form, in the first place. Throughout recorded history (and no doubt well before that) our sense of adventure has never been limited to the geographic, but also encompassed everything imaginable, including other worlds and beings both physical and spiritual.

It is clear that from very early on in this process we concluded that the multiverse is very much greater than our own restricted experience of our own world, that we ourselves are rather imperfect entities bound by physical and other limitations, and that there exist a wide range of animals and other beings capable of doing things we cannot (flying for example). It is also clear that exposing our minds to possibilities beyond those experienced directly through the body's sense receptors allowed our distant ancestors to open themselves up to the perception of, and communication with, living entities recognised as existing at least partly outside our physical world of Middle Earth. For pagans of all types, from ancient Sumeria to rather less ancient early England, ways of understanding the worlds, and what is real, were considered to be sufficiently comprehensive only if they included 'otherworldly' entities such as spirits of the dead, elves, fairies, giants, gods, and monsters. It did not matter if such beings were not always experienced in quite the same physical manner as more earthly beings, for people knew that our perceptive senses are limited, and that consequently communication with such beings might often most effectively be left to a minority able to specialise in such skills, whether priestesses, shamans, or magicians.

For Sumerians and Anglo-Saxons alike it appears that there was no insurmountable contradiction between believing in goddesses, gods, and a whole range of otherworldly entities on the one hand, and living a more mundane life in Middle Earth on the other. For the pagan early English, conceiving as they did of diverse and plural worlds, the certainty that *It's real if you can touch it* was complemented, not undermined by, knowledge of the gods. For farmers cutting crops and warriors cutting down enemies, for women undergoing labour pains and families seeing their elders die, there was no doubt that the physically experienced world is real. At the same time there was also no doubt that the worlds of the gods, and the gods themselves, were real as well, and that interaction between Middle Earth and (for example) Vanaheim was perfectly possible, as witnessed by the sending of Shef (Scyld Scefing) to Skåne (see chapter 2).

This interaction with the otherworldly did not consist of 'worship' of the gods, but rather an everyday acknowledgement of the importance of multiple beings and forms of existence, and their relevance to life on Middle Earth:

> "...the 'worship' required by the Norse pantheon was not adoration, or gratitude, or even unreserved approval, and was thus utterly unlike the Christian relationship to the divine. The religion of the Æsir and Vanir demanded only a recognition that they existed as an integral and immutable part of human nature and society, and of the natural world, and that as such they possessed an inherent rightness – perhaps even a kind of beauty. If one wished to avoid disaster, it was necessary to come to terms with the gods, and the terms would be theirs, not those of their followers." [522]

This pagan way of seeing the worlds is called 'materialist' in philosophical terms, meaning that the material, physical world, that experienced through the senses, is broadly accepted as reality, even allowing for imperfection in sensory abilities. It does not exclude the possibility of the existence of other worlds or otherworldly beings, or of interaction with those other worlds and beings. Communication with the gods may at times have needed to rely on specialist priestesses or shamans (just as the production of clothes required specialist weaving skills), but it was known that if on rarer occasion the gods might wish to communicate and interact with us, then they were fully capable of doing so. As 'otherworldly' as they might be, they were also material, corporeal, and able to play a part in the physical, 'real' world of Middle Earth, making themselves known to us, and touching the soil just like any farmer. The gods were both different from, and very similar to... us.

The various forms of paganism have always been 'materialist', accepting the reality of what we perceive, whether in the form of bricks and mortar, or interaction with the gods. There is however also a long history of other people taking a different view of reality. Like Germanic paganism, ancient Greek paganism was materialist and pluralist, describing multiple worlds and a wide variety of gods, but its cosmology was less dialectical and arguably correspondingly less intellectually flexible than the north European variety. In particular Greek pagans imagined that their gods were truly immortal, and perfect enough to live forever, unlike the northern deities doomed to die at Ragnarok, or earlier should they lose access to Idun's golden apples.

This Greek conception of divine perfection and immortality was developed further by the philosopher Plato (died 348 BCE), leading him to abandon paganism, pluralism, and materialism. Plato despaired not only of the imperfections so clearly inherent in the mundane world, but also of those so equally in plain view in the stories of the Greek gods. For Plato perfection was not the triumph of the void, but a desirable concept. He wanted to believe that the obtaining of perfection was not only theoretically possible, but also somehow ultimately actually achievable. The problem was that it was also very clearly incompatible with the reality of everyday life as experienced on earth. Real life was full of contradictions which it was impossible ever fully to resolve. The very nature of existence itself seemed to imply a disturbing lack of perfectibility. Death he perceived as an ultimately insuperable negation of any improvement in the quality of life, not only in physical terms but also spiritual. Even prior to death, whilst life still lasted, pain and suffering were inevitable in all their many forms: physical, mental, emotional, and spiritual.

Plato's need to see perfection as attainable drove him to assert that it must already exist – in the form of a single, flawless, God. Perfection, he realised, could not be plural. By its very nature it must be single and unitary in form, for there could not exist two or more different forms of perfection, for then each would be a contradiction and denial of the 'perfect' form of the other. For Plato, perfection and his single, unitary God were the same thing. Everything else, anything which existed outside of or beyond God was not only imperfect, but also at least partially 'unreal', for truly perfect reality could exist only as part of God, within Him, as part of His creation.

God was referred to as male, no doubt in part reflecting ancient patriarchal Greek culture and values, but possibly also because, for Plato and his followers, women were, because of their child-bearing function, necessarily more plural in nature than men, and therefore further away from their single, unitary, and perfect God. Mortals (most often referred to only as men) could aspire to move themselves closer towards God, and could seek to achieve this through theurgy (the use of magical ritual to influence divine intermediary entities such as Hecate in her form of the 'World Soul'), and intellectual and philosophical studies directed at the achievement of complete submission of a man's soul to God. This process of submission required acceptance of a need to comply with 'correct opinion' or belief, which again was not pluralistic but totalitarian and singular. Doing so would allow progress of the individual soul towards the achievement of total harmony, perfection and 'true reality', possibly expressed initially (some Platonists believed) in the form of mathematics and in particular in the perfection of numbers, and ultimately through complete submission to, communion with, and absorption within, God.

For Greek Platonists (and later Middle and Neo-Platonists) life on earth was at best only partially real, because ultimately only the one God was truly real. Knowledge of, and aspiration towards communion with God, allowed for some limited perception of true 'ideal' reality for individual souls still trapped in corporeal form on earth, but the 'illusion' of reality created for us by our senses was held to be largely unreal, as was indeed the very material reality being perceived by those senses. For Platonists the material, physical world itself was at least partially illusory. Life on earth, and indeed 'life' for souls trapped in the Underworld of Hades too, was less than fully real. Life only started to become real for those souls able to travel (after death) not down to the Underworld but up and beyond the moon to the celestial world of the heavens, where God dwelt.

Not only was the material world as perceived by pre-Platonic Greek pagans (trusting in their senses) determined by Platonists to be at least partially unreal, but so too were their pagan gods. Such gods, Plato declared, were too much like human beings to be truly, really divine. They were contradictory, always arguing, making war, having love affairs, and generally engaging in common, despicable activities. As such, like mortals, they could not be truly, perfectly real. To the extent that such gods might exist at all, they could do so only in the same way human beings do, as multiple, imperfect entities living in a less than truly real cosmos. The one true God by contrast did not have a necessarily corrupt, imperfect, physical form. He was pure spirit, purer even than mathematics and numbers. He existed as non-physical perfection in the form of a philosophical ideal.

This way of looking at the worlds, with its assertion that only the perfect 'ideal' is ultimately truly and fully real, became known as Idealism, and in its Greek Platonic form was very much a philosophical forerunner of monotheistic Christianity. Not only did Greek Platonic thinkers promote the concept of a single, perfect God, but they also clearly differentiated their God from that of other adherents of monotheism (such as the Jews), firstly by declaring the Greek one God to be also triplicate in form, and secondly by declaring the whole of mankind to be corrupted by 'unreality' from birth, and in need of salvation of the individual soul through total submission to God - which could only be achieved through obedience to the teachings of philosopher priest-magicians, based on theurgy, ritual, and intellectual study.

In Platonism the triplicate nature of the one God was expressed through Himself as Father, Himself as Son (called the "Demi-urge", a form created by Himself alone, in which He was able to impact on the lesser, material world), and His creation of the "World Soul" or Holy Spirit (often named as Hecate) which could act as an intermediary between individual mortal souls and God the Father. This was all later taken on board virtually unchanged by Christians, who rejected the Jewish one God in favour of the Greek triplicate form, but with the "Demi-urge" renamed as Jesus, and Hecate envisaged only as the "Holy Spirit".

Crucially Christians also adopted the Greek Platonist concept of individual souls needing to find eternal life and salvation in a celestial heaven through submission to God, declaring that to achieve this they must reject the single acknowledged alternative post-death scenario of descent into the Underworld. This message they reinforced by re-visioning the diverse lands of Hades as uniform and unchanging Hell, populated by fiery, eternally tormenting demons. Similarly, required Platonic obedience to the teachings of philosopher priest-magicians became obedience to the teachings of a new Christian hierarchy: a

Catholic ('universal') and Orthodox ('correct') Church. This Church was patriarchal. For the Church there was only one (triplicate) God and He was male. There was no room in this restricted 'Universe' for the goddesses to be found in any pagan multiverse. Priests must be male, and power, both ideological and coercive, was reserved to men only.

Whilst, as already stated, for Greek pagans (for farmers cutting crops and warriors cutting down enemies, for women undergoing labour, and families seeing their elders die) there was no doubt that the physically experienced world was real, Platonic philosophers and the Greek (and subsequently also Roman) Christian Church taught otherwise. The material world was simply too contradictory, difficult, and pain-imbued to be accepted as fully real. Mankind was born corrupted by, respectively, either unreality or 'original sin', and was condemned to sink into the Underworld or Hell upon death, though individual souls could be saved and gain eternal life in heaven through submission to the one God, as taught through total obedience to Him and (in Christianity) his Church.

The ideological conflict between materialist and idealist world views did not remain restricted to Greece and Rome, or to the Mediterranean and the Middle East. It was brought also to northern Europe and Anglo-Saxon England. Paganism in its early English form was doubtlessly at least as materialist and pluralist as the ancient Greek variety, or perhaps even slightly more so, with its Germanic insistence on the mortal nature of the gods. For both ancient Greek pagans and pre-Christian Anglo-Saxons the gods were real and many. They were also both goddesses and gods, defined in part by their sex and sexuality, and both the ancient Greek and early English versions of the multiverse allowed for rather more gender balanced interpretations of reality than the patriarchal Greek and Roman Christian churches.

Dissent, Diversity, Sex and Death

Looking back into history there can be a tendency to assume that the 21st century represents the peak of mankind's achievements, not just in technological matters, but also in terms of social and political formations, with a greater proportion of the planet's population than ever before enjoying liberal freedoms of both association and behaviour, including rights to be different, to think differently, and to engage more openly in a greater range of behaviours without suffering verbal condemnation or physical punishment. From studying the past it soon becomes clear however that in reality things have been rather more complicated.

Prior to the imposition of intolerant monotheistic ideologies by patriarchal elites, ancient and 'primitive' pagan interpretations of the worlds tended to be pluralistic, relatively diverse, and more gender balanced, with such understanding being reflected in a polytheistic recognition of disparate divinities, including many powerful goddesses. This is not to claim that ancient pagan societies were some kind of tolerant paradise. Inevitably conflicting interests, then as now, arose from varying and ever-changing environmental and economic factors, as well as conflicting perceptions of individual self-interest. 5,000 years ago the popularity of the 'great goddess' Inanna in Sumeria may well have reflected a society in which women had powerful roles, but 1,000 years later exclusively male power was coming to the fore, as reflected in an increasing emphasis on male gods and the demotion of goddesses.

The history of early English belief systems is similarly contradictory and complex. It seems that prior to migration to Britain (from around 450 CE) the early English predecessor tribes of the Anglo-Saxons predominantly revered the Vanir: fertility goddesses and gods exhibiting a wide range of social and sexual practices, including some later rejected, to a greater or lesser degree, by Germanic and Scandinavian pagans, such as incestuous sibling partnerships, homosexuality, and transgenderism. The Scandinavians came to honour the Æsir gods more than the Vanir, associating 'All-father' Odin in particular with their more patriarchal, warrior-based values. Inevitably this creed, based more on male coercive power than compromises between factional social interests as it was, necessarily developed a rather less diverse world view than the pre-Christian Anglo-Saxon Vanir based one, and the contradictions inevitably inherent in such ideological constraint came to be expressed through one figure in particular: Loki – the trickster, transgender, and tortured god.

Whilst Loki expressed the tensions arising from the narrowing of socially acceptable behaviours in Scandinavian societies, social tensions were also not unknown in early English culture, though given the possibly more tolerant and diverse routes available there for divergence and dissent, they did come to be articulated rather differently. Some individual early English aristocratic males for example could, if they wished, dissociate themselves from dominant masculine ideology, and elect instead to show an interest in elves, considered in pre-Christian times to be male but effeminate. Women, it was thought, could also step beyond standard social roles by learning magical *haegtesse* (witch) skills, including shamanic abilities to communicate with the gods.

Pagan Anglo-Saxon relative tolerance of diverse views and dissenting actions in relation to social, sexual, and gender roles, extended beyond both human and divine mortal cultures to understandings of what might be possible after death. The materialist world view, based on rational interpretation of actual experience in the context of the acknowledged limitations of physical sense-based information, inclined people to hypothesize a variety of post-death possibilities. For some these may have ranged from a limited survival in burial mounds whilst the body remained relatively intact, to forms of ongoing spiritual afterlives, whether in Freya's hall of Sessrúmnir, Odin's Valhalla, or the goddess Hel's frozen realm. However it is also possible that the general paucity of evidence of Anglo-Saxon concerns with the afterlife could reflect not just an inability of a largely illiterate society to transmit beliefs to later generations, but perhaps also a lack of concern with the individual's fate after death, reflecting material experience that it is children that provide by far the best evidenced guarantee of survival beyond the grave, and that it is the collective ongoing development of a people that really matters, not placing probably false hopes in any ideal, heavenly hereafter for individual souls.

The pagan consensus was clearly that everything has its time and that everything ends, to be replaced by new and different entities. Every generation is collectively succeeded by its children. Whether or not individual souls might survive bodily death for a while comes to seem relatively less important when it is acknowledged that all must eventually fully die anyway, at the latest when the very worlds we live in (whether Middle Earth or Asgard) come to an end.

A need to somehow reconcile comprehension of the soul as an entity not bound by physical form, with the actual encountering of death as the final ending of individual life, alongside the Germanic faith in the shamanic aspects of women, may explain the north European and no doubt Anglo-Saxon faith in supernatural female guardians such as the Disír (or in Scandinavia the hamingjur). Whilst Greek idealist philosophers sought to counteract the despair that consciousness of mortality brought them by alleging that individual souls could be saved from death and find eternal life through submission to one perfect God, many north European pagans preferred to face up to death by admitting its reality, but seeking solace firstly in the rational knowledge that children are our true collective immortality, and secondly in their spiritual experience of disír.

For pagan Anglo-Saxons bodily death could be expected to be followed by the reunion of the individual's soul with (at the abode of) their dís or supernatural female protector. Here the individual is initially accepted into the arms of their dís, before she leaves them to accompany instead another, still surviving, relation. This is surely a metaphor for the final acceptance of death. The deceased person no longer needs the protection of their dís, now that their life has finally fully ended in not just its physical but also its spiritual aspect ('body and soul'). They have in effect transferred whatever spiritual energy they had retained after bodily death to their dís, who by moving on to nurture another, probably very much younger, member of the family or tribe, reuses that donated energy in the most appropriate way that the deceased could possibly have wished for. In Germanic tribal culture it was not (as it was in Greek aristocratic Platonic and later Christian societies) the eternal survival of the individual soul which constituted the supreme spiritual purpose, but the collective further development of the people as a whole through successive generations.

It is worth remembering also the 'great goddess' Freya's title of Vanadís, the dís of the Vanir. Once it is understood that it is a key role of the disír to transfer spiritual energy from the dead souls they have nurtured and protected in life to young, still living, family and tribal relations, the meaning of the transfer of battle-dead souls to Freya's hall of Sessrúmnir becomes clearer: in these cases she is acting as their dís. Having fought and died for the collective interest of their family and tribe they may be paid an exceptional honour. Freya herself will act as their dís after death, with the goddess herself holding them in her arms to accept the necessary donation of their spiritual energy to their relations.

Ultimately the pagan Anglo-Saxon acceptance of death can be said to constitute a very positive world view. It is certainly 'heroic' in its determination to face up to and overcome the ultimate fear: that of ceasing to exist. For materialists it is also – crucially - realistic, being based on the evidence of actual experience as far as that is possible (the observation of death in others and the lack of experience of any real or long term survival of those others after bodily death, even though the soul's energy may be thought to linger before reunification with its dís). The pagan materialist's recognition of the finality of death may also be considered to be ultimately optimistic, in that it incorporates an understanding that this is the price that must be paid to ensure the collective ongoing life of family and tribe through succeeding generations. Deaths, at least for pagan Anglo-Saxons, could be understood as the midwives of births and new lives.

Bibliography

Author/Editor	Title	Publisher	Place	Date
Aðalsteinsson, Jón Hnefill	Under the Cloak – The Acceptance of Christianity in Iceland	Uppsala University Press	Uppsala, Sweden	1978
Anonymous	The Vinland Sagas – The Norse Discovery of America	Penguin	London	1965
Anonymous	Beowulf	Penguin Books	London	1973
Anonymous	Egil's Saga	Everyman	London	1975
Anonymous	The Exeter Riddle Book	Folio Society	UK	1978
Anonymous	Eirik the Red and other Icelandic Sagas	Oxford University Press	Oxford	1980
Anonymous	Eyrbygga Saga	Penguin	London	1989
Anonymous	The Saga of the Volsungs	Hisarlik Press	Enfield Lock	1993
Anonymous	Viking Gods	Quantum Books	London	1998
Anonymous	The Saga of King Hrolf Kraki	Penguin	London	1998
Anonymous	The Prittlewell Prince – The Discovery of a Rich Anglo-Saxon Burial in Essex	Museum of London Archeology Service	London	2004
Anonymous	The Wanderer – Elegies, Epics, Riddles	Penguin Books	London	2008
Anonymous	The Elder Edda	Penguin	London	2013
Anonymous	Njal's Saga	Wordsworth Editions	Ware	1998

Author/Editor	Title	Publisher	Place	Date
Arnold, C. J.	An Archeology of Early Anglo-Saxon Kingdoms	Routledge	London	1997
Aswynn, Freya	Leaves of Yggdrasil	Llewellyn	St. Paul, USA	1990
Bates, Brian	The Wisdom of the Wyrd	Rider	London	1996
Bates, Brian	The Real Middle Earth	Pan MacMillan	London	2002
Bede	Ecclesiastical History of the English People	Penguin	London	1990
Bennett, Mathew	Campaigns of the Norman Conquest	Osprey Publishing	Oxford	2001
Blain, Jenny	Nine Worlds of Seidr Magic	Routledge	London	2002
Blain, Jenny	Wights and Ancestors	Prydein Press	Runcorn	2016
Branston, Brian	Gods of the North	Thames and Hudson	London	1980
Branston, Brian	The Lost Gods of England	Thames and Hudson	London	1984
Buckland, Raymond	The Tree – The Complete Book of Saxon Witchcraft	Weiser	Maine, USA	1974
Care Evans, Angela	The Sutton Hoo Ship Burial	British Museum Press	London	1986
Carver, Martin	Sutton Hoo – Burial Ground of Kings?	British Museum Press	London	1998
Carver, Sanmark and Semple (Eds.)	Signals of Belief in Early England	Oxbow Books	Oxford	2010
Cater, Karen	Spirit of the Hare	Hedingham Fair	Hedingham	2010
Chadwick, H. Munro	The Origin of the English Nation	Cambridge University Press	Cambridge	1907

Bibliography

Author/Editor	Title	Publisher	Place	Date
Cohat, Yves	The Vikings – Lords of the Seas	Thames and Hudson	London	1992
Crossley-Holland, Kevin	The Penguin Book of Norse Myths	Penguin	London	1982
Crowley, Vivianne	Phoenix from the Flame	Aquarian Press	London	1994
Curry, Patrick	Defending Middle Earth – Tolkien: Myth and Modernity	Harper Collins	London	1998
d'Este, Sorita	Circle for Hekate	Avalonia	London	2017
Ellis Davidson, H. R.	Gods and Myths of Northern Europe	Penguin	London	1990
Ellis Davidson, Hilda	The Lost Beliefs of Northern Europe	Routledge	London	1993
Ellis Davidson, Hilda	Roles of the Northern Goddess	Routledge	London	1998
Evans, Bryan	The Life and Times of Hengest	Anglo-Saxon Books	Ely	2014
Fell, Christine	Women in Anglo-Saxon England	Basil Blackwell	Oxford	1986
Finberg, H. P. R.	The Formation of England 550-1042	Paladin	London	1976
Flavius Claudius Julianus Augustus ('Julian the Apostate')	Against the Galilaeans	Ostara Publications	ostara-publications.com, USA	2012

Author/Editor	Title	Publisher	Place	Date
Fletcher, Richard	Bloodfeud – Murder and Revenge in Anglo-Saxon England	Oxford University Press	Oxford	2003
Flowers, Stephen E.	The Secret of the Runes	Destiny Books	Vermont, USA	1988
Gaiman, Neil	Norse Mythology	Bloomsbury	London	2017
Gardner, John	Grendel	Gollanz	London	2015
Godden and Lapidge (Eds.)	The Cambridge Companion to Old English Literature	Cambridge University Press	Cambridge	1986
Goodison & Morris (Eds.)	Ancient Goddesses	British Museum Press	London	1998
Griffiths, Bill	Aspects of Anglo-Saxon Magic	Anglo-Saxon Books	Hockwold cum Wilton	1996
Guerber, H. A.	The Norsemen – Myths and Legends	Studio Editions	London	1994
Gundarsson, KveldúlfR Hagan (Ed.)	Our Troth Vol.1 – Gods, Goddesses and Wights	Ring of Troth Europe	n/a	1998
Hall, Alaric	Elves in Anglo-Saxon England	Boydell Press	Woodbridge	2007
Harasta and River (Eds.)	Athena – The History, Origins, and Evolution of the Greek Goddess	Charles River Editors	n/a	n/a (print on demand)
Heaney, Seamus	Beowulf	W. W. Norton	New York	2008
Herbert, Kathleen	Spellcraft – Old English Heroic Legends	Anglo-Saxon Books	Hockwold-cum-Wilton	1993
Herbert, Kathleen	Looking for the Lost Gods of England	Anglo-Saxon Books	Hockwold cum Wilton	1994

Author/Editor	Title	Publisher	Place	Date
Higham, N. J.	An English Empire – Bede and the Early Anglo-Saxon Kings	Manchester University Press	Manchester	1995
Higham, N. J.	The Convert Kings – Power and Religious Affiliation in Early Anglo-Saxon England	Manchester University Press	Manchester	1997
Hooke, Della	Trees in Anglo-Saxon England	Boydell Press	Woodbridge	2010
Howard, Michael	Mysteries of the Runes	Capall Bann Publishing	Chieveley	1995
Iles Johnston, Sarah	Hekate Soteira	Scholars Press	Atlanta, USA	1990
Jackson, Lesley	Isis – The Eternal Goddess of Egypt and Rome	Avalonia	London	2016
Jennings, Pete	The Norse Tradition – A Beginner's Guide	Hodder & Stoughton	Abingdon	1998
Jones, Kathy	The Ancient British Goddess	Ariadne Publications	Glastonbury	2017
Karlsdottir, Alice	Norse Goddess Magic	Destiny Books	Vermont, USA	2015
King, Bernard	The Elements of the Runes	Element Books	Shaftesbury	1993
Laing, Lloyd and Jennifer	Anglo-Saxon England	Granada Publishing	St. Albans	1982
Lee, Dave	Bright from the Well	Mandrake of Oxford	Oxford	2008
Mang, Andreas	Heathenism – Modern Philosophies, Concepts, Views	Eigenverlag Andreas Mang	Germany	2014

Bibliography

Author/Editor	Title	Publisher	Place	Date
Marsden, John	The Fury of the Northmen	Kyle Cathie	London	1996
Mathews, Caitlín	The Elements of the Goddess	Element Books	Shaftesbury	1989
Mayor, Adrienne	The Amazons – Lives and Legends of Warrior Women Across the Ancient World	Princeton University Press	New Jersey, USA	2014
McGrath, Sheena	Asyniur – Women's Mysteries in the Northern Tradition	Capall Bann	Chieveley	1997
McGrath, Sheena	Njörd and Skadi – A Myth Explored	Avalonia	London	2016
McNally, Michael	Teutoburg Forest AD 9	Osprey Publishing	Oxford	2011
Muir, Richard	Ancient Trees Living Landscapes	Tempus Publishing	Stroud	2005
Murdoch, Adrian	The Last Pagan – Julian the Apostate and the Death of the Ancient World	Sutton Publishing	Stroud	2005

Author/Editor	Title	Publisher	Place	Date
Murdoch, Adrian	Rome's Greatest Defeat – Massacre in the Teutoburg Forest	The History Press	Stroud	2008
Myres, J. N. L.	The English Settlements	Oxford University Press	Oxford	1986
Näsström, Britt-Mari	Freyja – the Great Goddess of the North	University of Lund	Lund, Sweden	1995
Newton, Sam	The Origins of Beowulf – and the pre-Viking Kingdom of East Anglia	D. S. Brewer	Cambridge	1993
Nixey, Catherine	The Darkening Age	Pan	London	2018
Orchard, Andy	Dictionary of Norse Myth and Legend	Cassell	London	1997
Owen, Gale R.	Rites and Religions of the Anglo-Saxons	Barnes and Noble	New York, USA	1996
Page, R. I.	Reading the Past – Runes	British Museum Press	London	1987
Page, R. I.	Norse Myths	British Museum Press	London	1990
Page, R. I.	Chronicles of the Vikings	British Museum Press	London	1995

Bibliography

Author/Editor	Title	Publisher	Place	Date
Paul, Jim	The Rune Poem	Chronicle Books	San Francisco, USA	1996
Paxson, Diana L.	Taking Up the Runes	Weiser Books	York Beach, Maine, USA	2005
Penry, Tylluan	The Magical World of the Anglo-Saxons	Wolfen-howle Press	Tonypandy	2012
Penry, Tylluan	An Introduction to Anglo-Saxon Magic and Witchcraft	The Wolfen-howle Press	Tonypandy	2014
Penry, Tylluan	Working with the Anglo-Saxon Runes	Wolfen-howle Press	Tonypandy	2016
Pollington, Stephen	Rudiments of Runelore	Anglo-Saxon Books	Hockwold cum Wilton	1995
Pollington, Stephen	The Elder Gods – The Otherworld of Early England	Anglo-Saxon Books	Ely, Cambridge-shire	2011
Porter, John	Anglo-Saxon Riddles	Anglo-Saxon Books	Hockwold cum Wilton	1995
Rance, Suzanne	The English Runes	Dragon House	*Amazon print on demand*	2017
Roderick Ellis, Hilda	The Road to Hel	Cambridge University Press	Cambridge	1943
Rodrigues, Louis J.	Anglo-Saxon Verse Charms, Maxims and Heroic Legends	Anglo-Saxon Books	Pinner	1993

Bibliography

Author/Editor	Title	Publisher	Place	Date
Rydberg, Viktor	Teutonic Mythology, Volume 1	Hardpress	Miami, USA	2016
Rydberg, Viktor	Teutonic Mythology, Volume 2	Book Jungle	Champaign, USA	n/a
Schledermann Peter	The Viking Saga	Weidenfeld and Nicholson	London	1997
Scott and River (Eds.)	Aphrodite – The Origins and History of the Greek Goddess of Love	Charles Rivers Editors	*Amazon print on demand*	n/a
Simek, Rudolf	Dictionary of Northern Mythology	D. S. Brewer	Cambridge	1993
Stenton, Sir Frank	Anglo-Saxon England	Oxford University Press	Oxford	1971
Stone, Alby	Ymir's Flesh – North European Creation Mythologies	Heart of Albion Press	Loughborough	1997
Storrie and Randall	Beowulf – Monster Slayer	Lerner Books	London	2009
Sturluson, Snorri	Edda	Everyman	London	1987
Sugimoto, David T. (Ed.)	Transformation of a Goddess – Ishtar-Astarte-Aphrodite	Academic Press Fribourg	Fribourg, Switzerland	2014
Sutcliffe, Rosemary	Beowulf: Dragonslayer	Red Fox (Random House)	London	1961 & 2001

Bibliography

Author/Editor	Title	Publisher	Place	Date
Sykes, Brian	Saxons, Vikings, and Celts	W. W. Norton & Company	New York, USA	2007
Tacitus	The Agricola and The Germania	Penguin	London	1970
Taplin, Oliver	Greek Fire	Jonathan Cape	London	1989
Teitler, H. C.	The Last Pagan Emperor	Oxford University Press	Oxford	2017
Thorsson, Edred	A Book of Troth	Llewellyn Publications	St. Paul, USA	1992
Todd, Malcolm	The Early Germans	Blackwell	Oxford	1995
Tolkien, J. R. R.	Finn and Hengest – The Fragment and the Episode	Harper Collins	London	1998
Tolkien, J. R. R.	The Monsters and the Critics	Harper Collins	London	2006
Tolkien, J. R. R.	Beowulf	Harper Collins	London	2015
Vanirdottir, Gefion	Fire Jewel – A Devotional for Freya	Asphodel Press	Hubbardston, Mass. USA	2013
Vikernes, Varg	Sorcery and Religion in Ancient Scandinavia	Abstract Sounds Books	London	2011
Waterfield, Robin and Kathryn	The Greek Myths	Quercus	London	2011
Welch, Lynda C.	Goddess of the North	Weiser Books	York Beach, Maine, USA	2001

Bibliography

Author/Editor	Title	Publisher	Place	Date
Wise, Terence	Men at Arms – Saxon, Viking and Norman	Osprey Publishing	Oxford	1979
Wolkstein and Kramer	Inanna – Queen of Heaven and Earth	Harper and Row	New York, USA	1983
Wood, Michael	In Search of the Dark Ages	Penguin	London	1994
Young, Serenity	Women Who Fly – Goddesses, Witches, Mystics and other Airborne Females	Oxford University Press	New York, USA	2018

Index

Index

References and Notes

[1] Gale R. Owen - *Rites and Religions of the Anglo-Saxons*, New York, USA, 1981, pp.32-33

[2] Viktor Rydberg, *Teutonic Mythology, Vol.1 – Gods and Goddesses of the Northland*, Hardpress USA 2016, p.120-123 (rewritten)

[3] Kathleen Herbert, *Looking for the Lost Gods of England*, Anglo-Saxon Books, Thetford, 1994 pp.15-16

[4] Owen, ibid. pp.32-33

[5] Herbert, ibid. pp.15-16

[6] Snorri Sturluson's "Edda"

[7] Rydberg, ibid. p.123 (rewritten)

[8] Völuspá (Poetic Edda)

[9] Raymond Buckland, *The Tree – The Complete Book of Saxon Witchcraft*, Maine, USA, 1974, p.16

[10] Herbert, ibid. p.18

[11] Herbert, ibid. p.19

[12] Rydberg, ibid. p.124 (rewritten)

[13] Owen, ibid. p.33

[14] Karen Cater, *Spirit of the Hare*, Headingham Fair, 2010, p.68

[15] Owen, ibid. p.51

[16] Roman historian Tacitus wrote *Germania* c.98 CE

[17] Herbert, ibid. pp.11-12

[18] Tacitus, *Germania* ch.40

[19] Herbert, ibid. p.18

[20] Hyndla's Lay, 35; Heimdallar Galdr., in the Younger Edda

[21] Eilif Gudrunson, Skaldskaparmal

[22] Auger: "a tool used to bore holes, as in ice or wood" - *www.thefreedictionary.com*

[23] "Evidence is presented... that Scef-Heimdal brought the fire-auger to primeval man" [Rydberg, ibid. p.126]

[24] Rydberg, ibid. pp.125-126 (rewritten)

[25] "culture" here seems to mean: settled living on and from the land – agriculture, as well as wisdom and knowledge. (Rydberg, ibid. chapter 21, p.124) (rewritten)

[26] Owen, ibid. p.33

[27] Or woman, e.g. the high status females in the Oseberg ship burial [https://en.wikipedia.org/wiki/Oseberg_Ship]

[28] Sam Newton, *The Origins of Beowulf and the pre-Viking Kingdom of East Anglia*, Cambridge 1994, p.97

[29] Preface to *Heimskringla*

[30] Newton, *ibid.* p.136

[31] Eliade, Patterns in Comparative Religion, p.32
[32] Newton, ibid. p.137
[33] Newton, ibid. pp.74-76
[34] Newton, ibid. pp.49-50
[35] Newton, ibid. p.51
[36] Rydberg, ibid. pp.124-125 (rewritten)
[37] Rydberg, ibid. pp.126-127 (rewritten)
[38] Social class in Nordic and Anglo-Saxon lands: see tables at
     https://en.wikipedia.org/wiki/Churl
[39] Rydberg, ibid. pp.127-128 (rewritten)
[40] *"The idea of a common fatherhood we find again in the question of Fadir's
     grandson. Through him the families of the nobility get the right of
     precedence before both the other classes. Thor becomes their progenitor.
     While all classes can trace their descent from Heimdal, the aristocracy can
     trace theirs from Thor as well, and through him from Odin."* Rydberg, ibid.
     p.128 (rewritten)
[41] Beowulf, trans. Seamus Heaney, Illustrated Ed. New York, 2008, p.213
[42] Tolkien, *"On Translating Beowulf"*, in The Monsters and the Critics, Harper
     Collins, London, 2006, p.49
[43] Tolkien, *Beowulf – A Translation and Commentary*, London 2015, p.142
[44] Tolkien, ibid. lines 7-8 p.13
[45] Tolkien, ibid. Commentary, p.254
[46] Heaney, trans. ibid. p.213
[47] Sarah Semple in *Signals of Belief in Early England* (ed. Carver, Sanmark,
     Semple), Oxford 2010, pp.24-25
[48] Beowulf, trans. Seamus Heaney, Illustrated Ed. New York, 2008, p.viii
[49] Tolkien, ibid. Commentary, p.328
[50] Tolkien, ibid. Commentary, p.323
[51] Julie Lund in *Signals of Belief in Early England*, (ed. Carver, Sanmark,
     Temple), Oxford 2010, p.60
[52] Heaney, trans. ibid. lines 175-80
[53] Tolkien, *The Monsters and the Critics*, Harper Collins, London, 2006, p.22
[54] Elder (Poetic) Edda, *Hávámal* verse 77
[55] Stephen Pollington, The Elder Gods, Anglo-Saxon Books, 2011, p.457
[56] Heaney, trans. ibid. lines 183-6
[57] Tolkien, Beowulf, ibid. Commentary, pp.170-1
[58] Tolkien, *The Monsters and the Critics*, ibid. p.38
[59] Heaney, trans. ibid. lines 850-1
[60] Tolkien, Beowulf, ibid. Commentary, p.298
[61] Hilda Roderick Ellis, *"The Road to Hel"*, Cambridge 1943, p.96
[62] Ellis, ibid. pp.86-7
[63] Tolkien, *The Monsters and the Critics* (quoting Ker), ibid. p.21
[64] Tolkien, *The Monsters and the Critics*, ibid. p.22

[65] Elder (Poetic) Edda, *Völuspá*, verse 57
[66] Elder (Poetic) Edda, *Völuspá*, verse 59
[67] https://en.wikipedia.org/wiki/Butterfly_effect (21/6/21)
[68] Terry Pratchett and Neil Gaiman, Good Omens, as per
    https://fs.blog/2017/08/the-butterfly-effect/ (21/6/21)
[69] Heaney, trans. ibid. line 455
[70] Tolkien, ibid. line 367
[71] Suzanne Rance, *The English Runes*, UK 2017 p.107 (my emphasis)
[72] Rance, ibid. p.107
[73] Rance, ibid. p.107
[74] Rance, ibid. p.107
[75] Tolkien, ibid. Commentary, p.244
[76] Tolkien, ibid. Commentary, p.243
[77] Tolkien, ibid. Commentary, p.245
[78] Heaney, trans. ibid. lines 572-5
[79] Tolkien, ibid. Commentary, p.256
[80] Tolkien, ibid. Commentary, pp.256-7
[81] Tolkien, ibid. Commentary, p.267
[82] Tolkien, ibid. Commentary, p.268
[83] Heaney, trans. ibid. lines 696-7
[84] Tolkien, ibid. lines 569-70
[85] http://www.heorot.dk/beowulf-rede-text.html, lines 696-7
[86] Tolkien, ibid. Commentary, p.267
[87] Heaney, trans. ibid. lines 2525-7
[88] Heaney, trans. ibid. lines 2573-91
[89] Heaney, trans. ibid. lines 3180-82
[90] Heaney, trans. Ibid. footnote to lines 234-6, p.17
[91] Tolkien, ibid. Commentary, pp.239-40
[92] Heaney, trans. ibid. lines 303-6 and footnote p.22
[93] Heaney, trans. ibid. p.230
[94] See for example the "Benty Grange" Anglo-Saxon helmet with its boar crest
    In Sheffield's Weston Park Museum - illustrated in Heaney (ibid.) p.20
[95] Heaney, trans. ibid. lines 403-5, 453, and footnote p.29
[96] Heaney, trans. ibid. p.220
[97] Heaney, trans. ibid. line 1042
[98] Tolkien, ibid. lines 850-1
[99] Tolkien, ibid. line 1101
[100] Tolkien, The Monsters and the Critics, ibid. pp.25-6
[101] See the story of the death of Baldr in Snorri Sturluson's *Prose Edda*
[102] Heaney, trans. ibid. lines 3180-3
[103] Tolkien, The Monsters and the Critics, ibid. p.28
[104] Tolkien, The Monsters and the Critics, ibid. p.31
[105] Tolkien, ibid. Commentary, p.326

[106] Beowulf, trans. Heaney, lines 2020-2050 and 2064-2066
[107] Tolkien, ibid. Commentary, p.327
[108] Tolkien, ibid. Commentary, p.331
[109] Tolkien, ibid. Commentary, p.330
[110] Tolkien, ibid. Commentary, p.337
[111] Tolkien, ibid. Commentary p.338
[112] Tolkien, ibid. Commentary p.328
[113] Tolkien, Beowulf, ibid. Commentary, p.179
[114] Tolkien, ibid. Commentary, p.328
[115] Tolkien, ibid. Commentary, p.328
[116] Tolkien, ibid. Commentary, p.328
[117] Tolkien, ibid. Commentary, p.329
[118] Tolkien, ibid. Commentary, p.329
[119] Tolkien, ibid. Commentary, p.330
[120] Tolkien, ibid. Commentary, p.330
[121] Tolkien, ibid. Commentary, p.331
[122] Tolkien, ibid. Commentary, p.337
[123] Tolkien, ibid. Commentary, p.338
[124] Heaney, trans. ibid. lines 941-5
[125] Tolkien, ibid. Commentary, p.295
[126] Tolkien, ibid. lines 969-76
[127] Heaney, trans. ibid. lines 1197-8 and footnote p.83
[128] Heaney, trans. ibid. lines 1226-31
[129] Tolkien, ibid. line 1020
[130] Heaney, trans. ibid. p.233
[131] Heaney, trans. ibid. lines 1926-43
[132] Heaney, trans. ibid. lines 2172-6
[133] Heaney, trans. ibid. lines 2369-72
[134] Heaney, *Beowulf* trans. ibid. line 1042
[135] Tolkien, *Beowulf* trans ibid. line 1101
[136] Gylfaginning (20ff.);
     https://en.wikipedia.org/wiki/%C3%86sir#List_of_.C3.86sir
[137] Rudolf Simek, *Dictionary of Northern Mythology*, Stuttgart 1993, p.230
[138] Sheena McGrath, *Njord and Skadi – A Myth Explored*, London 2016
[139] https://en.wikipedia.org/wiki/Nerthus
[140] https://en.wikipedia.org/wiki/Ska%C3%B0i#Gylfaginning
[141] https://en.wikipedia.org/wiki/Ska%C3%B0i#Gylfaginning
[142] Simek, ibid. p.95
[143] Simek, ibid. p.92
[144] Skidbladnir –
     https://en.wikipedia.org/wiki/Sk%C3%AD%C3%B0bla%C3%B0nir
[145] Gullinborsti - https://en.wikipedia.org/wiki/Gullinbursti
[146] Simek, ibid. p.379

[147] Freya Aswynn, *Leaves of Yggdrasil*, St. Paul MN, 1990, pp.95-97
[148] Simek, ibid. p.92, quoting Adam of Bremen, *Deeds of the Bishops of Hamburg* (1076)
[149] https://en.wikipedia.org/wiki/Ger%C3%B0r
[150] Simek, ibid. p.90
[151] https://www.godchecker.com/norse-mythology/GERSIMI/
[152] https://en.wikipedia.org/wiki/Freyja
[153] https://pantheon.org/articles/h/hildisvini.html, and https://en.wikipedia.org/wiki/Hildisv%C3%ADni
[154] Simek, p.71
[155] Simek, ibid. pp.90-91
[156] Simek, ibid. p.61
[157] Simek, ibid. p.339
[158] Simek, ibid. p.339
[159] *The Elder Edda*, Penguin 2011, p.8
[160] Andy Orchard, *Dictionary of Norse Myth and Legend,* London 1998, p.67
[161] Orchard, ibid. p.137, and: http://www.sacred-texts.com/neu/poe/poe03.htm
[162] *The Elder Edda*, Penguin 2011, p.8
[163] Simek, ibid. p184
[164] Rydberg, ibid. p.124-125
[165] Simek, ibid. p.351
[166] Sheena McGrath, *Njord and Skadi – A Myth Explored*, London 2016, p.148
[167] McGrath ibid. pp.150-151
[168] McGrath, ibid. p.118
[169] McGrath, ibid. p.149
[170] McGrath, ibid. p.151
[171] Hilda Ellis Davidson *Roles of the Northern Goddess,* London 1998, p.188
[172] McGrath, ibid. pp.118-119
[173] McGrath, ibid. p.142
[174] McGrath, ibid. p.125
[175] Stephen Pollington, *The Elder Gods*, Anglo-Saxon Books, 2011, p.60
[176] *"In comparative mythology, sky father is a term for a recurring concept of a sky god who is addressed as a "father", often the father of a pantheon... The concept is complementary to an "earth mother".* https://en.wikipedia.org/wiki/Sky_father
[177] Paul Bibre, *Frey and Gerd: the Story and its Myths,* 1986, in McGrath, ibid. p.114
[178] McGrath, ibid. pp.171-173
[179] McGrath, ibid. p.209
[180] McGrath, ibid. p.114
[181] See for example: Rydberg, ibid. pp.125-126
[182] McGrath, ibid. p.39

[183] McGrath, ibid. p.66

[184] Andy Orchard, *Dictionary of Norse Myth and Legend*, London 1997, p.160

[185] Simek, ibid. p184

[186] Snorri Sturluson, quoted in Orchard, ibid. p.101

[187] McGrath, ibid. p.209

[188] Orchard, ibid. p.123

[189] Orchard, ibid. p.123

[190] Orchard, ibid. p.124

[191] H. R. Ellis Davidson, *Gods & Myths of Northern Europe*, Penguin, 1990, p.75

[192] Kevin Crossley-Holland, *The Penguin Book of Norse Myths*, Penguin, 1982, p.198

[193] Freya Aswynn, *Northern Mysteries & Magic*, Llewellyn, 1998, pp.191/193

[194] Crossley-Holland, ibid. p.xvi

[195] Crossley-Holland, ibid. p.118

[196] Crossley-Holland, ibid. p.118

[197] Crossley-Holland, ibid. p.xvi

[198] KveldulfR Hagan Gundarsson (Editor), *Our Troth (Vol.1)*, Ring of Troth, 1998, p.51

[199] KveldulfR Hagan Gundarsson (Editor), Our Troth (Vol.1), Ring of Troth, 1998, p.51

[200] Gundarsson, ibid. p.50

[201] H. A. Guerber, *The Norsemen*, Senate, 1994, p.68

[202] Guerber, ibid. p.83

[203] Aswynn, ibid. p.193

[204] Crossley-Holland, ibid. p.217

[205] Crossley-Holland, ibid. p.192

[206] Simek, ibid. p.337

[207] Simek, ibid. p.337

[208] Orchard, ibid. p.167

[209] https://www.greekmythology.com/Other_Gods/Minor_Gods/Hesperides/hesperides.html

[210] https://www.greekmythology.com/Myths/The_Myths/Labours_of_Heracles/labours_of_heracles.html

[211] http://historylists.org/other/idun-and-the-golden-apples-of-youth.html

[212] Translation: Sheena McGrath, in We Are Star Stuff: *Idunn and Helen: People or Property?* (https://earthandstarryheaven.com/2017/03/08/people-or-property/)

[213] McGrath, *Idunn and Helen: People or Property?* (ibid.)

[214] Simek (ibid.) p.172

[215] https://en.wikipedia.org/wiki/I%C3%B0unn

[216] Only other reference to Ivaldi: the *sons* of Ivaldi created, at Loki's behest, Frey's ship *Skidbladnir*, Odin's spear *Gungnir*, and *Sif's golden hair*) [Andy Orchard, ibid.]

[217] https://en.wikipedia.org/wiki/Hrafnagaldr_%C3%93%C3%B0ins

[218] Jim Paul, *The Rune Poem*, San Francisco 1996, p.11

[219] Paul, ibid. p.10

[220] Paul, ibid. pp.8-9

[221] Bill Griffiths, *Aspects of Anglo-Saxon Magic*, Anglo-Saxon Books 1996, p.138

[222] Pollington, *The Elder Gods*, ibid. p.421

[223] Tylluan Penry, *The Magical World of the Anglo-Saxons*, Peterborough 2012, pp.113-114

[224] https://en.wikipedia.org/wiki/Rune_Poems

[225] https://en.wikipedia.org/wiki/Rune_Poems

[226] https://en.wikipedia.org/wiki/Rune_poem#Norwegian

[227] https://www.ragweedforge.com/RunNRPe.html

[228] https://en.wikipedia.org/wiki/Rune_Poems#English

[229] https://www.ragweedforge.com/rpae.html

[231] Paul, ibid. p.38

[232] Freya Aswynn, Leaves of Yggdrasil, Minnesota 1990, p.33

[233] Aswynn, ibid. pp.34-35

[234] https://www.ragweedforge.com/rpae.html

[235] Aswynn. ibid. pp.34-35

[236] Aswynn, ibid. pp.34-35

[238] Bernard King, *The Elements of the Runes*, Shaftsbury Dorset, 1993, p.124

[239] Books by Brian Bates include: *The Way of Wyrd* (1983), *The Wisdom of the Wyrd* (1996), and *The Real Middle Earth* (2002)

[240] www.dictionary.com – "cosmology"

[241] Aswynn, ibid. p.46

[242] Aswynn, ibid. p.79

[243] Aswynn, ibid. pp.105-6

[244] https://www.ragweedforge.com/rpae.html

[245] Nacht Engel, *Runes – The Magical Alphabet of the Ancient Peoples* of *Northern Europe*, pub. Runecast Copper, 2015 p.8

[246] Engel, ibid. p.8

[247] Aswynn, ibid. p.46

[248] Simek, ibid. p.265

[249] Della Hooke, *Trees in Anglo-Saxon England*, Boydell Press (Suffolk) 2010, p.3

[250] https://en.wikipedia.org/wiki/List_of_tree_deities

[251] https://en.wikipedia.org/wiki/Dryad

[252] http://www.thewhitegoddess.co.uk/articles/mythology_folklore/dryads_and_other_faery_folk.asp

[253] https://mythology.net/greek/greek-creatures/dryad/

254 See for example: https://lairbhan.blogspot.com/2016/05/robert-graves-influence-on-modern.html

255 https://en.wikipedia.org/wiki/Hyldemoer

256 https://www.godchecker.com/norse-mythology/HYLDEMOER/

257 Diana L. Paxson, *Taking up the Runes*, Maine, USA, 2005, p.86

258 Pollington, *The Elder Gods*, ibid. p.467

259 https://www.sciencefocus.com/planet-earth/how-many-trees-does-it-take-to-produce-oxygen-for-one-person/

260 https://www.nationalgeographic.org/activity/save-the-plankton-breathe-freely/

261 Richard Muir, *Ancient Trees and living Landscapes*, Stroud (Gloucestershire) 2005, p.57

262 Pollington, ibid. pp. 90-91

263 Hooke, ibid. p.11

264 Adam of Bremen, quoted in Hooke (ibid.) p.16

265 Freya Aswynn, *Leaves of Yggdrasil*, St. Paul, USA, 1994 pp.160-163

266 Andy Orchard, *Dictionary of Norse Myth and Legend*, London 1998, p.186

267 Simek, ibid. pp. 249 and 375

268 Simek, ibid. p.375

269 Hooke, ibid. pp.15-16

270 R. Muir, *Ancient Trees, Living Landscapes*, Stroud 2005, pp.55, 230

271 Hooke, ibid. p.21

272 Muir, ibid. p.230

273 Hooke ibid. p.26

274 Hooke, ibid. p.28 (my emphasis)

275 Hooke, ibid. pp.28-29

276 Hooke, ibid. pp.31-32

277 Hooke, ibid. pp.33-35

278 Pollington, The Elder Gods, ibid. pp.93-98

279 Britt-Mari Näsström, *Freyja – the Great Goddess of the North*, University of Lund, Sweden, 1995

280 Näsström, ibid. p.73

281 As told in *The Penguin Book of Norse Myths*, Kevin Crossley-Holland, London 1982, pp.65-69

282 Hilda Ellis Davidson, *Roles of the Northern Goddess*, London 1998

283 Hilda Ellis Davidson, *Gods and Myths of Northern Europe*, London 1964, pp.117-122

284 [Hindu] Rigveda, XVIII, 10. In H. R. Ellis Davidson, Gods and Myths of Northern Europe, ibid. p.92

285 Näsström, ibid. p.73

286 Hyndla's Lay: *"A short eddic poem... found in the late 14th century Flateyjarbók"* (Orchard, ibid. p.95)

[287] Kevin Crossley-Holland, *Penguin Book of Norse Myths*, London 1982, p.211 *(my emphases)*

[288] Crossley-Holland, ibid. p.211

[289] H. R. Ellis Davidson, *Gods and Myths of Northern Europe*, Penguin, London 1964, pp.98-9

[290] Orchard, ibid. p.121

[291] Simek, ibid. p.106

[292] Pollington, The Elder Gods, p.307

[293] Simek, ibid. p. 46

[294] Davidson, Gods and Myths of Northern Europe, ibid. p.116

[295] From *'Loki's Flyting'*, in Crossley-Holland, ibid. p.165

[296] Jesse Harasta and Charles Rivers (Eds.), *"Athena – The History, Origins, and Evolution of the Greek Goddess"*, Amazon (undated – print on demand), p.38

[297] Harasta and Rivers, ibid. p.39, 45

[298] David T. Sugimoto (ed.), *"Transformation of a Goddess – Ishtar-Astarte-Aphrodite"*, Academic Press Fribourg (Switzerland), 2014, pp.15-30

[299] Joshua J. Mark, https://www.ancient.eu/Inanna/

[300] Joshua J. Mark, https://www.ancient.eu/Inanna/

[301] Joshua J. Mark, https://www.ancient.eu/Inanna/

[302] Wolkstein and Kramer, ibid. pp.150-155

[303] Wolkstein and Kramer, ibid. pp.150-155

[304] Wolkstein and Kramer, ibid. p.158

[305] Wolkstein and Kramer, ibid. p.160

[306] Britt-Mari Näsström, Freya – the Great Goddess of the North, Lund (Sweden) 1995, p.26

[307] Näsström, ibid. p.26

[308] Wolkstein and Kramer, ibid. pp.161-162

[309] Näsström, ibid. pp.26-27

[310] Wolkstein and Kramer, ibid. pp.163

[311] Wolkstein and Kramer, ibid. pp.167

[312] Wolkstein and Kramer, ibid. pp.168

[313] Wolkstein and Kramer, ibid. pp.168

[314] https://www.ancient.eu/Inanna/

[315] Eiko Matsushima, in *"Transformation of a Goddess – Ishtar-Astarte-Aphrodite"*, David T. Sugimoto (ed.), Academic Press Fribourg (Switzerland), 2014, pp.1-14

[316] Joshua J. Mark, https://www.ancient.eu/Inanna/

[317] Joshua J. Mark, https://www.ancient.eu/Inanna/

[318] Patti Wigington, https://www.thoughtco.com/who-is-astarte-2561500

[319] Mark S. Smith, "'Athart in Late Bronze Age Syrian Texts" in *Transformation of a Goddess* (Ed. David T. Sugimoto), Fribourg, Switzerland, 2014, p.

[320] Smith, ibid. p.45

[321] Smith, ibid. p.56

[322] Smith, ibid. p.66

[323] Patti Wigington, https://www.thoughtco.com/who-is-astarte-2561500

[324] Patti Wigington, https://www.thoughtco.com/who-is-astarte-2561500

[325] Keiko Tazawa, *Astarte in New Kingdom Egypt*, in *Transformation of a Goddess* (Ed. David T. Sugimoto), ibid. p.110

[326] Tazawa, ibid. p.109

[327] David. T. Sugimoto, *The Judean Pillar Figurines and the "Queen of Heaven"*, in *Transformation of a Goddess* (Ed. David T. Sugimoto), ibid. p.143

[328] Sugimoto, ibid. p.153

[329] Sugimoto, ibid. pp. 153-154

[330] Elizabeth Bloch-Smith, Evidence for Phoenician Astarte, in Sugimoto, ibid. pp.191-192

[331] Bloch-Smith, ibid. p.170

[332] Bloch-Smith, ibid. p.182-183

[333] Sugimoto (ed.), ibid. pp.162-163

[334] Lesley Jackson, "Isis - The Eternal Goddess of Egypt and Rome", London 2016, p.44

[335] Jackson, ibid. pp.27-28

[336] Jackson, ibid. pp.58-59

[337] https://en.wikipedia.org/wiki/Isis

[338] https://en.wikipedia.org/wiki/Isis

[339] Jackson, ibid. p.16

[340] Jackson, ibid. (p.21, p.124)

[341] https://en.wikipedia.org/wiki/Assyrian_conquest_of_Egypt

[342] https://www.thoughtco.com/aphrodite-greek-goddess-of-love-beauty-111901

[343] Andrew Scott and Charles Rivers (Eds.), *"Aphrodite – The Origins and History of the Greek Goddess of Love"*, Amazon (undated – print on demand) p.29

[344] Scott and Rivers (eds.), ibid. p.19

[345] Scott and Rivers (eds.), ibid. p.20

[346] Scott and Rivers (eds.), ibid. p.30

[347] Scott and Rivers (eds.), ibid. p.30

[348] Patti Wigington, https://www.thoughtco.com/who-is-astarte-2561500

[349] Scott and Rivers (eds.), ibid. p.29

[350] Scott and Rivers (eds.), ibid. p.2

[351] Scott and Rivers (eds.), ibid. p.28

[352] Scott and Rivers (eds.), ibid. p.28-30

[353] See: Adrienne Mayor, *"The Amazons – Lives and Legends of Warrior Women Across the Ancient World"*, Princeton, New Jersey, USA, 2014.

[354] Scott and Rivers (eds.), ibid. p.38

[355] Britt-Mari Näsström, ibid. pp.23-28

356 Näsström, ibid. pp.23-24
357 Näsström, ibid. p.24
358 Näsström, ibid. p.25
359 https://www.greekmythology.com/Other_Gods/Minor_Gods/Hesperides/hesperides.html
360 Wolkstein and Kramer, ibid. pp.168
427 Sarah Iles Johnston, *Hekate Soteira*, Atlanta USA, 1990, pp.143-5
428 Sorita d'Este, *Circle for Hekate*, London 2017, pp.100-101
429 Sorita d'Este, *Circle for Hekate*, London 2017, pp.161-162
430 d'Este, ibid. p.162
431 d'Este, ibid. p.162
432 d'Este, ibid. pp.162-163
433 https://www.goddess-guide.com/crone.html
434 d'Este, ibid. p.159
435 d'Este, ibid. pp.159
436 d'Este, ibid. pp.87-88
437 d'Este, ibid. p.89
438 Introductory sources for 'Platonism':
    https://en.wikipedia.org/wiki/Plato
    https://en.wikipedia.org/wiki/Academic_skepticism
    https://en.wikipedia.org/wiki/Idealism
439 https://en.wikipedia.org/wiki/Middle_Platonism
440 Plutarch - Greek biographer and essayist (c. CE 46 – CE 120)
441 https://en.wikipedia.org/wiki/Middle_Platonism
442 Johnston, ibid. p.19
443 Johnston, ibid. pp.13-15
444 Johnston, Ibid. p.18
445 https://en.wikipedia.org/wiki/Neoplatonism
446 Johnston, ibid. p.36
447 Johnston, ibid. p.38
448 Johnston, Ibid. p.72
449 Johnston, ibid. pp.73-74
450 https://en.wikipedia.org/wiki/Edict_of_Thessalonica
451 Sarah Semple, *In the Open Air, in Signals of Belief in Early England*, eds. Carver, Sanmark and Semple, Oxford 2010, p.25
452 https://en.wikipedia.org/wiki/Loki
453 As at August 2020 the Wikipedia entry for Trickster Gods listed 46 such [en.wikipedia.org/wiki/Category:Trickster_gods]
454 Gylfaginning 32
455 Farbauti = 'dangerous hitter' (Simek, ibid. p.78)
456 Rudolf Simek, *Dictionary of Northern Mythology*, Cambridge 1993, p.186
457 Simek, ibid. pp.186-187

458 *Hyndluljod* (Poetic Edda), quoted in Andy Orchard, Dictionary of Norse Myth and Legend, London 1998, p.106
459 Orchard, ibid. p.106
460 Simek, ibid. p.195
464 Orchard, ibid. p.105
465 Kevin Crossley-Holland, *Norse Myths – Gods of the Vikings,* Penguin 1982, pp.194-5
466 McGrath, *Idunn and Helen: People or Property?* (ibid.)
467 Crossley-Holland, ibid. pp.185-186
468 Crossley-Holland, ibid. p.186
469 Crossley-Holland, ibid. p.229
470 Lokasenna verse 23 in *The Elder Edda*, Penguin, 2011 p.87
471 Lokasenna, ibid. verse 24, p.87
472 Roderick Ellis, ibid. p.115
473 Roderick Ellis, ibid. p.115
474 *Olaf's Saga Helga* XCI, in Roderick Ellis, ibid. p.114
475 Alaric Hall, *Elves in Anglo-Saxon England*, Woodbridge, Suffolk, 2009 ed. p.157
476 Hall, ibid. p.159
477 Hall, ibid. p.166
478 Doris Stenton, *The English Woman in History*, London, 1957
479 Christine Fell, *Women in Anglo-Saxon England*, Oxford, 1986, p.13
480 Fell, ibid. p.14
481 Fell, ibid. p.20
482 Hall, ibid. p.160
483 Hall, ibid. p.160
484 Hall, ibid. p.163
485 Hall, ibid. p.161
486 Hall, ibid. p.167
487 Simek, ibid. p.279
488 Chris Fern is a free-lance archaeologist and Research Associate at the University of York
489 Chris Fern, *Horses in Mind*, in *Signals of Belief in Early England*, eds. Carver, Sanmark, Semple, Oxford 2010
490 Fern, ibid. p.151
491 Fern, ibid. p.128
492 Fern, ibid. p.129
493 Fern, ibid. p.136
494 Fern, ibid. p.143
495 Jenny Blain, *Nine Worlds of Seid-Magic*, London 2002, p.19
496 Blain, ibid. p.90
497 Blain, ibid. p.129
498 Hilda Roderick Ellis, *The Road to Hel*, Cambridge 1943 and 2013, p.4

[499] Roderick Ellis, ibid. p.198

[500] Roderick Ellis, ibid. p.198

[501] Roderick Ellis, ibid. p.91

[502] Roderick Ellis, ibid. p.94

[503] Roderick Ellis, ibid. p.95

[504] Hilda Roderick Ellis, The Road to Hel, Cambridge 1943, p.75

[505] Roderick Ellis, ibid. p.71

[506] Roderick Ellis, ibid. p.86

[507] *Edda*, quoted in Simek, ibid. p.138

[508] Gylfaginning 33, quoted in Simek, ibid. p.138

[509] Simek, ibid. p.138

[510] Roderick Ellis, ibid. p.196

[511] Orchard, ibid. p.32

[512] Roderick Ellis, ibid. p.4

[513] Orchard, ibid. p.73

[514] Roderick Ellis, ibid. p.135

[515] Orchard, ibid. pp.49-50

[516] Roderick Ellis, ibid. pp.128-129

[517] Roderick Ellis, ibid. p.138

[518] *Wælcyrigan*: Anglo-Saxon otherworldly powerful female entities, similar to Norse Valkyries and Dísir.

[519] Pollington, The Elder Gods, ibid. p.437

[520] "*Sörla þáttr* is a short story in the later and extended version of the Saga of Olaf Tryggvason in the manuscript of the Flateyjarbók, which was written and compiled by two Christian priests... in the late 14th century." [https://en.wikipedia.org/wiki/Brisingamen]

[521] Doris Stenton (*The English Woman in History*), in Christine Fell, *Women in Anglo-Saxon England*, Oxford 1986, p.13

[522] N. Price, *The Viking Way*, AUN 31, Uppsala, 2003, pp.54-55, in Pollington, *The Elder Gods*, ibid. p.467

Printed in Great Britain
by Amazon